PENGUIN BOOKS

THE CARAVAN BOOK OF PROFILES

The *Caravan* was relaunched in 2010 as a journal of politics and culture.

Supriya Nair is an editor at Brown Paper Bag, and former associate editor at the *Caravan*. She lives in Mumbai.

THE CARAVAN BOOK *of* PROFILES

Edited by Supriya Nair

PENGUIN BOOKS

An imprint of Penguin Random House

PENGUIN BOOKS

USA | Canada | UK | Ireland | Australia
New Zealand | India | South Africa | China | Singapore

Penguin Books is part of the Penguin Random House group of companies whose addresses can be found at global.penguinrandomhouse.com

Published by Penguin Random House India Pvt. Ltd
4th Floor, Capital Tower 1, MG Road,
Gurugram 122 002, Haryana, India

Penguin Random House India

Published in Penguin Books by Penguin Random House India 2016

10 9 8 7 6 5 4 3 2

ISBN 9780143428152

Typeset in Bembo Std by Manipal Digital Systems, Manipal

Printed at Repro India Limited

www.penguin.co.in

FSC www.fsc.org MIX Paper from responsible sources FSC® C047271

This is a legitimate digitally printed version of the book and therefore might not have certain extra finishing on the cover.

Contents

Foreword

I am often asked by readers, writers, journalists, advertisers and friends: for whom is the *Caravan* really meant? Over the past eight years, the tone of the question has evolved from one of dismissal, when the magazine was just an idea, to sceptical caution in its initial years, and lately to appreciation, now that it is somewhat of a success.

Perhaps the tone of these questions has been informed by the reality that the magazine has always, in one way or another, moved against the prevailing trends in journalism. The late 2000s, when I first started to work on the idea of the *Caravan*, was the time for 24x7, sound-bite driven television and digital journalism. As I write this essay, clickbait-infested digital content development is having its moment. ('Nine cats pretending they weren't caught falling!') Who, in any event, would really like to read a magazine dedicated to long-form, narrative non-fiction?

This question has always remained relevant, and gained importance, to my mind, with each passing year. I have always found it very hard to justifiably articulate an answer about who the magazine is meant for. This is perhaps because I never thought consciously about the target reader, the market, the business plan, or any of the jargon they teach at management school, before I plunged into developing the magazine.

For me, it began quite simply with a personal fascination with the great American magazines of narrative non-fiction writing:

the *New Yorker*, *Atlantic*, *Harper's* and *Mother Jones*. These became my first and most convenient reference points when I had to explain my idea to a prospective writer or an editor.

'What kind of magazine do you want to start?'

'Something that is a cross-over of the *New Yorker* and the *Atlantic*?'

'Oh wonderful. But who is the magazine meant for?'

How could I not define who the magazine was meant for, when I was so clear what the magazine was supposed to be? There was, of course, an obvious answer—that it was meant for whoever would pay for it. But it really wasn't the entire truth, and hasn't affected what we choose to publish.

I found a fellow sufferer in Orhan Pamuk, who once wrote an essay titled, handily enough, 'Who Do You Write For?'. Pamuk writes that this question chased him, ever more fiercely, for over thirty years of his career. He considers it a bit of a trap, especially for literary writers from non-Western societies, often marked by inequality. If a writer didn't answer that they wrote for the poor and downtrodden, they might well be branded elitist. Further, if their work was available to a global audience, they might be criticized for 'exoticizing their country for foreign consumption and inventing problems that have no basis in reality'.

For Pamuk, the route to being authentic is for the writer to simply write for the 'ideal reader': someone who lives in the same world as the writer. Write, Pamuk says, for this ideal reader, 'first by imagining him into being, and then by writing books with him in mind'.

This implies, perhaps, that every writer arrives at their own conception of an ideal reader, who looks to the writer as an adviser, a counsel, a friend, and a storyteller; both the cause and the fulfilment of literary desire. For in the end, every honest writer writes, after all, for themselves.

The search for the 'ideal reader' isn't limited to writers. Publishers and editors of magazines can also share a similar, tortuous quest. Before a magazine becomes a product of larger publishing machinery, and before it has been passed down over successive generations of corporate control, in the very beginning, there is always that editor or publisher—often both roles combined in one person, the founder—who is imagining the magazine that he wants to publish, and the 'ideal reader' for that magazine. It wouldn't come as a surprise, therefore, that the ideal reader is again a reflection of the founder's own yearnings. One such case was that of Harold Ross, and the magazine he founded.

When Ross started the *New Yorker* in the early 1920s, America's newsstands were spilling over with magazines. Amongst the popular humour magazines there were *Life*, *Judge*, *Smart Set* and *American Mercury*, and then beyond the genre of satire, there were the giants like *Reader's Digest* and *Vanity Fair*. In spite of the obvious competition, Ross was keen on starting his own magazine, and set about raising money and enlisting writers for his 'comic paper'. His reasons were more personal than strategic, which he enunciated much later, in a letter to a friend: 'I started the magazine because I thought it would be so much fun to run a humorous magazine, you'd just sit and laugh at funny contributions all the time.'

So between the glut of humour magazines on the one hand, and sophisticated magazines like *Vanity Fair* on the other, Ross started work on his own magazine, which was to be a mix of local humour, and which would be on top of current events at the same time. He had no desire to make a magazine for anyone other than the residents of New York, his city, and that of his writers. The *New Yorker*, he wrote in a 1924 prospectus sent to potential subscribers and investors, 'is a magazine avowedly published for a metropolitan audience and thereby will escape an influence which hampers most national publications. It expects a considerable national circulation, but this will come from persons who have a metropolitan interest.'

I bring up Ross because of the influence his magazine had had on me, and most of the folks at the *Caravan*, and because of the way we think of our readers. In 2004, while studying politics at Columbia, I realized I was a person who had a metropolitan interest. I fell in love with New York, the city, and the *New Yorker*. I am not suggesting that the *Caravan* shares any actual DNA with Ross's cherished legacy. But perhaps what binds us together is the notion of who reads our writing.

~

The *Caravan* did not emerge out of a market survey exercise or need-gap analysis. It is the product of its makers' collective admiration of narrative journalism. As Tom Wolfe wrote, describing this style when it was still the 'new' journalism, it 'derived its extraordinary power from four devices: scene-by-scene construction; dialogues in full; third-person point of view; and recording everyday gestures, habits, manners, customs, styles of furniture, clothing, decoration, styles of traveling, eating, keeping house, servants, superiors, inferiors . . .'

It was years before I really understood the technicalities of producing magazines that published credible, immersive work along these lines. As an early reader of the delicious bundles of stories that made up the great American magazines of narrative journalism, I was oblivious to the huge editorial machinery and painstaking work that went into them.

After two years of acquainting myself with the business side of magazine publishing in Delhi, I couldn't help but think of starting my own version of the *New Yorker* in India. It was a blind plunge, not knowing what lay ahead. Some assurance came from the support of my family, especially my father, Paresh Nath, the editor-in-chief of the family enterprise, Delhi Press. I also had the financial security that a well-established publishing house lent. And then there was the legacy of the name. The '*Caravan*' was a highly popular magazine my grandfather, Vishv Nath, had begun in 1940, widely read until he closed it down in 1988. What I had in mind was completely different from his magazine, but I was sure about the name from the very beginning; many people remembered it so fondly, and accompanying their reminiscences was a sense of innocence and purity that I cherished.

Time slowed excruciatingly between mid 2007, when I started working on the magazine, and January 2010, when the magazine was formally launched in its current avatar. In December 2008, a pre-launch heralded a 'beta edition' that was different from the current *Caravan* in many respects, but served an important purpose. A cross section of the literary community—journalists, writers and editors—became aware that a small experiment in narrative non-fiction writing was under way. It was tenuous, and invited some scepticism—but it was a physical product, a real magazine.

It may not seem like it now, but this was really no small thing at the time. It was perhaps the cheapest marketing stunt anyone could have pulled off. Most importantly, it brought me closer to the people who believed in what I believed, and wanted to have a go at realizing the idea.

I met Vinod Jose, now the executive editor of the magazine, and my co-conspirator, when we published his master's project from Columbia Journalism School in the second issue of the *Caravan* beta edition. Like me, he dreamt of a magazine dedicated to narrative non-fiction. Snigdha Poonam, later the magazine's arts editor, got in touch with us in January 2009, when she was just twenty-three, because she too was smitten by the notion. Our first staff writer, the award-winning reporter Mehboob Jeelani, joined us as a young intern in May 2009. I call them the *Caravan*'s original team, not because they were the only ones who were part of that beta *Caravan*, but they have been the ones who best understood what I had set about doing, and who have given the most important years of their lives to the magazine.

Vinod is an exceptionally gifted journalist, and even better people's person: there could have been no one more apt as a partner in this mission. For eight years, he has been enlisting people to our cause—editors, writers, and most importantly, our contributing editors, who were kind enough to associate with a young magazine with an ambitious goal. With Vinod, we also started working on a brand new format for the magazine that we eventually launched, out of beta, in 2010.

I was introduced to Jonathan Shainin through Pankaj Mishra, who suggested that I meet an editor who had once worked at the *New Yorker* as a fact checker, and who was planning to move to India. To say that he was an exceptional choice is an understatement. Jonathan is a force of nature—an embodiment of everything that the editor of a literary magazine should be.

I won't yet write the book on the *Caravan*'s other members, but I will name a select few, if in passing. The magazine has been made, in various parts, by the efforts of our books editor, Anjum Hasan; our former fiction and poetry editors, Rajni George and Chandrahas Choudhury; staff writers, Rahul Bhatia, Krishn Kaushik and Praveen Donthi; associate editors, Jyothi Natarajan, Alex Blasdel, Supriya Nair, Sonal Shah, Ajay Krishnan and Roman Gautam; our arts director, Girish Arora; our photo editor, Srinivas Kuruganti; our graphic designer, Paramjeet Singh;

the ever-wonderful former editorial manager, Leena Reghunath; and our political editor, Hartosh Singh Bal.

The *Caravan* newsroom, at about twenty people, is bigger than that of most monthly magazines published from India. Almost everyone who has worked at the magazine started here when they were under thirty. For many, this is their first job in a magazine, and for some, their first job ever. This includes me, in a way; the *Caravan* has been my first editing experience. I mention this because I believe it has played a big part in defining our unique identity.

Everyone I've mentioned here believed, and believes, in the idea of a magazine not encumbered by the existing norms of journalism in India. They have wanted to go beyond the newsweekly cycle and the style of writing that reads like an announcer's voice; beyond newspaper reporting's five Ws and one H.

We all wanted the storyteller's voice, gave life to characters and immersed the reader in a sensory experience. Because, as I have said, we were all young when we began, we chose to experiment and be adventurous. And because we all loved the same kind of writing, we knew the readership we were writing for. All my time editing the magazine has been characterized by countless debates between these people, and many others, on what stories to tell, and how to tell them.

But the one thing that has rarely been debated, or rather what has never been ambiguous, is the *Caravan*'s ideal reader. This team is the very mix of ideal readers for whom we produce the magazine: smart, sophisticated, curious people, all of whom share a love of good writing.

We have all wanted to be a part of political and social change calling for an ever more fair, inclusive and free nation, one that demands accountability from its leaders.

Over the last seven years, we have taken on powerful national leaders and corporate giants, and investigated the workings of the government, political parties, state machinery and the private sector. Many of these stories have carried legal and pecuniary risks for the publishing house, and in some cases, physical risks for writers. As I write this, the courts are hearing two defamation cases against us. One is a response to a 2011 profile of the self-styled management guru Arindam Chaudhuri, who created a ponzi scheme of an educational empire called Indian Institute of Planning and Management, now exposed. The other is in response to our 2015 story about how Essar Corp bought influence with the government. We are fighting both cases.

More than a couple of dozen other stories have carried fairly high political and business risks. In one case, we were served three anticipatory notices by one of the most powerful business houses in the country, urging us to be cautious with the story we were about to carry. In 2015, when we were working on a long profile of one of the top leaders of the present National Democratic Alliance government, we were warned through various channels to back off. (This, I must say, was the first time that a very senior member of government actively tried to pressure us into killing a story.) Both, however, were published.

Over the years, for these and other reasons, the *Caravan* has come to enjoy the reputation of a punchy investigative magazine, one that is forever scouting for stories to take on people in power. Our pugnacity is perhaps overhyped. I think the magazine is an eclectic mix of some very fine writing on art, culture, literature, and most importantly, human-interest stories. This softer side of the *Caravan* is sometimes overlooked. Indeed, the stories in this book of profiles have been selected to present that well-rounded mix, representative of the magazine's true identity.

I am often asked how we manage to speak truth to power so often. My answer is that it is a mix of naivety and the institutional strength of the *Caravan*'s publishing house. I say naivety because beyond a point I don't like to think about the possible risks associated with a story. We ensure that our editorial process is robust, and leave no room for carelessness or bias. Beyond that, we like to take the plunge.

The other reason we can afford to take risks with the *Caravan*'s stories is because of the strength it derives from the institutional legacy of Delhi Press, the publishing house behind the magazine. In particular, my father and editor-in-chief of Delhi Press magazines, has unflinchingly backed and promoted the magazine. He, like his father before him, has never shied away from taking up important, and at times, perilous editorial battles.

My grandfather was a visionary and a fearless editor in every respect. He founded some of India's most well-respected magazines. At the age of twenty-two, he started the *Caravan* with his limited savings and some help from a friend. What started from a borrowed office in Connaught Place grew to become a publishing house with more than two dozen magazines, with a vast publishing infrastructure. The magazines that he most fondly edited, besides the *Caravan*, were *Sarita*, *Woman's Era* and *Champak*. A Hindi magazine on socio-political affairs, better known for its family-oriented fiction, *Sarita* was the field of his fiercest editorial battles.

For decades, he waged a war on religious obscurantism and political authoritarianism, and invited the wrath of political leaders and a vicious backlash from Hinduism's self-appointed custodians. He, and later my father, has fought their editorial battles with patience and fortitude. Much of the editorial strength that the *Caravan* therefore takes pride in derives from the institutional legacy of these two men, who created the world in which the *Caravan* can survive.

This book, and the magazine, is therefore dedicated to them.

Editor, *Caravan* Anant Nath
July 2016

Introduction

There was a time when, world over, everybody knew the standard protocols for what a newsperson called the 'celebrity profile'. To write the profile of a famous person engaged in the work of politics, culture or business, the journalist first went straight to the celebrity. They were routinely stonewalled by the celebrity's publicist, who set the rules of engagement: in almost every case, it meant the journalist would be given access to this luminary only on the condition that he or she would write something pleasing about them (the subject).

When published, these profiles sounded like run-on versions of long transactional Q&As. They contained little criticism of their subject, and the voice of the essay was that of the celebrity, not of the writer. Oozing across the pages, inevitably, were a few well-posed pictures, good enough for the appeased idol to frame the pages in glass, teak and rosewood, and tack them next to his certificates on the office walls.

The other sort of profile emerged later. Attempted with the greatest distinction by American magazines of narrative journalism, this style only grew to prominence in the mid-twentieth century. Investigative, critical, and often witty, the piece let the reader know, through its voice, that the writer–journalist was in command here, rather than the subject. Any material thrown up by way of a personal encounter with the subject was just one of a range of raw materials at the writer's disposal.

These works of journalism came closer than others to literature. Their character sketches were created through the imprints of strong imagery and scenes that were woven together in the fashion of a plot. The persons under investigation became not unlike the memorable, well-crafted figures of classic literature. This sort of writing became a genre unto itself.

For seven or eight decades, this variety of profile, part of American new journalism, established a tradition in the newsrooms in many Western nations. In India, however, the celebrity profile followed the old school for a very long time, except for a few random experiments. When the *Caravan* arrived in its relaunched avatar, the profile found a life of its own in Indian journalism.

To portray a life in something like totality, old rules of allegiance to the subject must fall by the wayside; as the Pulitzer Prize–winning journalist Jacqui Banaszynski said, with due respect to the subject, the writer's allegiance was now with the reader. There was no missing a subject's foulness, inconstancy and fury of wickedness. Human deceit became important, and in some ways central, to the deep profile.

These profiles made extensive use of investigative techniques. They deployed wit, irony and dramatic flair. They consigned the publicist to irrelevance. The resulting story was not just the chronicle of a life in itself. It was multilayered, and had many little stories in it, explaining a complex life by complex means. You reported close, and pulled back while writing. It made journalism a lot more liberating, but also several times harder.

Every aspect of such a story had to be based on credible sourcing, and put through rigorous fact checking. These stories were often reported after talking to forty or fifty people. There are the *Caravan* profiles that were written after talking to over a hundred people. If the character profiled was a complex personality or put hurdles in the way of reporting, if we found ourselves, for whatever reason, on unsure ground, the journalist worked harder. Profiles have taken anywhere from a customary three months (former governor of the Reserve Bank of India, Raghuram Rajan) to five months (liquor baron Ponty Chadha) to two years (Swami Aseemanand, in prison on charges of terrorism). Such reporting, which lay readers called research, for profiles was unprecedented in Indian journalism. Allowed time and space, they could not easily be found elsewhere; profiles in the *Caravan* constituted a genre within narrative journalism.

~

Across the world, there is a widely accepted set of dos and don'ts in journalistic ethics, which are then shaped more specifically by their cultural milieus. Indian English journalism is defined by what we may safely qualify as the domineering Lutyens' Delhi School of Ethics. This is marked by the principle that a journalist's grind for access to a power list of celebrities is directly proportionate to how much familiarity and social trust they have gained over the years.

In other words, the relationship is not even slightly that of two professionals talking to each other; instead, one of those professionals must play the ally. A celebrated columnist who regales readers with political gossip once played fixer to the Gandhi family, taking Indira Gandhi's daughters-in-law shopping. Later in her career, this columnist's allegiance shifted to the household of Atal Bihari Vajpayee, where she went as far as sorting out differences between politicians and acting as a go-between to many of them. The style and method suited her, and she has been distinguished in her pursuit by the degree of intimacy she achieved with her subjects, if nothing else.

Another way of securing access will be familiar to readers who tracked the story of the infamous Niira Radia tapes. On those recordings, acquired by tapping the phone of a high-profile publicist, a journalist–editor offers to do 'well-rehearsed' and 'fully scripted' interviews with, among others, Mukesh Ambani, the tsar of Indian business. 'What kind of story do you want?' the journalist asks the publicist Radia, all bluntness and tongue-in-cheek familiarity.

In this market, the *Caravan* had nothing to offer. Of the thirteen profiles in this anthology, writers gained access to their subjects only in eight cases. Two of these were from the current prime ministers of Pakistan and Nepal. The Indian who granted the most access did so from jail.

In another political profile where we got minimal access, our subject promised the reporter a longer second interview after their first meeting, then chose to inspire one of his crony businessmen to send us a barrage of legal notices before the story was published. The use of legal threat and intimidation to kill a story before it can hit the stands has a long tradition in India. In our case, we chose to ignore the threats and run the article.

Among our profiles of people involved in the economy, only Raghuram Rajan, a former academic, gave access. Cultural figures were uniformly more forthcoming, or as in the case of T.M. Krishna's essay on M.S. Subbulakshmi, drew on a complex personal and artistic history with the writer. As this makes clear, in India, A-list politicians and businesspersons, or A-, B- and C-lists alike, have a problem taking questions from independent journalists in one-on-one settings. Ironically, forfeiting personal access has worked largely to our advantage, just as some masters in the West turned the denial of access to their advantage.

Generally speaking, the *Caravan*'s profile writers were a fresh breed in Indian English journalism—young, often exposed to international standards and methods, and often keen to measure themselves against the classics of narrative journalism. *Vanity Fair* once reported that Gay Talese's famous profile of Frank Sinatra, published without writer ever having met subject, was often cited as the inspiration that steered generations of youngsters to a career in journalism. *Frank Sinatra Has a Cold*, published in *Esquire* in 1966, was written because Talese was tasked to profile Sinatra but was repeatedly given the brush-off by the singer's publicist. He completed the assignment, and created a classic of modern journalism by writing about trailing everyone around the great man instead.

The thumb rule for the *Caravan* profile is that access is good, but if it isn't given, the writer will have to be sanguine. Of course, they are often a little relieved that their story is now free of one of the most persuasive restraints on a writer: the potentially manipulative emotional influence of a direct conversation. Many Indian public figures, believing that a story would be discredited without their participation, turned us down. Perhaps few realized at the outset that a well-executed long story takes on a life of its own in the reader's mind, with the readers often remembering lines, dialogues and scenes, just as they did with literature and film.

Then there is the *Caravan*'s editing process, which I think it safe to say is unprecedented in Indian newsrooms. Here, editors dedicate their time to a writer as soon as an idea is hatched. Once the draft is filed, the editor busies herself with an elaborate three-layered editing process, working with the writer on content, structure and language.

Many writers exposed to international publishing standards immediately took to our thoroughness. Some Indian journalists, spoiled by long years of being subject to nothing more rigorous than a desk copy-edit, were initially resistant. In 2009, in the run-up to the relaunch of the magazine, while preparing a bank of long stories, I commissioned a senior journalist to write a profile of a prominent Indian politician. When the journalist received his editorial memo, he shot back with a furious text message: 'no one edited me in indian express, times of india. how dare you touch my copy? i will break (sic) hell if you publish it in my name.'

We killed that profile. But over the years, journalists have begun to recognize what we are doing, and how with a mighty, careful—and, in some cases thankless—effort from an editor, the pieces gain structure and a shelf life.

Institutionally, the *Caravan* has benefited a great deal from the diverse backgrounds of its editors, some Indian, some foreign. They have been former reporters, fact checkers, managers and more. Each contributed to the magazine's broad philosophy, and have left a little of their style and self in the newsroom, helping refine our process. Going chronologically, the tenures of Snigdha Poonam, Adam Matthews, Jonathan Shainin, Jyothi Natarajan, Alex Blasdel, Supriya Nair and Sonal Shah, as well as the current team of Ajay Krishnan and Roman Gautam, have all made the *Caravan* an editor's magazine reputed for a dogged pursuit of perfection. Shainin, for example, who helped take the *Caravan* editing to a new level when he came on board by the end of 2010, developed a reputation for sending memos to writers which were longer than their drafts. All these editors demonstrated a profound literary sensibility which complemented the reportorial excellence we sought very nicely. The intellectual and creative engagement of writer and editor is one of the many beautiful things about long-form narrative journalism, and it is the dictum of the *Caravan*'s editing philosophy.

And, lastly, a newsroom could have a mighty vision, but it would be of little use without a publisher willing and able to execute it. The greatest possible esteem must be reserved for the support the magazine has received from the Delhi Press family, especially the face of its third generation: the *Caravan*'s editor and publisher, Anant Nath. When I was offered the job to lead the *Caravan* in January 2009, I was the third professional Anant tried out for the position, with the first two leaving after very short stints.

Since its inception in 1939, Delhi Press has been renowned as a publisher of general interest magazines, with thirty-six titles published in ten languages. Popular titles like *Grihshobha*, *Sarita*, *Champak* and *Saras Salil* are read around India, and are the face of Delhi Press. The prejudices of English-speaking Indians may not, perhaps, have allowed many to expect this publishing house to back a major innovation in Indian English journalism: some of my own friends tried to dissuade me from taking up Delhi Press's offer. For many, a mainstream press looks like the *Times of India*, or *India Today*, or the *Indian Express*, not this. But the wisdom of 35 million loyal readers, and the company's insistence on standing by strict principles for over seven decades—from taking a stand against religious obscurantism to refusing highly lucrative liquor or tobacco ads, for example—is no joke. Anglophile or not, in a postmodern India where glitter glosses over substance, I realized that Delhi Press was one of the rare publishing groups where a conversation on ethics and principled journalism is possible.

I chose to spend the first three weeks of my time in Delhi Press writing what I called a vision document, a blueprint for our grand idea that detailed at length the kind of new journalism we would practise. This was to articulate, at the outset, the kind of journalism the *Caravan* would practise, forging its own style in a category replete with great and distinctive examples, whether it was the *New Yorker*, *Granta* or the *Atlantic* and many others. What the *Caravan* would do and wouldn't do—one had to have the clarity early on itself. It was also to settle major questions on the extent to which we would experiment with the form, reporting time and editorial freedom, balancing our risks while keeping in mind that the magazine was going to be primarily Indian and had to be commercially viable and in consonance with the ethos of the publishing company. This clarity was vital for the professionals who would make the momentous decision to leave behind tried-and-tested newsrooms to try something totally new with us.

I remember, clearly, an evening in early 2009 when I finished a twelve-page draft of this document, which included the first mention of our showcasing of long, well-rounded profiles. I went out on a drive with Anant, who read it at one go, sitting in the Delhi traffic. The working relationship between professionals and business owners is one strong rivet in the links that bind the chain of an institution: this one, between an executive editor and a publisher–editor, has held fast. So have the rivets formed by the wonderful team of professionals which joined us and strengthened us, meeting and then exceeding the challenges each of them faced.

~

The free press in India is certainly better than its counterparts in monarchies, theocracies and dictatorships, but let's compare apples with apples. This, I'm afraid, produces a dismal scenario in a democracy whose self-image is so intimately concerned with close comparisons to established, industrial democracies in the West.

In India, fearing retribution, the standard 'source' on whose shoulders a story stands—the powerful celebrity, the insider at a corporation, the wheeler-dealer in a political party—habitually remains anonymous. Where it isn't threat at work, it's personal ambition. One of the people I spoke to for a profile was a very senior politician who lived in Gurgaon—a desirable address in some professions, but worse than Tihar jail for someone who was once a Lutyens' Delhi insider. The man was deadwood, cast off in the wilderness: yet at the end of the interview, when he insisted on anonymity, I realized that this octogenarian was still hoping to come in from the cold, repatriated to the land of the living with a gubernatorial position or some other decoration.

Journalists seeking attributed accounts have been at the receiving end of such systemic unwillingness. (An additional complication arises at the *Caravan* due to our dislike of the airy newspaper habit of ascribing things to 'sources' who said them, and to changing names. This is why, instead of 'Mr X', you hear from 'a senior party general secretary who was witness to the discussion', or 'an industrialist from eastern India who funded the leader' and so on, in our reportage.) We look for material that outlines a whole life, its characteristics, its ups and downs, its encounters, how a particular character behaves at key points in his life.

How much easier the convention of he-said, she-said journalism is, which stops at putting out opposing points of view. But this sort of journalism is only as good as its sources, and the cheap compromises and peculiar hollowness of Indian public life have not served our press or our democracy well. A President or prime minister only has to exit office in other democracies for hundreds of people in his administration to open up on their experiences in the regime, eager to clear the record for a variety of motives. Of the thousands who exit our political or corporate system year on year, only a few are open to recalling their work with any measure of frankness. Our lack of interest in thinking deeply about the past, in learning as a people from our experiences, and our shyness about candid conversations have made us less wise as a people—and the job of a profile writer more stressful.

Even with the challenges faced, the *Caravan* profiles have drawn laurels from reading, thinking Indians and international audiences. From the *Guardian*, the *New York Times* and *The Economist* to the great intellectuals of our times, many have praised us for publishing India's finest journalism. Still, a small constituency of Lutyens' Delhi's ethicists, seizing on this quality, have accused us of 'hatchet jobs' or '*supari* journalism'. To characterize this faction of critics who disapprove of our having broken protocol, I shall borrow a comment from Abhinandan Sekhri, a senior editor and satirist at *Newslaundry*, who once described a certain class as 'Indian elites of the 70s and 80s, who would be like "Hey dude, how dare you ask me questions? You think I will need to explain myself?"'

After making interview requests respectfully, and hearing back in the negative with almost bureaucratic regularity, the *Caravan*'s profile writers said—so be it. This spirit—of irreverence, of audacity—was also needed. By doing this, you were performing a democratic duty. By labouring to produce the results in a long, artfully constructed story, you were bringing pleasure to your reader. Some people like us for the former, some for the latter. For some, myself included, it's the mix of the two that contains the kick.

~

We are nearing the end of the second decade in the twenty-first century. This industry, and this profession, are facing a sea change that is perhaps second only in its impact to the arrival of the printing presses half a millennium ago. The journalist's primary role—that of sending information from a site of action to the consumers of that information who are further away—is no longer quite as fundamental. The citizen on the street can now fulfil that function through her phone. The reader need not be beholden to a few oligarchic suppliers for his news.

There are several answers to the question of what we should do now. One, for certain, is that reporters would do well to don the additional hats of writer and intellectual. In this regard, I hope the *Caravan*'s profiles also offer something like an idea for the future. In spite of the similarity in the processes of reporting and writing, as I look back on these stories, I am struck by how different each one is. This is because each profile was produced by someone who assumed all three roles—reporter, writer, intellectual—in their approach to the story, and each person's individual style determined the balance of power between the three.

There is evidence that this might be the way forward. Our profiles, which make the major chunk of the *Caravan* cover stories, are shared and read widely, every month. The last numbers available for 2014 on Twitter show that the *Caravan*'s cover stories were shared over 50,000 times; newsweeklies with four times as many issues per year did fewer than 10,000 shares. The value of doing well-rounded journalism, profile or otherwise, perhaps is one of the few ways to validate the profession itself.

The *Caravan*'s profiles have, in recent years, prompted two leading national newspapers to hire staffers for a hitherto unknown designation in India: profile editors. They commission profiles similar to the *Caravan*'s, if not as thorough as ours. The whole Indian situation is not many miles removed from American newsrooms in the 1960s, which mocked narrative journalism as a 'bastard form' before asking their own reporters to start writing like narrative journalists on their daily beats. At any rate, I hope the profile, whether at the *Caravan* or on other platforms, is here to stay in Indian journalism: I'm confident of its key role in bettering the discourse so crucial in a democracy.

By the summer of 2016, six years after its relaunch, the *Caravan* had published 110 profiles by seventy-eight writers. Each is a unique accomplishment, but constrained by space, we had to choose a few to represent what they have accomplished. We enforced two rules in their selection: only one piece per author, and a roughly equal distribution of these thirteen stories between politics, business and culture. Also, a look behind the scenes and a current update on where these profiles stand today, from the writers.

For these obvious reasons, many exceptional works are not included here, and I trust our readers will enjoy digging through our archives online to find many essays equally or more enjoyable. But I'm afraid with very little modesty I must say that most of the profiles in this book are classics of journalism in their own right now. Here, for your consideration, is the *Caravan*'s Praveen Donthi on Finance Minister Arun Jaitley; the *Caravan*'s Leena Reghunath on Swami Aseemanand; the *Caravan*'s Krishn Kaushik on former attorney general Goolam Vahanvati; Mira Sethi on Pakistan Prime Minister Nawaz Sharif; Deepak Adhikari on Nepal Prime Minister Prachanda; Mark Bergen on former Reserve Bank governor Raghuram Rajan; Samanth Subramanian on media mogul Samir Jain; the *Caravan*'s Mehboob Jeelani on liquor barren Ponty Chadha; the *Caravan*'s Rahul Bhatia on cricket entrepreneur N. Srinivasan; T.M. Krishna on musician M.S. Subbulakshmi; Ali Sethi on ghazal queen Farida Khanum; Baradwaj Rangan on Tamil superstar Vikram; and myself on former prime minister Manmohan Singh.

This is an opulent history, and, as is evident, an ambitious creative endeavour: the result of each of these writers using every tool in the shed, including some we didn't know were waiting to be hefted. Above all, this anthology, capturing a few important lives in our times, was designed for pleasure. Happy reading.

Executive Editor, *Caravan* — Vinod K. Jose
August 2016

RAGHURAM RAJAN became a far bigger deal than I had ever anticipated. I would like to claim that at the onset of the reporting, more than three years ago as I write this, I had the foresight to predict that the bookish government adviser would soon be named governor of the Reserve Bank of India (RBI), casting him in the central role during a critical economic moment for India. I would like to say I knew that the role would make Rajan, a reserved academic for much of his previous public career, the subject of intense scrutiny, and a sudden darling of the media. I did not. Nor did I, or anyone, foresee the tangled political contest Rajan would face with the Modi administration, which would ultimately end his tenure at the RBI.

Instead, I was drawn to the ways Rajan's ideas about monetary and fiscal policy reflected major economic debates unfolding in India and globally. This is, admittedly, a dry topic. But it had boost from political drama: here was, on the surface, a staunch free-market economist, rising in the ranks of a party not historically fond of free-market ideologues. What I learned in my reporting, and what his RBI stint has showed, is that Rajan is a technocrat, not an ideologue.

No article before the *Caravan*'s had unpacked his economic positions alongside his personal history and character, one that turned out to be surprisingly rich. Then a confluence of events—the RBI appointment, the sharp descent of the rupee and late 2013's pending economic crisis—helped make that portrait a timely snapshot of a man and a nation moving through a time of crisis.

MARK BERGEN

Mark Bergen wrote about economics and business from Bangalore for two years for Reuters, the New York Times, *the* Wall Street Journal *and other publications. He currently covers technology for Bloomberg News in San Francisco. He is from Ohio.*

Line of Credit

Raghuram Rajan Takes Charge at the RBI

By MARK BERGEN | 1 October 2013

I

When the rupee struck 60, the lines tethering Mint Road to North Block drew taut. Relations between the Reserve Bank of India (RBI), in Mumbai, and the ministry of finance have rarely been without friction, but as the currency fell past a dramatic threshold against the dollar at the end of June, they were frantic and heated. The government in Delhi, already under siege from all sides, faced a new barrage of public criticism as the plummeting rupee touched new lows almost every day.

Six weeks earlier, the US Federal Reserve chairman, Ben Bernanke, announced that his bank's third round of quantitative easing, an unorthodox tactic to stimulate the American economy, would soon wind down. Investors who had poured into emerging market nations for juicier yields now started to flee en masse. The retreat stung currencies from Turkey to Brazil, but India was particularly exposed, with a current-account deficit fresh off a record high and increasingly dependent on short-term foreign investment.

With the currency commanding unprecedented attention and talk of another 1991 growing louder, Delhi took action. According to several people working with the finance ministry, RBI officials were summoned to North Block with unusual frequency—and on 15 July, the central bank intervened.

The RBI initiated a series of dramatic measures to drain liquidity from the market and defend the battered rupee. The moves were abrupt, haphazard and ineffectual: as the central bank fumbled from strategy to strategy over the following month, the rupee kept tumbling.

Close observers of the Indian economy have many disagreements—over why growth stalled, who is to blame and what must be done—but here they reached a consensus. A chorus of former officials, economists and investors told me that the RBI had been strong-armed by a politically anxious finance ministry. The liquidity moves came as an utter surprise to the Technical Advisory Committee (TAC), a seven-member body that counsels the central bank, two of its members said. The bank's public statements were sporadic and clumsy, uncharacteristic of the then RBI governor, Duvvuri Subbarao—solid evidence, one person with close knowledge of the RBI told me, that its hand had been forced by the government.

In Indian financial circles, where the RBI was seen as the sole government institution whose credibility had remained intact, the feckless moves that began in July signalled that its credibility was unravelling.

If those exaggerated anxieties have since been reversed, the turnaround began on 6 August, when the flailing government surprised its fiercest critics by naming Raghuram Govind Rajan as the next head of the central bank. Rajan, a distinguished professor at the University of Chicago's Booth School of Business, had been hailed as 'the oracle of the financial crisis' for his prescient warnings three years before the 2008 collapse. He had spent the past year as the government's chief economic adviser, a post that many presumed was a brief stopover on his way to Mint Road.

But his appointment was not a fait accompli. While the names of other candidates were floated in the media, the deepening sense of crisis may have given the final push to Rajan's installation, diminishing doubts that had been aired over his relative lack of bureaucratic experience and his short time in India. When he took charge on 4 September, announcing his arrival with a confident and sweeping inaugural speech, markets gushed. Stocks sprung up and the rupee recovered 10 per cent of its value in a week. Headlines proclaimed a 'Rajan rally' and analysts marvelled at the power of 'the Rajan effect'.

Officially, the private sector praised his promise of clarity and consistency in the central bank's decisions. Unofficially, as one former bank analyst wrote in an email, many were 'thirsting for an adult' in the government. Confidence in the Indian economy, which had drooped to toxic lows, was partially resuscitated—and the credit was placed squarely on the shoulders of a man who decidedly does not want it there. A vocal critic of the extraordinary stimulus measures undertaken by central banks like the US Federal Reserve, Rajan's defining intellectual trait is an insistent pragmatism. One suspects that nobody distrusts the power of 'the Rajan effect' more than Rajan himself.

On the day of his appointment, a dreary Tuesday in August, he met the press inside North Block and gave a short, solemn statement. The government and the RBI, he said, did not have a 'magic wand to make the problems disappear instantaneously'. He left without taking questions.

By the time I met Rajan at the RBI's offices in Mumbai on 13 September, he was an unlikely celebrity. His modest disavowal of the 'magic wand' had been forgotten by the media, and Rajan had become 'The Guv'. The overheated market for speculation about Rajan's superhuman powers peaked earlier that morning, when the *Economic Times* published a column by Shobhaa De crowning the handsome RBI governor India's newest sex symbol. ('The guy's put "sex" back into the limp Sensex,' De wrote. 'His chiselled features are as sharp as his brain.')

We met in the RBI visitor lounge, an angular room on the eighteenth floor of the bank's headquarters, whose windows offered a sweeping view of south Mumbai; Rajan's own office, across the hall, peers over the rest of the city and the sea. Rajan—Raghu to anyone who shakes his hand—sat in front of a wall of small portraits of the governors before him. The painting of his predecessor, Subbarao, had yet to be completed.

When Rajan took over nine days earlier, he immediately introduced measures that many credited with undoing the damage wrought during Subbarao's last months on the job. The 'Rajan rally' made good copy, but he was characteristically cautious in describing his shift in direction: when I asked if the policies introduced in July and August had been reversed, he replied they had merely been 'fine-tuned'.

In conversation, Rajan is direct but distinctly professorial. His answers come in complete paragraphs, typically prefaced by 'I think' or 'My sense is'. Asked about his rapturous reception in the press, he deflected towards the more comfortable territory of economic theory. 'We must remember that sentiment is important, whatever the cause for the sentiment,' he said. 'Markets are not impersonal. There are people making decisions. How they think, how they form expectations, is important.'

But he was aware that he was still in the midst of a honeymoon. 'There's only so long that expectations can carry you before translating into reality,' he told me. Rajan has long been a sceptic of the true reach of central bankers, and while he didn't address them directly, he attempted to defer the oversized expectations that met his arrival. 'What I can do is offer some stability to the currency,' he said, quickly adding, 'And I mean stability not just in external value, but the domestic value of the currency, which means inflation.'

A week after our meeting, in his first monetary policy statement, Rajan defied market expectations and raised the nation's central interest rate, citing the threat of continued inflation. At the same time, the new governor lowered the marginal standing facility, the rate of last-resort lending for banks, which the RBI had abruptly raised on 15 July as part of its inept rupee defence.

Though analysts naturally differed as to the wisdom of Rajan's first big decision, on paper he had cemented his stature as an independent reformer. He had stood down industry, which was clamouring for rate cuts, and likely disappointed Finance Minister P. Chidambaram, who is widely believed to have been the fiercest lobbyist for lower rates over the past year. It looked as though he had deemed the RBI's earlier liquidity measures unwise, and moved to reverse them.

For those familiar with Rajan's views, his first move should not have come as a surprise. His wariness of inflation is well documented, as is his cynicism about central bank efforts to juice growth with loose monetary policy.

Among close observers of the RBI, the more important questions concerned his willingness to defy pressure from Delhi and restore clarity to the central bank's objectives. Since his appointment in August, speculation has swirled around his role in the RBI's clumsy July manoeuvres. If the government had forced the bank's hand, as many insiders insisted, had its chief economic adviser gone along?

Rajan arrived in Delhi in August 2012 with a reputation for voicing dissent and an enviable aptitude for predicting financial disaster before it struck. 'He always speaks his mind in meetings,' one of the economists on his staff at the finance ministry told me. 'He's very evident, and people know it.' Yet there is no concrete evidence that Rajan, who spoke to Chidambaram on a near-daily basis, raised alarm bells in July.

Ashima Goyal, a TAC member who called the sudden liquidity measures 'overkill', told me she believes Rajan supported them inside the finance ministry. 'He was very strong in supporting the need to defend the rupee,' Goyal said. At a university event in Delhi, shortly after the decisions, she approached Rajan and raised concerns that a similar defence undertaken by the RBI in 1998 had suppressed growth. 'He seemed to think that the liquidity movement was necessary.'

In public appearances, Rajan toed the ministry's line: during a brief television interview on 26 July, he endorsed the policies as necessary but temporary efforts to stabilize the rupee, with 'minimal damage' to growth. 'He's a pretty orthodox chap,' said Jahangir Aziz, an economist with J.P. Morgan, which backed the RBI's decision. 'He likes to finish doing things inside the box before moving outside the box.'

Ajay Shah, a former finance ministry economist who has known Rajan for more than a decade, saw the July moves as a disaster orchestrated by the government, a glaring sign of the RBI's lack of autonomy. 'The last six months of macro and finance policies are the biggest blunders in Indian history,' Shah told me in August. 'I don't know where Raghu stood.'

Others who know Rajan believe he was personally opposed to the decisions, and his advice behind closed doors was ignored. They saw his public comments as a necessity for anyone working inside the government, rather than an omen of his compromised independence.

When I asked Rajan about his stance on the July moves, he was tactful but evasive. 'Without being more specific than needed,' he began, 'the finance ministry and RBI have been discussing a lot of things over the last year. And I'd say there's been substantial amount of understanding and cooperation. Not necessarily agreement on everything, but certainly understanding on everything that is done. You can debate for a long time where would we be without it—would we be in a better place or a worse place.'

He added, with a chuckle: 'I don't think it's the appropriate time to have that debate.'

His reticence during our interview was carefully calibrated. By mid July, he was likely aware of the decision to come a month later, an appointment he almost certainly expected when he arrived in Delhi a year earlier. Though he was a frequent critic of the government's economic and financial policies before his return to India, Rajan is, above all, a pragmatic and politically savvy economist.

But the debate he would prefer not to have—at least in public—is unlikely to vanish. When he took charge of the central bank on 4 September, India was mired in its worst monetary situation in recent memory, and debate about the RBI's role had reached an apex. The spectre of 1991 lingered over the government. Although India's foreign reserves had grown considerably since the days of its worst balance of payments crisis, chatter persisted that the country might need to turn to the International Monetary Fund (IMF), where Rajan once served as chief economist.

The 'Rajan rally' dispelled the worst of these fears, but distrust of the government's ability to manage the economy remains strong. For all the native pride at his return, Rajan remains an outsider, a figure of Davos rather than Delhi. Yet for over a decade, he has quietly worked with the government, advising the country's economic decision-makers.

Among the youngest in a close-knit generation of Indian economists who have found tremendous success abroad, he has now come back to assume a position he has long sought, to which he brings an embrace of capitalism far outside the Indian mainstream. In the two paramount debates in international economics about the crisis of 2008—what caused it, and what to do in its wake—Rajan has been a controversial central character. And he is now cast as the saviour of the Indian economy, a burden he is determined not to carry.

II

In October 1955, India's first chief economic adviser, J.J. Anjaria, hosted a dinner party for an American guest. The economist Milton Friedman was visiting Delhi from the University of Chicago, sent by the US President, Dwight Eisenhower, to assess and advise the eight-year-old nation. Friedman, whose tenure in Chicago would last another two decades, was already closely associated with the ideology for which he and the university would later become synonymous: a love of free enterprise and disdain for government regulation.

After three weeks in Delhi, Friedman drafted a memorandum on the Indian economy that fit his reputation. It scolded the government for its heavy hand in industry, rigid controls on the private sector, and erratic monetary policies. When Anjaria invited him over, Friedman met 'some eight of the eighteen or nineteen' economists working on the government's Second Five-Year Plan, he recalled in his 1999 autobiography. None of them agreed with his recommendations.

The story of India's subsequent economic trajectory is a familiar one: decades of woeful growth, held down by the Licence–Permit–Quota Raj, until a balance of payments crisis in 1991 forced the curtain to lift. Two decades of robust expansion followed, until the slowdown that began in 2011.

But this well-worn narrative is incomplete. For its first fifteen years after Independence, India's rate of growth was on par with other newly created agricultural nations. The economic malaise arrived around the start of Indira Gandhi's prime ministership, along with her nationalization of industry and consolidation of power. But it ended, and rapid growth began, when she returned to office a decade before 1991.

'Starting around 1980, the Indian economy became a veritable dynamo,' Rajan said in a 2006 speech in Mumbai. 'Despite the inevitable unfavourable comparisons with China, very few countries have grown so fast for such a prolonged period of time, or reduced poverty so sharply.' Arvind Subramanian, a friend and frequent collaborator of Rajan's, wrote a landmark paper in 2005 with the Harvard economist Dani Rodrik, which traced India's total factor productivity, a metric of growth. It accelerated 2.1 per cent faster than the average country for two decades after 1980, after lagging nearly a per cent behind the rest from 1960 to 1980.

As Rajan put it in his 2006 speech, echoing the conclusions reached by Subramanian and Rodrik, the spurt came when 'government attitudes towards the economy' shifted under Indira and then Rajiv, with 'pro-business reforms' that signalled a more favourable atmosphere for private industry.

The 'pro-competition' reforms of 1991, to use Rajan's phrase, dramatically opened up the economy, building on the smaller steps taken a decade earlier. But the failure to follow through with 'second generation' reforms after the Congress-led United Progressive Alliance (UPA) came to power in 2004 eventually caught up with India in the wake of the global economic crisis.

'For a few years [after 2004] the momentum created by previous reforms, together with strong global growth, carried India forward,' Rajan wrote last summer. Politicians concluded that additional reforms were unnecessary and politically radioactive. While the UPA's re-election in 2009 cemented what Rajan dubbed a 'lurch towards populism', government came to be seen as 'a source of sporadic handouts rather than of reliable public services'.

Among economists, at least, this broad diagnosis evokes little disagreement. The more contentious issues have to do with who bears the blame for the complacency that preceded the slowdown, and how much the government's policies since 2010 have exacerbated it.

Few commentators have positive words for Pranab Mukherjee's tenure as finance minister, which began in 2009 and seemed to mark the nadir of the shift towards populism. A consummate Congressman who had long been the government's reliable political firefighter, Mukherjee has been blamed for doing too few of the right things to push forward reforms, doing too many of the wrong things after growth began to slide, and generally failing to hold the line against surging deficits. D.K. Mittal, who was the financial services secretary in the ministry, put it more charitably than most: 'He was busy with other things.'

'He was not focused on the economy,' said Ila Patnaik, a professor at the National Institute of Public Finance and Policy. 'He was a politician, and not really an active finance minister.' By her reckoning, Mukherjee came into office as a bubble was set to burst. Driven by an influx of foreign capital, growth accelerated too quickly. And the government, with its eye on the 2009 Lok Sabha elections, refused to slow spending and waited too long to raise interest rates or pull back its stimulus after the financial crisis. 'The economy was overheating,' she said. 'Ten per cent growth was faster than what the economy could take.'

The contrary view holds that double-digit growth would have continued had the government not snuffed it out. Surjit Bhalla, a loquacious, contrarian economist and investment manager, does not buy the bubble theory. By the end of 2009, as the crisis loomed, retail inflation was touching 15 per cent, and the RBI, which had begun to cut rates after the collapse of Lehman Brothers in September 2008, decided to reverse course. From March 2010 until October 2011, the RBI hiked the repo rate thirteen times by a total 375 basis points, among the fastest inclines on record.

In Bhalla's view, they completely misread the numbers and misdiagnosed the underlying cause of inflation, which he blames on a sharp rise in agricultural procurement prices orchestrated by Congress president Sonia Gandhi's National Advisory Council. In a 2011 study, Bhalla argued that a 10 per cent hike in procurement prices, timed to benefit farmers before the 2009 elections, led to a 3 per cent rise in consumer inflation.

'What did the RBI do?' Bhalla bellowed. 'They said, "Oh my god! There's excess demand, the economy is overheating!" It was nonsensical.'

As inflation soared, the then chief economic adviser, Arvind Virmani, felt much like Milton Friedman once did. Back in 2006, when growth was still near 10 per cent, Virmani had authored a Planning Commission report warning that it risked hitting a plateau unless immediate reforms arrived. Three years later, in his final economic survey as chief economic adviser, Virmani issued a further caution, in softer language—requisite for government documents, he assured me—on the need to contain the fiscal deficit while growth was still under way. The budget deficit, which had been targeted at 2.5 per cent of GDP in February 2008, hit 8.2 per cent a year later.

'Growth couldn't be taken for granted,' Virmani told me when we met in Delhi. 'But they ignored the warnings on the slowdown.' While things still looked good, Virmani said, clear signs of imminent trouble were entirely missed.

Though Rajan has written that the boom was not 'an aberration'—contrary to the bubble theory—he does not seem to agree with those who believe the economy was humming along in good health until the government spoiled the party. 'Strong growth tests economic institutions' ability to cope,' Rajan wrote in April, 'and India's were found lacking.' His own speeches and columns have emphasized the structural deficiencies in the Indian economy that were not repaired while growth was still booming, and badly exposed when it slowed down. As he said in a 2009 interview, referring to the crisis in America, 'It's at the point when people say there's no problem that in fact all the problems are building up.'

'We kept patting ourselves on the back that 8 per cent growth was our birthright,' said Pratap Bhanu Mehta, the president of the

Centre for Policy Research in Delhi. 'All the bodies that should have been thinking objectively did not do that in the lead-up to the crisis.'

A minor awakening arrived last September, when Chidambaram called in the emeritus economist Vijay Kelkar, who penned the first government report to spell out the dire fiscal situation. That same month, the finance ministry announced its 'big bang': further liberalization of foreign direct investment and plans to reduce costly diesel subsidies. But the economists I spoke to were distinctly unimpressed. As a slice of GDP, foreign direct investment inflows are less than 2 per cent.

Ashok Desai, who was chief economic adviser in Manmohan Singh's finance ministry during the 1991 crisis, scoffed at the government's belated moves. Over the past two decades, Desai told me, 'the word "reforms" became a sort of holy term', drained of its significance by politicians eager to claim its mantle. 'Everyone used it without meaning it.'

On 14 April last year, a small gathering was held in Delhi to celebrate the re-release of a book of essays honouring Desai's finance minister. Rajan stepped up to the podium, began with brief words of praise for Manmohan Singh, and then swiftly bore down on the failures of his government. New reforms had been held back by 'an unholy coalition' between 'the connected' and the Congress, Rajan declared, in what one observer described as 'a near tongue-lashing' of the prime minister. 'We need to become paranoid again, as we were in the early 1990s,' Rajan concluded.

Four months later, he became the next Chicago economist summoned to Delhi.

III

In 1966, three years after his third child, Raghuram, was born in Bhopal, R. Govindarajan was posted to Indonesia. A failed coup the previous year had sparked off a frenzy of violence, which targeted communist supporters of the Indonesian President Sukarno and claimed more than half a million lives. 'I remember the sound of machine guns in the evenings,' Rajan told me. 'My mother bore the brunt of the uncertainties. You had soldiers with a lot of authority moving around. It wasn't clear that they would respect diplomatic immunity.'

Profiles of Rajan invariably describe him as the son of an Indian diplomat, whose further assignments took the family to Sri Lanka and Belgium. Growing up, Rajan assumed his father worked for the ministry of external affairs. But Govindarajan, who topped his 1953 Indian Police Service batch, was an officer in the Intelligence Bureau (IB); he would have been dispatched to Indonesia as a spy, not a diplomat.

When the IB was split to create a separate external intelligence agency in 1968, Govindarajan became one of the original 'Kaoboys'—the first men to join the new Research and Analysis Wing (R&AW) under the legendary spymaster R.N. Kao, for whom Rajan's father was officer of staff, according to a former R&AW director.

When Rajan was seven, the Tamil brahmin family moved to Sri Lanka. He recalled it as 'a time of turmoil' in the country. 'One of the years I was there, there was no school, so we played,' he said. Rajan's younger brother, Mukund, was born in Chennai in 1968; he is now a top executive at Tata Sons, where he serves as brand custodian, chief ethics officer and spokesman. (Rajan's older brother now works for a solar company in the US; his only sister is a French teacher in Delhi, married to an Indian Administrative Service officer.) After Sri Lanka, the family moved to Brussels, where the children attended a French school, and then returned to Delhi in 1974, eleven months before Indira Gandhi declared the Emergency.

In Rajan's narrative of his own life, delivered in interviews, speeches and his own writing, his encounter with the dysfunctional Indian economy of the Emergency years plays a pivotal symbolic role. It's a kind of origin myth for the economist he would later become: a champion of capitalism who is acutely aware of both the unintended consequences of government intervention and the risks of unregulated financial markets.

The Rajans were certainly not suffering: his father was a senior government employee, with income sufficient to buy a car but influence too weak to jump the waiting list. But the shortages of certain goods came as a shock: the children took turns each day searching for shops selling bread. 'I went from seeing the supermarket filled and toys galore [in Brussels] to a country where you had to hunt for bread, and milk was a luxury,' Rajan told *Businessweek* in 2011.

As Rajan tells the story in his bestselling 2010 account of the global financial crisis, *Fault Lines*, Indira Gandhi's puzzling policies turned him towards his eventual profession. 'I thought there might be some grand design I did not understand,' Rajan wrote, 'but the government's policy clearly was not working, because India was still poor. I was determined to learn more, so I became interested in economics.'

But the young graduate first took a far more conventional route. Rajan went to the Indian Institute of Technology (IIT) Delhi and studied electrical engineering, graduating in 1985 with the prestigious Director's Gold Medal, awarded to the best all-round student. He did well academically, one classmate told me, but he was not 'one of the nerds'. He was an avid quizzer, and a decent bowler. Anant Jhingran, who won the President's Gold Medal, given to the top-ranked student, recalled that 'many of us excelled in studies, but Raghu was by far the best all-rounder'.

According to one of Rajan's close friends from the university, IIT was the first place where Rajan faced people who outperformed him academically. 'Raghu thought he would be number one,' the friend said. 'He ended up about 25th—not at all at the top of the class. That, for him, was a very sobering experience.'

IIT was also the stage for Rajan's first lesson in Indian politics. He struggled with Hindi, a language he learnt only after arriving in Delhi. His classmates did not let this pass. 'Of course we made fun,' Jhingran recalled, laughing. In his final year, Rajan contested elections to head the Student Affairs Council. At the time, the school was divided between English- and Hindi-speaking factions, Rajan's friend told me. Rajan ran as the de facto English candidate, against a Hindi speaker, who defeated him. 'He was very disenchanted about IIT after that,' his friend said.

But Rajan's education in Indian politics continued after the election. The victor was revealed to have taken kickbacks from a school canteen supplier, and promptly ejected from office. Rajan's friends urged him to run again, and he agreed—but only on the condition that no one contested against him, his friend recalled. In the end, another Hindi speaker challenged him anyway, but this time Rajan won.

After graduating, Rajan went on to the Indian Institute of Management (IIM) Ahmedabad, where he earned another gold medal for his master's work. As at IIT, he is remembered fondly there, as a congenial pupil and peer. Samir Barua, a retired dean who taught Rajan in an advanced mathematics course, told me he was 'an extremely bright student'. At the time, the financial sector was contracting, and many students were contemplating careers in academia, which Barua considered a natural move for Rajan.

Barua's expectations were not widely shared. 'He was not a bookish kind of guy,' one of his IIM classmates told me in July. 'I would never fathom him in this particular role. I thought he would be a corporate guy.'

For a brief time, Rajan was. After IIM, he joined Tata Adminstrative Services as a management trainee. In a 2006 talk at the Forum for Free Enterprise in Mumbai, Rajan related a telling anecdote from his brief time there—an episode that he claimed prompted his departure from Tata, and then from India:

> A CEO of one of the group companies berated the engineers in the group of management trainees he was taking around, arguing that we had wasted the nation's money by taking a precious engineering place and then departing to the ranks of management. While he was showing us around the factory, however, we noticed two elevators going up. We appeared to be waiting for the elevator on the left even though the elevator on the right was available. When asked why, he replied, 'We are waiting for the management elevator, this one is for the engineers and workers.'

Rajan went on:

> So despite all the rhetoric about socialism, government policies were of the few, by the few, and for the few. I have argued that this may have been unintended, but perhaps I am being charitable. Perhaps indeed the consequences were fully intended, but were cloaked in the rhetoric of social purpose, and the public confused with smoke and mirrors.

In the fall of 1987, he departed for a doctoral programme in management at the Massachusetts Institute of Technology's (MIT) Sloan School of Management.

By the time Rajan was preparing to leave India, his father had ascended to the top ranks of R&AW. The agency's director, S.E. Joshi, was set to retire in June 1987, and Govindarajan was in line to succeed him. But according to two published accounts, which were confirmed by a former R&AW chief, his ascent was suddenly derailed earlier that year by an unexpected development: the eruption of the Bofors scandal.

On 16 April, Swedish Radio aired its first report on the kickbacks paid by Bofors to Indian officials and politicians. Late that same night—after midnight, according to Prashant Bhushan's book *Bofors: The Selling of the Nation*—Rajiv Gandhi summoned his IB chief and the acting director of R&AW, Govindarajan, to an urgent meeting at his house:

> They were immediately ushered into the Prime Minister's office. The Prime Minister was wide awake and quickly asked them what was happening. Govindarajan, who had just returned from out of town the previous night, was taken by surprise. He had no idea what the Prime Minister wanted to know.

As a result, Gandhi superseded Govindarajan and installed a more junior officer, A.K. Verma, as the R&AW chief. Govindarajan was instead made chairman of the government's joint intelligence committee, where he remained until his retirement.

(In his memoir of the spy service, *The Kaoboys of R&AW*, the late B. Raman provides a less detailed account of the same episode without naming Govindarajan, referring instead to an 'officer of the Tamil Nadu cadre' who was superseded because Gandhi was annoyed that 'he was unaware of the Bofors scandal when it broke out in the Swedish electronic media'.)

When I first mentioned his father's career in R&AW, Rajan was taken aback; it seemed possible nobody had put the question to him before. ('He's very uncomfortable talking about himself,' one of Rajan's old friends told me.) He confirmed that his father had been in line to head the spy agency, but denied that the Bofors story had anything to do with Gandhi's decision.

'My father's experience in bureaucracy was a good one,' Rajan said, uncomfortably, when I asked if it had in any way influenced his decision to return to India. 'But that didn't—I didn't join the bureaucracy. So it wasn't what I wanted to do. I wanted to read, write, think.'

Rajan completed his PhD at MIT the year that the Indian economy opened up, when he was only twenty-eight. His thesis, 'Essays on Banking', examined the particular nature of the relationship between banks and lenders at a time when broad deregulation had dramatically altered the banking sector in industrial nations. Deregulation was presumed to increase competition, and competition presumed to increase efficiency, Rajan wrote in the introduction. Each of the book's three essays, however, considers a situation in which this might not be the case, due to the unique nature of the relationship between banks and creditors, which is more than merely transactional. By focusing on what he would later call 'the plumbing underlying the industrial economy', it was possible to understand why it was not always as frictionless as advertised—an insight that allowed him to see the dangers of risk accumulating on bank balance sheets before the financial crisis.

In one chapter, Rajan contemplated the repeal of a US law that mandated the separation of commercial and investment banking. The argument for increased competition would suggest that commercial banks should be allowed to compete with investment banks to underwrite corporate offerings. (Indeed, the US repealed the law in 1999, though some have argued it should be reinstated in the wake of the financial crisis.) Rajan's analysis argued that while repealing the law appeared to increase competition, the naturally monopolistic character of banking relationships would make its actual impact ambiguous. The conclusion is not atypical for academia, but it would become a trademark of Rajan's academic career, where his findings often landed as deeply informed scepticism: *we just don't know*.

He settled in Chicago in 1991, where he became assistant professor of finance at the Booth School of Business. Rajan and his wife, Radhika, a fellow IIM Ahmedabad graduate, socialized in Hyde Park, the university neighbourhood where they lived with their two children. The svelte Rajan ran along the lakeshore nearby and played squash with a typical competitiveness, his colleague and co-author Luigi Zingales told me. He did little else. 'I don't think he had a lot of excitement in his life, besides work and family,' Zingales said.

Rajan published regularly on arcane banking and finance topics and lent an occasional quote to the press, though rarely on issues involving India. He extended his reach in 2003, with the publication of his first book, *Saving Capitalism from the Capitalists*, co-authored with Zingales. Both an ode to competition and an indictment of the entrenched interests, business or political, that seek to stifle it, the book gained some traction among economists and policymakers. Bruce Bartlett, a conservative economist who worked under Ronald Reagan and George H.W. Bush, called it 'one of the most powerful defences of the free market ever written'. But it was hardly a popular tract. 'The book struck a chord with a lot of people in high places,' Zingales told me. 'It was not read on airplanes.'

Among his fellow economists, Rajan's reputation was steadily growing. His profile rose further in August 2003, when he was unexpectedly appointed as the chief economist at the IMF, the youngest person to occupy the post, and the first born in an emerging-market nation.

Rajan arrived at the IMF in the midst of an ongoing intellectual brawl. His predecessor, Kenneth Rogoff, had been engaged in a public spat with Joseph Stiglitz, the former chief economist at the World Bank. At the time, the IMF was recovering from a soiled reputation in the wake of the East Asian crisis a few years earlier. Stiglitz, a liberal macroeconomist and Nobel laureate, loudly criticized the IMF's typical austerity recipe for developing countries—forcing deficit reductions, removing controls on capital inflows and hiking interest rates. Rogoff shot back with a famously combative open letter to Stiglitz, but left his position soon thereafter.

Rajan brought a calming force. He kept the IMF's austerity policies largely intact, without the drama. Joshua Felman, an Asia economist at the IMF, characterized his former colleague in similar terms to many others I interviewed. 'He's very approachable. He gets into debates, but it's very hard not to like him,' Felman said.

In interviews, Rajan frequently harks back to his IMF tenure as a sign of his willingness to leave the comfortable confines of academia for the hurly-burly of public life. 'I remember, when I went to the Fund,' he told me, 'Gary Becker [a Nobel laureate and colleague of Rajan's at Chicago] asked me, "Are you nuts?" This time he was more complimentary. But I think the general sense in academia is "You must be crazy."'

It was at the IMF that Rajan first showed his flair for subtle defiance. In 2005, he and Arvind Subramanian published a paper that bucked the conventional wisdom on the efficacy of foreign aid, which they concluded had an adverse impact on developing countries, hindering their competitiveness. 'It came very close, in people's eyes, to saying motherhood is wrong,' Felman recalled.

An economist who was then working in the Fund's China division told me that the paper aired an unspoken understanding within the organization about the deficiencies of foreign aid, but failed to provide an alternative way forward for rich lenders dealing with poorer countries. 'You're not telling me what the right thing is,' the economist said. 'It did leave people hanging, worried about the silence.'

The following year, Rajan and Subramanian released another contrarian study, which could also be seen to have upturned a consensus without providing any replacement. It focused on capital controls, barriers to foreign investment inflows that Rajan had assailed in his first book with Zingales. This paper reached a radically different conclusion. Contrary to the orthodox view among economists—which informed the IMF's austerity recipes—the paper found that non-industrial countries that opened themselves up to foreign capital typically grew slower than those that did not.

In his short time as RBI governor, Rajan has been lauded for his definitive stances, but conclusions like these are the hallmark of his intellectual positions, which often insist there is no one-size-fits-all theory to guide economic policy. Rather than certitude, his academic career has been defined by a blend of scepticism, pragmatism and caution, traits that will surely mark his tenure at Mint Road—and infuriate his inevitable critics.

IV

At least until a few weeks ago—when Rajan gave his inaugural speech in Mumbai and woke up the next day to find his picture on the front page of nearly every newspaper in India—the defining moment of his career came in a small Wyoming resort town.

In August 2005, the US Federal Reserve gathered for its annual symposium in Jackson Hole. Alan Greenspan, who had been the Fed's chairman for the previous eighteen years, would be making his final appearance at the conference, which took on the character of a sentimental farewell tribute. The American economy was soaring, and Greenspan was its esteemed chieftain. Many of the financiers and economists in attendance attributed the era's sustained global growth to the financial innovation ushered in by Greenspan's policies. Four years earlier, the famed Watergate journalist Bob Woodward had penned a book-length portrait of the Fed chairman, simply titled *Maestro*.

And then Raghuram Rajan, the forty-two-year-old IMF chief economist, stood up and laid into the maestro's work.

The paper that Rajan delivered was titled 'Has Financial Development Made the World Riskier?' His answer was a decisive yes. Deregulation, competition and new innovations like securitization had created distorted incentives for bankers to take on excess risk in pursuit of short-term gains, Rajan argued, placing the entire economy at the mercy of a crisis. Three years later, the system imploded almost exactly as he had warned.

'I exaggerate only a bit when I say I felt like an early Christian who had wandered into a convention of half-starved lions,' Rajan later wrote in *Fault Lines*. Larry Summers, the former US treasury secretary who was until recently the leading contender to fill Greenspan's old seat, dismissed Rajan's concerns as 'slightly Luddite' and 'largely misguided'. Donald Kohn, a Federal Reserve governor, was even harsher, chiding Rajan as woefully nostalgic.

At that point, Greenspan was 'the king', the Princeton economist Alan Blinder said in a 2009 interview. 'So when you disagreed with Greenspan,' Blinder recalled, 'you were up there on the foothills of Mount Olympus disagreeing with Zeus.'

Blinder was the only economist to publicly defend Rajan at the Fed symposium, remarking on the 'unremitting attack he is getting here for not being a sufficiently good Chicago economist'. But after the crisis, when the anti-regulation views associated with the university's economists came into disrepute, Rajan was the only one whose credibility remained undamaged.

The Jackson Hole episode neatly illustrates the difficulty of pinning down Rajan's economic ideology. A champion of capitalism and free markets, he has also argued, as he did in Wyoming, for firmer regulation. *Fault Lines*, a treatise on the causes of the financial crisis, begins with a chapter focused on rising US income inequality—a concern associated with the American left, not the right. In Rajan's diagnosis, risky economic policies were put in place by politicians attempting to compensate voters for their diminishing faith in social mobility. 'Easy credit', one of the book's chief villains, becomes a way to reassure 'those left behind by growth and technological progress', but it introduces unsustainable levels of risk into the financial system. 'If you read *Fault Lines*, it reads like an absolutely classic Marxist critique of capitalism,' Pratap Bhanu Mehta said.

But in the biggest post-crisis economic battle in the US, Rajan is entrenched firmly in the rightward camp. Because he sees easy credit—in the form of low interest rates and government efforts to make loans available to low-income homebuyers—as one of the chief culprits in the crisis, he has loudly opposed the Federal Reserve's efforts to keep rates near zero and boost employment and growth with quantitative easing.

Rajan's theory of the post-crisis recession holds that persistent unemployment is 'structural'. In other words, the bubbles that inflated and then burst in certain sectors of the economy—including housing, construction and finance—will not return, and workers who lost their jobs need education and training to get new ones elsewhere.

The opposing camp holds that unemployment is 'cyclical', caused by a drop in consumer demand that could easily be rejuvenated by government spending if stingy politicians would allow it. The chief proponent of this view is Paul Krugman, the Princeton Nobel laureate and *New York Times* columnist who has repeatedly berated Rajan for his opposition to further stimulus and low interest rates during a time of high unemployment and stunted growth.

In July 2010, as the Federal Reserve prepared its second round of quantitative easing, Rajan wrote an op-ed in the *Financial Times* urging Bernanke to raise rates instead—lest the US repeat 'the same monetary policies that led to disaster'. Liberal economists tore into Rajan: Krugman called the argument 'depressing', and argued 'it would be an utter disaster for the economy'.

Neatly placing Rajan on the ideological map in India is not so simple. He stayed out of the fray in this summer's exaggerated battle between Jagdish Bhagwati and Amartya Sen, and his views suggest sympathies with both sides of the rather oversimplified 'growth versus welfare' debate. Rajan's ideas are broadly in line with Bhagwati's argument for growth as the main driver of development, and it's hard to imagine him as an enthusiastic supporter of the UPA welfare measures that have been blamed for inflating deficits.

Yet he has couched many of his indictments of the Indian economy in Sen-like terms. In a 2008 speech in Mumbai called 'Is There a Threat of Oligarchy in India?', he pointed to the troubling number of billionaires whose fortunes were made by their control over land, resources and government licences. He has repeatedly emphasized the need for government to provide better healthcare and education, two of Sen's standbys—one could easily imagine the Bengali Nobelist saying that 'our entire bureaucratic system of provision of public goods is biased against access by the poor', as Rajan did in the same Mumbai speech.

This is the Rajan several in India want to see: the free-market champion who rails against oligarchy. 'In India, the defence of capitalism has become the defence of crony capitalism,' Mehta told me two days after Rajan's RBI appointment. 'Indian capitalism really needs to be saved from capitalists.'

Rajan's first engagement with Indian economic policymaking came in the autumn of 1998, in the Boston apartment of his old IIT classmate Jayant Sinha. The newly appointed Bharatiya Janata Party (BJP) finance minister, Yashwant Sinha, was visiting his son in the midst of a US tour, and Jayant invited his friend Rajan to come from Chicago.

In Boston, the elder Sinha asked the young economist for ideas. Rajan gave him two major recommendations, according to the finance minister's 2007 memoir. The first was to ease the process for income tax filing to broaden the pathetic collection rates; the second was to boost home ownership. Sinha soon introduced a one-page filing form for taxpayers; in his next budget, he unfurled an increase in interest deductions on home mortgages.

Soon Rajan also began advising the RBI and the Securities and Exchange Board of India (SEBI). In 2002, Sinha invited Rajan to consult with the finance ministry. Ajay Shah, then an economist in North Block, told me that he worked with Rajan to craft two pieces of banking legislation.

Their partnership was interrupted when Rajan was offered the IMF job in 2003. But it was around when Rajan's time at the IMF ended, in 2006, that he began to write more often about his own country. Two years later, he met Manmohan Singh in Neemrana, at an annual economic conference that Rajan had helped launch. After the collapse of Lehman Brothers triggered the global crisis, Rajan was appointed an 'honorary economic adviser' to the prime minister.

That job involved writing policy notes at Singh's request. In 2010, the deputy chairman of the Planning Commission, Montek Singh Ahluwalia, assigned an economist to work part-time with Rajan on the notes. 'That was the time when his intellectual ideas on India developed,' the economist, who went on to work for Rajan at the finance ministry, told me.

Shortly after Rajan met Manmohan Singh in Neemrana, Ahluwalia drafted him to head a government committee on financial sector reforms. The resulting 200-page report, *A Hundred Small Steps*, was broad in scope yet detailed in directives. 'It was much more suave and polished', than an earlier effort on the same subject that had failed to gain traction, said Ajay Shah, who worked on both reports. It captured the style Rajan has taken within institutions: bold yet pragmatic. The financial press praised the report for targeting small experiments beneath legislative concern—what the report called 'low-hanging fruit'—over familiar but implausible reforms. It also contained a recommendation that became freshly relevant when Rajan became RBI governor. Monetary policy, the report said, should have a 'clearly defined primary objective': taming inflation.

As Rajan's involvement in Indian economic policy slowly deepened, he began to speak out more acidly on the country's failings. The Indian edition of *Fault Lines* features an entire additional chapter on the country, in which Rajan pillories the government for its cosiness with the 'rich' and 'powerful'. In April 2012, the same month that he lambasted the UPA government's policies before an audience that included the prime minister, Rajan deployed even stronger language in a graduation address at the Indian School of Business in Hyderabad. In India, he lamented, 'We keep repeating failed experiment after failed experiment.'

Though Rajan's growing body of speeches and writings on India provides a useful summary of his insights into the country's economic and political issues, there are several key subjects he has rarely, if ever, addressed. There are few references in his writing to the rising fiscal deficit, which he had warned of in 2004 while at the IMF. As an economist who has specialized in banking and finance, one might have also expected more commentary from Rajan on the increasingly dangerous expansion of bad loans on the books of Indian banks.

Throughout much of this time, Rajan was sending missives to Raisina Hill. What went unsaid in his public writing may have crept into private statements. When I asked Rajan about his memos to Singh, he was characteristically discreet about their contents, though his remarks suggested a deepening appreciation of the political challenges facing Indian policymakers. The memos were 'primarily updates on what was going on in the world economy', Rajan told me. 'There were some India-specific suggestions. But of course, from the outside, it's harder to see the constraints,' he said. 'I don't think the recommendations changed substantially in some time, partly because I think it was difficult to get a lot done here.'

Rajan has not divulged the moment when he decided to come to India, where difficulty persisted, and leave the confines of academic stardom: after the publication of *Fault Lines*, he was in high demand on the speaking circuit—earning about $40,000 per appearance.

'I don't want to make it sound as grandiose as giving back,' he told me when I asked what prompted his return. 'The way I think about it, if I woke up at age sixty-five and saw either a very successful country or a very unsuccessful country, either way I would have tremendous regret in not having played a part—either for the good or preventing the bad.'

V

On 14 April, Chidambaram set off for a weeklong trip across the Atlantic. His companion, and the broker for many of his meetings, was his chief economic adviser. It was the final leg in an international tour for Chidambaram, which included several public appearances and a quiet but determined effort to court foreign investors, touting a turnaround in the Indian investment climate.

Rajan's central role on the tour provided another example of his global reputation, the trait many suspect was the prime motivation for his recruitment. 'What you get with him, for free, is this international image,' an economist who worked under Rajan in the finance ministry told me. 'We were all aware of that.'

Before Rajan's appointment as RBI governor was announced, several people close to him told me that had he not received the job, he would have swiftly packed his bags and returned to Chicago. His stint as chief economic adviser was merely 'a stop-gap before heading to the RBI', said the economist Laveesh Bhandari, who heads the research firm Indicus Analytics. As an outsider, Rajan needed to tally some experience in the Indian bureaucracy to help overcome any resistance to his appointment.

'He had wanted to come back to India, clearly, for a much longer amount of time,' Aziz, the J.P. Morgan economist, told me. 'But there are very few openings in India where Rajan can fit in, given who he is, given his stature.'

Rajan's staff at the finance ministry described him as both an unrelenting workhorse and an effective manager, who welcomed their ideas and invited them to meet the cast of luminaries parading through his office, like Nouriel Roubini, another prophet of the financial crisis, and the *New York Times* columnist Thomas Friedman.

Inside the ministry, Rajan was more pragmatist than renegade. 'There was this expectation in the media that he was Chicago style, and would come in and blast UPA's leftist policies,' one of his economists told me. 'That's not how he worked.'

The chief economic adviser's main task is to produce the government's annual survey. Rajan's is a foreboding document that pleads for 'urgent steps' to reduce government spending and subsidies and lays out a few recommendations—labour law repeals, vocational training, formal apprenticeships—to direct Indians from agriculture to services and skilled manufacturing jobs. It predicts a dire future if further reforms don't arrive soon.

Several people with knowledge of the finance ministry's workings told me that Rajan carried considerable influence in North Block, and was more actively involved in internal decisions than prior chief economic advisers. But that degree of involvement did not guarantee his advice led to action.

'His impact is very marginal, simply because the government itself is not functioning,' Bhandari told me in July. Mittal, the retired finance ministry secretary, told me that 'it was not possible to say he has a very large influence on the government'. His tenure wasn't long enough, and his international stature had a consequence: according to Mittal, Rajan spent roughly half his time outside India. (That included teaching a course on corporate finance back in Chicago.) 'But he's a very bright and very nice man,' Mittal added quickly. 'No question about that.'

Rajan's staffers preferred to describe his lack of sweeping influence inside the ministry as a sign of tactical savvy. 'He picks his battles inside,' one of the economists who worked for Rajan told me. 'He had a good relationship with Chidambaram.'

One battle that Rajan picked, and presumably lost, involved the government's Food Security Bill. From his academic work, it is clear that Rajan is inclined to support direct cash transfers rather than subsidies, and his concerns about the rising fiscal deficit surely angled him against the programme. 'I know for a fact that Rajan was upset about the Food Security Bill,' the economist Swaminathan Aiyar told me.

If so, his displeasure took typical Rajan form: an affront through academic rigour. His office asked the Bharti Institute of Public Policy in Hyderabad to conduct a thorough study of food distribution. When I spoke to Prachi Mishra, a senior economist in the office of the chief economic adviser, she avoided Aiyar's strong language about Rajan's views, but admitted that she worked closely with Rajan to review the food bill. Her study of the measure, whose findings she published in the *Economic Times*, argued that the government had ignored the non-subsidy costs of setting up and implementing the programme, and therefore underestimated its price tag by at least Rs 1.43 lakh crore (Rs 1.43 trillion) over three years.

The economists who worked under Rajan insisted that the finance ministry welcomed all ideas, and on particular policies, like the Food Security Bill, would let grievances be fully aired. But although it remains open to dissent, the ministry, like the UPA itself, dawdles along through consensus.

If Rajan ever became angry with this reality, his staffers claimed they never saw it. 'I'm sure he's had his moments of extreme frustrations,' one told me. 'Look, he's come from a completely different world to this jungle.'

Rajan used a softer metaphor to describe his time in Delhi. 'Government is a big ship,' he told me. 'Not every part of government flows in the same direction.' When I asked him for concrete examples, he declined to provide them. 'There are places where we take a long time coming to a decision,' he said. 'Sometimes that's because consensus-building takes time; sometimes it's just because that's not on the front burner. And sometimes it's just plain sloth. To that extent, we want to eliminate the sloth.'

In the days after we met, Rajan looked very much like a man fighting sloth, or at least complacency. On 18 September, Bernanke startled the world by delaying the 'taper' of quantitative easing. It was a gift to the Indian economy, but two days later, Rajan declined to accept it and raised interest rates.

That decision swung stocks in the opposite direction of his first RBI speech. The original 'Rajan rally', Rajan surely knows, was powered by personality and luck. Many of the details in the agenda he laid out were not new; they had long been in the works at the RBI. Rajan had merely packaged them together, but his decision to prioritize these plans, combined with his vaunted reputation, drove expectations that they could be realized. He also happened to arrive at the moment when the threat of American military action in Syria faded, calming market jitters across the world.

'Many of those measures have been taken to try to boost confidence in the system,' the former RBI governor Bimal Jalan told me. 'They are not long-term steps. But they give the country time to take measures it needs to take.'

The financial press cheered Rajan's first outing, yet the Mumbai investor class took a wait-and-see stance. Two days after his big speech, Rajan's office quietly released a two-paragraph statement announcing that a $15 billion credit line swap with the Bank of Japan, unfurled last December, would extend by $35 billion. 'This is a more meaningful development than the speech he gave,' said Ritika Mankar Mukherjee, an economist with Ambit Capital. 'It tells you how well planned and systematic he is.'

It also reveals a calculated cooperation with Delhi, which was needed to stamp the swap deal. Of the five prior RBI governors since 1991, the only one to have a thoroughly cordial relationship with his finance minister was C. Rangarajan, who served alongside Manmohan Singh.

I failed to find anyone who would describe Rajan as uncongenial. He has a strong working relationship with the Congress party's economic leaders. Should the BJP come to power, Rajan may rely on the support of Yashwant Sinha, one of the party's leading economic figures. But in all my interviews, not a single person suggested that Rajan would be subservient to Delhi.

Rajan is now heading a behemoth bureaucracy that elicits a wide range of appraisals. As juggler of growth and inflation, some analysts judge it among the world's best, as *The Economist* did last year. Several Indian economists regard it as the worst. Many people consider it to be one of India's most efficient bureaucracies, though a few others take the opposite view.

'It's a bit like the Soviet Union,' said Shah, a vociferous critic of the central bank. 'Everyone has to say nice things, or it will all fall apart.' When we spoke in July, he wondered why his former research partner would want the governorship. 'It's a crown of thorns,' Shah told me. 'If someone offered it to me on a platter, I would say no.'

A. Seshan, a former officer-in-charge at the bank's economic analysis wing, told me in an email that the pressures on the RBI from Delhi, both 'overt and covert', have substantially escalated in recent years. In a study released last month by the Bank of Korea, two economists assessed the autonomy of ninety central banks, and judged the RBI to be the world's least independent.

When I asked Rajan about the study, he acknowledged that the 'explicit structure' of the bank might support that conclusion—the governor is appointed, and can be easily fired, by politicians in Delhi. But Rajan argued this view overlooked more implicit arrangements that prove the RBI governor commands respect and independence. 'The finance ministry will keep proposing their way of looking at things in the economy,' he said. 'But the central banker has the decision of whether he or she accepts them.'

'I don't think the differences [with the government] are as large as they are played out in the press,' Rajan continued. 'But if they are, that does reflect a great amount of independence. If the central bank was under the thumb of the finance ministry, there would be no differences.'

Rajan's first break with Delhi, his decision to raise interest rates, has already come under heavy scrutiny. Yet monetary policy is only a slim portion of his job. Much of the Indian economy churns outside the control of formal interest rates, and the central banker's role in regulating the banking and finance sector likely has a more significant effect on the large informal economy.

For some financial observers, this is disconcerting—they doubt Rajan's ability, as a bureaucratic outsider, to steer and challenge India's stodgy scheduled banks. For Rajan, the academic tenured on his banking expertise, this gamut of control is the central allure of the RBI governorship.

One of Rajan's initial proposals in this arena faces considerable hurdles. In July, three industrial houses—Aditya Birla, Reliance Capital and Tata Sons—applied for new bank licences that the RBI had recently made available. Chidambaram strongly backs letting them in, while Subbarao and the RBI have stood opposed. Rajan, with his concerns about India's tilt towards oligarchy, is widely considered to share his predecessor's stance. His maiden speech introduced plans for 'on-tap' licensing, a process that, in essence, allows small banks to cut the line for licences. It will, one RBI veteran said, bring immense resistance from Mumbai's most powerful corporate houses.

It will also be the first major test of how Rajan handles his relationship with the finance ministry. His outsider status has earned praise internationally, but his lack of 'intensive India experience' is a severe handicap, said Bhandari of Indicus Analytics. 'You need people who you can pick up the phone and call,' he told me. 'You need those sorts of relationships.'

On 23 June, Rajan was away from Delhi, delivering a lecture on 'unconventional monetary policy after the crisis' at the Bank of International Settlement in Basel.

The talk was trademark Rajan. It focused on a 'debt-fuelled crisis' driven by easy credit that had been doled out by 'shortsighted' politicians, and it ended with nothing more definitive than a question mark:

> The bottom line is that unconventional monetary policies that move away from repairing markets or institutions to changing prices and inflationary expectations seem to be a step into the dark.

By this point, it was an open secret that Rajan was a leading contender to head the RBI: his staff would hold back laughs at his public appearances when the media invariably asked Rajan about the job, and he invariably refused to comment. In the days after his appointment, one of his staff economists bemoaned the 'hero-worshipping' under way, which unfairly put the burden of restoring the economy on a man who cannot do it alone.

Perhaps Rajan anticipated this. In hindsight, his Basel speech reads as a prescient prediction, personal defence and, maybe, apology. He ended with a lengthier exposition on the 'magic wand' he would soon deny possessing:

> When the central banker offers himself as the only game in town, in an environment where politicians only have choices between the bad and the worse, he becomes the only game in town. Everyone cedes the stage to the central banker, who cannot admit that his tools are untried and of unknown efficacy. The central banker has to be confident, and will constantly refer to the many bullets he still has even if he has very few. But that very public confidence traps him because the public wants to know why he is not doing more.

Central banks took their 'step into the dark', Rajan said, out of 'hubris'—a word he had used five years earlier in Mumbai as a warning of what might bring India to her knees. In Basel, Rajan asked if this same hubris had also convinced central bankers they possessed a 'Midas touch'. His answer went unsaid, but it was definitive.

When I went to Ambala Central Jail in early 2012, hoping to meet **SWAMI ASEEMANAND**, I had no idea what awaited me. I was taken aback when this holy man, in jail awaiting trial for his suspected role in terror attacks allegedly perpetrated by Hindu extremist groups, bared his heart to me, believing that I was an admirer. He put my courage, honesty and sanity to severe test. In the next two years, I would often open Janet Malcolm's *The Journalist and the Murderer* and read it like it was the Bible. Was I committing the sin of being a 'kind of confidence man, preying on people's vanity, ignorance, or loneliness, gaining their trust and betraying them without remorse?' He imagined that I was a believer in the cause.

The story made some waves when it broke, and its revelations were discussed and debated on prime-time TV. It provides a rare first-person account into the innards of Hindutva ideology, and its extreme means and ends. But, as I feared when I was reporting the story, it changed little. It pains me that, maybe, to many of my fellow countrymen—who may or may not believe in the Rashtriya Swayamsevak Sangh and its strident version of patriotism—this story must have been too fantastic to believe.

I also regret giving the National Investigation Agency (NIA), a key player in this story, a respect that it has done nothing to deserve in the intervening years. As this story gained attention, the NIA told the *Caravan* it was keen to use the taped conversation as evidence in their case. We waited months for them with copies of the tapes on CDs and pendrives. They never showed. As I write this, neither they, nor any other agency, has shown any interest in investigating Aseemanand's startling statements. Last August, the NIA decided to not challenge Aseemanand's bail in the Samjhauta bombing case. He remains in judicial custody, as he is yet to obtain bail in the other terrorism cases that he is involved in. His trial is in progress and many of the important witnesses of the case have turned hostile. Meanwhile, the NIA is back to investigating the role of Pakistan's ISI in the case, in spite of having abandoned that theory once already. I will be unsurprised, in the present circumstances, if Aseemanand becomes a free man again.

LEENA REGHUNATH

Leena Gita Reghunath is a journalist and former lawyer. She was the editorial manager at the Caravan *while she was working on this story.*

The Believer
Swami Aseemanand's Radical Service to the Sangh

By LEENA GITA REGHUNATH | 1 February 2014

I

'*Swamiji ko bulao*,' the jailer ordered. Call the Swami. Two police constables scurried out of the jailer's office and onto the grounds of the prison. A deafening noise reverberated through the room, as if a hundred men outside the walls were howling at the same time. It was visiting hours in early January 2011 at Ambala's Central Jail.

After a few minutes, Swami Aseemanand, the Hindu firebrand accused of plotting several terrorist attacks on civilian targets across the country between 2006 and 2008, stepped into the doorway of the jailer's office. He wore a saffron dhoti and a saffron kurta that hung down to his knees. The clothes were freshly ironed. A woollen monkey cap was pulled down over his forehead, and a saffron shawl was wrapped around his neck. He looked bemused to see me. We exchanged namastes, then he ushered me through a door into an adjoining room, where clerks in white dhoti–kurtas were poring over titanic ledgers. He sat on a large wooden trunk behind the door, and instructed me to pull a chair from a nearby desk. He was informal, like a good host, and asked me about my visit. 'Somebody has to tell your story,' I said.

This was the beginning of the first of four interviews I had with Aseemanand over more than two years. He is currently under trial on charges including murder, attempt to murder, criminal conspiracy and sedition, in connection with three bombings in which at least eighty-two people were killed. He could also be tried for two other blast cases; he has been named in the chargesheets, but not yet formally accused. Together, the five attacks killed 119 people, and worked as a corrosive on the bonds of Indian society. If convicted, Aseemanand may face the death penalty.

In the course of our conversations, Aseemanand became increasingly warm and open. The story he told of his life was remarkable and haunting. He is fiercely proud of the acts of violence he has committed and the principles by which he has lived. For more than four decades, he has loyally promoted Hindu nationalism; during much of that time, he worked under the banner of the Rashtriya Swayamsevak Sangh's (RSS's) tribal affairs wing, the Vanvasi Kalyan Ashram (VKA), spreading the Sangh's version of Hinduism, and its vision for a Hindu Rashtra. Through all this, Aseemanand, who is now in his early sixties, has never diluted the intensity of his beliefs.

After the assassination of Mohandas Gandhi, Nathuram Godse and his accomplice Narayan Apte were executed by hanging and cremated at the Ambala jail, in 1949. Their co-conspirator, Godse's brother Gopal, was sentenced to eighteen years' imprisonment. 'I'm kept in the same cell as Gopal Godse,' Aseemanand proudly told me. Today, Aseemanand is perhaps the most prominent face of Hindu extremist terrorism. Journalists who met him in the years before the bombings described him to me as an extraordinarily arrogant and intolerant man. What I saw in the dark records room of the jail was a man subdued by his imprisonment, but void of remorse. 'Whatever happens to me, it's a good thing for Hindus,' Aseemanand told me. '*Logon me Hindutva ka bhaav aayega*'—it will stir Hindutva among the people.

On the night of 18 February 2007, the Samjhauta Express started on its usual course from platform 18 of the Delhi Junction railway station. The Samjhauta, also known as the 'Friendship Express', is one of only two rail links between India and Pakistan. That night, almost three-quarters of its roughly 750 passengers were Pakistanis returning home. A few minutes before midnight—an hour after the train started its journey—improvised explosive devices (IEDs) detonated in two unreserved compartments of the sixteen-coach train. Barrelling through the night, the train was now on fire.

The explosions fused shut the compartments' exits, sealing passengers inside. 'It was awful,' a railways inspector told the *Hindustan Times*. 'Burnt and half-burnt bodies of the passengers were all over in the coaches.' Two unexploded IEDs packed into suitcases were later discovered at the scene; the devices contained a mixture of chemicals including PETN, TNT, RDX, petrol, diesel and kerosene. Sixty-eight people died in the attack.

This was the second, and deadliest, of the five attacks in which Aseemanand is implicated. He is now accused number one in the Samjhauta train blasts; accused number three in a bombing at Hyderabad's Mecca Masjid that killed eleven people, in May 2007; and accused number six in a blast at the dargah in Ajmer, Rajasthan, that killed three people, in October 2007. He is also named, but not yet charged, in two attacks in Malegaon, Maharashtra, in September 2006 and September 2008, that together took the lives of thirty-seven people.

Many of these cases have been investigated by multiple agencies at different points in time—including the Mumbai Anti-Terrorist Squad (ATS), the Rajasthan ATS, the Central Bureau of Investigation (CBI), and the National Investigation Agency (NIA). At least a dozen chargesheets have been filed in the five cases. Thirty-one people have been formally accused, and two of Aseemanand's close associates are among them—Pragya Singh Thakur, who was a national executive member of the Bharatiya Janata Party's (BJP) student wing, the Akhil Bharatiya Vidyarthi Parishad (ABVP); and Sunil Joshi, who was a former RSS district leader in Indore. All of the investigative agencies determined that Aseemanand played a central role in plotting the attacks. Aseemanand, by his own account, hosted planning sessions, selected targets, provided funds for the construction of IEDs, and sheltered and otherwise aided those who planted the bombs.

In December 2010 and January 2011, Aseemanand made two judicial confessions, to courts in Delhi and Haryana, in which he admitted to planning the attacks. At the time of his confessions, Aseemanand refused legal representation. He spent forty-eight hours in judicial custody, insulated from investigating agencies, before making each statement, thereby giving him an opportunity to change his mind. Both times, Aseemanand resolved to confess, and had his statements recorded in court. His confessions, and the confessions of at least two of his fellow conspirators, allege that the attacks were planned with the knowledge of at least one senior member of the RSS.

On 28 March 2011, Aseemanand accepted legal representation. The next day, he retracted his confessions, claiming that they were coerced by torture. An application he submitted before the trial court read, 'the leak of Aseemanand's alleged confession to the media, which is shocking and deliberate, is a part of the design to politicize and hype the case, conduct and conclude a media trial, and to create, at the global level, the notion of Hindu terror for the political purposes of the ruling party'. Aseemanand and several of the defence lawyers working on the Samjhauta case told me that the lawyers are all members of the Sangh; one of them said that they manage the case in meetings of the Akhil Bharatiya Adhivakta Parishad, the RSS's legal wing.

When I interviewed him, Aseemanand denied being tortured, or that his confessions were coerced. He said that when he was arrested for the bombings, by the CBI, he decided it was 'a good time to tell all about this. I knew I could be hanged for it, but I'm old anyway'.

Over the course of our conversations, Aseemanand's description of the plot in which he was involved became increasingly detailed. In our third and fourth interviews, he told me that his terrorist acts were sanctioned by the highest levels of the RSS—all the way up to Mohan Bhagwat, the current RSS chief, who was the organization's general secretary at the time. Aseemanand told me that Bhagwat said of the violence, 'It's very important that it be done. But you should not link it to the Sangh.'

Aseemanand told me about a meeting that allegedly took place in July 2005. After an RSS conclave in Surat, senior Sangh leaders including Bhagwat and Indresh Kumar, who is now on the organization's powerful seven-member national executive council, travelled to a temple in the Dangs, Gujarat, where Aseemanand was living—a two-hour drive. In a tent pitched by a river several kilometres away from the temple, Bhagwat and Kumar met with Aseemanand and his accomplice Sunil Joshi. Joshi informed Bhagwat of a plan to bomb several Muslim targets around India. According to Aseemanand, both RSS leaders approved, and Bhagwat told him, 'You can work on this.' Indresh added, 'You can work on this with Sunil. We will not be involved, but if you are doing this, you can consider us to be with you.'

Aseemanand continued, 'Then they told me, "Swamiji, if you do this we will be at ease with it. Nothing wrong will happen then. Criminalization *nahin hoga* (It will not be criminalized). If you do it, then people won't say that we did a crime for the sake of committing a crime. It will be connected to the ideology.

This is very important for Hindus. Please do this. You have our blessings.'"

Chargesheets filed by the investigative agencies allege that Kumar provided moral and material support to the conspirators, but they don't implicate anyone as senior as Bhagwat. Although Kumar was interrogated once by the CBI, the case was later taken over by the NIA, which has not pursued the conspiracy past the level of Aseemanand and Pragya Singh. (Joshi, who was allegedly the connecting thread between several different parts of the conspiracy—including those who assembled and those who planted the bombs—was killed under mysterious circumstances in December 2007.)

Since allegations first emerged in late 2010 that Kumar had a role in the attacks, the RSS has closed ranks around him. Bhagwat, in an unprecedented act for an RSS *sarsanghchalak*, participated in a dharna to protest the accusations against Kumar. The BJP has also defended him, and the BJP national spokesperson Meenakshi Lekhi was his lawyer at the time he was named in the chargesheets. A lawyer for one of the accused told me that Kumar is 'highly ambitious', and 'in waiting to be the sarsanghchalak'.

An officer at one of the investigating agencies, on the condition of anonymity, allowed me to inspect a secret report submitted to the ministry of home affairs (MHA). The report requested that the MHA send a show-cause notice to RSS authorities, asking why the organization should not be banned in light of the evidence against them. The MHA has not yet acted on the recommendation.

The fear of being banned—as the organization briefly was after the assassination of Gandhi, in 1948; during the Emergency, in 1975; and after the demolition of the Babri Masjid, in 1992—looms over the RSS leadership. Whenever terrorist violence has been attributed to its members, the Sangh has taken a tack similar to the one they used with Nathuram Godse: there is no question of owning or disowning the perpetrators, the RSS says, because they have all previously left the Sangh, or were acting independently of the organization, or alienated themselves from it by embracing violence.

Aseemanand poses a serious problem to the RSS in this regard. Since it was founded in 1952, the VKA has been in the nucleus of the Sangh family, and Aseemanand has dedicated almost his entire adult life to serving the organization. At the time he planned the attacks, he had been the national head of the VKA's religious wing—a position created especially for him—for a decade. Even before the inception of the terrorist plot, organized violence (including coordinated communal riots) was a well-known part of his methods.

Bhagwat and Kumar were allegedly aware of Aseemanand's involvement in the plot by mid 2005. Aseemanand was not excommunicated—far from it. In December of that year, according to a report in *Organiser*, the RSS's weekly mouthpiece, he was honoured with a Rs 1 lakh award marking the birth centenary of M.S. Golwalkar, the RSS's second and most venerated chief; the veteran BJP leader and former party president Murli Manohar Joshi gave the ceremony's keynote address. Even if Kumar remains insulated from a full inquiry into the allegations against him, there can be little question of the RSS convincingly denying its brotherhood with Aseemanand.

Denouncing terror attacks launched in the last decade by members of the Sangh, Swami Agnivesh, a prominent Hindu reformist, told me that the RSS 'will harm themselves and others of the Hindu society' through militant Hindutva. 'It is deplorable,' he said. The political scientist Jyotirmaya Sharma, who has authored three books on Hindutva, said, 'The RSS involves itself in both covert and overt functions. But the organization's central premise is the sort of hit-and-run guerrilla warfare advocated by Ramdas, the guru of Shivaji. And the problem is that we don't have enough liberal institutions within the country—from political parties to even strong enough media—to counter such acts of terror waged so blatantly in the name of Hindu religion.'

Despite such condemnations, the Sangh has come a long way since the ignominy of 1948. Through their efforts at man-making and nation-building, the RSS and its affiliates, particularly the BJP, now seem to represent a major current in the mainstream of Indian society. Aseemanand, too, is in many ways a product of those efforts, and he shares the RSS's aims—albeit in magnified form: his vision for the future, he told me, is a global Hindu Rashtra.

II

Aseemanand's passionate belief in the Hindu Rashtra, and his commitment to violence as a means of securing it, emerged from two connected but radically different streams in Indian thought—the ecumenical karma yoga of the Ramakrishna Mission, and the Hindutva of the RSS. Aseemanand was shaped by both of these currents, and in some sense he chose to combine the ascetic life of the former with the extreme politics of the latter. This partly had to do with his early participation in a local RSS *shakha*, and it was also, in some measure, a rejection of the values of his father. In Aseemanand's own account, it was a sort of awakening—to Hinduism as a political force.

Aseemanand was born Naba Kumar Sarkar in the Hooghly district of West Bengal, sometime in late 1951. He is the second of seven sons of the freedom fighter Bibhutibhushan Sarkar, a Gandhian who told his children that Gandhi was his god. The village where they lived, Kamarpukur, was also the birthplace of the nineteenth-century sage Ramakrishna Paramhamsa, who preached '*yato mat, tato path*' (many faiths, many paths to god). Ramakrishna's most famous disciple, Swami Vivekananda, established the Ramakrishna Mission in 1897, to carry on the work of karma yoga—service through selfless action. Aseemanand grew up around the corner from the mission's local branch—a place of pilgrimage for Ramakrishna devotees—and spent many of his evenings listening to the monks there singing devotional songs.

Bibhutibhushan and his wife, Pramila, wanted their son to join the mission's holy orders—a source of pride for many devout Bengali families. But Aseemanand and his brothers were also drawn to the RSS, whose own version of social service was burgeoning under the leadership of M.S. Golwalkar. 'I have gone after ideologies in my youth and lived by them,' Aseemanand recalled his father telling them. 'So I understand when you are influenced by an ideology and want to follow it. But the RSS is the organization that killed Gandhi, so it is my duty to warn you against it.' The boys nevertheless grew close to local RSS workers, who often ate with the brothers at the Sarkar house, and they began participating in local shakhas. Aseemanand's elder brother joined the RSS full-time. Aseemanand and his younger brother Sushant Sarkar, whom I met in Kamarpukur, told me that their father didn't try to prevent this, but he issued a stern warning: they were never to introduce him to a member of the Sangh.

The balance of Aseemanand's beliefs tilted dramatically during his twenties, under the mentorship of two Sangh members. The first was Bijoy Adya, an RSS worker who guided Aseemanand towards radical Hindu politics. In his office in Kolkata, where he now edits the Bengali RSS newsweekly *Swastika*, Adya told me that he first met Aseemanand in 1971. Aseemanand was studying for his bachelor's degree in physics at a local university—he eventually got his master's degree as well—but 'his parents always understood that he was different from their other sons', Adya said. 'They knew that there was no way he would lead a normal life like the other brothers.' Aseemanand was also still a regular at the Ramakrishna Mission. 'It was in fact from his house that I read all the major literature on Vivekananda,' Adya said.

One of the books in the Sarkar library was *A Rousing Call to the Hindu Nation*, a collection of Vivekananda's writing and speeches edited by Eknath Ranade, a stalwart of the Hindutva movement whose colleagues gave him the nickname 'underground sarsanghchalak' for his leadership of the RSS during its prohibition following Gandhi's assassination. The book emphasized Vivekananda's call to Hindus to 'Arise! Awake! And stop not until the goal is reached.' The Ramakrishna Mission had wrongfully made Vivekananda a secular figure in order to get government funding, and it took Ranade's text to correct this, Adya said. (At the behest of the RSS chief Golwalkar, Ranade also oversaw the construction of the Rs 1.35-crore Vivekananda Rock Memorial off Kanyakumari, which was completed in 1970.) Adya encouraged Aseemanand to read the book.

'According to Ramakrishna Mission every religion is equal,' Aseemanand told me. 'They used to celebrate Christmas, Eid—so I used to do the same. When Adya said that this was not what Vivekananda preached I did not believe him.' He then took up Ranade's text. One particular line from Vivekananda dominated Aseemanand's reading: 'Every man going out of the Hindu pale is not only a man less, but an enemy the more.'

'I got a huge shock after reading this,' Aseemanand said. 'In the days that followed, I gave this a lot of thought. Then I realized that it is not in my limited capacity to realize or fully analyse

Vivekananda's teachings, but since he has said it, I will follow it all my life.' He never visited the Ramakrishna Mission again.

If Ranade's version of Vivekananda became the soul of Aseemanand's political conviction, its form was provided by an RSS worker and ascetic named Basant Rao Bhatt, who had moved to Calcutta from Nagpur, in 1956, to work under Ranade. Bhatt was fiercely dedicated to the mission of the RSS, but had a soft, disarming charisma; Aseemanand told me that even his father once remarked, 'It is hard to believe that an organization that has people like Basant working for it could be bad.' In Bhatt, who eventually became the chief of RSS operations for West Bengal, Aseemanand found an example of how to unite the ideology of the Sangh with the sort of pastoral service practised by monks of the Ramakrishna Mission.

When Indira Gandhi imposed the Emergency and banned the RSS in 1975, she started cracking down on its members. Thousands of Sangh workers were thrown in jail, including Aseemanand. Bhatt followed the example of his mentor, Ranade, and began operating underground, providing for the families of the imprisoned. When the ban was lifted at the end of the Emergency, Bhatt started a new wing of the VKA, to cover Bengal and the North-east. Soon after, Aseemanand moved in with him and began working full-time for the organization. In 1978, they founded the first VKA ashram in the north-eastern part of the country, in the forests of Baghmundi, near Purulia, West Bengal.

The push towards the North-east was part of a nationwide expansion of the VKA into tribal areas. Since it was founded in Jashpur (now in Chhattisgarh) by the RSS leader Balasaheb Deshpande—who began his work with a dozen children of the Oraon tribe—the organization has strived to counter the influence of Christian missionaries and to prevent tribals from converting.

Christianity, the Sangh believes, is a threat to the integrity of the nation, breeding separatist movements like those that have long operated in the North-east. The VKA's methods are largely derived from the successful model of Christian evangelists: it runs playgroups, primary and middle schools, hostels and health services that also serve as centres for proselytization. Its goal is to promote Hindutva and thereby increase the cultural and political capital of the RSS.

Aseemanand spent most of the next ten years working in Purulia to advance these aims. But he also decided to follow some version of the monastic path his parents intended for him, and at thirty-one he resolved to take *sanyaas*. Bhatt told him that if working with tribals and furthering the Sangh's cause was his mission, he didn't need to join a holy order. But Aseemanand had made up his mind, and left Purulia for the ashram of the Bengali guru Swami Paramananda. 'I chose him to be my guru because he followed Ramakrishna's teachings,' Aseemanand said. 'He worked mainly with the Dalits, but he was also involved in the propagation of Hinduism.' Paramananda administered the vows of sanyaas to Naba Kumar Sarkar, and renamed him Aseemanand—'boundless joy'.

After taking sanyaas, Aseemanand returned to Purulia and his work with the tribals. His life at the ashram there brought him into contact with the top leaders of the VKA, including its all-India organizing secretary, K. Bhaskara Rao, who was also for much of his life the RSS chief for Kerala (which today boasts over 4,000 shakhas—more than any other state). Impressed by Aseemanand, in 1988, Rao and the VKA president, Jagdev Ram Oraon, asked him to extend the VKA's *dharma jagran*—its work of spiritual awakening—to the Andamans.

Since colonial times, many of the more than 500 islands in the Andaman and Nicobar archipelago have been settled by Indians from the mainland. To build townships for the settlers, tribals from areas in what is now Chhattisgarh were often shipped in. By the 1970s, the Sangh feared that tribal migrants to the Andamans were becoming increasingly enthralled by Christian missionaries, making the islands hostile to Hindus and Hindutva, Aseemanand told me. The islands had been represented in Parliament for more than a decade by a Congressman, Manoranjan Bhakta. Aseemanand was to go and establish a foothold for the RSS.

'When I landed in the Andamans for the first time, there was no place to work from, no people to work with,' Aseemanand said. He set about forming bonds with tribal settlers through a combination of folksiness and unvarnished religious zeal. Although he didn't go into detail, he told me that even in the Andamans he was using the threat of violence to coerce tribals into embracing Hinduism. He called these reformations '*ghar vapasi*'—homecomings. (The Sangh maintains that adivasis are fundamentally Hindus, not animists, and talks about 'reconversion'.)

Aseemanand also employed more sophisticated types of propaganda. He lived among the tribal settlers, seeking out older members of the community who had not fully embraced their new religion. 'They told me that though they had converted to Christianity, they still wanted to keep their traditions alive—the festivals, their dance,' he said. 'So I told them that it is my job to get this done.'

Armed with the goodwill of these community elders, Aseemanand recruited half a dozen young girls, then sent them to a Vivekananda centre in Kanyakumari to teach them bhajans and get them to 'start believing in Hanuman', he said. Afterwards, he took them to the VKA headquarters at Jashpur, where they learned about Hindu culture for three months. Aseemanand and the girls then began a sort of roadshow, circulating through Andaman villages to lead bhajans and recruit another set of children. Because Aseemanand felt it was not right to travel in the company of young single women, the girls were married off, and the next batch of children—trained by the girls—were around eight years old.

Aseemanand then set about formalizing the Hindu community by building permanent spaces for worship and creating official bodies to look after them. In Port Blair, a man named R. Damodaran became the president of the local temple committee, and a Bengali named Bishnu Pada Ray became the secretary.

Aseemanand lived full-time in the Andamans until the early 1990s. He said his efforts there laid the groundwork for Ray to become the territory's first BJP parliamentarian, in 1999. 'I told him that it's good for him to go into politics, and so he went to Delhi and met Vajpayeeji,' Aseemanand told me. 'Politics is also part of our work.' Damodaran was unanimously elected the chairman of the Port Blair Municipal Council in 2007.

Even after leaving the Andamans, Aseemanand frequently returned, sometimes to hand out medicines and food following natural disasters. But he callously restricted his relief efforts to those who declared themselves Hindu. He told me one story about the aftermath of the tsunami in 2004. 'A Christian woman came for milk for her child,' he recalled. 'My people said no. She said that the kid had not had any food for three days, and pleaded that it would die if we didn't give some milk. So please give some. Then they said go ask Swamiji. I told her that what they are doing is right. You won't get any milk here.' It is a story he likes to repeat.

III

The Dangs is the smallest, least populated district of Gujarat, and lies in its southern tail, bordered by Maharashtra to the east and west. Seventy-five per cent of its population of roughly 2 lakh lives below the poverty line, and 93 per cent is adivasi. Like other tribal areas, it has seen a disproportionate share of conflicts over resources and ideology. The British first subdued the area's tribal kings in the 1830s, and obtained the rights to exploit the Dangs' teak-rich forest, which still covers more than half the district, in 1842. Apart from Christian missionaries, the British banned all social workers and political activists from the area, fearing the influence they might exert over adivasis' sense of entitlement to the land. The first mission school there was founded in Ahwa, the district headquarters, in 1905, and Christian evangelists of many denominations have been active in the area ever since. According to Aseemanand, Christians used to call the Dangs '*Paschim ka Nagaland*'—the Nagaland of the west. 'The threat was as big as in the North-east,' he said.

Aseemanand first visited the Dangs in 1996, while touring the country on behalf of the VKA. The organization's leaders had asked him to take his successful conversion programmes into every tribal area in India; they had even created a *Shraddha Jagran Vibhag* (faith awakening wing) and installed him as its president. But Aseemanand thought he could have a greater impact working in a single area, and felt a strong pull to the Dangs. The Dangs 'had the kind of work that I am good at—staying among the tribals and working with them', he said. 'One should always do the work from which one gains contentment.' Unlike the North-east, he told me, there was still a chance to reclaim the Dangs from Christians.

First and foremost, however, Aseemanand was loyal to the Sangh, and his superiors were worried that he would be unable to fulfil his national mandate from the forests of Gujarat. Aseemanand didn't convince them to let him focus his operations on the Dangs until 1998. Their anxiety proved unwarranted: less than a year after setting up in the district, Aseemanand managed to galvanize Sangh cadres across the country with his combination of evangelical outreach and violent coercion. Rao, the VKA organizing secretary and Kerala RSS chief, called it 'an example for the whole nation', Aseemanand recalled.

By the time Aseemanand stationed himself at a VKA ashram in Waghai, in 1998, religious differences were already straining adivasi communities in the Dangs, many tribals told me. Christian proselytization in the area had been relatively limited before the 1970s; but since 1991 the Christian population in the Dangs had been growing by roughly 9 per cent each year, according to census figures. When parents died, brother would fight brother over what sort of funeral rites they should perform. In the year before Aseemanand arrived, twenty attacks on Christians had been reported in the district, and they continued sporadically throughout 1998.

Every year, the VKA ashram housed around two-dozen tribal boys, providing them with free food and accommodation so they could attend a local government school. A day at the ashram began with Aseemanand leading the boys in chanting the Ekata mantra, an ode to Bharat Mata and prominent Indians—from Gandhi to Golwalkar—sung by RSS *swayamsevaks* to open every session at the shakhas. One of the students that Aseemanand met at the ashram was Phoolchand Bablo. Aseemanand credited Bablo, who became a sort of guide and aide-de-camp for the swami, with much of the success of his work in the Dangs.

When I visited the Waghai ashram last year, Bablo came from his village to meet me. He was plump, with a round face and a smile whose warmth reflected in his eyes—the sort of person I felt I could trust to give me directions in a strange land. Even the most disturbing stories Bablo told me were imbued with this warmth.

Aseemanand's methods were similar to those he used in the Andamans. He trusted Bablo to guide him to communities where he would be easily welcomed and could recruit aides to extend his influence throughout the forests. He and his volunteers would then hike to remote tribal villages, where they camped for up to a week at a time, eating with the adivasis and sleeping in their huts. Aseemanand preached Hinduism; distributed chocolates, Hanuman lockets and copies of the *Hanuman Chaalisa* to children; sang bhajans; and told the villagers that they should not be converting to Christianity. In every village, Aseemanand and his aides would make lists of people who could be baptized into Hinduism. The lists were closely monitored by Aseemanand. When he left for the next settlement, his aides would make sure that the adivasis' huts were flying the saffron pennant of the Sangh.

Aseemanand married these comparatively soft methods to fear-mongering. 'He talked of real-life situations like that in the districts on the borders of Bengal,' Bablo said. 'Over there, the entire Hindu community had to flee because of the Muslims who keep coming in from the other side.' In pamphlets that he printed in the thousands and distributed throughout the district, Aseemanand also denounced Christians. The header on one flier, announcing a massive rally in June 1998, warned: 'Come Hindus, Beware of Thieves'. The invective below read: 'The most burning problem of Dangs District is the establishments being run by Christian priests . . . Wearing a mask of service these Satans are exploiting the adivasis . . . Lies and deceit are their religion.' Aseemanand soon turned these execrations into violence.

On Christmas evening 1998, the Deep Darshan High School, in Ahwa, was attacked by members of the Vishwa Hindu Parishad (VHP), the Bajrang Dal, and the Hindu Jagran Manch (HJM), an offshoot of the VKA. Sister Lily, one of the Carmelite nuns who ran the school, said more than 100 people armed with stones participated in the rampage, breaking windows and destroying the roof of the school's hostel for tribal boys. 'Even after all these years I can still visualize it,' Sister Lily told me when I visited her at the school. 'I was so frightened that day.'

Thirty kilometres away, in Subir, another school was attacked; a grain shed there was looted and then set on fire. In Gadhvi village, a mob of reportedly 200 people demolished the local church and then set it ablaze; afterwards, they went to a neighbouring village and burnt down the church there. The church in Waki village was torched the next day; a forest department jeep was reportedly used in the attack. The day after, six village churches in the Dangs were destroyed. The homes of Christian tribals were pelted with stones. Christian and Muslim businesses were destroyed, and Christian tribals were assaulted.

The destruction carried on like this for a total of ten days. Between mid December 1998 and mid January of the next year, '40,000 Christians got converted to Hinduism', Aseemanand proudly claimed. 'We demolished thirty churches and built temples. There was some commotion.'

The violence had started with three HJM rallies on Christmas morning—one in Ahwa and two in tehsils of a neighbouring district—organized by Aseemanand. According to Dasharath Pawar, who was then general secretary of a BJP unit in the Dangs, 3,500 Sangh members wielding trishuls and lathis participated in the Ahwa rally. Slogans echoing Aseemanand's anti-Christian rhetoric were raised. The town's main road was hung with saffron banners. Local priests had petitioned the district collector, Bharat Joshi, to intervene. Instead of defusing the situation, he graced the dais at the Ahwa rally with his presence.

The scale of the rioting that followed the rallies owed a great deal to Aseemanand's skill as an organizer. Before he arrived, there were only a handful of Sangh workers in the district; Aseemanand pumped energy into the Hindutva movement and turned it into a force with thousands of members, Pawar said. 'His words were powerful enough to awake the sleeping Hindutva in you.'

'To stop conversions is an easy job,' Aseemanand told me. 'Use the route of religion. Make the Hindus *kattar* [fanatic]. The rest of the work will be done by them.'

One of the accomplishments Aseemanand claimed in this respect was the founding of the HJM, which was set up to look like a purely tribal organization. Because of the violence involved, 'we couldn't do all the Sangh's work through the VKA,' he said. 'So we had to make the HJM for this with tribals. This Janubhai'—the ostensible HJM president—'didn't know a thing. What plan of action to undertake, what to print in the pamphlets, all those decisions were taken by us. We just kept him as a face since he is a tribal. Adivasis used to do all the Sangh's work.'

Whether by inspiration or intimidation, Aseemanand's ghar vapasi programmes also became increasingly popular. For the next three to four years, whenever they had a roster of fifty to 100 potential converts, he and his aides would gather them up and haul them in open trucks and jeeps to the Unai temple in Surat. After a dip in a perennial hot spring next to the temple, and a *tilak-pooja*, the tribals were declared Hindu. They were packed back into the vehicles with a photo of Hanuman and a copy of the *Hanuman Chaalisa* under their arms. On the way back, bhajans blared from the vehicles so that the whole programme became a spectacle. The carnivals would stop at the Waghai ashram, where Aseemanand hosted a feast and gave each convert a Hanuman locket.

Aseemanand's concern for the tribals rarely extended farther than the question of whether they were praying to Jesus Christ or to Ram. In an interview with the *Week*, in January 1999,

Aseemanand said, 'We are not interested in poverty alleviation or developmental activities. We are only trying to uplift the tribals spiritually.' This approach, backed by Aseemanand's participation in local communities, had a powerful appeal. 'I have never seen a person live a more difficult life than Swamiji,' Bablo said. 'With utmost devotion, he goes and stays with the most backward community. He stays there, eats there and mingles with them—and makes those people his own. The people end up getting confident that now we, too, have someone to stand up for us.'

Aseemanand described the Dangs to me as one of the most beautiful places in India. Many journalists who worked there in the late 1990s agreed. When I visited the area in June 2013, the forest was grey and bare. ('You should see it during the monsoon,' Aseemanand told me in Ambala jail.) What stood out to me were the region's roads—miles and miles of world-class highways carved into the mountains. They were built by the government of Aseemanand's most important political patron, Narendra Modi.

Around the time Aseemanand moved to the Dangs, in early 1998, the BJP politician Keshubhai Patel was sworn in as Gujarat's chief minister. For most of the period since Independence, the state had been a Congress stronghold, although Patel had also headed it for seven months in 1995. In March 1998, when Vajpayee became the prime minister—and the ideological compromises of his government were still in the future—there was a surge of expectation in the RSS cadre that their vision for India was coming into being.

The Christmas riots in the Dangs seemed in some small measure to herald the change they desired. An early indication of Aseemanand's success was the appearance of Sonia Gandhi, who travelled to Ahwa to condemn what she called the 'heartbreaking' violence. Other politicians and celebrities followed suit. The news coverage significantly raised Aseemanand's public profile—and his esteem within the Sangh. Not long after, the RSS granted him its annual Shri Guruji award, another honour named after Golwalkar.

To quell the uproar in Delhi over Aseemanand's riots, L.K. Advani, then the home minister, was forced to intervene. 'When my conversion stories made national news, and when Sonia Gandhi flew down to make speeches against me, there was a lot of discussion in the media,' Aseemanand said. 'Then Advaniji was the home minister and asked Keshubhai Patel to rein me in. So then he started stopping us from working and even arrested my people.' But Modi was already waiting in the wings, and sharpening his knives. Aseemanand said that Modi approached him at a senior RSS gathering in Ahmedabad, and told him, 'I know what Keshubhai is doing to you. Swamiji, there is no comparison to what you are doing. You are doing the real work. Now it has been decided that I will be the CM. Let me come and then I will do your work. Rest easy.' (Repeated attempts to contact Modi through his office went unanswered.)

Modi became the chief minister in October 2001. When the anti-Muslim riots that killed over 1,200 Gujaratis began at the end of the following February, Aseemanand orchestrated his own attacks north of the Dangs, in the Panchmahal district, he claimed: 'The wiping out of Muslims from this area was also overseen by me.'

Later that year, Modi came to the Dangs to help consolidate Aseemanand's influence. In October 2002, Aseemanand started construction on Shabari Dham, a sacred precinct dedicated to the tribal woman believed to have helped Ram during his legendary fourteen-year exile. To raise funds for the precinct's ashram and temple, whose centrepiece would be a statue of Ram, he organized an eight-day *Ramkatha* (Ramayana recital) by the celebrated rhapsode Morari Bapu. The performance attracted at least 10,000 people. Modi, in the midst of campaigning to regain his chief ministership—his government had dissolved that July, in the aftermath of the riots—appeared on stage to help kick off the performance.

Part of Modi's election manifesto that year was the Gujarat Freedom of Religion Bill, which proposed that all religious conversions be approved by a district magistrate. Four months after Aseemanand's fundraiser, Modi's trusted aide Amit Shah brought the bill before the state assembly; the bill passed, and was signed into law in April 2003. Soon, Aseemanand, with the help of Morari, Modi and the leadership of the RSS, began planning a high-profile ghar vapasi in the Dangs.

At the end of his Ramkatha, Morari had proposed a new Kumbh Mela at Shabari Dham. The festival, which took four years to prepare for, would be a demonstration against conversion and a celebration of Hindutva. Aseemanand took it upon himself to organize the mela, together with the RSS.

In the second week of February 2006, tens of thousands of Indians flooded into the forest village of Subir, 6 kilometres from Aseemanand's ashram at Shabari Dham, to attend the inaugural Shabari Kumbh Mela. Like the four traditional Kumbh Melas which it was meant to emulate, the Shabari Kumbh centred on an act of ritual purification; by ceremonially plunging themselves into a local river, adivasis would signal their return to the Hindu fold. Thousands of people from tribal districts across central India were trucked to the event; the response to an RTI application I filed stated that the Gujarat government spent at least Rs 53 lakh to divert water into the river—making it ample enough to accommodate the crowds.

The Shabari Kumbh was also a show of unity within the Hindu right: over the three-day mela, well-known religious figures (such as Morari Bapu, Asaram Bapu, Jayendra Saraswati and Sadhvi Rithambhara), top leaders from the RSS and the broader Sangh Parivar (including Indresh Kumar, and the hard-line VHP leaders Pravin Togadia and Ashok Singhal) and senior BJP politicians (including the chief minister of Madhya Pradesh, Shivraj Singh Chouhan) shared the dais. Hundreds of full-time RSS members and thousands of the organization's volunteers managed the event. As one pair of researchers put it, the Shabari Kumbh was a 'confluence of . . . sadhus, Sangh and sarkar'.

On the festival's opening day, Modi told the audience that every attempt to take tribals away from Ram would fail. Behind the stage was a giant mural of the Hindu deity firing an arrow into a ten-headed Ravana. The then RSS chief, K.S. Sudarshan, took a more belligerent line. 'We are up against a *kapat yuddha* [deceitful war] by fundamentalist Muslims and Christians,' he told a gathering of sadhus, adding that this had to be 'combated with everything at our command'. Sudarshan's deputy, Mohan Bhagwat (who became sarsanghchalak when Sudarshan retired in March 2009), told the group, 'Those opposing us will have their teeth broken.'

According to news reports, anywhere from 150,000 to 500,000 people attended the Kumbh, although few reconversions were witnessed. Today, there are barely any devotees flocking to the Shabari Dham temple, and the temple cannot afford support staff. The ashram where Aseemanand lived has been demolished. Pradeep Patel, who assists the temple's chief pujari, told me that the temple has become notorious because of its association with Aseemanand, and this has kept away all the generous Gujarati contributors the temple used to attract. The few Maharashtrians who visit the place barely drop a Rs 10 note in the *bhandaar*, having spent all their money on travelling to the Dangs. A disappointed Aseemanand told me, 'It is my mistake. I couldn't build it properly.'

There is nevertheless a flurry of activity in the area. The Gujarat government seems to think that temples are what the region needs the most, so that the Dangs can earn its bread and butter through religious tourism. In 2012, the state inaugurated the Rama Trail project, a government initiative to commemorate the journey undertaken by the mythological characters of the Ramayana, and Shabari Dham features prominently in the plan.

The response to an RTI petition I filed revealed that under the Rama Trail project, the Shabari temple received Rs 13 crore from the state government to build a Shiv temple, four fountains, a service road and compound wall, a huge parking lot, and a seating plaza—and to cover the costs of sanitation, flooring, electrification and water supply. In contrast, Modi's government is yet to submit plans that would allow it to deploy a Rs 11.6-crore grant handed out by the central government, under the Backward Regions Grant Fund scheme, to foster development in the Dangs. The money has been lying unclaimed for the last six years. Local Christian institutions have also been shut out by the state. 'From 1998 we have been blacklisted in Gandhinagar,' Sister Lily, at Deep Darshan High School, said. 'We have been putting up files for new grants for the school every year, but they don't give us anything.'

The Unai temple in Navsari, where Aseemanand carried out his mass conversions, also received Rs 3.63 crore under the Rama Trail project. Work on the main building was completed by the time I visited, in June 2013. The new structure was magnificent, imposing. Behind its walls, it hid the humble old temple where Aseemanand brought his tribal bands for reconversion. A priest at the temple told me grimly that the number of visitors to the temple has spiked in recent years, but the hot springs have dried up for the first time.

IV

For the three years preceding the Shabari Kumbh, alongside preparing for the festival, Aseemanand had been meeting with several other long-time Sangh workers to discuss a problem far more distressing to them than religious conversions. At the core of this group were Pragya Singh Thakur, the executive member of the ABVP; and Sunil Joshi, the former RSS district leader in Indore.

In early 2003, Aseemanand received a phone call from Jayantibhai Kewat, who was then a BJP general secretary for the Dangs. 'Pragya Singh wants to meet you,' Kewat told him. Kewat arranged for them to visit his house in Navsari, Surat, the next month.

Aseemanand remembered bumping into Singh at the house of a VHP worker in Bhopal, in the late 1990s. He was struck by her appearance—short hair, T-shirt, jeans—and her fiery rhetoric. (In a characteristic tirade delivered sometime after 2006, Singh declared, 'We will put an end to [terrorists and Congress leaders] and reduce them to ashes.') In Navsari, Singh told Aseemanand that in a month's time she would visit him at the VKA's Waghai ashram.

It was Aseemanand's ardent championing of Hindutva, his '*Hindu ka kaam*', Singh told me, that first drew her to him. 'He was a great *sanyaasi*, doing great work for the country,' she said, when we met last December in Bhopal.

After the Navsari meeting, Singh soon arrived in the Dangs as promised. Three men accompanied her. One was Sunil Joshi.

People who knew Joshi described him as 'eccentric and hyperactive', according to news reports. Singh told me he was like a brother, and that they met through the RSS. Aseemanand recalled that, in later years, when he sheltered Joshi at the Shabari Dham ashram, Joshi would spend all day incanting bhajans and performing poojas while Aseemanand roamed the forest, visiting tribals. Around the time Joshi and Singh first started spending time with Aseemanand, Joshi was wanted for the murder of a Congress tribal leader and the Congressman's son in Madhya Pradesh, a crime for which the RSS reportedly excommunicated him.

Another member soon joined their group. While working in Canada, an administrative professional named Bharat Rateshwar had also heard about Aseemanand's work in the Dangs; he decided to give up his life abroad and return to India to help. Rateshwar built a house, in nearby Valsad district, where Aseemanand's collaborators would stay on their way to his ashram.

Aseemanand and Pragya Singh both told me that they met frequently in the years leading up to the Kumbh. Above all, they discussed the growth of the country's Muslim population, which Aseemanand considered the biggest threat to the nation. 'With Christians, we can always stand together and threaten them,' Aseemanand told me. 'But Muslims were multiplying fast.' He continued, 'Have you seen the videotapes in which the Taliban slaughter people? Yes, I did talk in meetings about that. I said that if Muslims multiply like this they will make India a Pakistan soon, and Hindus here will have to undergo the same torture.' The group explored 'ways to curb this', he said. They were also angered by Islamic terrorist attacks, especially on Hindu places of worship such as the Akshardham temple in Gandhinagar, Gujarat, where thirty people were killed in 2002. Aseemanand's solution to this problem, which he advocated frequently, was to retaliate against innocent Muslims. His refrain was *bomb ka badla bomb*—a bomb for a bomb.

The group's conversations continued over the next two years, as Aseemanand made preparations for the Kumbh. Soon, Mohan Bhagwat and Indresh Kumar gave their sanction to the plot, according to the account Aseemanand gave me. While they took centre stage at the Kumbh along with other leaders of the Hindu right, Aseemanand retreated to his ashram. Despite his seniority and popularity within the Sangh, he had agreed with Bhagwat and Kumar that he should publicly distance himself from the RSS. 'It was a strategy that we took at the time,' Aseemanand told me. Instead of participating in the Kumbh, he was to focus in secret on planning the attacks.

Less than a month after the Shabari Kumbh, two bombs exploded in Varanasi, killing twenty-eight people and injuring a hundred more. One of the explosives was placed at the entrance to a Hindu temple. Aseemanand, Singh, Joshi and Rateshwar immediately convened at Shabari Dham, where they decided to conjure up a reply.

In his confession, Aseemanand said that Joshi and Rateshwar agreed to head to Jharkhand to purchase pistols, and SIM cards to be used in detonators. Aseemanand gave them Rs 25,000. He also suggested that they try to recruit other radical sadhus to the conspiracy. (In the end, the Ram bhakts he nominated chose to stick to vitriol.) In Jharkhand, Joshi contacted his friend Devender Gupta, the RSS chief of Jamathada district, who helped them secure fake driving licences with which to purchase SIM cards.

In June 2006, the team rallied at Rateshwar's house. Joshi and Singh arrived with four new members of the conspiracy—Sandeep Dange, Ramchandra Kalsangra, Lokesh Sharma and a man known only as Amit. Dange, whose nickname was 'Teacher', was the RSS district head in Madhya Pradesh's Shajapur area; Kalsangra was an RSS organizer from Indore.

According to chargesheets, Joshi formed three task forces to carry out the blasts. One group would motivate and shelter young men whom they would recruit to plant the bombs; one would procure materials for the bombs; and the third would assemble the devices and execute the attacks. Joshi agreed to be the only connecting thread between the various parts of the conspiracy. He then suggested that they target the Samjhauta Express in order to kill the maximum number of Pakistanis. Aseemanand proposed Malegaon, Hyderabad, Ajmer and Aligarh Muslim University.

Several months went by in the Dangs without news. Then, during Diwali celebrations, Joshi came to meet Aseemanand at Shabari Dham. According to Aseemanand's confession statement, Joshi claimed responsibility for two explosions in Malegaon, on 8 September, that killed thirty-one people. Dange, along with Kalsangra, had helped Joshi procure bomb-making materials, assemble the explosives, and execute the attacks, according to chargesheets.

On 16 February 2007—a Shivratri day—Joshi and Aseemanand met again, at the Kardmeshwar Mahadev Mandir in Balpur, Gujarat. 'There is going to be some good news in the next few days,' Joshi told Aseemanand, according to the confession. Two days later, the Samjhauta Express was bombed. A day or so after that, Joshi, Aseemanand and some members of the larger conspiracy met at Rateshwar's house, where Joshi took credit for the attack. This time he told Aseemanand that Dange and his aides carried out the blast. Attacks continued over the next eight months; in May, the group bombed Hyderabad's Mecca Masjid and, in October, they bombed the Ajmer dargah.

On 19 February 2007, Singh had sat down to watch breaking news of the Samjhauta blast with her sister and her aide Neera Singh, according to a witness statement given by Neera. When images of the destruction brought Neera to tears, Singh asked her not to cry, because all the dead were Muslims. When Neera pointed out that there were some Hindus among the dead, Singh replied, '*Chanay ke saath ghun bhi pista hai*' (Worms get ground with the gram). Then Singh treated her sister and Neera to ice cream.

At the end of 2007, things in the conspiracy took a turn for the worse. On 29 December, Sunil Joshi was shot dead on an isolated stretch of road near his mother's house in Dewas,

Madhya Pradesh. Joshi had four aides—Raj, Mehul, Ghanshyam and Ustad—who lived with him and were almost always in his company. (Raj and Mehul are wanted by police for the Best Bakery arson attack, in which fourteen people were burned alive during the Gujarat riots in 2002.) All four mysteriously disappeared after Joshi's killing.

When he learned of Joshi's death, Aseemanand, looking for information about the killing, dialled the telephone number of a military intelligence officer he had met at a meeting of the militant RSS offshoot Abhinav Bharat, in Nasik—Lt Col. Shrikant Purohit.

Purohit is a mysterious figure. For the last three years, he has been behind bars for planning the second Malegaon blast, of 2008. Time and again, he has claimed that he was acting as a double agent under orders from his army superiors. 'I have done my job properly, have kept my bosses in the loop—and everything is on paper in the army records,' he told *Outlook* in 2012. 'Those who need to know, know the truth.' Pragya Singh's lawyer, Ganesh Sovani, told me they are treading carefully with Purohit: 'We don't know what his real intentions are.' According to Aseemanand's confession statements, Purohit told him that since Joshi was involved in the murder of the tribal Congressman, this must have been an act of revenge.

Five months later, three bombs exploded in Maharashtra and Gujarat—two in Malegaon, and one in Modasa—killing at least seven people and injuring roughly eighty. Aseemanand soon received a call from Sandeep Dange, who asked Aseemanand to shelter him at Shabari Dham for a few days. Aseemanand was on his way to Nadiad in Gujarat and didn't think it wise to leave Dange in the ashram in his absence. Dange asked Aseemanand to pick him up from a bus depot in Vyara, 70 kilometres from Shabari Dham, and drop him in Baroda. In Vyara, Aseemanand met a very worried Dange, along with Ramchandra Kalsangra. They said they were coming from Maharashtra. Aseemanand later recalled to police that throughout the three-hour journey to Baroda they remained completely silent.

Singh was the first of the main conspirators to be captured, in October 2008, in connection with the second Malegaon bombing, after the Mumbai ATS determined that a scooter used in the blast belonged to her. Allegations soon emerged that she had been brutally tortured while in police custody. The news deeply disturbed Aseemanand. In the first week of November, the Mumbai ATS made another major arrest in the case—Purohit. He is alleged to have trained the terror suspects in bomb assembly, and supplied RDX from army stocks. Later that month, the ATS arrested a conspirator named Dayanand Pandey. Then the arrests suddenly came to a halt; Hemant Karkare, the celebrated chief of the Mumbai ATS, who was heading the investigation, was shot dead on 26 November during the terrorist attacks in Mumbai.

Little changed until April 2010, when the Rajasthan ATS, while investigating the Ajmer bombing, arrested Devendra Gupta, the RSS district head from Jharkhand who had provided fake identification to Joshi and Rateshwar, and two others. The NIA took over the Samjhauta case that July. Meanwhile, the CBI was investigating the Mecca Masjid case, and conducting surveillance on several members of the conspiracy, including Aseemanand.

By now, Aseemanand knew that things were closing in; Phoolchand Bablo told me that in the months before his arrest Aseemanand was very disturbed. 'He would be silent, resolutely silent about the news and investigation, and we did not ask him anything,' Bablo said. Aseemanand, who was almost sixty at the time, soon left Shabari Dham and began moving around the country in order to evade arrest. The constant travel weakened him, and his health deteriorated. Eventually, he settled in a village outside Haridwar, where he lived under an assumed name until the CBI tracked him down that November. 'They had arrested everyone connected to Sunil,' Aseemanand told me. 'I was the last one to be nailed.'

Aseemanand was thrown in a Hyderabad jail and soon confessed. 'The CBI already knew the whole story,' Aseemanand told me. One statement Aseemanand made included a surprising account of why he decided to confess. A few days after his detention, he met a Muslim boy named Kaleem, who was also imprisoned in Hyderabad. Kaleem was accused of the Mecca Masjid blasts which Aseemanand had plotted. Kaleem used to wait on Aseemanand, and his kindness aggravated Aseemanand's conscience. He was confessing, Aseemanand claimed, out of remorse.

When I mentioned this incident in our first interview, Aseemanand gave me a mischievous look. 'So how big was the news about Kaleem?' he asked. He said the story was completely fabricated by the police. 'Kaleem knew that I was in the same jail, but I couldn't meet him,' Aseemanand said. 'How will I ever say such things to a Muslim boy?'

After his confession, Aseemanand drafted two letters—one to the President of India claiming responsibility for the Samjhauta blasts, and one to the President of Pakistan, which read: 'Before the criminal legal system hangs me, I want an opportunity to transform/reform Hafiz Saeed, Mullah Omar and other jihadi terrorist leaders and jihadi terrorists in Pakistan. Either you can send them to me, or you can ask the Indian government to send me to you.'

V

Superintendent of police Vishal Garg's office is a modest cubicle in the NIA's swanky Delhi headquarters. Against one glass wall of the office is a filing cabinet with four drawers labelled 'Ajmer Blast', 'Samjhauta Blast', 'Sunil Joshi Murder', and 'Stationery'. A white board behind Garg's desk tracks future court dates for the

Samjhauta and Ajmer cases, in which Garg is the investigating officer. On another wall is a 'wanted' poster featuring Sandeep Dange, Ramchandra Kalsangra and a man named Ashok who are still absconding in the Samjhauta case. The reward for information leading to the arrests of Dange and Kalsangra is one million rupees each.

'We often refer to the Aarushi case here,' Garg said when I visited his office last year. 'Three days after the crime happened, the CBI was given the case and they reached the crime scene. You can imagine what valuable evidences must have been lost.' Garg looked every bit the part of a counterterrorist IPS officer—down to the aviator sunglasses. 'We took over the Samjhauta case three years after the crime,' he continued. 'You can imagine how difficult the investigation must have been for us.'

Garg continued, 'We have not been able to nail the money trail so far, as these are not bank transactions or ones that are documented. You can call it the limitation of the investigation. We know that Aseemanand has handed over cash to Sunil Joshi, but no idea of how much it was.' The source of the explosives used in the blasts is also still under investigation. Pointing to the 'wanted' poster, Garg said, 'These Rs 10-lakh-award guys are the main brain and main executives of the crime. We need to catch them to get a better picture.'

The NIA is facing a number of obstacles. In July 2012, the Supreme Court restrained the agency from interrogating Pragya Singh in the murder of Sunil Joshi, on the technical grounds that the case's FIR was lodged before the inception of the agency in 2009. The court has also blocked the agency from questioning Lt Col. Srikant Purohit and another accused. The NIA prosecutor and legal adviser Ahmed Khan has advised the agency to club all the cases together and try them in a single court, but no further steps have been taken in this direction.

The NIA says supplementary chargesheets naming more conspirators will be filed soon, and Garg told me he was working hard. 'Last week one of my subordinates met me at the lift and said, "*Saab, aaj aap bade smart lag rahe ho.*" I told him he could also look sharp if he gave up sleeping.' He broke into a laugh, then told me that he once had a commanding officer who used to tell him that if he slept, he should dream of the good time his suspects must be having.

When I asked Garg why the NIA never questioned Indresh Kumar, he said that it was an internal matter and would not discuss it.

After Pragya Singh was arrested, in 2008, Congress leaders such as P. Chidambaram and Digvijaya Singh began decrying what they called 'saffron terror'. RSS and BJP officials rushed to defend their organizations from the taint—first denouncing and then defending the accused.

'I am shocked and it is shameful that the BJP is disowning her and all their organizations are disowning her,' the senior BJP leader Uma Bharti said following Pragya Singh's arrest. 'When they wanted, they used her.' The BJP spokesperson Ravishankar Prasad countered, 'There is no question of owning or disowning her. She left ABVP in 1995–96.' The party was later embarrassed when recent photographs surfaced showing Pragya Singh in the company of the BJP president, Rajnath Singh, and Shivraj Singh Chouhan. Another showed her sharing a dais in Gujarat with Narendra Modi during his post-riots election campaign.

When allegations emerged that Pragya Singh was tortured, the BJP changed tack. L.K. Advani condemned the 'barbaric treatment' meted out to her, and said that it was clear the investigating agency 'was acting in a politically motivated and unprofessional manner'. (The political scientist Pratap Bhanu Mehta later commented, 'Nothing diminished L.K. Advani before the last election more than his artless, passionate and entirely a priori defence of Sadhvi Pragya.')

But the RSS launched its most vehement public protest (and one of the largest in its history) a week and a half before Aseemanand was arrested, in November 2010—on behalf of Indresh Kumar, whose name had begun cropping up in media reports about the investigations. The Sangh's chiefs marshalled a nationwide protest. According to *Organiser*, more than a million people participated in over 700 dharnas across the country; virtually the entire leadership of the RSS and the VHP appeared on stage at the rallies. At a demonstration in Lucknow, Mohan Bhagwat stressed the importance of his own participation in Kumar's defence. 'For the first time in the history of the organization, a sarsanghchalak has not only attended a dharna but also addressed the meetings as a conspiracy was being hatched to tag terrorism with the RSS,' he said. The dais was adorned with a poster featuring the face of Mohandas Gandhi. Bhagwat continued, 'Hindu Samaj, saffron colour and the Rashtriya Swayamsevak Sangh—all these terms are opposite in meaning to the term terror.'

The CBI and ATS investigations produced valuable leads and witness statements that clearly point to Kumar's role in the bomb blasts. The NIA's own chargesheets indicate that he was the mentor to several of the leading figures in the conspiracy (especially Sunil Joshi), and the CBI has interrogated him. In late July 2011, it was widely reported that the NIA, too, intended to question Kumar. But he was already taunting the agency in the press: 'When NIA has strong evidences against me in terrorists' act, why isn't it arresting me?' He went on to claim that he, along with Pragya Singh and Aseemanand, had been falsely implicated. The agency is yet to question him.

The RSS and the BJP have taken every opportunity to call the ongoing investigations a witch-hunt instigated by the Congress-led government. If this is true, the half-hearted way in which the cases are being handled make one wonder what influence the government really has over the agencies.

When I interviewed Kumar last year, he complained that journalists only ask questions about the RSS's politics, and aren't interested in the organization's social initiatives. 'Then they just print those questions and murder the story about our work,' he said. 'Now the media is slowly realizing that they have been wrong in ignoring such a diversified organization as the Sangh.' When the conversation turned towards his role in the blast, he said, 'I warn people to be careful when they write about me.' His tone was aggressive. Later, when I telephoned him to ask about the meeting in which he and Bhagwat allegedly gave their blessing to the terrorist attacks, he went completely silent. Mohan Bhagwat's office asked me to email them for comment, but at the time this article went to press they had not responded.

On Friday, 24 January, a special NIA court in Panchkula, Haryana, framed charges against Aseemanand in the Samjhauta blast case. After three years in Ambala jail and thirty-one months of legal hearings, his trial can finally move forward. In an NIA court in Jaipur, he has been under trial for the Ajmer case since September 2013. His trial in the Mecca Masjid case is not yet under way; last November, he made his first visit in two years to the Hyderabad court that is hearing the case.

Pragya Singh, who is accused number one in the 2008 Malegaon blast, has approached the Bombay High Court to challenge the NIA's constitutionality. She also claims to be suffering from cancer, and is currently under treatment at an ayurvedic hospital in Bhopal. She has filed various bail applications that are being contested by the NIA.

At this point, it seems the trials may drag on for several more years. Lawyers from both sides blame each other for delaying court proceedings. Over the year and a half that I travelled back and forth from the Panchkula court, there were few newsworthy developments until the framing of the charges.

In Ambala, Aseemanand is now being held in a special B-class cell with Ram Kumar Chaudhary, the Congress parliamentarian from Himachal Pradesh who is accused of murdering a twenty-four-year-old woman in Haryana in November 2012. They share a cook, who prepares them meals on request, and they are only on lockdown during the night.

In our last interview, in January 2014, he asked if I would like some tea. Before I could answer, a lean teenage boy, incarcerated for petty crimes, thrust a plastic cup filled with sweet chai into my hands. Aseemanand pulled him close and said, 'This is my boy. He will be released soon.' He looked into the teenager's face and added, laughing, 'This *chaiwala* might grow up to become Narendra Modi.'

During our interviews, prison officers often stopped by to ask Aseemanand how he was doing. 'They all tell me "*jo hua accha hua*",' Aseemanand said—whatever happened is good. 'They don't know whether I have done it or not, but they believe that whoever did it, did the right thing.'

When I visited Kamarpukur, Aseemanand's village in West Bengal, his family members were largely reluctant to speak with me. But as I left, his younger brother Sushant said to me, 'Wait for a few months. Once Modiji comes to power I will put a stage in the village centre and shout from the loudspeakers all that Aseemanand has done.'

In one of our meetings, Aseemanand paraphrased the last words of Nathuram Godse: may my bones not be discharged into the sea until the Sindhu river flows through India again. He has assured Phoolchand Bablo that although his trial might take time, he will definitely be released. And he told me that the work of people like him, Pragya Singh and Sunil Joshi will continue: 'It will happen. It will happen on time.'

My editors were looking for a cricket writer who could do this story. I tried to convince them that a cricket writer should be the last person to turn to. For descriptions of a cover drive or a hard life overcome? Yes. For a critical story about the source of such a writer's livelihood? No.

They were unimpressed. So I went to Chennai, the base of **NARAYANASWAMI SRINIVASAN**'s schemes. The first person I met showed me old pictures from a time when Srinivasan was just entering the world of cricket administration. Those pictures became the story's opening. Things got better after that. People really want to talk about men like Srinivasan because the list of his slights is long. The challenge really was to discover how many people it was humanly possible to speak with.

What emerged from reporting was not only a story about Srinivasan, but also a picture of the Indian cricket board at work. As we have discovered over the last couple of years, it is not a happy story. I had hoped our profile of Srinivasan and his business would lead to some call for change. I write this in the midst of a fierce season of upheavals in Indian cricket. To my dismay, however, it appears that people have ignored the politicking and gaming that this article describes, determining instead that Srinivasan's story was a great how-to guide.

RAHUL BHATIA

Rahul Bhatia, a writer in Mumbai, was a staff writer for the Caravan.

Beyond the Boundary

How N. Srinivasan Became Cricket's Biggest Hitter

By RAHUL BHATIA | 1 August 2014

I

It was 1993, and Sunil Gavaskar and Motaganahalli Jaisimha were lounging in a hotel room in Chennai. Two of India's sporting greats, they came from different generations, but their careers on the Indian cricket team had overlapped for precisely eleven frenetic days in Trinidad and Barbados in 1971, during India's legendary series victory against a rampant West Indies side. Between Jaisimha's time and Gavaskar's, Indian cricket had steadied itself.

The torch had now passed to their successors, and they were free to sit in the groggy afternoon, reminiscing and laughing. With them in the room was a third man, a large but unobtrusive spectator who, from all available evidence, admired them unstintingly. Narayanaswami Srinivasan was forty-nine years old, and had loved cricket for a great many years. In time, he would come to see this love as a kind of patriotism, and everything he would do for cricket as a form of service to his country.

He listened quietly to them. He was dressed for summer, and his hair was not quite a mullet, but certainly business up front and a party in the back. This was all, in fact, Srinivasan's party. One of Chennai's most famous businessmen, he had generously agreed to sponsor a Tamil Nadu cricket player's benefit match, and got to hang out with a clutch of sporting heroes in return (Gavaskar brought along Michael Ferreira, the national billiards champion).

The match was held the following day. It began competitively but ended in farce, as benefit matches often do. Srinivasan turned up at the after-party sunburnt, and lingered in the company of international cricketing legends, some of them former captains of their national teams. There were others who had come close, also-rans who should have made it to the top but hadn't. The happy stories of the stars drowned out the sadder tales of the might-have-beens. All this was new for Srinivasan, even though his company, India Cements Limited, owned several local clubs in the city and had paid salaries to their cricketers for decades. Moments like these were unusual for people who dealt in clinkers and kilns.

That evening Srinivasan flitted between cricketers, holding a tall drink in one hand and a tobacco pipe by its bowl in the other. Gavaskar dug a hand into his own pocket, shut his eyes and sang while a band played. A cake was brought out. Fifteen flimsy cricketers populated the green icing. The first slice was from long on, and it was presented to Srinivasan with ceremony.

From there, his ingestion of cricket began.

The Srinivasan who walked into the meeting of the International Cricket Council (ICC) at its headquarters in Dubai on 9 January this year looked like a different man. Time had left him sunken-eyed and serious. He was now the president of the Board of Control for Cricket in India (BCCI), the most powerful cricket board in the world; but it had been a difficult year, and the annoyances were piling up. His presumptive leadership of global cricket was under threat. He even had a cataract to take care of.

For the two decades since the benefit match, Srinivasan worked to fuse himself with the sport in a way that no cricket administrator had in the past, and outplayed some of the most formidable men in the business. Jagmohan Dalmiya, a supremely wily strategist, had been Srinivasan's boss at the BCCI once, but had been relegated to relative obscurity. The redoubtable Sharad Pawar, chief of the Nationalist Congress Party and one of India's toughest politicians, had been the BCCI president, and then the ICC chief in 2010, but Srinivasan had outflanked him, too. And Lalit Modi, Srinivasan's most vocal rival and the manic architect of the money-spinning, short-format Indian Premier League (IPL), was living in exile in London—a circumstance for which he blamed Srinivasan.

Every once in a while, the shark tank of Indian cricket administration is invaded by an exceptional individual, the kind of leader who directs the current away from old habits and instincts and resets the terms of the game. Dalmiya had been the first of them—an obdurate power player, more familiar with Indian cricket's constitution than any of his peers. He had come to prominence just as satellite television arrived in India, with marketers and agents in tow. The money that cricket promised to attract was greater than even Dalmiya could imagine. It took an inventive mind like Lalit Modi's to think of the many ways in which such wealth could be multiplied: logos above logos, shirt sponsors, hotel sponsors, image rights, even a version of the game that would make its more conservative loyalists shudder. But all that money needed a manager with a mind like an abacus, a man who understood what it was really worth and what it was good for. Srinivasan turned out to be that man.

No cricket administrator rose more quickly from practical obscurity to international fame than Srinivasan. He served as member on four committees of the ICC, the sport's apex body, to which all national cricket boards belong. Back home, having muscled his way into the Tamil Nadu Cricket Association (TNCA) and then the BCCI, he took firm hold of every important decision-making process in both organizations. It was often difficult to discern the limits of his influence on the game. In the most telling example, India Cements, the company of which he is now the vice chairman and managing director, gained ownership of the IPL's Chennai Super Kings franchise in 2008, when Srinivasan was BCCI secretary. This became possible after the board changed provisions barring administrators from taking any commercial interest in Indian cricket to exempt the IPL. An editor who has covered cricket for nearly two decades summarized for me the roots of Srinivasan's domestic power. 'The boards'—those governing the regional cricket associations in India—'are incompetent,' he said. 'Among them, Srinivasan is a powerful, charismatic figure. He tells them, "Without me, you will not get money."'

But, in recent months, Srinivasan's rapid ascent up the leaderboards of cricket administration had slowed. Since May 2013, practically every newspaper and news channel in India had clamoured for Srinivasan's resignation from the BCCI after his son-in-law, Gurunath Meiyappan, a senior official for the Chennai Super Kings, was arrested on the charge that he had placed illegal bets on IPL games. Mumbai police suspected that Gurunath had leaked confidential team information to fixers. At a raucous press conference, Srinivasan insisted that Gurunath, whose family owned Chennai's oldest movie studio, was simply 'very enthusiastic'. But the din of the unbelievers kept swelling. For two months, newspapers reserved front-page space for Srinivasan, whose assessing eyes stared coldly out at the nation from his photographs. Finally, in June 2013, he offered to 'step aside'—a kind-of, not-quite resignation.

Investigators hand-picked by the BCCI soon cleared him and Gurunath of any wrongdoing, and Srinivasan resumed office in September. But even as he carried on—pausing only occasionally to tell reporters to 'stop hounding' him—in October the Supreme Court acted on a petition filed by the Cricket Association of Bihar which contended that, with Srinivasan in charge of the BCCI, a meaningful inquest could not be expected. The court appointed a retired high court judge, Mukul Mudgal, to investigate the allegations credibly.

The considerable weight of all this scrutiny bore down on Srinivasan as he entered the ICC meeting in January. His counterparts from other national boards were wary. They were all well versed in the art of surviving the vagaries of power—the fixture from Zimbabwe is Robert Mugabe's man—but Srinivasan was more than a match for them. He always prepared well for meetings, he could think like an accountant, he kept his advisers close, and almost never failed to ensure that his supporters were happy and well rewarded.

Three different people—a prominent cricket commentator, an editor at a popular sports website and an ICC official—told me as much in interviews. 'I haven't known any BCCI secretary or president reading meeting papers as thoroughly as Srinivasan,' the ICC official said. 'He's more prepared than anyone else.' The official did not wish to be named; when we spoke in March, it seemed certain to him that Srinivasan, in spite of the quagmire of corruption charges threatening him at home, would soon be his new boss. News had already broken that the ICC was resurrecting a lapsed office, that of chairman—a step above the president and the CEO—and it was all but confirmed that Srinivasan would be its newest occupant.

The January meeting began with the chairmen of the English and Australian boards explaining a new plan, and then explaining themselves. The Financial and Commercial Affairs Committee of the ICC, one of four committees on which Srinivasan sat, was introducing a proposal to radically reorganize the council, and so revise the balance of power in international cricket. 'India, England, and Australia,' the tabled document stated, 'have agreed that they will provide greater leadership at and of the ICC.' Put plainly, the three biggest markets in global cricket would manage the cricketing affairs of the ICC's more than one hundred member nations.

Then came the money talk. The document explained that India contributed 80 per cent to the ICC's revenues. The next largest market, England, had a single-digit share. 'The current revenue model is lopsided,' Srinivasan told his unsettled listeners. 'India gets the same amount as Bangladesh and Zimbabwe.' To bring some balance to the distribution of profits, he suggested, 25 per cent of the organization's global revenues would go into India's purse.

A Pakistani official present that day recalled that the representatives of England and Australia seemed oddly apologetic. They said, as he remembered it, that 'this proposal was the only way of keeping India within the international tent'. (The official declined to be identified because, he said, 'we are trying to improve our relationship with the BCCI'.) Foreseeing resistance from the other administrators, the big three had packed an Excel table, full of spectacular revenue projections, into their twenty-one-page vision document. They pointed out that they expected the ICC to earn from $1.5 billion to $3.5 billion between 2015 and 2023. From 2007 to 2015, they estimated, the ICC's revenues would total $2 billion. These riches would be shared among the member nations (which meant, first and foremost, that the richest boards had every chance of getting richer). Najam Sethi, the chairman of the Pakistan Cricket Board at the time, waved away all this talk; it was clear under the proposal that the three big boards would control all meaningful decision-making. 'This is a take-it-or-leave-it situation for us,' Sethi reportedly told the gathering.

The proposal to modify the ICC's power structure simply represented, at the highest level, what was more or less Srinivasan's modus operandi wherever he worked. As president of the TNCA, he had used an absolute majority of loyalists to remove term limits; this year, he was elected chairman of the group for the fourteenth consecutive time. As president of the BCCI, he altered rules that barred elected representatives from seeking re-election. At every step, he had succeeded by pushing the boundaries with little regard for popular opinion.

In February this year, the Mudgal commission published its report on the IPL spot-fixing charges, making grave allegations of wrongdoing against Srinivasan, as well as twelve others. A Supreme Court bench called it 'nauseating' that Srinivasan was still in power at the BCCI, and barred him from the presidency of the organization until it could complete further investigation into the allegations. Then, on 26 June, Srinivasan was elected the chairman of the ICC unopposed. No Indian cricket administrator had come so far, leaving so much chaos in the wake of his ambition.

II

In the official history of India Cements, Srinivasan's father, T.S. Narayanaswami—they called him TSN—is one of the company's two founders, alongside a man called Sankaralinga Iyer. Both men are described as pioneers, who created a cement empire that began with a single factory in Talaiyuthu, 'an almost unmapped tiny hamlet in India's southern-most district'.

Talaiyuthu, in Tamil Nadu's Tirunelveli district, is the type of town that's on the way to somewhere else. It sprung up around the factory in the 1940s and 1950s, and its landmarks suggest a bias towards an older version of the facts. Up the main road is the Sankar Nagar police station; the cricket stadium near Sankar

Higher Secondary School has a patchy field; the women's hostel at Sankar Polytechnic College is about half a kilometre from the men's. In his 2013 book *Cement Uncements*, R. Natarajan, a former assistant editor at *The Hindu,* attempts to set the record straight on Iyer's and Narayanaswami's real places in the company's history. He asks: 'If TSN was the founder of India Cements, what was Sankaralinga Iyer? Was he TSN's assistant?' No, Natarajan replies to his own query. 'The fact is otherwise. Iyer was its founder and TSN was his assistant.'

The name of India Cements is entwined tightly with Srinivasan's career in cricket. The company sponsors the Chennai Super Kings, and its logo emblazons the jerseys of its players. These include Mahendra Singh Dhoni, the captain of the Indian national team, who also leads the Super Kings, and was made the vice president of marketing at India Cements in 2013. Srinivasan's rise to the top of his company, in some ways, foreshadowed his later rapid ascent through cricket.

Cement manufacturing was a matter of national concern through the Second World War and in newly independent India. Armed with one of only six licences issued to new cement manufacturers by the government, Sankaralinga Iyer founded India Cements in 1946, and asked Narayanaswami to join him soon afterwards. By 1949, the company had expanded, under a leadership that practised a form of 'benign autocracy', as noted in an unpublished company record. Employees 'were not highly paid, but the company took care of them in a way a parent would his family. The employees too reciprocated with dedicated service without expectation of reward.' Srinivasan was immersed in this culture from early on; in later years, similar language would be used to describe his cricketing endeavours by many club owners and journalists, in whose eyes he was a patriarch who took care of those he considered 'family' within the BCCI.

Narayanaswami left India Cements around 1950 for a venture started by Biju Patnaik, the future chief minister of Odisha, but soon attempted to return. Iyer had cooled to him, and it took a year of pleading and persuasion by relatives and mutual friends for Iyer to take Narayanaswami back. Once reinstalled, though, Narayanaswami made a good impression on the company's leaders, who nominated him to the board in 1959. The company rode into the 1960s fully formed, with factories producing over a million tonnes of cement a year.

In 1968, Srinivasan, then in his twenties, was named the company's deputy managing director. He reported to K.S. Narayanan, Iyer's eldest son. The two young men had an uneasy relationship, which culminated in a public battle over company matters in 1979. Srinivasan came under severe scrutiny from the India Cements management. *Cement Uncements* claims that when Narayanan pulled Srinivasan up about a particularly questionable deal, he was 'nonchalant, if not insolent. To get off the heat, he took a jaunt to Singapore.' Doubts over this deal were serious enough for the board to call a shareholders' meeting to vote on Srinivasan's dismissal.

This battle, and the complications that followed, bore several hallmarks of Srinivasan's style—rule-manipulation, a talent for persuasion and persistent allegations of political influence bolstering his business. At the meeting, to the board's dismay, several shareholders rose up one by one to make themselves heard—a tactic meant to run out the clock. They went on about 'relevant and irrelevant things', Natarajan writes. 'The chairman could not stop them.' Shareholders read from a script, and swore at company management. The distraction continued until the management of the hotel hosting the meeting told India Cements its time was up. The gathering dispersed without voting on Srinivasan's removal.

Natarajan, whom I spoke to earlier this year, told me that a number of the most vocal shareholders 'were people from the DMK'—the Dravida Munnetra Kazhagam, a powerful party then in the state's opposition. Whispers of Srinivasan's political machinations in Tamil Nadu, largely linked to the DMK, surfaced regularly through subsequent years. For example, in 2002, allegations that he laundered undeclared income for DMK leaders came to light. Jayalalithaa Jayaram, then the chief minister of Tamil Nadu, accused her predecessor and DMK patriarch M. Karunanidhi of signing agreements that were supposedly biased in favour of 'one individual'. According to a report in *The Hindu*, Jayalalithaa stated, 'It was well known that Mr. Srinivasan was Mr. Maran's benami'—a conduit for illegal funds for the veteran politician Murasoli Maran, Karunanidhi's nephew.

In 1979, Srinivasan, like his father before him, left India Cements, but he returned in 1989. Several people I spoke to in Chennai attributed the return to his political connections, in particular to Maran. Only one person claimed otherwise. A.S. Panneerselvan, who covered politics in Tamil Nadu for many years and is now the readers' editor of *The Hindu*, was convinced that Srinivasan's connections couldn't have helped him. 'The Maran connection has nothing to do with what he is today,' he told me. In 1998, Panneerselvan had been more certain about the nature of Maran's relationship with Srinivasan: in a story for *Outlook* magazine, he described Maran as Srinivasan's 'godfather', and wrote, 'He uses his political connections very subtly so that very few notice the series of coincidences.'

When I asked him if these alleged political connections had anything to do with Srinivasan's career as a sports administrator, he seemed sceptical. Panneerselvan reasoned that Srinivasan's accumulation of power within cricket truly began after Maran's death in 2003. 'Maran's sons'—the media baron Kalanithi and the politician Dayanidhi—'are not in favour of him at all. Everyone talks about their friendship, but the thing is, the nature of their relationship has not been documented.'

In years to follow, many would feel the brunt of such 'series of coincidences'. Srinivasan often seemed like a chess player thinking several moves ahead of everyone else. In 2010, the sports journalist Sharda Ugra wrote a short profile of him on the cricket news website Cricinfo. It began:

> If ever a movie was made about the rise of N. Srinivasan, it would have to feature a scene reflecting the man's ambition. The actor playing the man would be standing around with his aides in the Tamil Nadu Cricket Association (TNCA) office and charting out before them the course of his destiny. 'All of you are fools,' he would say, and then tell them how it was going to be. 'First the treasurer, then the secretary, then vice-president, after which the President.' Cutting through the deferential silence, the denouement would arrive with a drumroll, 'Then I will try for the ICC.'

In Chennai this March, I met Bharath Reddy, a fifty-nine-year-old who managed players for the first-division cricket teams of the Sanmar Group, a conglomerate owned by Sankaralinga Iyer's family. He was dressed in a pastel green shirt and carried a company badge, but his battered fingers gave the game away. As a young Tamil Nadu cricketer, thirty-five years ago, Reddy was India's main wicketkeeper during a 1979 tour of England. His international career lasted for less than eight weeks, although he continued to play for Tamil Nadu until 1986. He retired when he was barely thirty-two.

After that, Reddy became a cog in Tamil Nadu's cricket machine, and in the process became one of Srinivasan's earliest allies. In 1993—the year that Srinivasan sponsored the benefit match—Reddy was campaigning to be named secretary of the TNCA. The odds were stacked against him. The TNCA's leadership had traditionally been dominated by a club of influential local businessmen, such as A.C. Muthiah, head of Southern Petrochemicals Industries Limited, and K.M. Mammen, of MRF Limited. Between them, Muthiah and his father, M.A. Chidambaram, had run the association for forty-two of its forty-six years.

In 1993, Reddy's rival for the post of secretary was the industrialists' candidate, a former international fast bowler named Prabhakar Rao. Rao's backers were entrenched in the system, and had financial resources that Reddy couldn't match. 'Secretaries of all clubs are not well-to-do people . . . You have to get them drinks, you have to—' he broke off. 'I'm not willing to spend money. I can give my hard work, but I'm not prepared to give money to win votes. At that time you need a godfather.'

In the twenty years since, contesting TNCA posts has only become more expensive. 'At that time it did not cost a lot to run for office,' Reddy said. 'Now a vote alone goes for one crore thirty lakhs.' I asked how he knew this. His glance was withering. 'I'm talking to you about it. That's a fact. That's the last quoted price. You can't buy the district votes outright, but you can buy them by spending money on them: entertainment, helping them with ground-lease renewals.'

Reddy needed an investor. He approached Srinivasan to fund his campaign, and struck a deal. 'He was relatively young,' Reddy said. 'So I spoke with him. I think he also wanted to come in'—to the fold of the TNCA. 'Cricket was always one of the top things for people to get into the limelight. Otherwise why else would industrialists want to get involved?'

In 1994, a year after Reddy won his election, his benefactor campaigned to enter the association as vice president, but failed. The TNCA nominated vice presidents from two geographies, the Chennai clubs and the districts; Srinivasan campaigned from the city, but found the opposition to his candidature too great. A.S. Venkateswaran, an association lobbyist, remembered: 'We were against Srinivasan because he was blindly supporting Bharath Reddy.'

The defeat rankled, and Srinivasan and one of his confidants, Kasi Viswanathan—later secretary of the TNCA—set out to understand the reasons for it. 'He planned meticulously,' a Chennai club owner told me this March. 'There was very stiff opposition to NS'—Srinivasan—'in the districts. There were thirty districts, each of which had a vote. Barring three of them, nobody wanted him.' Viswanathan collected information on clubs and parleyed with owners on Srinivasan's behalf. He reached out to old friends for information of value—anything that explained voting history, what the electors needed, or who their friends were. 'He wanted to know what happened earlier in the TNCA,' the club owner said. 'He wanted to know about the elections, about the members.' He wanted to know more about alliances, too. 'Gather, assimilate, dissect, understand member-club secretaries. What X needs, what Y needs, what Z needs. Every man has a soft spot. Every man has a weakness.'

Srinivasan set about influencing the districts outside the city by supplying them with cricket equipment. These were times when a little largesse went a long way. The rewards for electoral support were typically so scant, and clubs so depleted, that simple acts of kindness such as providing lunch money and arranging water for players could win friends. The districts could nominate two vice presidents to the TNCA; in 1995, two years after Srinivasan lost his first campaign, he was their nominee.

Reddy said the vice presidency was a dummy post for Srinivasan, more or less a stepping stone to the real prize—the president's chair. For his part, unable to be re-elected to the post of secretary, he hung on to Srinivasan for a while. Upon becoming vice president, Srinivasan tried to convince Muthiah to replace the association's new secretary, an accountant named Ashok Kumbhat, with Reddy. 'Initially, Muthiah agreed,' the club owner told me. But club secretaries complained to Muthiah's father, M.A. Chidambaram, calling the change unnecessary. So Muthiah forbore to appoint Reddy.

According to the club owner, Srinivasan's campaign to unseat Muthiah in the next election, in 1997, owed something to how slighted he felt by this. Srinivasan stepped his campaigning up by an order of magnitude. Standing drinks and underwriting kit was relegated to amateur hour; he was now strengthening his position by buying clubs outright. 'Very meticulously,' the club owner said, 'he created his own support base with Egmore, Gandhi Cricket Club'—both clubs he acquired. 'Now he owns thirteen or fourteen clubs. Now he has the entire association under his thumb.'

Despite his efforts, Srinivasan lost the 1997 election, too. But, in 2001, less than a decade after he first sought entry into the TNCA, Srinivasan became president of the association, and has remained at the post ever since. Venkateswaran, the TNCA vote-gatherer, said of the sea change, 'Barring half a dozen people, everybody will vote for Srinivasan today.'

The Chennai club owner said Srinivasan was persuasive because he was 'a great actor'. When we met, he impersonated Srinivasan angling for the presidential post: 'I am here only for the welfare of you and cricket.'

'He has mastered the technique of getting votes,' Venkateswaran added. That view was shared by a former BCCI media manager who had worked with Srinivasan. 'He knows only two things. He is either here—' he clutched his feet. 'Or here—' he feigned a two-handed chokehold.

III

In 1999, Muthiah was named president of the BCCI, thanks to the support of a man who had loomed large over both Indian and international cricket for years—Jagmohan Dalmiya. Dalmiya, a power player from West Bengal, had been named ICC president in 1997. The prime of his administrative career coincided with possibly the biggest development in cricket history—the explosion of the market for cricket broadcasting, particularly in the newly open Indian economy. Dalmiya was instrumental in bringing the World Cup to the Indian subcontinent in 1996, when it was co-hosted by India, Pakistan and Sri Lanka. By this time, Dalmiya had attracted the attention of the whole cricket-playing world; in his book *Sticky Wicket*, the former ICC CEO Malcolm Speed described him as 'without doubt one of the most resolute, able, difficult, prickly, and unpredictable men' he had met.

Over the next decade, Srinivasan's relationships with Muthiah and Dalmiya, antagonistic and convenient by turns, helped him consolidate his power, both at the TNCA and within the BCCI. 'Our group brought Dr Muthiah to power,' at the BCCI, a former senior official of that organization from Rajasthan, known for his mining and construction interests, told me. 'That's Dalmiya, Arun Jaitley,'—the senior BJP leader who headed the Delhi District Cricket Association for over a decade—'all of us. We voted for him.' Badri Seshadri, one of the founders of Cricinfo, realized that Dalmiya was the real power behind the throne when he once took a proposal to Muthiah. '"You must convince Dalmiya,"' Seshadri recalled being told. 'He made it very plain.'

But Muthiah and Dalmiya began to drift apart almost immediately after the former's election. 'Dalmiya probably thought that because Muthiah has been brought into power by him, he would be consulted on all matters,' the senior official said. 'Which Muthiah did not do. To that extent, Muthiah was correct. But his knowledge of cricket was very limited, and he, in turn, started taking impulsive decisions.' Like many others, this official did not want to be identified, even though he had stepped away from cricket after being voted out of his post. It seemed an unspoken code among most cricket administrators that the safest place to be, after years of handling large contracts and currying favour, was underground.

In 2000, Muthiah's opponents on the board grew unhappy with what they saw as his independent streak. With the Indian team going through a funk, Muthiah invited the retired Australian opening batsman Geoff Marsh to become a consultant for the country's new National Cricket Academy. 'That led to a lot of complications,' the official said.

Hoping to undercut Muthiah by strengthening an opponent on his home turf, his BCCI critics turned Chennai-wards, to Srinivasan at the TNCA. Muthiah's term limit as TNCA president meant he would have to leave office in 2002, and it was widely known that his succession plans did not include Srinivasan. 'We thought, if anyone could beat Muthiah in the TNCA, Srinivasan could,' the Rajasthan official remembered. 'We started to pep him up in a big way.'

Meanwhile, apparently dissatisfied with Muthiah's leadership of the BCCI, his former mentor, Dalmiya, also decided to withdraw his support. In the next BCCI elections, held in Chennai in 2001, Dalmiya won the presidency even though he was widely expected to lose to Muthiah. Two former cricket officials—Venkateswaran, and a confidant of Dalmiya's—told me that Palaniappan Chidambaram, the former Indian finance minister, was in the hotel where the election was held at the time of the vote. The minister's wife, Nalini, a Supreme Court advocate, was the election observer, but Chidambaram's presence was perceived as a real show of Dalmiya's strength. One senior journalist I spoke to, who was present that day, claimed, 'It was clear: you don't vote for me, you get raided by income tax.' When I contacted Nalini Chidambaram, she denied her husband had ever been at the hotel. 'No, no, no,' she said. 'He has got nothing to do with it.'

Defeated, Muthiah left the BCCI, but he continued to scrabble for purchase within the organization—something that changed his attitude to Srinivasan. In the 2002 TNCA election, held that June, Muthiah surprised his supporters and rivals by vouching for Srinivasan. The organization's club representatives, used to thinking of the two as enemies, were taken aback; rumours about the volte-face still buzz around today, even a dozen years later. As part of the deal, Srinivasan apparently agreed to help one of Muthiah's men into the position of association secretary.

One of the people he called on to get this done was Bharath Reddy. 'He wanted me to support Muthiah's candidate,' Reddy said. The memory clearly agitated him. 'I told him I will not do it.' He held his arms tightly at his sides, and said, 'He wants people to stand like this. I was not prepared to do it.'

During this election, Srinivasan displayed an uncanny ability to play difficult situations to his advantage. Ashok Kumbhat, the association secretary who had once expected to succeed Muthiah as president of the TNCA, decided to run independently. According to a person involved with Kumbhat's campaign, six months before the election, 'Srinivasan called us. He said, "Please don't have a contest."' Kumbhat disregarded the request, and continued his preparations.

However, before the elections could be held as planned, in June 2002, they were stopped for reasons that went beyond cricket. Tamil Nadu was then ruled by the All India Anna Dravida Munnetra Kazhagam under Jayalalithaa, who had already cast aspersions on Srinivasan as a financial conduit for her rivals' undeclared income. Shortly before the elections, Venkateswaran told me, Jayalalithaa made it known to Muthiah that the elections could not go ahead. He recalled the panic with which Muthiah called him. '"Madam wants me to stop it. What do I do?" I advised him to calm down. Let us find a solution.'

Muthiah decided to postpone the elections, and left Venkateswaran to tell Srinivasan that the deal was off. He did so the next day, at a gathering of the association's members, where he pulled Srinivasan aside after a round of drinks. To his surprise, Srinivasan insisted on going ahead with the elections. 'He wasn't upset,' Venkateswaran said. 'He just said, "We'll fight it out."'

At this point Srinivasan had, to all appearances, a reasonable majority over Kumbhat—but not an insurmountable one. Venkateswaran told me that when he heard the elections might be delayed, Srinivasan grew restless. In order to calm his mind, Srinivasan resolved to turn Kumbhat's backers. Practically every night for the next month he hosted dinners for different groups of club secretaries and owners. The month passed tensely, but elections went ahead as scheduled. In the end, Kumbhat won sixty-one votes. Srinivasan won over 120.

'In that one month, several of Kumbhat's supporters became Srinivasan's supporters,' the Chennai club owner said. 'How, we don't know.'

Within a couple of months of the 2002 TNCA elections, Srinivasan announced he wanted to enter the BCCI as one of its vice presidents. According to Venkateswaran, he spoke with representatives from five states, and asked for their support at the board's yearly general meeting, slated to take place in Kolkata that September. As once before, with his entry into the TNCA, there was no majority waiting to put him in place. Venkateswaran remembered telling Srinivasan, before he left, 'It doesn't matter if you don't become vice president. The finance committee chairman of the BCCI is leaving to become the secretary of the BCCI. Why don't you aim for the vacant post?' By the time they spoke again the following night, Srinivasan had done precisely that, and secured the office.

With the TNCA behind him and the BCCI awaiting, Srinivasan's next major alliance seemed inevitable. The man at the centre of the BCCI was Dalmiya, so Srinivasan turned to developing a friendship with him. 'TNCA's votes, which were in the opposition, began to come to Mr Dalmiya,' the BCCI official from Rajasthan said. 'Because he said'—to Srinivasan—"I'm going to support you and I'm going to remain loyal." He became very loyal, and very close. And the man is—' the official paused. 'He's a diligent man. Otherwise he couldn't have lasted this long. He has got to have some merit in him. Lot of merit in him.'

Srinivasan arrived at the BCCI right at the time when Indian officials were reassessing the worth of the one thing for which they commanded any price they wished: television broadcast rights for matches played in India. Numbers were growing in every dimension—viewers, screens, discretionary income. Indians who bought things had more to pay advertisers. In turn, advertisers had more to pay channels. The coffers of the BCCI swelled accordingly.

The finance committee turned out to be a worryingly good fit for Srinivasan, at least as far as some of its other members were concerned. In 2004, when Srinivasan had been on the committee for two years, the board invited bids for broadcast rights. The subsequent machinations and fallout clearly demarcated the gulf between Srinivasan and men such as Dalmiya. Both the board as well as those who did business with it understood that Srinivasan would not scruple to exceed his remit; he wanted to control how the board spent its substantial income.

The television-rights battle would prove a major step in achieving this objective. The senior official who told me the story was convinced that this was the moment when the balance of power in Indian cricket altered irrevocably—the moment in which Dalmiya set in motion a series of events that would prove his own undoing. In 2004, Srinivasan, Dalmiya and Kishore Rungta, then the BCCI treasurer, were part of the marketing committee, charged with selling television rights to the highest bidder. Two well-matched rivals went up against each other in this fight. On one side was ESPN-Star Sports, a monster venture involving both Disney and Rupert Murdoch's News Corporation. On the other was Zee TV, India's first home-grown private broadcaster, which had become one of the country's largest media companies. Zee had tried to acquire television rights for cricket in India and abroad before, but failed; the 2004 bid was a real chance at redemption. Subhash Chandra, the company's founder, attended the meeting in person. Rungta and Srinivasan reportedly favoured Zee, while Dalmiya wanted to award the rights to ESPN-Star, who had sent a team of executives to make their channel's case.

'We made tough conditions,' the official remembered. 'The main purpose of those conditions, in my perception, was to eliminate Zee.' The broadcast requirements, published in a tender document, were stacked against Chandra's company. For example, the BCCI wanted bidders to have at least two years' experience in producing cricket broadcasts. Zee had none.

The BCCI's members were concerned by rumours that Chandra desired not just to bid for rights, but to have a say within the board. The official told me that the thought of a broadcaster becoming a peer repulsed them. When they found that Zee's bid was higher than ESPN's on a year-by-year basis, the members asked ESPN-Star 'if they were prepared to pay the same price for three years instead of four'. Rungta and Srinivasan objected to this, saying that Zee deserved a chance to raise its bid too. A senior executive from Zee, who was involved in preparing the channel's bid, confirmed this to me. 'Srinivasan said Zee were the highest bidders so they should be awarded the rights,' he said. However, 'Dalmiya was not inclined towards that. We didn't get a warm feeling from Dalmiya.'

When the board's members met later that day, they reasoned that their conditions were probably too stringent for Zee to accept, according to the official. The potential revenues could not possibly cover the cost of the unprecedented bid; ESPN-Star would win anyway.

The next morning, Chandra returned with his reply. He said he would match ESPN's offer, and agree to the conditions the board had laid down. The official said he could tell by Dalmiya's body language that 'this put off Mr Dalmiya to a very large extent. If I remember correctly, he requested Srinivasan to chair the meeting when the discussion took place. A kind of authority was given to Srinivasan to deal with this subject.'

Dalmiya's tenure as chief of the BCCI was scheduled to end in a few weeks, and he was poised to become the board's first 'patron-in-chief', a nominal position. For some time until then, the board's younger members—it is unclear if Srinivasan, aged around sixty at the time, was among them—had tried persuading Dalmiya to step aside and allow them to take decisions for the board.

When the Zee executive recalled the scene at the meeting, he remembered a room full of BCCI officials ready to give Zee the bid. The senior official had a slightly different recollection. Srinivasan, he said, quickly laid out the conditions under which the board would negotiate with the channels. 'Srinivasan had power to chair the meeting only,' the official continued. But he overstepped his boundaries—he 'faxed a letter of intent to award Zee the contract on the basis of that so-called authority without asking Dalmiya. The letter was completely ignored by Dalmiya, who wrote letters to the contrary. It became about the prestige of Srinivasan versus Dalmiya.'

IV

It wasn't long before politics, always hovering at the edges of cricket, insinuated itself right into its midst. As Dalmiya attempted to shore himself up against his opponents—some of much longer standing than Srinivasan—the tectonic plates of the sport shifted once again. A new giant had stepped on to the field—this time, no less a personage than Sharad Pawar. The politician 'was pulled into battle' by Chandra and Srinivasan, the senior official told me. Pawar's career in Maharashtra and national politics spanned four decades by this time. He had almost been the prime minister of India at least once, and ruled his turf in western Maharashtra with an iron fist. Everywhere he went, allegations of corruption and financial wrongdoing followed. Nothing, though, ever stuck.

'Pawar would never have come in if it wasn't for Zee. Pawar had no interest in cricket,' the Zee executive said. He added, expansively, 'Until 2004, Pawar didn't even know what the BCCI was.' According to him, it was the first time the media highlighted the kind of money that was being bid. In a matter of days, Pawar decided to run for BCCI president, just as Dalmiya was leaving.

The election that followed was among the closest and most dramatic in the board's history. In the end, Pawar lost owing to a technicality. Dalmiya, by virtue of his position, was able to cast four votes—the last of which gave his candidate, Ranbir Singh Mahendra, a one-vote majority over Pawar. But Pawar, having entered the field, proved unwilling to exit it. He was far better prepared for the 2005 election, which he swept. He turned to his associates and reportedly asked, 'What is to be done after the office is elected and the committees are being formed?' After hearing them out, he told his advisers that he wanted Srinivasan overseeing the board's accounts as treasurer.

Pawar's decision to appoint Srinivasan to his team did not prove popular. It stood to reason that Pawar saw Srinivasan as an acceptable ally, but the new president's confidants had watched Srinivasan's rise, and they doubted both his loyalty and his motives. Among Pawar's advisers was Harish Thawani, a media entrepreneur who ran a television production company called Nimbus, which operates the two NEO sports channels. Thawani's shaved head, full face, deep tenor and crisp articulation add up to give him the appearance of a reformed soccer hooligan. When we met, he recalled telling Pawar, 'You are making the biggest mistake of your life. This snake needs to be finished now.' Pawar received this advice with tranquillity. Srinivasan had his drawbacks, he told Thawani, but seemed to be a good administrator.

Once Pawar left the BCCI in 2010 to become the president of the ICC, he was replaced by a lawyer from Nagpur named Shashank Manohar, who came to be considered very close to Srinivasan. (The ICC official from Pakistan told me that, during an ICC meeting, Manohar suddenly changed his mind about a controversial technology-aided umpiring system just after Srinivasan leaned over and whispered in his ear.)

Even as secretary, Srinivasan's influence was pervasive, and his opinions were taken seriously. Nimbus had bid over $600 million—about Rs 2,700 crore—for the rights to telecast cricket in India from 2006 to 2010, but that was in the past; Srinivasan was unimpressed by Nimbus's delayed payments. At a meeting, Srinivasan told Thawani he should expect an official fax stating that if Thawani didn't pay up, the BCCI would encash the company's bank guarantee.

'When you leave this room,' Thawani replied, 'I will be waiting for you outside and I will personally break both your legs. Then you won't be able to walk home and you won't be able to send me the fax.'

In spite of this, Nimbus once again won the right to broadcast Test and one-day matches in India for four years, at a price of $436 million—roughly Rs 2,000 crore—in 2010. This was an ambitious bid, based on an optimism belied by the company's financial health. By 2011, it once again began to default on its payments. As luck would have it for Thawani, Srinivasan was by now firmly in charge of the casino.

BCCI presidents are elected for two-year terms, with the possibility of a one-year extension. Srinivasan had thrown his hat into the ring as the man to succeed Manohar. In spite of a conflict-of-interest case filed by Muthiah at the Supreme Court, which questioned Srinivasan's purchase of the Chennai Super Kings IPL team while he was a BCCI official, support for Srinivasan was strong. Six regional associations nominated him for the post. In a last reversal of whatever Dalmiya's intentions may have been for his rival, Shashank Manohar backed him too.

'Shashank and Srini were inseparable,' Thawani told me, about this period at the BCCI. 'Shashank trusted Srini like he trusted his own wife. I'd fly to Nagpur and have lunch with Shashank on a Saturday and I'd say: "What the fuck, Shashank? How can you forget?"' He meant the wariness of Srinivasan that Pawar's circle had once nurtured. 'Who are you defending?' Thawani was upset that Manohar was now openly supporting Srinivasan as his successor. 'And he'd say, "Srini's not like that any more. He has changed, you know? You come under the influence of good people and there is a good side in you that comes out."'

The Supreme Court's initial decision on Muthiah's petition was a split verdict, and Muthiah filed another petition in August 2011 to nullify Srinivasan's bid to officially take over the BCCI. The Supreme Court cleared Srinivasan to take up his post in September. Later that month, Srinivasan took over from Manohar as president. Two months later, the BCCI cancelled Thawani's contract. Thawani says the board didn't inform the company before calling it off.

By all accounts, Srinivasan had worked himself into positions of proximity to past presidents, making himself indispensable as the brains of BCCI's operations. 'When he was the secretary, he controlled things,' the senior editor who has covered cricket for years told me. 'Even when he was a treasurer, he controlled. He managed to remain in control no matter what his designation was, which is highly unusual.'

Now, as president, he was unencumbered by the shackles of reporting to anyone else. Even to outsiders, the ease with which Srinivasan jumped between warring groups was disconcerting. 'Look at Srinivasan,' the Zee executive said. 'He was with Dalmiya, then Pawar, then Lalit Modi; and then Pawar moved to the ICC and then Shashank was the president. He started working with Shashank but against Lalit and Pawar.'

The Zee executive told me that Srinivasan was the only BCCI member his company had felt it could talk with. 'We were in touch with him,' he said. 'They asked us to pay one hundred crore in two days' time with whatever the bidding conditions were, and we accepted that. We paid the money and after that we went to the courts.' There had been little wrong with the letter of intent Srinivasan had sent in Zee's support; after all, the room in the India Cements office where these matters were decided had been filled with BCCI officials who had agreed to give Zee the rights. But ESPN-Star took the BCCI to court over the legality of the agreement, and an excruciating legal tussle followed. In 2014, the memory of how that contract was handled still annoyed the Zee executive. 'Institutions like these should be run by the sports ministry,' he told me.

Srinivasan's critical eye, and his efforts to shore up power, ensured that this kind of drawn-out conflict did not occur again. A former Nimbus employee who had witnessed negotiations with Srinivasan told me, 'He used to be very tough. The only guy in that room who used to see what's best for the BCCI. Others would skip over small details. He would say, no, it's important that we are transparent and show propriety. Harish used to hate it.'

The cricketing globe, as seen on television in India, is carved up between a handful of Indian broadcasters. For cricket played in the country, an audience must tune in to Star. For games in the Caribbean, Zee's Ten Sports. Zee's eponymous network is the official cricket broadcaster for five other cricket boards, including South Africa. Every cricket administration has a preferred broadcaster. Dalmiya fought in ESPN-Star's corner; Pawar's BCCI accommodated Nimbus. If any such preference were ascribed to the BCCI in the Srinivasan era, the evidence would point to Star India, the News Corporation company that was once half of ESPN-Star.

In April 2012, soon after Nimbus's contract was cancelled, the BCCI's marketing committee awarded television rights to the network for Rs 3,851 crore—higher than the losing bid of Rs 3,700 crore, although not in any significant way when broken down by price per match, which is the unit by which broadcasters evaluate bids.

A week after the winner was announced, Life OK, a Hindi entertainment channel run by Star India, became a sponsor of the Chennai Super Kings. According to the deal, the channel's logo would appear on every player's 'non-playing arm'—the sleeve that does not face the camera when a player is at bat. This was an unusual decision for a channel that was 'hoping to stand out in the cluttered GEC'—general entertainment channel—'space through this sponsorship deal', as a channel press release said. Life OK's general manager, Ajit Thakur, told *The Hindu*, 'When India Cements offered this sponsorship, we saw it as an opportunity.'

The apparent conflict of interest did not end with the sponsorship. Rajeev Shukla, a journalist turned politician whose family owns several news and entertainment channels, happened to be on the BCCI committee that gave the rights to Star India. In October 2012, employees of the advertising sales division at Shukla's channel News24 were told to resign, a high-ranking ad sales officer who was laid off told me. According to the *Economic Times*, it was decided that Star would run the channel's ad sales in return for a minimum guarantee each year. This was not an unprecedented situation; Star had cut similar deals with other news channels in the past. The difference was that News24 was a minor player, with virtually no ratings to benefit an entity selling advertising on its behalf.

A former Star executive explained that the deal may have taken place because 'the more vulnerable a channel is, the better the deal you can extract'. I asked him if he felt awarding the rights to Star indicated a conflict of interest, given that Shukla's channel was to enter into an agreement with Star shortly afterwards. He told me that Shukla's television production company 'used to supply content to Star for a very long time. We don't know if he recused himself from discussions about awarding the rights.' Shukla did not reply to a request for an interview, and did not answer my phone calls.

But it was world cricket's single biggest draw last year, and the off-field machinations that surrounded it, that raised the volume of questions about the BCCI's favouritism and grudge-bearing to a crescendo. Sachin Tendulkar, India's most popular player in the modern era, announced his intention to retire at the end of 2013. The match that was to be Tendulkar's two-hundredth and final Test was to be played on tour in South Africa in December. It promised to be a marquee series—two strong teams, a number of exciting young cricketers, and the departure of the man widely considered to be India's greatest cricketer of all time.

Then, before the tour, the BCCI announced that it would host Tendulkar's farewell series at home instead. International cricket calendars are scheduled years in advance, but the BCCI's officials justified their decision by claiming that Tendulkar wished to end his career at home. It went unsaid that the new series would benefit Star at Zee's expense: Tendulkar's last Test would obviously garner ratings not seen in nearly a decade. The Zee executive calculated his network's loss of potential earnings at over Rs 35 crore. Meanwhile, media buyers estimated that Star's advertising rates for the match would be five or six times higher than normal. At Tendulkar's farewell ceremony after the match, the retiring legend was given a trophy to thank him for his service to the great game. It was handed to him by Uday Shankar, the CEO of Star India.

V

This March, during a Supreme Court hearing related to the Mudgal report, a justice asked, 'Why is Srinivasan sticking to the chair? If you don't step down, we will pass an order.' The report, commissioned the previous October, had come out in February, after its authors had investigated the spot-fixing charges. It was damning as far as Srinivasan was concerned.

Srinivasan's earlier reinstatement had been made possible by the inquiries of a BCCI-appointed committee, much to the derision of its critics. The Supreme Court reopened the investigation and appointed its own three-member committee, which is expected to submit its report by the end of this month. But the censure of the apex court did not extend to its barring Srinivasan's candidature for ICC chief. In June, when the ICC asked the BCCI to reconfirm its nominee to the post, the board remained steadfast in its support of its de facto president. A Press Trust of India report quoted unnamed BCCI sources as saying they had assured the ICC that putting Srinivasan on the ballot would not stand in contempt of the Indian Supreme Court. Some observers objected on principle. The cricket journalist Lawrence Booth wrote in the *Daily Mail*: 'If Srinivasan is considered unfit to run the BCCI, he should not be handed the reins at the ICC, an organisation which—in theory at least—sits higher up the food chain.' Yet, once again, both the niceties and the votes were on Srinivasan's side; he was rubber-stamped into the position unanimously.

Over the course of reporting this story, a number of messages and phone calls asking to meet with Srinivasan proved fruitless. His confidant Kasi Viswanathan, a former secretary of the BCCI and an India Cements employee, told me that he wasn't ready to speak with reporters.

Earlier this year, just days before the court recommended that he step down, Srinivasan allowed Prabhakar Rao, now a TNCA vice president, to speak with me on his behalf. We met at Rao's office, a large space dominated by an outsize desk. He pulled out a list of safe talking points and said, 'We will not embarrass him. He doesn't believe in pulling anyone down. He likes to help cricketers. He has sponsored a number of boys in their careers. I was told the board was spending Rs 9 crore a month on pensions.' Rao added that Srinivasan really looked after the districts that first nominated him. 'TNCA gave each district fifty thousand as a subsidy to run cricket,' he said. 'When we attended the golden jubilee of Salem District Cricket Association, he announced at the meeting that the subsidy will go up to two lakhs a district.' Rao spoke as though Srinivasan were the panacea to all of cricket's ills. 'Lots of private clubs are suffering due to rising costs. We spend 26 lakhs once in two years on kits for them. How many tournaments he sponsors! He has a very large heart.'

An India Cements employee who was 'loaned' to the BCCI when Srinivasan took over the board told me, referring to the spot-fixing controversy, 'We don't have the need to know if the allegations are true or not. As long as we know our managing director, why should we bother with the media?' Srinivasan's attitude, he said, had always been that 'cricketers have made this money, so they should benefit'. He added that only a few people are against Srinivasan. 'Most people are very happy.'

This is undeniable. Srinivasan has worked to share the wealth more than any other cricket administrator in India. He has raised the pensions that appear electronically—magically, one former player told me—in retired cricketers' accounts on the same date month after month. He has funded associations generously to build new infrastructure. During his tenure as BCCI president, stadiums in towns such as Ranchi, Rajkot and Dharamsala were upgraded to international-standard venues.

Over the course of dozens of interviews, I was sometimes told that Srinivasan is an unreasonable man, and sometimes that he could be reasoned with. I heard that he was tough and sharp; I heard he was given to unexpected acts of kindness. He was a dodgy dealer, in a way that made you chuckle. An official from an IPL franchise told me that once, a young nephew of Srinivasan's back in Chennai found himself in a spot of trouble. He had a swim meet to attend, but was unable to postpone a school exam happening the same day. The nephew was incredibly lucky, the official said, laughing. The swim meet was postponed after a cow was found paddling in the pool.

But I also saw, first hand, the hesitation his name often occasioned. Former players, and others involved with the sport, called me after interviews, worried that they had said too much. One man, who is over seventy years old, told me that changes to the BCCI constitution, such as the tweaking of the conflict-of-interest clause, 'were made to suit the long-term interests of one individual', and then requested that I not print his statement because, 'at this age, I cannot attract controversies'.

When the Supreme Court barred Srinivasan from the BCCI presidency, it recommended the appointment of two ex-cricketers to hold the reins until its investigation was complete. The former bowler Shivlal Yadav had the general run of the BCCI; the former batsman Sunil Gavaskar was put in charge of IPL affairs. The appointments occasioned a brief surge of public optimism, but none of it was in evidence in my interviews. Srinivasan's hold over the game goes so deep that not even the aged or the distant felt truly beyond his grasp if he chose to tighten it. 'Every member of the BCCI is at his feet,' an associate of Srinivasan's told me. 'He doesn't need to be anything to call the shots.'

On 16 July, at six o'clock in the evening, Yadav joined officials from a number of regional associations to toast Srinivasan, now the ICC chairman, at Chennai's Chepauk stadium. They were 'competing to praise him', the associate told me. A portrait of Srinivasan was ceremonially presented to the man himself. Surveying the venue was another large picture of Srinivasan, hanging in the background. Yadav turned to him. 'I pray to god that the bad period that we are only reading about in the media will be over as soon as possible,' he told the man under investigation, 'and you will take over from me.'

For a few years, **PONTY CHADHA** was the emperor of northern India's liquor trade until he was killed in a shoot-out on 17 November 2012. He was murdered on the same day Bal Thackeray died; in the midst of round-the-clock reporting and banner headlines for the Shiv Sena leader, newspapers and TV networks found ample space to cover Chadha's ghoulish death in a Delhi farmhouse. Initial reports suggested that Chadha was killed by his brother Hardeep over a property dispute; Hardeep was killed in turn by Chadha's bodyguards. There were allegations of conspiracy; fingers were pointed at Chadha's aide Sukhdev Singh Namdhari, suspected of the killings for financial gain.

The drama faded out of the headlines soon, leaving most people with only the vague sense of a gangster-movie tragedy: a bloody fratricide involving mysteriously wealthy men. I also forgot about Ponty Chadha until the day I came across a photograph of him, posing near a birdcage with his left arm missing from the shoulder. The reminder of his little-known disability made me curious about his journey.

I began to wonder what it took Chadha, a boy from a Moradabad family of liquor traders, to overcome the loss of a limb and fight his way past the wild frontiers of his trade in the battlefield of Uttar Pradesh (UP). Few knew of him before his successes—closely linked to his growing political influence across states—began to shape his reputation. But there is a long history to the trade, and to the deals that made Chadha rich, and kept UP's thirst slaked. More meaning could be derived from the story of Ponty Chadha's death once the story of the Chadha family and their old, shadowy business was uncovered.

With Ponty and his brother gone, the reins of the multimillion dollar business are in the hands of his son Manpreet Singh Chadha, who's also known as Monty. He is working hard to reinvent the image of his family business through enterprises such as his self-proclaimed 'ultra-modern' real estate ventures. Meanwhile, Namdhari, his father's henchman, was remanded to a fourteen-day judicial custody in early spring. He is suffering from Hepatitis C and has become suicidal.

MEHBOOB JEELANI

Mehboob Jeelani is a journalist based in Istanbul, Turkey, where he writes features for TRT World. Before this, Jeelani extensively covered Indian politics for The Hindu *and the* Caravan, *and also wrote about business for* Fortune *magazine in New York.*

Under the Influence

Ponty Chadha's potent mix of liquor and politics

By MEHBOOB JEELANI | 1 November 2013

I

Perhaps there is no better way to divine the significance of a regime change than to observe the reshuffling of courtiers who thrive off and influence power. For many journalists and political analysts, then, the high-profile guests entering the grounds of Lucknow's La Martiniere Boys' College on 15 March 2012 revealed a lot about whom the new Uttar Pradesh government would smile upon, and how it would function, in the ensuing five years. Nine days earlier, the Samajwadi Party (SP) had won a majority in the state's sixteenth legislative assembly elections since Independence, and the scion of the party's ruling dynasty, Akhilesh Yadav, was preparing to be sworn in as the new chief minister. Hundreds of celebrating SP workers in red Gandhi caps danced and sang songs before a stage draped in flowers.

Sitting in a special enclosure were some of the country's most prominent politicians, bureaucrats, police officers, film stars and industrialists. The previous day, the *Times of India* reported that the Yadav family had 'doled out invitations to every celeb known to them'. When the billionaire mogul Anil Ambani showed up, SP supporters shepherded him to a seat next to Akhilesh's father, the party patriarch, Mulayam Singh Yadav, who had led the state at three different points.

Ambani was also present at Mulayam's swearing-in ceremony for his third stint as chief minister, in 2003. The following year, Mulayam supported Ambani's successful bid for a Rajya Sabha seat, and granted him the rights to build a 3,500-megawatt power plant in Gautam Buddh Nagar district, where the Uttar Pradesh government had purchased land at cheap prices for 'public purpose'. The project had been stalled by farmers demanding higher compensation for the 2,500 acres making up the site, 40 kilometres from the national capital, but Ambani and Mulayam remained close.

Another billionaire, Subrata Roy, the chairman of Sahara India Parivar, was also spotted chatting with Mulayam and shaking hands with party leaders. Roy, who rose to prominence in Uttar Pradesh, acquired vast landholdings in the state during the third period of SP rule, which lasted until 2007.

Conspicuously absent from the roster of billionaires paying their respects at La Martiniere was the liquor baron and real estate tycoon Ponty Chadha. Chadha had also been close to the Yadavs and, like Roy and Ambani, enjoyed great patronage under Mulayam's third government. But these old ties had been eclipsed by Chadha's subsequent association with Mayawati, the charismatic Bahujan Samaj Party (BSP) leader who ousted Mulayam in 2007.

When Mayawati came to power, almost every top bureaucrat and police officer who had ties to the Yadavs was transferred out, and businesses that blossomed under the previous regime were stifled. Many believed that Chadha's fortunes would also take an ill turn. But he swung things in his favour. While Ambani and Roy saw various projects scuppered under Mayawati's rule, Chadha was awarded a monopoly over distribution for the state's Rs 14,000-crore liquor market. In addition, he was given control of 30 per cent of the alcohol retailers across the state, and was allowed to purchase a number of distressed but viable state-owned sugar mills at a price below their fair-market value. He also received a Rs 10,000-crore contract for distributing food under the state's midday meal scheme for children and pregnant women—in violation of an earlier Supreme Court order—and landed vast tracts of prime real estate just outside Delhi at a loss to the public, state Congress leaders claimed, of Rs 40,000 crore. Both Chadha and the BSP government made enormous sums from the booze trade in particular—excise tax on the 10 million cases of liquor sold every year generated roughly Rs 10,000 crore annually for Mayawati's government—and within the state administration Chadha became known as 'Mayawati's financier'.

With the SP back in power, many believed Chadha would now suffer. After abandoning Mulayam for Mayawati, it was far from clear that Akhilesh would let him back into the SP fold. During poll stops, Akhilesh had frequently expressed his displeasure with the state's liquor policy, which had allowed Chadha to drive up retail prices. At a public meeting in Bhimnagar, he promised the crowds that he would cut the cost of their '*shaam ki dawai*' (evening medicine) if voted in.

In fact, the pressure on Chadha seemed to begin in the weeks leading up to the election. In January, the Comptroller and Auditor General (CAG) issued a report saying Chadha's sugar mills had been auctioned off at a loss to the public of somewhere between Rs 1,200 crore and Rs 2,000 crore, and recommending that the case be taken up by the enforcement directorate. Then, on 1 February—the same day that Mayawati kicked off her re-election campaign at a huge rally in Sitapur—a group of roughly twenty officials from the Income Tax Department arrived at Noida's Centrestage mall, which is owned by Chadha's Wave Group. After flashing their identity cards and gaining access to the 350,000-square-foot building, the officials rushed into the basement, where they reportedly found a secret vault. At the same time, at least a hundred of their fellow officers were raiding eighteen other Chadha-owned properties (including farmhouses, malls and nightclubs) scattered across Uttar Pradesh, Punjab and Delhi.

While the officials cut into the vault at Centrestage with a high-powered gas torch, fifty-five-year-old Chadha—a tall, corpulent, grizzly bear of a man with close-cropped hair and beard—was having a drink with a friend at the friend's office in South Delhi's Defence Colony. He had been tipped off about the raid. 'He was sitting in his office and we were exchanging poetry,' the friend, who runs a petroleum business, told me. 'I asked him whether he was worried about the raid and he said, "I have seen such gimmicks long ago. I know where it's going to end."'

Early news reports claimed that the tax officials had recovered Rs 100 crore from the vault, along with various unspecified documents. There were rumours in the papers that the cash had been laundered by family members through various companies in Dubai, where Chadha had properties and investments. If the confiscated paperwork could prove this, it might threaten Chadha's empire, which was valued at somewhere between $1 billion and $10 billion. And, intentionally or not, some of the blowback was bound to catch Chadha's political patron, Mayawati, as she mobilized her party ahead of the polls.

In the end, Chadha's equanimity seemed justified. Two weeks after the raids, newspapers reported that almost nothing was recovered from the mall. 'There were only two Rs 50 notes in the vault,' an Income Tax Department official told the *Economic Times*. Whatever the truth, the episode was an embarrassment for the department, and Chadha emerged unscathed. The week following the raid, he held a lavish wedding for his daughter Harleen, at which senior politicians from the SP and the BSP, and from Punjab and Delhi were in attendance.

Mayawati fared less well. The BSP lost 126 of their 206 assembly seats (out of a total of 403) and, with them, the chief ministership. There was a growing sense that, as the SP swept into power, those who had prospered (perhaps illicitly) under Mayawati, including Chadha, might be swept out.

Shortly after Akhilesh took the oath as chief minister and left the stage at La Martiniere, ecstatic SP supporters stormed the platform and set fire to the dais. Many of the most important guests retreated to a grand after-party at Sahara Shahar, Subrata Roy's 375-acre Lucknow estate. En route to the bash, Akhilesh held a press conference at which he proclaimed, 'Organized corruption as happened in the previous regime never took place in the state [before] . . . UP is now celebrating democracy.' At Roy's, senior politicians, serving bureaucrats, stars and business moguls mingled. Imported whisky was served all night, and several party leaders passed out on white couches spread across the property's lush lawns. They were later escorted home in white Mercedes sedans, the house transport.

At one point, a group of Indian Administrative Service (IAS) officers gathered on the grass began chatting about the people who had vexed the Yadavs when they were out of power, those who had remembered the family and helped them win the election, and the candidates for top ministries and administrative posts. They also briefly discussed Chadha. Because of his closeness to Mayawati, the officers agreed that his ascendancy in Uttar Pradesh was coming to an end. But not all the signs pointed in this direction. It was rumoured that Chadha had, in fact, been invited to Akhilesh's swearing-in. Chadha's son, Manpreet, who goes by 'Monty', arrived late to the inauguration, but managed to show his face. (According to some reports, Monty had flown in to Lucknow on a private jet with a 'well-known Mumbai industrialist'.)

The auguring of public appearances and celebrity guest lists aside, Chadha was, according to some, too big to fail. 'Ponty always had a strange magnetic force that pulled him into relevant circles,' S.A.T. Rizvi, a former IAS officer who served in Uttar Pradesh for more than two decades, told me. 'His ever-rising money and muscle power made him indispensable.' Rizvi wasn't the only one who thought so. Within the wealthy and politically connected circles in which he moved, Chadha had gained a surpassing reputation for the kind of entrepreneurial success that is born of great intimacy with power. He built the bulk of his fortune in the span of two decades by forming close relationships with north India's ruling personalities on the promise of benefits that only liquor could bring. Booze dispensed on the campaign trail could more or less be counted on to deliver votes, and liquor sales were the easiest way to pump funds into government coffers. Across north India, excise duties on alcohol are the second-largest source of state revenue (after sales tax), since most other taxes go to the Centre. Illegal kickbacks from contracts in other industries might line the pockets of individual politicians, but nothing could rival booze for legitimately enriching an entire government—whether or not those funds were later siphoned off for less than official purposes.

All this gave Chadha more ballast against the shifting winds of political favouritism than many other magnates in India. Party leaders, serving legislators and bureaucrats from across the political spectrum wore expensive watches or hung on their walls paintings gifted to them by Chadha. 'He even imported Scotch with his name, Ponty, inscribed on the bottles and gifted them to almost every politician, businessman and friend in town,' Tony Jesudasan, a spokesperson for Anil Ambani, told me. Political rivals would bump into each other when they attended Chadha's Gatsby-style farmhouse parties, to which they were sometimes flown at his expense on privately chartered planes. The former SP general secretary Amar Singh, who once wielded great influence with Mulayam, explained Chadha's political buoyancy to me in simple terms: 'He gives 70 per cent of his bribes to the party in power and 30 per cent to the opposition.' If you mattered and could help Chadha expand his interests, then he would throw his weight behind you—regardless of party, identity or ideology.

Chadha's friends in public office proved more than willing to help pay him back. By 2012, his empire had expanded into an almost absurd array of enterprises. In addition to being a liquor baron, sugar miller, real-estate giant, and food distributor, he became a paper miller, soda bottler, large-scale poultry farmer, Bollywood film producer, public transport operator, hydroelectric dam builder, mall and multiplex erector, educationist, philanthropist and African-land speculator. He also owned a professional hockey team. 'Ponty always saw three 50-paisa coins in one rupee,' Mahesh Gupta, a former excise commissioner of Uttar Pradesh, told me. If in a few of his projects Chadha seemed to turn a profit only after assuming significant risks and benefiting the economy at large, many of his ventures got going through contracts effected by the state on ludicrously favourable terms.

That it was Chadha who eventually leveraged these advantages to obtain outrageous wealth might have come as a surprise. He was a college dropout contending with two brothers and a host of cousins for space in a family business that was itself subject to violent external competition. He was also an amputee—a childhood accident deprived him of his left arm below the elbow and left him with two partial fingers and part of a thumb on his right hand—who had to hold his own in the physically aggressive culture of Moradabad, western Uttar Pradesh, where he grew up. But he was intelligent, and later gained a reputation for his orderly mind. 'He planned everything in his head and had this amazing memory power,' Jesudasan said. 'He would never forget his meetings or appointments. He had this clock constantly ticking in his head and it always alarmed him about his plans.'

Chadha, who was universally known as Ponty—he once told a reporter that the nickname was given to him by his father, and he liked it because 'it was easy to remember and gelled with the trade'—learned early on never to yield an inch. The common perception is that whoever got in his way was either induced into an alliance or pushed out of business. 'His strength was that he was brutal on the street and very sober with the government,' Gupta said. By the time he was killed, 10,000 armed men reportedly guarded the family's many enterprises. Some of Chadha's rivals had been murdered, and accusations of guilt were inevitably laid at his feet. The president of the Lucknow Sharab Association, Anil Agarwal, said Chadha had entered 'the most outrageous domains of the liquor business', in which any act of violence was possible. At other times, Chadha showed a willingness to betray his own kin.

Chadha often compared himself with a lotus that bloomed from the mire. His closest aide, Sweety Singh, told me a story that he seemed to consider an illustration of this moral decency. One of Chadha's business rivals had hired a group of contract killers to assassinate Chadha. 'The contract killers knew who Ponty was,' Sweety said, brimming with pride. 'They called him and revealed the name of their client and asked if Ponty wanted him killed once and for all. But Ponty is such a great man that he said, no, don't do him any harm. He was very kind-hearted.'

One way or another, Chadha's interests were enforced. He eventually held sway over significant parts of the liquor business in Uttar Pradesh, Punjab, Haryana and Chandigarh; had liquor operations in Rajasthan, Uttarakhand and Chhattisgarh; and amassed a king's ransom through his other enterprises.

Following Akhilesh's appointment, it soon became clear which way the winds would blow for Chadha. A month after the swearing-in, Mulayam received Chadha for breakfast at his Lucknow home. The meal was dominated by silence: Mulayam spoke rarely, mostly complaining about his insomnia and other health problems; Chadha kept quiet. According to a senior SP leader who has been privy to many meetings between the two men, it was like a 'father and son having a usual meal and communicating in hints and codes known only to them'. You don't calculate the profits and losses at a meeting like that, the SP leader said. 'You just need to convey that you are loyal to the politician—and Ponty had mastered that art.'

In the following months, Akhilesh backtracked on his campaign promises, allowing the liquor distribution policy that Mayawati had instituted to Chadha's great advantage—and which she had renewed just months before the elections—to remain the law of the land. He then publicly denied that there were grounds for investigating the sugar mill auctions, effectively blocking an official probe; cleared all the Noida real estate projects that Chadha had initiated under Mayawati (which he had earlier promised to review); and renewed Chadha's monopoly over the distribution of midday meals.

Though Akhilesh's accommodations were a boon, Chadha was anything but complacent. At the same time that the new chief minister was applying more grease to the wheels of Chadha's various enterprises, Chadha and his son, Monty, were working hard to shed the less seemly aspects of the family's reputation, and to achieve a new respectability through enterprises such as their self-proclaimed 'ultra-modern' real estate ventures.

But Chadha was not to see the full fruits of this labour. His attempts to refashion the family image were still under way in mid November 2012, when he was gunned down by his brother Hardeep in a shoot-out at one of the family's many Delhi farmhouses. It was a violent, high-profile end to a life that began rather modestly in post-Partition Uttar Pradesh, and it seemed to fix the liquor baron's reputation as a rags-to-riches gangster. But the killing, and the stories that emerged in its aftermath, also began to shed some light on how Chadha, largely a cipher to the public, had accomplished his remarkable rise.

II

Moradabad is a battered city of small-time brass, copper and steel producers about three hours east of Delhi. The small district centre of roughly 900,000 straddles a highway that runs from the capital to Jim Corbett National Park, along which a bunch of hotels, glittering with signboards, have recently sprung up. Once you enter the city, bicycles, scooters, cars and autorickshaws fight slowly through narrow roads. Driving past Moradabad's famous market for brass utensils, you hit dense neighbourhoods such as Adarsh Colony, where Ponty Chadha grew up, in the early years of Mulayam's ascent.

Ponty was born Gurdeep Singh Chadha, in Moradabad, on 22 October 1958. The town had a history of intense Hindu–Muslim rioting that stretched back at least a century, and many of the people Chadha grew up around had been scarred by the violence of Partition. The Sikh families who migrated from newly formed Pakistan were confined to a refugee settlement in Adarsh Colony. Those I spoke with said their community had always focused on business: they drove trucks, fixed cars and motorbikes, and opened small iron- and steel-producing units.

During Partition, Chadha's grandfather Gurbachan migrated to Moradabad from Rawalpindi, where he was forced to leave behind his livelihood: a herd of cattle and buffaloes. In the United Provinces, he somehow managed to acquire new stock, and began selling milk. Around the time that the state was renamed Uttar Pradesh, in 1950, he had enough capital to begin producing bhang and country liquor. He was known for his staunch faith in God and his acts of charity, and never turned away beggars desperate for a dram. For a single peg of desi whisky, he would ask them simply to utter the holy word. A mendicant would shout 'Satnam!' and Gurbachan would pour spirits into his cup.

Chadha's father and his two uncles took over the alcohol business in the early 1960s. The family—including the brothers' respective wives and about a dozen siblings and cousins—lived under one roof. From producing country liquor for a single local shop, they moved into buying alcohol from larger distilleries and wholesaling it to several small outlets. By the 1970s, the family controlled a major proportion of the liquor distribution in Moradabad town. Early on, they decided to restrict the operation to blood relatives. Chadha was sent to boarding school in Nainital along with his cousin Gurjeet, who was known as Teetu. 'Ponty was good at mathematics and he enjoyed geometry,' sixty-one-year-old Gurdyal Singh, the Chadhas' next-door neighbour in Adarsh Colony, said. 'The family had great expectations from Ponty and Teetu both, but no one ever imagined that Ponty would go so far.'

Teetu and Chadha were family, friends and fierce competitors. Around the time they were ten, Teetu told me, they both nearly died in the accident that led to Chadha's disfigurement. One evening while the rest of the family was busy with prayers, they went up to the terrace of the house to challenge one another to a rock-slinging contest. They tied a long string to a stone and took turns hurling it from the balcony. On his go, Chadha took a great swing, which was followed by a loud thud. Chadha had collapsed. A few moments later, Teetu fell unconscious. The string had tangled in a high voltage power line and the cousins were electrocuted. 'Look at this hand,' Teetu said, holding up his left limb, which had only two fingers. 'I got crippled, too.'

After the accident, Chadha struggled with his handicap. Holding a spoon or holding a pen—he had to clasp his world between two fingers. He learnt to do it well: by his early twenties, he rode a gearless bike around Moradabad, played neighbourhood cricket, and kept guns. 'He was a very good shooter,' Darinder Singh, Chadha's school friend and neighbour in Moradabad, who is known as Para, said. 'He loved hunting musk deer. We would often set up a barbeque and roast the prey.' To hunt, Chadha wore an artificial arm with a sharp tip. He would rest the barrel on this arm and pinch the butt in his armpit. 'Then he would pull the trigger with his two fingers,' Para said. 'Those two fingers were as strong as pliers.'

After finishing high school in 1978, Chadha and Para enrolled in the undergraduate economics programme at HSB Inter College in central Moradabad. The majority of the students at the college were Hindu Jats. They teased Chadha for being crippled. 'They called him *loola*, *tunda*,' Para said. 'In the beginning he ignored them but a few days later it started bothering him a lot.' Chadha and Para hatched a plan to beat up the student who antagonized Chadha the most. They ambushed the student while he was having lunch inside a classroom. Chadha locked the door, and kicked the student's table so hard that he mangled it. Chadha then asked Para to grab the student. Para, who is still tall and muscular, held the young man from behind. 'Then Ponty headbutted him a couple times,' Para said.

News of the assault quickly spread, and soon a large group of Jats wielding knives, steel rods and hockey sticks began searching for Chadha and Para. 'We went into hiding,' Para said. They sought help from Para's older brother, who ran a transport company in town and employed a few dozen Jats, and he negotiated with the leader of the Jat students. The price for Chadha's safety was that he never went back to college.

If Chadha's formal education was at an end, a more important one was just beginning. He and Teetu spent much of the 1980s as enforcers in the family business, raiding retail liquor shops to execute embargoes on bottles smuggled in from the borders of Punjab and Haryana, where alcohol was cheaper than it was in Uttar Pradesh. Shops with which the Chadhas contracted could only stock brands the family distributed, and anyone who infringed this rule soon watched his entire supply dry up.

As the family expanded its distribution network, Chadha's remit grew. To help carry out his work, he founded a gang of informants, which he earnestly called 'the vigilance team'. 'He developed a strong intelligence network of spies across the town,' Mahinder Singh, the chief excise officer in Moradabad district, told me. Team members were given motorcycles to patrol the highways for smugglers, or bicycles to pedal from shop to shop as they kept a check on distribution. At the same time, Chadha was learning to use the local administration to his advantage. He was in close touch with Singh and other excise officers in Moradabad, and would tip off inspectors about smuggled liquor. 'His team still shares its information with us,' Singh said.

By 1987, Chadha was completely consumed by the family business, which was pulling in significant amounts of cash. Under the guidance of his uncle and Teetu's father, Harbhajan Singh, Chadha earned a decision-making stake. Chadha's overriding ambition, a neighbourhood friend named A.K. Khanna told me, was 'to bring order to the liquor trade of Moradabad'.

Harbhajan helped school Chadha in the value of political goodwill. He was the first in the family to establish contact with Mulayam Singh Yadav, who became chief minister in 1989, at the head of the Janata Dal alliance. Since Independence, Uttar Pradesh had been largely dominated by the Congress party and its brahmin hierarchs. Mulayam and his contemporaries represented a new breed of identity-based state politics in which muscular party leadership embodied hopes of caste empowerment. Yadavs, a peasant and pastoral caste who were seen by upper castes as uncouth and lacking in respect for the law, soon gained the whip hand in the state. Accusations of bribery, extortion, kidnapping and murder were common.

Chadha was eager to form his own links with these new powers. As a reward for his dedication to the family business, Harbhajan sent him on an important errand in advance of the 1989 elections: delivering Rs 8 lakh (worth roughly Rs 27.5 lakh or $45,000 today) to Mulayam. 'The elections were close and Mulayam needed that cash,' Teetu's son chipped in when I asked his father about the incident. When Mulayam defeated the Congressman N.D. Tiwari, and entered into a coalition with the Bharatiya Janata Party (BJP) to form a government, Chadha brought him another present. 'Mulayam didn't have a car back then,' a close associate of the Chadha family told me. 'Ponty gifted him one.'

After taking over as chief minister, Mulayam enacted a policy of 'caste-based business tenders' that gave lower-caste communities living on riverbanks the exclusive right to extract sand and pebbles for resale. Thickets of new commercial and residential buildings were sprouting up along the north-western edge of Uttar Pradesh, where Delhi was expanding eastward into Noida, and the projects (which would soon be fertilized by economic liberalization) required massive amounts of sand for concrete. Govind Pant Raju, a senior journalist based in Lucknow who was then a small-town newspaper reporter covering the operations of local mafias, said that Chadha 'immediately pounced on this policy' and was awarded a claim. 'Everyone wondered how he managed to get this contract from the government,' Raju said. 'The policy was meant for lower castes living along rivers and there was no scope for subcontracting.'

The sand mines were a boon for the liquor business. 'We made good profits,' said Teetu, who would accompany Chadha to his extraction sites, spread along the Gola river in Nainital district. 'In return, we just had to give the government some royalty.' Chadha pumped revenues from the mines back into his liquor distribution network, which needed capital in order to spread to other markets, where the established players were backed by vicious gangs. He also began to cultivate a relationship with western Uttar Pradesh's most powerful liquor baron, Kishan Lal Wadia. 'Ponty was a small-time operator of Wadia in the early nineties,' a senior SP leader told me. 'It was from Wadia that Ponty learned to cajole politicians, and it's because of Wadia's liquor money that Mulayam managed to influence the politics of western Uttar Pradesh.' Wadia's backing gave Chadha the confidence to expand into the northern part of the state, which later became Uttarakhand.

Before he could push north, however, Chadha required muscle, and that muscle required leadership. 'He first employed a group of notorious criminals,' the senior SP leader said. 'Then he needed someone to lead these criminals.' In 1993, a violent dispute broke out in northern Uttar Pradesh between Harbhajan Singh Cheema (a politician who was also in the mining business) and Gurbachan Lal Sharma (a well-known and deeply feared gangster) over a few acres of land. For the next two years, the two waged a bloody gang war in which dozens of men were killed. As a politician, Cheema had to appear frequently in public and needed a bodyguard. Sukhdev Singh Namdhari, a man with a reputation for violence, took the job.

In February 1995, Sharma was murdered by unidentified gunmen. Police arrested Namdhari, but he was quickly bailed out. 'The common perception was that Namdhari gunned down Sharma,' Raju, the journalist, said. Here was Chadha's much-needed man. Later that year, Chadha hired Namdhari—who eventually had fifteen cases registered against him for crimes including criminal intimidation, dacoity and murder—to oversee his liquor and sand-extraction projects in the north. Under the tutelage of Wadia, and with Namdhari by his side, Chadha expanded his distribution network from Moradabad to eighteen districts in western and northern Uttar Pradesh—an achievement that would soon seem modest.

III

Chadha's uncle Harbhajan, a stout, turbaned man with a well-waxed snow-white beard, is still a wholesaler of foreign liquor in Moradabad. Sitting in his office, a small room with finely polished walnut furniture on the first floor of a two-storey cinema hall that the family built in the 1970s—the first big investment the Chadha family made outside the liquor trade—he seemed to me to be frozen in that earlier era. Devotional songs played from somewhere beneath his desk. (He said he always listens to holy music at work.) The building, now drab, was veined with cracks.

Behind Harbhajan's desk there was a glass cupboard. Inside, a framed picture showed two young men—Harbhajan and Mulayam. When I asked him whether he was still in contact with the SP leader, he said he wasn't: 'I lost touch with him because of Ponty. One day he told me that since he and Teetu were taking good care of the business, I should stay away from Mulayam. He said, "Mulayam doesn't like to entertain too many people for one purpose."' Harbhajan then told me how Chadha, as he expanded into northern Uttar Pradesh in the mid 1990s, broke away from parts of the family. 'He betrayed me,' Harbhajan said. 'He took a 40 per cent share from Moradabad and refused to give me anything from Uttarakhand.'

The mid 1990s marked the beginning of Chadha's decade-long ascension from a small if politically well-connected regional player to a shaping force in north India's politics. This coincided with a period of radical upheaval that threw Uttar Pradesh open to new alignments of power. As the old order of the Congress was overturned by the identity politics of the SP, BSP and the Hindu nationalist BJP, opportunities arose for local interests that had been outside Congress coteries to gain influence and office. Bitter contests broke out over control of the lucrative machinery of the state. Between 1993 and 2003, there were eight chief ministerships and three periods of President's rule, all of which were accompanied by intense administrative churning. In 1995, the year that Mayawati first came to power, at least 500 officials were transferred around—or out of—the state bureaucracy; when she came back to power in 1997, after a year and a half of President's rule, she transferred nearly 800.

In time, Chadha took advantage of many of these new alignments. His first order of business in the late 1990s, however, was to keep expanding his liquor operations, laying the groundwork for the distribution monopoly that he would later achieve.

State policy was to auction off wholesale liquor licences on an annual basis. The number of outlets a wholesaler could serve was strictly limited, so in order to bag large numbers of licences at a single go, Chadha pioneered a system called 'playing proxy': gather as many trustworthy people as possible and load them up with cash to outbid rivals. Through these cartels, which became known as 'liquor syndicates', Chadha snapped up most of the alcohol distribution licences in western Uttar Pradesh.

More territory meant Chadha could harness his liquor business to forge new political alliances, reaching out not only to Mulayam and Mayawati, but also to Rajvir Singh (son of the two-time BJP chief minister Kalyan Singh), whom he reportedly made a partner in the liquor distribution of Aligarh district (where his father's constituency was). (Rajvir denied this association with

Chadha, telling me, 'I have never worked with him. He had his own contacts and people like me never mattered to him. He was better off without the support of my father. He had already gained enough power in previous regimes.')

Chadha also hoped to push his distribution network and its influence into other parts of the state but, for the time being, he was blocked by equally powerful rivals, such as the Mulayam supporter (and future SP politician) Jawahar Lal Jaiswal. Instead, he found a frontier in Punjab, where a tussle over liquor and politics had erupted between Sukhbir Singh Badal (son of the chief minister, Parkash Singh Badal) and his brother-in-law, Adesh Pratap Singh Kairon. In 2001, with the elder Badal's five-year term nearing its end and fresh assembly elections around the corner, the family's Akali Dal party began searching for new candidates.

In business and in politics, Sukhbir supported the Akali Dal old guard, which was affiliated to the biggest liquor distributor in Punjab, Jagdish Singh Garcha, who also served as the state's minister for technical education. Kairon, who was the excise and taxation minister, lobbied to get party tickets for business associates who wanted to enter politics, but were frozen out by Garcha's control over liquor distribution. Kairon's candidates could only woo voters if he tapped his own booze supplies. 'To break Garcha's monopoly,' said K.S. Chawla, a journalist based in Ludhiana who has covered the Badal–Kairon row, 'he brought Ponty to Punjab.'

A couple of months before the elections in early 2002, there was to be an auction of Ludhiana retail liquor shops at which Garcha and Chadha were expected to face off as agents for Sukhbir and Kairon. Chief Minister Badal postponed the auction three times, hoping that he could arbitrate a truce between his son and son-in-law. But the clashes persisted, and the auction was eventually held in nearby Patiala. It was Chadha's first foray into Punjab. Bidding liberally, he and his syndicate snaffled up shops worth Rs 16 crore per year. 'Ponty never cared about the market,' Garcha, now in his late seventies, told me. 'For a liquor shop worth 10 lakh rupees, he would propose 50 lakh.' After acquiring large wholesale licences, Chadha would then co-opt the small middlemen who connected distributors to hole-in-the-wall shops. 'He was loaded with a lot of money and he bought almost every small-time contractor,' said Garcha, who for a while managed to hold on to half the district's retail stores.

As it turned out, neither Garcha's liquor and Sukhbir's votes nor Kairon's votes and Chadha's liquor could keep the Akali Dal in power, and Sukhbir's father was shunted out of office by the Congress politician Amrinder Singh. This didn't seem to matter much to Chadha, however. He now had a foothold in Punjab and set about playing the game he had mastered in Uttar Pradesh: massaging politicians' egos while aggressively pursuing market share. He quickly established a strong bond with the chief minister, with whom he socialized frequently. On one occasion, Singh, after disappearing from Punjab without alerting even his own security officers, suddenly issued a press statement from Dubai announcing that he was attending the wedding of someone close to Chadha. But Chadha's influence was also percolating down through the state's liquor apparatus: excise officers overseeing local auctions would hold the bidding for hours if Chadha needed to turn up late. Over the course of the next three years, Chadha poached almost all the contractors from Garcha's network.

In the late summer of 2005, in the middle of Singh's reign in Punjab, Chadha attended the golden jubilee celebrations of the Dhudial Khalsa Senior Secondary School in Patiala, where he had won his first retail shops. There, a politician from the Akali Dal who was close to Kairon baited Chadha by accusing him of running a liquor mafia in Punjab. Ponty answered politely, 'The mafia doesn't care about generating revenue for the government.

In my case, I care a lot about the government. I run this business and add huge sums to the state exchequer.' Here, distilled, was the political genius of Chadha's enterprise. Before leaving the event, he announced that he would renovate the school, which was dilapidated, and build it a new storey.

In 2003, as Chadha was taking advantage of his opening in Punjab and raking in cash through his monopolies in Uttarakhand and western Uttar Pradesh, a BSP–BJP coalition government under the leadership of Mayawati, which had come to power following a remarkably close election the previous year, was struggling to maintain its integrity. In late August, the BJP withdrew its support for the chief minister, and the coalition crumbled. Amid calls for dissolution of the assembly, Mulayam rallied, gathering enough support to stave off fresh elections and regain power in Lucknow.

Shortly afterwards, Mulayam and Amar Singh, the SP party general secretary, began distributing favours to their dearest benefactors. Singh lobbied on behalf of the real estate dealer Ashok Chaturvedi, who was given a large tract of land in Noida. 'The arrangement between Singh and Mulayam was that except for [the industrialist] J.P. Gaur and Chaturvedi, no one would ever enter into the real estate sector in Noida,' a close associate of Singh's told me.

In addition to trying to bolster his friends, Singh hoped the agreement would stifle Chadha, who had just begun to funnel profits from his liquor empire into other industries, including real estate. 'Amar tried his best to turn Mulayam against Ponty,' the former SP leader told me. 'He would often say, "Why are we helping this man? He changes his colour like a chameleon."' But Mulayam and Chadha went back to the days of NE 1000, and the chief minister soon publicly inaugurated one of Chadha's first real estate projects, the 314,500-square-foot Wave Mall in Lucknow, one of five Wave malls that Chadha would eventually build.

Singh, his close associate said, was 'disgruntled', but the chief minister proved indifferent to his constant grumblings against Chadha. 'Mulayam doesn't care a damn about loyalties,' the former SP leader said. 'All he cares about is his own share—and when it comes to distributing money, Ponty's record was always clean.' Singh confirmed this view of Chadha, telling me that Chadha was a 'transparent and honest creator, distributor and maintainer of ill-gotten wealth'. (When I asked him about Chaturvedi, he said he knew him and other players from a distance: 'Chaturvedi would come and meet me just like anyone would meet me. These guys—Ashok, Ponty and J.P. Gaur—they had direct contact with Mulayam. I was never part of that circle.')

Chadha did well under Mulayam, but the real explosion in his wealth took place when Mayawati came back to power. Propelled by a number of convenient decisions by her BSP government, Chadha was able to force out his remaining opponents in Uttar Pradesh's alcohol distribution market, bag a significant portion of the state's retail liquor shops, massively extend his real estate ventures, and gather into his ever-expanding arms a whole range of new enterprises, including the sugar mills and food distribution contracts. A hallmark of several of these endeavours seemed to be vertical integration: liquor sold in his new Model Wine shops was supplied by his distribution company; instead of small change, Model Wine customers were given little snack packets made by his new food processing plant; and the Bollywood films he produced were distributed through his new film distribution company and shown at his eleven Wave multiplexes. Every link in these chains could be exploited to disguise profits through financial misreporting of one kind or another. For example, Chadha quickly developed a reputation for distributing some of the country's worst movies (such as *Jism II*); it was easy to claim that such tripe sold poorly at the box office, especially when Chadha was the one collecting the ticket stubs, but a senior SP leader told me that the films earned more than critics or tax collectors ever thought.

If malfeasance fuelled much of this acceleration in Chadha's interests, scandal was its inevitable by-product. One of the most significant improprieties that emerged from Mayawati's association with Chadha at this time involved the sugar mills. In 2010 and 2011, her government held auctions of twenty-one underperforming state-owned refineries, sixteen of which were bought by seven firms that turned out to be a cartel controlled by Chadha. Many of these companies had common shareholders and directors, shared a single address, and paid to participate in the auctions using demand drafts with consecutive serial numbers issued by the same bank branch on the same day. This lack of competition alone cost the state an estimated Rs 200 crore, according to the CAG report later filed in the case. Although the details are complex, at least a dozen improprieties were identified in the sale of the mills, including undervaluation of the land and other assets, and disclosure of the minimum acceptable bid. In total, the CAG said that the state lost more than Rs 2,000 crore through its illicit management of the auctions.

In another high-profile case, the Mayawati government violated a Supreme Court ruling in order to permit Chadha's Great Value Foods to become the sole supplier of lunches for the state's midday meal scheme. The supply contracts, which were supposed to go to certain kinds of local community groups and feed more than 2 crore children and pregnant women, were worth roughly Rs 10,000 crore. Later, it turned out that the food Chadha was providing fell far below the prescribed nutritional standards.

The biggest bonanza to which Mayawati helped Chadha was in the liquor trade. The year after she was appointed as chief minister, the state's liquor distribution policy was changed to ban wholesalers from directly purchasing liquor from distilleries. Instead, the government handed over wholesale and distribution rights for the entire state to the government-owned Uttar Pradesh Cooperative Sugar Factories' Federation, which in turn subcontracted the job to Blue Water, a private beverage company whose ownership ultimately answered to Chadha. 'The government did not advertise the subcontracting, and the entire trade was handed over to Ponty,' said S.P. Singh, the president of the Lucknow Wine Association and a distant relative of Chadha's, who became a staunch adversary of the baron after Chadha shafted him in a distribution deal. 'The lifeline of every distributor was in his hands. It was his wish to choke us, drown us or simply ignore us. He played those games very well.'

Chadha used his new monopoly to add 10 to 15 per cent to the maximum retail price of liquor—a levy that became known as 'Ponty prasad' or 'Ponty tax'. This allowed him to generate his own substantial profits while at the same time pumping money into the state exchequer and rewarding Mayawati for her patronage. Between 2008 and 2012, state revenues on liquor excise increased more than 70 per cent to Rs 8,139 crore. (One Lucknow liquor distributor who worked under Chadha told me that price hikes always work, because 'people need alcohol like cars need petrol'.)

Perhaps understandably, the excise commissioner of Uttar Pradesh during much of this period, Mahesh Gupta, saw Chadha in a somewhat rosier light than S.P. Singh. Soon after Gupta took up his post in 2008, Chadha came from Delhi to pay his respects in person at Gupta's official residence in Lucknow, and the two men visited with one another on several subsequent occasions. 'He was a very careful human being,' Gupta said. 'He would fix an appointment with you, though he could have simply called and met us whenever he felt like it. But he would always follow proper procedure.'

The 'proper procedures' became even more lucrative for Chadha after Mayawati changed the retail rules so that he could corner all the liquor shops in the western part of the state. Chadha could now buy alcohol from distilleries and sell it direct to consumers at his own shops. Allegedly, Chadha also cut a number of backroom deals to boost his profits; according to S.P. Singh, he made a secret agreement with Vijay Mallya to promote the latter's Kingfisher beer and McDowell's No. 1 whisky over other brands. Before Chadha's death, Singh said, 'You couldn't find Radico Khaitan in the market. Their 8PM brand had become a dream.'

The takings from these monopolies were a boon for Wave Infratech, Chadha's real estate business, which initiated three major projects in Noida during the period of Mayawati's reign, including two commercial complexes of more than 2 million square feet each. A fourth project, Ghaziabad's Wave City, was officially launched only two months after her tenure as chief minister came to an end. In all of these cases, Mayawati was accused of selling the land off to Chadha at absurdly low rates.

In Moradabad, Chadha's uncle Harbhajan told me that, to his death, Chadha continued to exclude him from the conspicuous riches that these new projects had brought. 'I met him a thousand times over the issue—that my son's heart burns when he sees your shopping malls and wealth; you should give us our share,' Harbhajan said. 'Even his father agreed that we deserved an equal share, but Ponty kept playing with me by delaying the proceedings.'

IV

Chadha's dispute with Harbhajan was by no means the most heated, or the most intimate, of the family arguments that seemed to come to a boil as the Chadha fortune grew. In 2010, Chadha's brother Hardeep began pressuring their father, who was suffering from Alzheimer's disease, to dictate that the family's holdings be evenly split between Chadha, Hardeep, and their third brother, Rajinder, according to a report later published in *India Today*. Chadha bristled: it was his leadership that grew the family's alcohol distribution network from a single small town in western Uttar Pradesh into the largest liquor monopoly in north India; it was his hard graft that pushed the frontiers of their empire into other lucrative industries, such as sand mining and real estate; and it was his influence that seeped behind the lace curtains and into the back seats of cherry-topped Ambassadors in Dehradun, Chandigarh, Lucknow and Delhi.

Hardeep eventually prevailed on their ailing father, and Chadha felt compelled to accede to his dying wishes. But he did so in bad faith: when their father passed away, in April 2011, Chadha reneged on the deal. For the next sixteen months, the brothers argued face-to-face and through intermediaries over what they were each due. According to Balbir Singh Kohli, a close relative of the Chadha family, Chadha felt Hardeep was being manipulated. 'Some people are misleading him against me,' Chadha told Kohli. 'I want him to understand that.'

If forty-five-year-old Hardeep was susceptible to manipulation, perhaps it was because he ached to step out of Chadha's shadow. 'Wherever Hardeep went, people always recognized him as Ponty's brother,' Ravi Sodhi, a spokesperson for Chadha's largest company, Wave Group, told me. 'He wanted his own identity.' As a result, he became increasingly imperious. 'Hardeep would shout and yell at his servants just to say that he was someone important in the family,' Sodhi said. He had also taken to stroking a cat while sitting in a throne as he received guests at the Chhatarpur mansion he shared with the family and, on a recent occasion, he had inexplicably set fire to carpets worth lakhs of rupees. 'With every passing month, the dispute grew bigger,' Kohli said.

The brothers' larger quarrel over the family's empire soon began to centre on a pair of farmhouses that Hardeep intended to dispose of against his brother's wishes. Chadha, who was magnanimous with friends and enemies alike but could brook no impudence, was furious. Although the homes were a negligible part of the fortune he had accumulated over his two and a half decades of canny business leadership and oily political lobbying, he had resolved to keep them in the family.

On 15 November 2012, with the brothers' acrimony reaching a fever pitch, family members prevailed on them to meet at a Delhi gurdwara. Remarkably, a second settlement was reached: according to *India Today*, Chadha agreed to buy Hardeep out of the business for something between Rs 400 crore and Rs 1,200 crore. It must have seemed like a small price to pay to rid himself, and the empire he built, of his brother's meddling. But whatever relief there was didn't last long. The next day, another meeting was called between Chadha and his brother. Hardeep, reportedly hectored by the people counselling him against Chadha, annulled the payout deal. It was the final nail.

Shortly after 9.50 a.m. on Saturday the 17th, Chadha convened a meeting of armed men at his family's Chhatarpur mansion, on Delhi's south-western outskirts, where he lived with his mother and both his brothers. In attendance was his long-time henchman, Sukhdev Singh Namdhari (who was now serving as Uttarakhand's minorities commissioner), as well as at least eleven others. According to chargesheets later filed in a Delhi district court, Chadha divided his and Namdhari's men into two detachments and directed them to storm the contested properties, forcibly evict anyone present, and seize control, while he and Namdhari stayed back and waited for news.

Arriving at 42 DLF Farms, the squad assigned to the property overturned a white Maruti parked in front of one of the property's several gates, and then set about smashing all the gate locks. They rushed onto the grounds and busted into the house, viciously beating as many of the staff and security guards as they could find, stripping them of their mobile phones, and then forcing them off the property. According to statements made by several of the staff members, there were thirty to forty men in the raiding party, who carried rifles, pistols, revolvers, hockey sticks, dandas and swords. After seizing the farmhouse, new locks and cans of black paint were distributed to some of the men. They painted over a 'For sale' sign that Hardeep had put up and a plaque outside the house that bore his name, then secured all the gates. But one of the staff members who had been assaulted managed to escape with his mobile phone and get word to Hardeep, who was soon racing to the property from his office in Noida.

Once the house was locked down, Chadha and Namdhari were called. At 12.30 p.m., they reached the locked rear entrance in a dark green Toyota Land Cruiser. Sachin Tyagi, a twenty-seven-year-old Uttarakhand police constable assigned to Namdhari as a personal security officer, was in the front next to the driver, strapped with a nine-millimetre carbine rifle. One of Chadha's aides, Narender Ahlawat, soon arrived to open the gate. Just as he popped the lock, Hardeep charged up in a Mercedes. According to witness statements, Hardeep sprung out of the car brandishing a pistol, and approached Ahlawat, hurling abuses. Then he shoved Ahlawat, and shot him in the leg.

Chadha began to climb out of the Land Cruiser, but Hardeep was now facing him. Hardeep cursed his brother, then pumped seven shots into his legs, abdomen, back and chest. He then turned towards the open gate. Namdhari levelled his pistol—a .30-bore that he had licensed illegally using a forged ration card—at Hardeep. Tyagi, too, put Chadha's brother in his sights. Then they opened fire, hitting him twice. A slug that entered through Hardeep's back tore a track through his lungs, filling them with blood, before exiting briefly through his right armpit and then boring clean through his arm.

Chadha was haemorrhaging wildly, but he was apparently still alive. Namdhari and Tyagi secured him in the Land Cruiser as Hardeep, suffocating with his own blood, took shelter in a guardhouse by the gate, where his body was later found. The Land Cruiser then tore off in the direction of Fortis Hospital, in Vasant Kunj, with Chadha bleeding out in the back seat. At 1.05 p.m., doctors at the hospital declared him dead on arrival.

By that evening, hastily reported accounts of the fratricide were vying for air on prime-time news shows with obituaries of the Shiv Sena demagogue Bal Thackeray, who died in Mumbai that afternoon. As word of the killings spread, Chadha-controlled businesses across north India closed their doors amid uncertainty over what would befall the decapitated empire in the coming hours and days. Wave cineplexes ceased screenings, Wave malls were emptied out, and police officers were dispatched to stand guard by shuttered Model Wine shops across Uttar Pradesh. Allegations of conspiracy soon began to emerge, with some claiming that Namdhari had orchestrated the shoot-out in order to expropriate millions of rupees that Chadha had invested in his name.

Namdhari was arrested in Uttarakhand two days after the killing, at a press conference where he was pleading innocence in the shootings. In the next two weeks, Delhi police detained twenty more people in connection with the crime. Three chargesheets have since been filed, but the case remains sub judice, and Namdhari continues to maintain his innocence. For its part, the Chadha family seems convinced that, in effect, brother killed brother. 'It's just two minutes of anger that destroyed a beautiful family,' Paramjeet Singh Sarna, a close relative, told me. He said the fraternal dispute over money and influence within the family was almost resolved.

Two days after Chadha's and Hardeep's deaths, it was announced that Chadha's son, thirty-three-year-old Monty, would take the reins of the company. A high-school dropout who seems to have passed much of his youth behind the red-velvet cordons of Delhi's most expensive nightclubs, Monty had spent the past couple of years trying to help his father slough off the Chadha family's notorious reputation. When the Wave City project was conceived, the company made Monty the face of it, and he became the man journalists wanted to interview. Chadha handled the back-end operations, keeping tabs on the money and clearing up a million little hurdles the government puts in the way. Following the tax department raids, it was Monty's idea to hire the spokesman Ravi Sodhi, who had previously worked for Anil Ambani, and to set up the Wave Group's first public relations department. Monty now works closely with his childless uncle, Rajinder, who was immensely loyal to Chadha, but Sodhi told me that Monty's decisions are final.

Earlier this year, I went to the Wave Group's Noida headquarters to meet Monty and ask him about his father and the future of his father's empire. As I entered the office, a multi-storeyed glass building inaugurated a few months after Chadha's death, two big garlanded portraits of Chadha and his late father, Kulwant, welcomed me. Sodhi appeared and shepherded me through a long corridor that led to a thick metal door, where he stopped to scan his fingerprint on a small box. The door opened, and we walked into another corridor, by a meeting room labelled 'Chanakya'. Suddenly, a door to the room slid open. Inside, Monty, in a maroon turban and plush-looking brown shoes, was sitting at a round table with one of his employees, whose name and job description I never got.

During our conversation, Monty, with his alert eyes and softly rasping voice, discussed the sense of great responsibility with which his father's sudden death left him. At present, the company's main target is to finish its ambitious Wave City project, which Monty pitched to me as 'something like downtown Manhattan'. The first phase, which is presently under construction, has 1,400 apartments, two office buildings and a shopping mall. Monty's top priority, he said, is to finish this project by 2016. He then asked me why I was interested in writing about his father, and listened quietly to my response with his head down. When I finished, Monty raised his head and said that he would discuss the matter with his senior officers. 'Sorry,' he said, offering me a firm handshake. 'We want some time to think.' He never got back to me.

Although the killing of Chadha and Hardeep seemed to cement the less admirable qualities of Chadha's reputation, it may also have freed Monty from the legacy of his father's corruption. Shortly after Chadha's death, Akhilesh Yadav quashed all outstanding investigations into Chadha's business dealings, leaving Monty free to pursue greater respectability. But the Uttar Pradesh chief minister renewed the Chadhas' liquor monopoly in early summer, projecting record-high excise revenues for the state. Regardless of where Monty says he wants to focus the family business, the economics of the liquor industry and the political conditions out of which the Chadha empire grew persist, and it isn't clear that anyone who finds his hand on the tap and his mouth at the spigot can find the will to let go.

In a way, of course, every work of journalism is a singular challenge, but a profile of **SAMIR JAIN** was especially unique. Has there been anyone in the history of modern India who has shaped its sensibility so thoroughly and still remained so obscured from the public eye? Jain wasn't just the proprietor of the largest English-language newspaper in the world. He was the man who cast the *Times of India* in its modern image: avaricious, compromised, shallow, unreliable. When it turned out that this model of publishing could earn pots of money, other newspapers hurried in its wake, to the inarguable detriment of news reporting and writing. In the long haul, Jain may well go down as the man who both created and destroyed modern Indian newspaper journalism. Since this piece was published, Jain has, according to many accounts, withdrawn somewhat from his empire. But Bennett, Coleman & Co. Ltd's media properties—its newspapers and magazines, its radio stations, its shrill English news channel—still reflect many of Jain's priorities.

Despite his dominance over the industry for three decades, nothing significant had been written about Jain at all when I began work on this story. He is ferociously reclusive, and his colleagues and family tend to honour his desire to remain deep backstage. This posed some technical questions for me. If he refused to be interviewed, how could I write about his life, his temperament and his views on journalism? If nearly everything I discovered about the man was fresh material, how was I to decide what was necessary to relay and what wasn't? The final piece presented here was the result of nine months of work, cut down from its original 19,000 words to its present 16,000. Even at that length, I hope, it is an intimate profile, a portrait of a man of complicated flaws and virtues.

SAMANTH SUBRAMANIAN

Samanth Subramanian is a writer and journalist living in Dublin. His writing has appeared in the New Yorker, *the* New York Times, *the* Guardian *and* Caravan, *among others. His latest book is* This Divided Island: Stories from the Sri Lankan War.

Supreme Being

How Samir Jain created the modern Indian newspaper industry

By SAMANTH SUBRAMANIAN | 1 December 2012

I

In the collective memory of *Times of India* journalists, the notebooks loom large; no conversation about Samir Jain can be complete without mentioning them. If Jain, the vice chairman of Bennett, Coleman & Company Limited and publisher of the *Times of India*, invites you into his office for a chat, you're expected to carry a notebook, and you're expected to take notes. 'We all had our Samir Jain notebooks, and anxious managers outside his cabin would hand us new ones in case we'd forgotten ours,' said an editor who worked at the newspaper during the 1990s. 'I even remember the type: Ajanta No. 3 notebooks, spiral-bound, in different colours.'

New initiates into Jain's meetings have made the mistake of decorating the pages of their notebooks with aimless doodles; old hands learn at least to scrawl down key words, lest they be quizzed the next day or the week after. It can be a chore; it can also be downright galling. After a cordial conversation in 1986, when Jain was still finding his feet around the paper, he pointedly told one editor, decades his senior: 'It's so nice discussing these matters with you. But when others come to see me, they bring a notebook. Maybe you should too.' In response, the editor told me, his voice still bearing embers of anger, 'I said: "You may own the paper, but this is not tolerable." Then I came downstairs and wrote out my resignation letter.'

Really diligent scribes can leave Jain's office with aching wrists. In large gatherings elsewhere, Jain prefers to remain a passive observer, but in these little conclaves, he can talk, in mixed English and Hindi, for an hour or more at a time. He is nothing if not discursive; his homilies have ranged over editorial matters, brand-building and marketing, the nature of art, the psychology of his readers, sex, literature, and—most commonly—religion and spirituality.

Over the last two and a half decades, Jain has imprinted himself indelibly onto the *Times of India*, and thereby onto Indian journalism. In his newsroom, Jain is sometimes referred to, discreetly, as 'Supreme Being', and his will can be difficult to fathom. He preserves an Olympian detachment from his newspaper's coverage of politics, and editors attested to me that he never once calls to inquire about the next day's headlines, let alone to push a line in favour of one party or another. Simultaneously, though, Jain has been exacting and forceful in his mission to shape the *Times of India*—its editorial philosophy; its news priorities; its gimlet-eyed focus on the bottom line—in his image. His demands can sound abstract or whimsical, and he is frequently elliptical about spelling them out, but he is insistent that they be met.

Jain, who will be fifty-nine in March, has a capacious memory, and he recollects, nearly verbatim, much of what he has read. 'The active Samir is a treat. He likes debate. If he argues with you on some point, it means he's willing to be convinced,' said M.D. Nalapat, once the coordinating editor of the *Times of India*. Nalapat left the newspaper in the late 1990s, although he remains close to Jain. 'But total silence means deep disagreement, and there's no convincing him. If you're smart, you'll shut it down and not go any further.' Jain is always polite and soft-spoken, but he watches his audience keenly, a former *Economic Times* editor told me; his eyes constantly flit around the room, 'and just when you think he isn't looking at you, you'll find that he is, to see if you're listening. It's very unsettling.'

Strict rules of engagement govern Jain's meetings, some of them even written out explicitly as instructions from Bennett, Coleman's management and distributed to new editors. 'You aren't supposed to look at your watch, for instance,' said Vidya Subrahmaniam, a former staffer on the editorial page and now an associate editor at *The Hindu*. 'Even if you have an appointment with the prime minister, that is secondary.' No crosstalk is allowed. You don't scrape your chair along the ground, and you accord Jain rapt attention. In *Behind the Times*, a frothy, cinnamon-dusted history of the newspaper, Bachi Karkaria, one of its columnists, describes a discussion in Jain's Mumbai office, during which an editor had slumped a few degrees too many in her chair. Jain slid 'a folded slip [of paper] to her across the desk. In his spidery handwriting, it read, "Very discreetly, and without seeming to be reacting to this note, please do not sit with your knees pressed against the edge of the table."'

These assemblies have been pleasant for some; one former editor said that Jain was 'one of the best teachers I have ever had. Talking to him focused your mind. It made you think through your position on something.' For most participants, they were harrowing, like a subtle but perpetual test of obedience. 'He never directly dictated the edit line. He engaged you in long conversations, and you had to read between the lines, absorb the message, come back down, and write your edit,' Subrahmaniam said. One editor quit the paper because the constant effort to glean Jain's meaning grew too wearying. 'I'd come out of some of these sessions just ashen-faced,' he said. 'I was rattled. I couldn't handle that intensity.'

A coded lexicon evolved to describe these councils and their cast. In a 'darbar', Jain met his full court of editors; in a 'darshan', a pilgrim walked into Jain's sanctum alone. K. Subrahmanyam, the late strategic affairs analyst who worked on the opinion page, called Jain's business managers '*pakkavadyams*', referring to the cluster of accompanists around the main performer in a Carnatic music concert. Less charitably, Subrahmanyam, who survived one bout with cancer, labelled these sessions with Jain—supposedly beneficial, always sapping—as 'chemotherapy'.

Sometimes these meetings are conducted at Sujagi, Jain's residence opposite the Taj Mahal Hotel in central Delhi, a tasteful but austere house with few idiosyncrasies. (One of them, though, is piped music; a visitor in the early 2000s swears that he heard, to his surprise, Buddha Bar trickling out of the speakers.) More often, the meetings will happen in Jain's office on the fourth floor of the Times Group building in New Delhi, or in its equivalent in the handsome Mumbai premises near Chhatrapati Shivaji Terminus.

From these offices, Jain administers the Bennett, Coleman empire, India's largest media house. In the year ending March 2011, Bennett, Coleman earned revenues of Rs 47.49 billion and an after-tax profit of Rs 9.75 billion. (By comparison, HT Media, which owns the *Hindustan Times*, registered revenues of Rs 18.15 billion, and Network18 Media & Investments, which owns CNN-IBN and CNBC-TV18, earned Rs 14.84 billion.) Bennett, Coleman, a private limited company, owns some stray real estate firms and brokerage houses, produces movies and music, dabbles in web commerce via Indiatimes, and runs a mysterious subsidiary, Times Yoga Ltd, whose purpose and nature I was never entirely able to establish.

Almost all of Bennett, Coleman's money is earned by its newspapers—the *Times of India*, the *Economic Times*, *Navbharat*

Times, sundry city tabloids—and, to a lesser extent, by its television channels such as Times Now and ET Now, a sheaf of magazines, and FM radio stations. In 2010–11, Bennett, Coleman's dailies commanded 54 per cent of the English-language market in India's eight biggest cities. The *Economic Times*, with a daily readership of more than 800,000, is India's biggest business newspaper. The *Times of India* is the country's highest-circulated English-language newspaper and also the highest-circulated English-language newspaper in the world, with a daily run of over 3 million copies. Its readership is nearly double that of its nearest rival, the *Hindustan Times*, and its sheer dominance in India, a country with more than 11,000 English newspapers and periodicals, is something of a marvel.

These are not laurels upon which Jain is content to rest; having conquered the metropolises, the *Times of India* is opening editions in towns like Visakhapatnam, Aurangabad and Nashik. There are now fifty editions across forty cities; the *Times of India* has localized itself across a country in a way no newspaper has ever done before. Jain is also throwing himself afresh into the vernacular space, having long neglected his Hindi and Marathi dailies; a few weeks ago, Bennett, Coleman launched *Ei Samay*, a Bengali daily, to compete with the venerable *Ananda Bazar Patrika*. 'I think Samir regrets not having spotted the growth of vernacular newspapers,' the head of a competing media house told me. 'We saw it eight years ago, and we were surprised, frankly, that he didn't. We were always waiting for him to catch up.'

Playing catch-up is not Jain's style; there is little in the Indian newspaper business over the last twenty years that he has not pioneered. He has touched off explosions in circulation by pushing into new towns and into new reader segments, helping India become the world's largest English-language newspaper market. He spotted, before any of his peers, the necessity of burnishing a brand, and his single greatest accomplishment lies in making the *Times of India* the country's foremost media brand. He has, with his cash reserves, kept newspaper prices ruinously low; a weekday issue of the *Times of India* costs Rs 4.50, or 8.3 cents, in New Delhi. This forces publishers to wring every possible rupee out of advertisers, and at this blood sport, Bennett, Coleman has proven the most proficient. Separately, and well before other newspapers, the *Times of India* became adept at celebrity journalism, filling its supplements with movie-star gossip and cocktail-party photos and other exalted banalities.

Jain was also the first newspaper baron in India to tinker with the interstitial spaces between editorial and advertising, smudging the line between the two departments. A junior editor in the mid 1990s recalls one of Jain's corporate managers, 'articulating the wisdom of the palace, saying unapologetically: "The job of the newspaper is to deliver the reader to the advertiser."' Such a mission can be a slippery slope, and its critics claim that the *Times of India* has tumbled joyfully down it—that its editorial coverage can be bought, and that, in its pages, advertising can be paraded as news. Ravi Dhariwal, Bennett, Coleman's CEO, has had to respond to these charges so often that he has developed a flat but exasperated tone in which to deliver his denial. No editorial space in the main *Times of India* paper can be purchased, he told me. He hinted further that this was not necessarily the case with other Indian dailies: 'I think we're the cleanest media house there is.'

In running his newspapers, Jain anticipated, by many years, the questions that nip at the ankles of the print media today: about the sort of news a newspaper needs to cover, about the readers it should aim to please, and about its very purpose in our lives. Jain has discovered unequivocal answers to these questions for himself, but he continues to be excoriated, Dhariwal believes, only because these answers—brutally commercial in nature—have been so disruptive. 'It's a complex psychological reaction to our strength,' he said. 'But they all follow us. Every single media company wants to emulate what we do.'

Dhariwal isn't wrong. Success as lavish as Jain's has given other publishers no option but to replicate parts, or all, of his model. 'I don't think any paper wholeheartedly followed down his path,' said the head of a competing media house, 'but now we do have to think of the newspaper as a consumer product, as Samir did. Samir made papers look at their readers and say: "If you want me to dumb it down, I'll dumb it down. Film, sex, fashion—whatever it takes."' When, in 2005, Jain started Private Treaties—by which Bennett, Coleman swaps advertising space for small stakes in companies—other media houses fulminated, but they 'waited and watched' before following suit, this competitor of Jain's said. Since then, the Network18 Group, HT Media, New Delhi Television (NDTV) and the Dainik Bhaskar group have all practised variants of Private Treaties. The pressure to mimic the *Times of India* can be as intense in newsrooms as in boardrooms. 'Whatever the *Times of India* did, we had to do two days later,' said a former *Hindustan Times* editor. 'Every single morning in my edit meetings, it was: "What did *TOI* do? What did *TOI* do? What did *TOI* do?"'

I never got a chance to ask Jain about his thoughts on any of this; my requests to interview him proved futile. Jain is fanatically reclusive, and he makes himself particularly unavailable to reporters. The last major interview he gave was a quarter-century ago, to the British journalist Nicholas Coleridge, who devoted a chapter in his book *Paper Tigers* to the Indian newspaper industry. Even then, Jain was souring on the idea of being covered by the media. Raju Narisetti, who attended the Times School of Journalism in 1988 and is now managing editor of the Wall Street Journal Digital Network, recalls Jain telling his class: 'The one thing I have learned from Girilal Jain [then the *Times of India* editor-in-chief] is to never give interviews. That's why they keep publishing the same old photograph of me.' Images of Jain continue to be rare today. The few that exist show a trim, dapper man, his salt-and-pepper hair neatly battened into place, his eyes masked by his spectacles' browned-over lenses.

In direct proportion to this bashfulness is Bennett, Coleman's litigious streak; the company eagerly pursues legal action over any perceived slight, however inconsequential or well founded. Vineet Jain, Bennett, Coleman's managing director and younger to his brother Samir by twelve years, once promised to sue *Maxim* because it had printed—without naming him—a photo from one of his pool parties, showing him and a friend in the water with two models. Pradyuman Maheshwari, a columnist in Mumbai, shut down his small, chatty media blog after Bennett, Coleman threatened to sue him unless he removed nineteen posts about the company. 'They said, "You've been running this campaign against us,"' Maheshwari told me. 'One executive there had this habit of filing suits from Sikkim. They were going to file across the country!' The company has now announced plans to sue Zee News after a Zee Business editor was caught, in a sting video, telling Jindal Steel officials: 'ET *mein to front-page stories bik rahi hain aaj kal* (Even front-page stories in the *Economic Times* are being sold).' Fear of the Jains' legal reach is endemic. As a result very few of the people I spoke to—numbering roughly fifty, including phalanxes of editors, managers and journalists, both bygone and present-day—agreed to be identified by name.

Samir Jain evokes, from those who have known him, a bewildering assortment of reactions. Some cannot be critical enough, either of him or of his stewardship of his newspapers. One former editor started out talking about Jain civilly enough, but he rediscovered so many buried grievances over the next ninety minutes that he became, by the end of our conversation, a spluttering Roman candle of invective. (Not surprisingly, he too asked to remain anonymous: 'I don't want all the legal weight of the fucking *Times of India* jumping on me.') Others swear affection to him, saying that Jain is unfairly maligned; they recount stories of his generosity and his razor-keen intelligence. Still others stud their narratives with caveats and assertions and counter-assertions and sentences that begin: 'He's a very difficult man to know, but . . .' The complexity of these responses is to be expected, because it matches the complexity of the turmoil he has sown, single-handed, in Indian journalism. 'The entire newspaper industry in this country since the 1990s,' Chandan Mitra, editor of the *Pioneer*, told me, 'is essentially the creation of Samir Jain.'

II

One day in the late 1990s, an assistant editor on the *Times of India*'s opinion page dredged up the courage to complain to Samir Jain that his paper was being dumbed down, crammed to its brim with irrelevant articles. 'Samir sent a minion off to fetch a *Times of India* from twenty years ago, and we sat down and compared the first page of the day's paper with the first page of the paper from twenty years ago,' the assistant editor said. 'And the twenty-year-old one was full of rubbish! It was all, "The prime minister said this, the President said that." It was very government-driven, very *sarkari*.'

The most popular way to talk about the *Times of India* is to wail about its decline under Jain, but this trope relies on an erstwhile excellence from which the newspaper supposedly fell—an excellence that, to twenty-first-century eyes, appears partly mythical. In the early 1980s, the *Times of India* reported faithfully—too faithfully—upon government policies and the state-run economy, but on little else. Journalists never ventured out of the cities, and their copy was smug and lifeless. Pritish Nandy, now a film producer, joined the Times Group in December 1982 and went on to edit its *Illustrated Weekly*, and he remembers that 'conversation in the office was all about who went and met Indira Gandhi for a cup of tea. They were all bloated frauds. And the paper reflected that. It was pompous and questionable.'

Nobody reading the *Times of India* today can deem it guilty of pomposity. Instead, the paper feels slight, its vast breadth of subject matter diminished by its frustrating lack of depth and its higgledy-piggledy approach of delivering even the most complex news. Stories carry slugs that might have been gleaned from pulp magazine covers: 'Beed Shocker', shrieked a recent front-page example, about a female foeticide case in the district of Beed in Maharashtra. Pages are overwhelmed by advertising. There is always distraction and entertainment to be found in the *Times of India*, but rarely does it leave a reader replete or satisfied.

The *Bombay Times and Journal of Commerce* was founded in November 1838, and published twice a week, by a syndicate of small companies and British barristers. It was renamed the *Times of India* in 1861 by its editor Robert Knight, an Englishman who was an acid critic of British imperialism and who, according to his biographer, built 'a vigorous, thoughtful and conscientious newspaper'. (Knight went on to start the *Statesman* in Calcutta.) The *Times of India* changed hands several times until, in 1892, Thomas Bennett and F.M. Coleman formed a company that owned the newspaper as well as jute concessions and other assets. In 1946, as British owners of Indian businesses drained hastily out of the country, Bennett, Coleman was sold for Rs 20 million to its first Indian owner, the sugar magnate Ramkrishna Dalmia.

Within the expanse of Dalmia's realm, the *Times of India* sat like a gleaming vanity purchase. 'He never expected any profit from it,' Subhash Chakraborty, an old *Times of India* hand, said. 'His attitude was: "There's no dearth of capital. What do you want to do?" They had correspondents in Washington, London and China.' But Dalmia couldn't enjoy his newspaper for long; he owed money to an insurance company, and he paid off that debt by selling Bennett, Coleman to his son-in-law Shanti Prasad Jain in 1948. The Dalmia–Jain group had been one of India's largest business houses; when the Monopolies Inquiry Commission examined the country's conglomerates in 1965, the Calcutta-based Sahu Jain family—of which Shanti Prasad Jain was the scion—owned twenty-six companies, with assets of Rs 678 million and interests in cement, jute, paper, chemicals and mining.

Like Dalmia, who was later imprisoned for embezzlement, Jain was tripped up by the law. In the early 1960s, after *Times of India* editors confided to the government that Jain was selling newsprint on the black market, he was briefly sent to jail. The government took over the newspaper: Half the directors on the board were appointed by the state, and its chairman was a Bombay High Court judge. In a 2009 essay, T.N. Ninan, a former editor of the *Economic Times* and now chairman of the *Business Standard*, wrote that the tattling of Jain's editors 'was something that the proprietor's descendants were not going to forget, a quarter-century later'. Ninan quoted Rupert Murdoch, who once said, when his editor was revamping the London *Times*: 'He thinks it is his paper, it is mine.' A similar sentiment, Ninan wrote, was 'now burned deep in Indian proprietorial hearts'.

The newspaper remained in its peculiar receivership until 1976, the thick of Indira Gandhi's Emergency, when it was released back into the hands of Ashok Jain, Shanti Prasad's son and Samir's father. The timing was not incidental. 'A lot of people had taken to calling us the Times of Indira,' a former resident editor said, 'and one or two editorials in praise of Sanjay Gandhi had been smuggled in.'

Newsprint profiteering aside, Shanti Prasad Jain hewed to the editor's ideal of an owner: remote, preoccupied with his ancillary businesses, disinterested in his paper's contents. The journalist Kuldip Nayar, in his memoir *Beyond the Lines*, wrote that Sham Lal, the *Times of India*'s editor in the 1970s, had said he was 'never rung up by Shanti Prasad Jain . . . and that the latter did not even remotely suggest to him which line he should adopt on any particular subject'. Ashok Jain, Nayar wrote, was somewhat different: 'He was committed to commercial success and would ensure that the newspaper did not come into conflict with his business interests or those he promoted.' But editors from the 1980s recall an earnest ham-handedness in Ashok Jain's attempts to bend editorial to his bidding, and an amiability that made him easy to turn down without fear of reprisal.

Primarily, the newspaper offered Ashok Jain an addictive proximity to power. 'Being able to walk into any minister's house was a sort of validation for him,' a former editor said. 'There's a directors' lunch table on the fourth floor of the Times building in Delhi. You can only get in if you're invited by the Jains. So the smart journalists in Ashok's time would bring in some minister, or some official, and get an invitation to lunch. If you managed a Supreme Court judge, your career was assured.'

But Jain was also an awful businessman who, as this editor said, 'drove his industries into the ground'. In 1983, around the time Samir began to involve himself more deeply in the *Times of India*, Bennett, Coleman's turnover was Rs 680 million—not inconsiderable but, as another senior editor who knew Samir well pointed out, also not sufficient to maintain the Jains' status among the country's wealthy Marwari families. The Jains' jute mills were ailing, and their cement and chemical factories in Bihar had started to shut down in the mid 1980s. 'The reference point for Samir was the set of Marwari kids he grew up with in Calcutta,' the editor said. 'The family had become sort of a laughing stock among the Marwaris. That's what drove him. He once told me: "The family doesn't need to make money. But it needs to show that it can make money."'

The Jains' ancestral house on Alipore Road in Calcutta, where Samir Jain grew up, was a vast edifice of marble and lawn, rumoured to be, after the Governor's residence, the city's second-largest home. A frequent visitor in the 1960s remembers the family as energetic hosts of parties and get-togethers, their house forever bright with social activity. Jain was a slight boy, prone to catching colds, but he was more convivial than he is now, this visitor said. 'He'd organize these group events for us when we were children,' she recalled. 'So to help some cause, we'd all sit down and make these craft projects and sell them for charity—and Samir would be the one organizing all this.' In *Paper Tigers*, a friend of Samir's grandfather remembers him as 'rather a pert boy, a chatterbox, a know-it-all. People were always ticking him off for talking too much.'

After school, Jain attended St Stephen's College in New Delhi, but he led such a retiring life there that several of his peers don't remember him at all. He was bright but a mediocre student, said a member of the Delhi University faculty at the time. 'Three of my friends needed to coach him privately to help him get his BA degree,' he said. 'One of these was somebody named Rao, and Samir didn't like his strong Telugu accent. So he told his mother, "I won't learn from him. I don't like his accent," and Rao was fired. Even then, Samir had very strong likes and dislikes.'

Details from the period of Jain's life between his graduation from St Stephen's and his formal entry into the newspaper in the early 1980s are sparse. He worked in Bennett, Coleman's outposts, in its jute division and in its paper and cement factories in Bihar. It must have struck him early that these limbs of the company had atrophied beyond measure, said one person who knew Jain well, because he lost interest in them rapidly. 'Then he looked around for a business that he thought would do well, and he saw the *Times of India*.'

In 1975 or 1976, Jain began visiting the newsroom, dropping in for conversations or to familiarize himself with the paper. An editor from the time recalled occasional 'pleasant chats' and added: 'At least he didn't cross anybody's path back then.' In fact, he said, Jain found himself condescended to; the attitude 'among the editors was "*Yaar train karenge, akhbaar chalane ka*" (We'll train him how to run a newspaper).' When Jain tried to learn about the newspaper's corporate affairs, for instance, he was handed thick volumes of company and income tax law and asked to satisfy himself with that.

Unsurprisingly, Jain didn't take kindly to this. He left New Delhi in 1982, putting himself through a rotation of newsrooms in the West—notably the *New York Times* and the *Wall Street Journal*, and then *The Times* in London—to understand journalism. 'Whenever he visited, he'd come with bundles of foreign newspapers,' said the then editor of a smaller Times Group publication. 'At the *New York Times*, he realized that the publishers were just as strong as the editors, which influenced him deeply. When he came back to the *Times of India* around 1984 or 1985, he came back with a vengeance.'

Disillusioned journalists of the era will recount, as if narrating the onset of some great blight, the first signs of Jain's increasing influence. He started to call extended meetings, where he told his editors, 'We can hire anybody to write. My editors shouldn't waste time writing,' or 'Newspapers are being run to impress the prime minister. I have no interest in impressing the prime minister. My interest is the man who has a used car to sell or a daughter to marry off or a business in Chawri Bazaar to promote. That man should advertise with us.' Chandan Mitra, an energetic new hire in the *Times of India* newsroom in the late 1980s, said that Jain wanted editorial staff to get more involved in marketing the newspaper. 'He'd circulate photocopies of articles in some American marketing journal, related to brand-building or the future of newspapers or something like that,' Mitra said. 'And he'd quiz us on them the next day. "Have you read it? What did you think of this point? Internalize these ideas."'

Already, Jain had become fond of repeating the analogy he is most well known for, which even today is the guide rail of the *Times of India*: A newspaper is a product just like a cake of soap, and it should be marketed as such. Raju Narisetti recalled Jain saying as much to his class at the Times School of Journalism in 1988. In *Paper Tigers*, Coleridge wrote: 'Of all the newspaper owners in the world, I met no one so single-mindedly wedded to marketing as Samir Jain.' Coleridge described a 150-minute soliloquy, during a meeting of Jain's board, in which he covered a whiteboard with algebraic notations and Venn diagrams, talked about 'synergy of innovation', and explained that the ancient Egyptians took '2,000 years to develop the water clock into the sand clock' because 'they had no marketing department'. Jain's directors, seemingly nonplussed, did little but take silent notes.

To journalists of the time, who viewed branding and marketing as the murkiest of the dark arts, the bleed of Jain's ideas into the editorial department proved distressing. Nobody was angered more than Girilal Jain, the editor of the *Times of India* and no direct relation to the Sahu Jain family. A pipe-smoking bull of a man, Girilal Jain would be described, in his *Guardian* obituary in 1993, as an editor with a weakness for Indira and Rajiv Gandhi, but also one with an avowed belief in editorial independence. In September 1987, he wrote an op-ed arguing that, in the media, 'editorial and management can be separated if the proprietor so desires, as has been the practice in this newspaper'.

Even as that piece was published, Samir Jain was turning into rubble the dividing wall between editorial and management. There were squabbles over appointments: Darryl D'Monte, named resident editor of the Bombay edition in 1988, said that he was hired only to stymie Girilal Jain, who did not quite get along with D'Monte and had wanted somebody else. At the time, 'Samir was smarting under Giri's condescension. I became a pawn in a bigger game,' D'Monte said. There were daily frictions, and there were unsubtle exercises of power: One day, Chandan Mitra said, 'in smaller font on either side of the lettering of the *Times of India* masthead, the words "Let" and "Wait" were added, with a message saying "See Page 16". It was a back-page advertisement for Cadbury's. "Let the *Times of India* Wait, Eat Cadbury's First"—that was the message. Giri was livid, because for him, it was the masthead! It was the most sacrosanct thing!'

There are also accounts of the editors' peremptory handling of Samir Jain, and they can be read as origin myths for his deep resentment of editorial power. The story most commonly told, but also the most difficult to verify, involves a standoff in an editorial meeting, from which Girilal Jain ejected Samir Jain, telling him brusquely that management had no place in these conferences. On another occasion, when Samir Jain asked his editors what he could do to improve the newspaper, he was told that the toilets needed cleaning. Jain also bristled when the newspaper's longest-serving journalists, who had known him since he was a boy, continued to call him 'Samir', rather than anything more formal.

'So he started this rule that people in the office should be called by an abbreviation of their title,' an editor said. 'Samir became JMD—joint managing director.' The rule has hardened into a tradition; Jain is still called VC, for vice chairman, and his brother Vineet is called MD, for managing director.

'I think all this burned deep,' said a former Times Group editor who remained on good terms with Jain until recently. 'And this came on top of the editors who had complained about his grandfather and sent him to jail. He also didn't like the fact that journalists still looked to the government's wage board to fix their wages, rather than negotiating directly with their management. So with all this in mind, Samir believed: "My editors aren't loyal to me."'

In a dynastic company, a face-off between the editor and the owner's son could only end in one way. Kuldip Nayar recalled, in *Beyond the Lines*, that Girilal Jain had asked him to intervene with Ashok Jain, 'to get Samir Jain, his son, off his back . . . I flew to Bombay and spoke to Ashok, who frankly said he would have no hesitation in supporting his son because the latter had increased the revenue tenfold, from Rs 8 lakhs to 80 lakhs. "I can hire many Girilal Jains if I pay more, but not a Samir," said Ashok.'

When the dismissal came, it was swift. In the most dramatic rendition of the tale, which I heard from several people, Girilal Jain, pushing sixty-five, was first forced to go on 'leave preparatory to retirement'. Then, in the midst of this leave, he was telephoned at home one night, by a desk hand, and told: 'Your name isn't being carried as editor in tomorrow's edition.' To the newsroom, the move felt 'decisive and surgical', Mitra recalled. 'Everybody was stunned into silence. Nobody was talking, and there was a sullen atmosphere in the newsroom. People were standing around in little groups and whispering.' It was 1988; the previous year, Samir Jain had become vice chairman of Bennett, Coleman, but only with this flexion of muscle did he establish his control over the *Times of India*.

Once upon a time, 'Samir Jain may have been as passionately in love with newspapers as Rupert Murdoch was said to be,' said one editor who was close to Jain. 'But in those early years, when he wasn't accepted by the newsroom, that love really withered away.' Much later, Jain would confide in this editor that he had genuinely tried to persuade his journalists about the soundness of his ideas, and to participate in his fresh vision for the newspaper. In return for his efforts, Jain felt that he received only lip and disdain. 'So Samir decided then: "I'm no longer going to try to convince people to see my point of view. I'm just going to tell them what to do."'

III

On a microfiche, browsing chronologically through the *Times of India* archives of the 1980s and the 1990s is instructive; do it fast enough, and it can feel like unfurling a Samir Jain flip-book, his influence blossoming before your eyes. In the opening leaves, the *Times of India* is dour and statist: It carries the full, plodding text of speeches made by the prime minister or other high-ranking ministers, organizes its content sloppily, and shuns any colour in its reportage. There is no mistaking its advertisements for editorial content, though: In the issue dated 13 February 1981, an article by R.S. Mathur, the registrar for cooperative societies, about the high glories of the cooperative movement in Uttar Pradesh, carries an underlined header: 'A SPONSORED FEATURE'.

Six years down the line, the newspaper has livened up considerably. Reporters bring more diverse stories from the Indian hinterland, and the tone of the editorials is punchier, although they are still written in filigreed English. (Jain hated this. The writer Naresh Fernandes, who worked two stints in the *Times of India*, recalled Jain stressing: 'Our articles should be in Indian English. The problem with journalists is that you think readers want good writing. Readers want lazy writing.') Days such as 24 October 1987, with death and destruction flooding the front page, have become rare, because Jain believes that bad news doesn't sell. (On that black day, the front-page headlines read: '13 IPKF men die in blast'; '13 more killed in Punjab'; 'Man shot dead in Faizabad'; '7 hurt in factory fire dead'; 'Santipur civic chief beaten to death'.) 'Nobody wants to wake up in the morning to see blood and gore on the front page,' a former *Economic Times* editor remembered Jain saying. Fernandes told me that Jain even briefly appointed a 'good-news editor'.

Around this time, the paper has also become heavily freighted with advertisements, and they have been sold more strategically; in one issue of *Saturday Times*, a lifestyle supplement, an article on dupattas runs above spots for two clothing stores. The supplements themselves are new: *Career and Competition Times*, for students preparing for the professional world; *Saturday Times*; *The TOI Offspring*, each issue produced by the pupils of a different school. The most prized of Jain's supplements during this time is *Section 2*, which functions almost as a stand-alone newspaper, and which is more extravagantly produced than its parent. Chandan Mitra, who was *Section 2*'s opinions editor, recalled Jain saying: 'If these supplements are read, well and good. But they should be like Persian cats. They should be stroked and displayed. Somebody should feel good that something so beautiful has come out.' But *Section 2* was 'never fully formed', recalled Mitra. 'That's why it flopped. After a year, when it was struggling, Samir said: "Doesn't matter, shut it down." But he told me: "Chandan, it won't be long before every paper starts doing this." And he was right. Now we all have supplements.'

By 1992, advertorials have begun to be tagged 'Response Features', 'Response' being the name that Jain gave to his marketing department. It is not immediately clear that these are paid articles; on 6 May 1992, nothing distinguishes the Response Feature on the benefits of computer education from the paper's other editorial content, even though it sits above three advertisements for computer courses. The news covers a wider range of topics than before, echoing Jain's belief that a newspaper ought to be like a *thali*, with something in it for everyone. By 1996, part of the editorial page is ceded to a column called Speaking Tree (sample headlines: 'The scriptures through women's eyes'; 'Wrestling with the dark mystery of death') and to Sacred Space, which carries pieces discussing spiritualism in delicate secular tones. Reporters cover their city more strenuously, and some of that news makes it into supplements called *Bombay Times* and *Delhi Times*. It isn't until 1998, however, that these supplements create India's Page 3 culture, featuring private parties next to their reams of film-world gossip. When that happens, it is as if the final tumbler has fallen into place. To anyone who has paged through two decades of back issues, the *Times of India* from 1998 thrums with sudden familiarity, having become the most complete template for the *Times of India* we know and read today.

Whenever I met somebody who had worked closely with Samir Jain, I would ask them: 'What drives his vision for the *Times of India*?' This was like flashing them a white card with an inkblot on it; people would mull over the question's nebulous outlines and furnish me with wildly conflicting responses. One former editor at the *Economic Times* told me that Jain sees his newspapers as an establishment parallel to the state, protecting the rights of the individual: 'He believes the Indian state is a predator, that it has too much power.' M.D. Nalapat said that Jain once wanted the *Times of India* 'to be so powerful that it could choose the next prime minister, or the next cabinet, like *The Times* of London in the late 1920s'.

Others scoffed at the suggestion that Jain craves such momentous political influence. Ravi Dhariwal said he decided to join Bennett, Coleman, in 2001, only because Jain had 'no political agenda, no industrial agenda . . . He just wanted it to be a good business.' This was not even the business of news, necessarily. 'Samir would say: "See, my business is selling space. I can bring out a paper even without any journalists,"' the former *Economic Times* editor told me. Simultaneously, he also remembered Jain saying: 'The *Times of India* is aspirational. Our readers should display it. They don't even have to read it.' Sanjaya Baru, once associate editor of the *Times of India* and the *Economic Times* and a former media adviser to Prime Minister Manmohan Singh, believes that Jain has wanted 'different things at different times, for his newspaper. But basically, he wants his paper to entertain his audience.'

Still others maintained that Jain cares only about how much money the paper makes—a view that syncs perfectly with the stereotype of the hard-nosed Marwari businessman, and that is nourished by anecdotes about his thrift. Dhariwal cannot understand this perception either. 'From time to time, I go and tell him: "This is what's happening. We're having a good year, or we're having a bad year. This is what we're going to end up with,"' Dhariwal said. 'And he just says: "Okay." He's not fussed about it at all. It may have been like this twenty years ago, when he was very keen on how much money . . . But the company makes a lot of money. The two brothers are very frugal, very austere. They don't have private planes or yachts. They don't need the money.'

Instead, it is money not so much as crackly mattress stuffing but as a marker of relative success that seems to spur Jain. Dhariwal acknowledged that Jain is 'very competitive', and one of Jain's rival proprietors told me that he always 'wanted to be the sole media mogul. It has always been: "I won't let you survive."' An editor who works at the *Times of India* recalled a recent brand valuation exercise that the company conducted. 'Samir said: "Do it. But the truth is: It doesn't matter if the brand value is 200 or 300 or 400 crore rupees. What matters to me is if it's going up or down." It's like a basketball game for him. Either you win or you lose.'

Jain has never been reluctant to extend his proprietorial reach into the editorial department; even in 1988, Narisetti told me, 'the idea of separating church and state was never part of the ethos of how he saw his media'. But where other owners intervene to promote a politician or a party, Jain has steadfastly refused to do so. One former editor, who joined the *Times of India* in the early 2000s, recalled being told in his very first meeting with Jain that 'he liked his paper to be soft. He told me specifically that he didn't want the *Times of India* to be an auditor to the nation.' Unlike Ashok Jain, Nalapat said, Samir isn't eager to mix with ministers or cosy up to government. 'In that sense, he was the ideal boss for an editor to have,' he said. Only in the gory thick of Gujarat's communal riots in 2002, when the Bharatiya Janata Party (BJP) leaned heavily upon the Jains to be less critical of Narendra Modi, did journalists receive veiled messages to, as Vidya Subrahmaniam put it, 'pipe down'.

That seems to have been an aberration; a senior editor who has worked for the Times Group for over a decade said that, in all his time there, 'Samir has never once asked what's going on the front page the next day.' Another editor recounted that, during his time, 'there was so much work that we did which no one ever interfered with. All the Coke and Pepsi stories [about pesticide levels in their colas] were broken on the front page. There was an air reporter and a water reporter. By and large, if you wanted to do a good day's work, you were allowed to do it.'

Reporters still break stories consistently: the abuses of power surrounding the Commonwealth Games and the Adarsh Housing Society allotments, the Maharashtra irrigation scam that forced the state's deputy chief minister to resign, and the ongoing travails of the BJP president Nitin Gadkari have all been doggedly investigated in *Times of India* articles. Even some of its fiercest critics admit that they read the *Times of India* to know what is happening in the country. Talking to journalists there, I frequently caught an aggrieved tone that their good work is never acknowledged by the industry at large, and that the liberty to pursue these big political stories is never remarked upon. One editor in New Delhi told me: 'We take ourselves damn seriously, man.'

It might be a canny realization on Jain's part that even a thali of a newspaper must be arranged around a core of hard journalism, and that such journalism needs a certain latitude. But he hasn't shied away from eating into editorial independence in other ways, most egregiously in 1997 and 1998, when the Enforcement Directorate was investigating Ashok Jain for unauthorized foreign exchange transactions. In retaliation, according to petitions filed with the Press Council of India, the *Times of India* began a systematic campaign against the enforcement directorate in its pages, alleging human rights abuses by its officers. H.K. Dua, then an editorial adviser to the *Times of India* and now a Rajya Sabha member, claimed that he was fired in May 1998 for refusing to assist Ashok Jain, Samir's father, in his bid to stay out of prison.

In a March 1998 letter to Bennett, Coleman's executive directors, parts of which were later published in *Frontline*, Dua wrote that Jain asked him to lobby with political leaders and to 'write articles in his favour to create a helpful climate before the Supreme Court takes up his cases'. A few weeks later, Dua fired off another letter, protesting that his editorial responsibilities were being curbed 'because I have refused to be of any help to Mr Ashok Jain'.

More consistently, Jain has sought to shape the *Times of India* according to the eccentric contours of his views on life and journalism. He waged patient wars of attrition, for instance, on two of his journalists who supported M.F. Husain's right to paint the goddess Saraswati nude; one resigned, and the other was forced to recant in print. ('It suddenly worried him, during this time, that the Saraswati on the Jnanpith Award [a literary prize established by the Jains in 1961] was also nude,' one of these journalists told me. After hectic consultations, it was decided that the Saraswati was not really nude because 'she was draped in pearls, which satisfied all parties'.)

Loath as he is to announce bad news in large headlines, he detests even more the media's treatment of sudden catastrophes, preferring to adopt a cosmic view of such events. On 11 September 2001, an editor recalled, 'Samir said: "You know, 180,000 people died yesterday. Today 182,000 people have died. It's a blip, that's all."' Instead, Jain was happy to have his papers 'be about the three Fs, as he called them—food, fashion and fuck. Although he wouldn't say "fuck", he'd just say "Eff".' Jain's directives to his corporate managers emphasized this. A participant at a conference in Mumbai in 2005 remembered Pradeep Guha, then the president of Bennett, Coleman, stating in a speech: 'My task has been to move the *Times of India* from being a real good paper to being a feel-good paper.'

Jain holds fixed views on whom his journalists should write for, and what this imagined body of readers would want in his newspaper. One opinion-page writer who told me that Jain hated to valorize the state added, after a beat, that he was keen instead to 'valorize CEOs. "Who are your readers?" he'd ask. "Your readers are not the Karol Bagh masses or the rural masses. Your readers are elite urban Indians."' These readers, Jain believes, have little appetite for the cerebral writing that journalists often wish to practise. They want short sentences, brief articles and English that 'even a fifth standard boy can understand', one editor told me.

In that vein, Jain has advised slipping deliberate spelling errors into the copy, to 'make the reader feel more comfortable'. Dhariwal said that Jain often recommends 'putting in words of Hindi, to reflect the way people speak'. Another editor moaned that Jain pushed for his pages to be a hodge-podge of articles: '"The Indian mind likes clutter," he would say. "Just look at our markets."' Jain even suggested, very recently, a liberal use of emoticons. 'He still sends in hare-brained ideas like these,' a senior *Times of India* editor said. 'It's amazing the trivial stuff he'll get obsessed by. But because he's had outstanding success in the past, you feel odd in automatically assuming that it's stupid.'

Jain's model reader, in other words, is really Jain himself: contemptuous of government, detached from politics, intolerant of intellectualism, fond of gimmicks, hungry for success and eager to be reassured about the material well-being of his world. His shrewdness lies in having predicted—as early as 1990, even before the economy was liberalized—that the numbers of such readers would multiply. These are the readers who have swollen the ranks of his subscribers.

Along the way, Jain has upended the crucial assumption from which all journalistic enterprise proceeds: that a publication's editor will, with insight and accumulated experience, know best what reportage will serve a public need. Jain and Dhariwal are both dismissive of this premise. 'Then you're writing for your clan rather than the reader,' Dhariwal said. 'That's where I think we have succeeded to a large extent—and I think we've tried very hard, in the *Times of India*—where our editors today write for the reader.'

This has been the other great guiding principle of Jain's interventions over the years: to deflate what he perceives as the bloated egos of journalists, to yank them off their self-installed perches of importance. Some of this resentment was seeded in the late 1980s, when Jain found the old guard of the *Times of India* arrayed against him. Certainly also, braggadocio such as that displayed by Dileep Padgaonkar, the *Times of India* editor who famously told the BBC that he was 'the second most important man in India', cannot have helped. One former editor, who has now left the mainstream media entirely, admitted that 'the craft of journalism, as practised in India, deserved to be knocked. Journalists needed a Samir Jain to wake them up. There was a lot of complacency, and I think some amount of criticism was good.'

To be sure, Jain can be sincerely solicitous of his employees' well-being, and he is known for touching acts of care and generosity. An Indiatimes executive remembered that, during a recent meeting, Jain cast a concerned look at his burgeoning waistline and prescribed him a diet. 'Around a month later, somebody from his office actually called to check if I was following the diet, and if it was working.' When Jain spotted another unhealthy eater—an editor who frequently worked late—he dispatched dinner every evening, from his house to the editor's office. In *Behind the Times*, Pradeep Guha tells Karkaria about the day his father passed away in Mumbai. Jain arrived 'the same night from Delhi, and came straight from the airport to my Bandra flat. He had carried a large tiffin carrier with him and handed it to me saying matter-of-factly, "You all must not have cooked or eaten anything since morning."'

But when he wanted to cut journalists down to size, Jain could be both theatrical and petty. He would, I learned from several people, keep telling editors: 'You guys are cost centres. It's the marketing guys who're bringing in the money.' Editors remember baulking at being put to work addressing invitations to Bennett, Coleman functions. In 2003, after an assistant editor in Mumbai inadvertently angered Jain, he redesignated an entire batch of them as feature writers and sent in a crew of carpenters—within the hour—to tear down the cubicles to which these feature writers were now no longer entitled. On the opinion page, Jain ordered that the first-person pronoun 'I' be shrunk into lowercase, to symbolically diminish the writer's ego. Not surprisingly, one editor said, Jain loves *The Economist*, with its lack of identifying bylines—and thus the ultimate sublimation of the journalist.

Under Jain, titles were reworded, such that the editor of the newspaper's Delhi edition came to be called 'Editor—Delhi market'. Indeed, conflating editorial with marketing was one of Jain's stratagems of choice—not only because it allowed him to blur the distinctions between the two departments, but also because it forced journalists to examine a side of newspaper production that they considered beneath them. Chandan Mitra recalled the consternation among his fellow journalists when Jain announced, in the late 1980s, a system of having editors and managers exchange roles for a few weeks. Jain repeated the move with Sanjaya Baru when he was the *Times of India*'s business editor in 1994, swapping his position with that of Vijay Jindal, a corporate director. 'Possibly it was a plan to show journalists they were expendable, or it was just a whim,' Baru said. 'Samir liked to be whimsical.'

The most dramatic consequence of such a whim came in 1994, when Padgaonkar was going on leave and an interim replacement was needed. Instead of a journalist, Baru and D'Monte told me, a director from the board was put in charge. 'He was so profusely embarrassed about it,' Baru said. 'He would come down and chair our editorial meetings, but he would just let us make the decisions.' D'Monte told me that bitterness against Jain's belittling of his editors had been percolating for some time already, and that this anointment of Padgaonkar's understudy proved to be the breaking point. Padgaonkar, D'Monte, and a handful of other editors and journalists quit, but that didn't faze Jain. After the walkout, an *Economic Times* editor recalled, Jain told his staff: 'We're the market leaders. And the market leader doesn't need a first-class editor. It can do with a second-class, or third-class, or even fourth-class editor. We don't need editors.'

IV

The energy that Jain has poured into the consideration of what a newspaper should do has only been surpassed by that devoted to the question of how it should be sold. Since 1990, he has staffed Bennett, Coleman with managers from companies that have nothing to do with journalism and everything to do with the blunt art of the hard-sell: Pepsi, ITC, Shoppers Stop, Unilever, Trent. When a team from Pepsi visited the *Times of India* in Delhi, to rebut the Centre for Science and Environment's accusations about pesticides in their colas, an editor remembered that Jain was smitten by their presentation. 'He likes people like that,' the editor told me. 'Later, he told a couple of senior management fellows: "I don't think there's anybody on our staff who can give a presentation like that."'

One of Jain's most persistent legacies has been the price we pay for our newspapers. In 1994, Jain slashed the cover price of the *Times of India* in New Delhi from Rs 2.30 to Rs 1.50

per copy. The move, to better compete with the *Hindustan Times*, boosted circulation in the city from 30,000 to 170,000, and it proved cut-throat in more ways than one; that July, after newspaper vendors called a boycott of the *Times of India* because the price drop hurt their commissions, one vendor was knifed and others beaten up for defying the boycott. Similarly, Jain set the price of the relaunched *Economic Times*, in the early 1990s, at Rs 4, and Chandan Mitra recalled him saying: 'We'll slash the price after some time, after we establish that the *Economic Times* isn't just for Press Information Bureau handouts.' When other business dailies began to dust themselves off and gear themselves to cover a new Indian economy, Jain halved his price. 'He was so sure nobody would have an answer for it,' a former editor said. 'It was like going for the jugular.'

Jain replayed this gambit of predatory pricing every time the *Times of India* rode in to conquer a new town, its saddlebags sloshing with cash. He made the case, one editor told me, that he was only helping to grow the base of English-newspaper readers. 'But clearly, it's not like that was his larger belief,' the head of another daily said. 'If that was so, why didn't he also drop the price in Mumbai, where the *Times of India* had a monopoly?' Narisetti reckons that Jain's wilful devaluation of his product pressured 'the rest of the industry to be beholden to advertisers. The history of how the newsroom has become subservient to advertisers starts with this pricing model, when a newspaper is cheaper than a cup of tea.'

Undercutting his rivals on price is part of Jain's conviction that they should be given no quarter. In *Paper Tigers*, Coleridge describes Jain asking his board what they should do with a surplus gravure press and then supplying the correct answer himself: 'We will destroy it. We will hammer the machine. And why will we hammer it? Can no one tell me? The reason we will hammer it is to prevent some other publishing house from laying their hands on it.' Jain even started a whole new daily in Mumbai—the short-lived *Independent*, in 1989—just to shut down a rival, the *Indian Post*, whose senior staff he had hired away nearly in toto. 'It was an ego thing,' Mitra, who briefly edited the *Independent*, told me. But there was also a practical aspect to Jain's move. 'It was started to mop up the Mumbai ad market. For a hundred bucks, if you were buying an ad in *TOI*, you could spend an extra ten bucks and the same ad would appear in the *Independent* also.'

Jain so deeply believes the business to be a zero-sum game that he virtually considers it a war—a metaphor he once animated by setting up, next to his cabin in Delhi, a full-fledged war room in which to discuss strategy. One former *Economic Times* editor recalled that, during his stint at the paper, this room used to contain a table, 'slightly bigger than a billiards table', on which was set out the apparatus of a naval war game. 'There were several fleets,' he said. 'In the middle was this white fleet, with an aircraft carrier right in the middle, a flag on it saying "TOI Bombay". This was the mother ship, and to protect the mother ship, there would be other boats, submarines and gunboats. One would be "ET Chennai", one would be "Illustrated Weekly", that kind of thing. In the corners of the table, there'd be a black fleet for the *Hindustan Times*, a yellow fleet for the *Indian Express*, and so on. The thing is: Nobody reacted to the ludicrousness of the game.'

Once every week—'Fridays, if I remember rightly', this editor said—Jain invited into the war room representatives from each of his newspapers and from various departments. Then he grilled them on strategy. On one occasion in 1993, the Reliance group, which then owned a daily called *Business & Political Observer*, was poised to eat into the *Times of India*'s market share. 'So Samir was standing there, with one of those little sticks in his hand, and there was a new set of ships called Reliance,' the editor told me. 'He pushed them towards the white fleet and said: "This fleet is advancing towards us. What should we do?"' Jain didn't get the answer he was looking for, 'because he said: "No, I think none of this is going to work. So we'll do something else." One of the bigger ships next to the mother ship was labelled the *Illustrated Weekly of India.* He took his pointer and pushed that ship down. That very day, the *Illustrated Weekly* was closed. It was killed on the table.'

Jain had, of course, decided the loss-making *Illustrated Weekly*'s fate well before this meeting. But his rationale for scuttling the magazine at that moment in time was an intricate one. The *Illustrated Weekly* was such a prestigious brand within the Times Group stable, the editor remembered Jain explaining, that its sudden demise would unsettle his rivals. 'Any competitor would think: "*Saala*, what is his strategy here? He has something up his sleeve. So let's wait. Let me not launch an attack." So when this happened, Reliance stopped in their tracks.' Out of wariness, this editor said, the Ambanis did not market the *Observer* as strongly as they might have. 'They retreated. That was the impact it had.'

V

In the mid 1990s, Times Group editors started to spot Vineet Jain in the newsroom with increasing frequency. The younger Jain had studied marketing at the small and obscure American College of Switzerland—a liberal arts college attended by the children of genealogical and financial blue-bloods, where a young Sylvester Stallone once coached women's athletics. He had also earned a reputation for being more accessible, sociable and glamorous than his brother—a prime specimen of the very Page 3 culture he helped to create. 'With Vineet, what you see is what you get,' an editor who works at the *Times of India* told me. But another editor from the late 1990s, after admitting that he had several run-ins with Vineet, said that he was a shallow man, and that Samir Jain's tendency to leave day-to-day decisions to his younger brother meant that 'show started to come at the expense of substance. Samir at least reads books, discusses philosophy, that kind of thing. Not Vineet. If you have a conversation with Vineet about India and China, his eyes will glaze over. But if you want to talk about whether a heterosexual can ever become a homosexual, he'll engage you for hours.' I thought this was an exaggeration until I found a 1,700-word blog post Vineet Jain wrote for the Indiatimes portal in 2009, titled: 'Being gay—is it free choice or a natural inborn preference?'

Even more than Samir Jain had done in the late 1980s, Vineet Jain has discomfited his editors. Sanjaya Baru left the Times Group in 1997, he said, 'partly because of the seven-year itch, but also because Vineet started interfering a lot in an insistent manner. Samir would only ever hint or advise, never insist.' In keeping with his image as a man about town, another editor told me, Vineet Jain pressed the *Times of India*'s supplements to cover parties and 'tits and babes' and demanded that the main paper chase sensational stories. In *Behind the Times*, Bachi Karkaria writes, it was at the insistence of Vineet Jain that the television channel Times Now executed 'its carpet bombing coverage of the rescue of Prince, the little boy trapped in a Kurukshetra borewell for 48 hours'. Through those two days, Jain delivered his instructions right into 'the earpiece of the anchor, Arnab Goswami, upping the ante by telling him to flood the screen with viewer reactions'.

The Times Group's television channels, as well as its Internet enterprises, have been Vineet Jain's babies. 'Samir never liked television very much,' one former *Economic Times* editor said. 'He blocked it, in my view, for at least five or six years. He wanted to stick to the group's core competence. And in some ways, he was right, because they're not yet making money on their news channels or on the Internet.' But they will, Vineet Jain believes. 'I keep telling my people that you may be earning your revenues from print, but it is actually the digital space that you are here for,' he told *Business Today* in a rare interview in 2008. 'It will be your salvation.'

Vineet Jain also conceptualized Medianet, the scheme by which advertisers and public relations agencies can, in certain supplements, buy coverage disguised as news. By many accounts, Medianet is the most miasmic development in Indian journalism in decades. In the varicose veins of the industry, anecdotes clump up, like bad blood, about how Medianet has even infiltrated the main paper, such that the generosity of an advertiser can be rewarded with positive coverage—implicit bargains that are impossible to prove or to track. Dhariwal and two *Times of India* editors categorically denied this, insisting that Medianet operates only in the paper's supplements. Medianet's practices have also spread outside the Times Group to rival newspapers and television channels. 'The difference is that they do it tucked away behind bushes,' Karkaria writes in *Behind the Times*, while Bennett, Coleman 'does it as "*khullam khulla*" [openly] as reckless lovers'.

Medianet played upon two of Samir Jain's most constant apprehensions about his newspapers: that they were, in just the regular process of reporting upon people or companies, providing them free and quantifiable publicity; and that his journalists were making a side income by writing pieces in exchange for money or other benefits. (On the latter count, he has not been wrong; in 2003, an *Economic Times* journalist was arrested in Mumbai while collecting the second instalment of a Rs 2.5 million payoff to spike stories about a financial services firm.) A repeated and unfortunate victim of Samir Jain's fears has been the *Times of India*'s book-review page over the years. An editor recalled Jain grumbling, in the mid 1990s, that these pages had degenerated into parlours for the mutual scratching of backs by reviewers and authors. 'He'd complain: "You always review books that sell in the thousands, never in the lakhs."' In early September, the book-review page of *Crest*, the *Times of India*'s weekend magazine, was axed because, according to people in the newspaper, reviews often discussed books available on Flipkart but not Indiatimes—the equivalent, in Jain's eyes, of giving comfort and succour to the enemy.

For similar reasons, the *Times of India* adheres to a strict policy of not mentioning brands of any sort in its journalism unless they are crucial to the story. A book launch occurs at 'a Vasant Kunj bookshop' and not at Landmark; a charity event raises money at 'a south Mumbai hotel' and not at the Oberoi. 'I want my story to be as pure and newsworthy as can be,' Dhariwal told me. 'The moment I write "Taj Hotel", I may get a free meal, I may make them feel obliged. I don't want any of that. We don't want even potential quid pro quos.'

The same philosophy applied, Dhariwal said, in perhaps the *Times of India*'s most extreme—and most farcical—fulfilment of this policy: its refusal, earlier this year, to refer to Indian Premier League (IPL) teams by their full names. A senior team official told me that Bennett, Coleman had tried—and failed—to browbeat the IPL management, threatening to elide the team names unless the IPL bought more advertising. Until the very final stages of the tournament, therefore, the Deccan Chargers were called Team Hyderabad, the Kolkata Knight Riders were called Team Kolkata, and so on. Joy Bhattacharya, the Kolkata Knight Riders team director, tweeted after the English Premier League final between Manchester United and Manchester City: 'Today, *TOI*'s sports page headline should read "In a thrilling finish, Team Manchester pip Team Manchester to the EPL title!"'

Dhariwal denied that there had been any attempt to gouge advertising out of the IPL: 'In the main *Times of India* there will never be a connection between what we write and advertising.' He then mounted an impassioned but somewhat muddled defence of the newspaper's policy on IPL team names. 'Look, you want publicity, you want your name in the paper, then you can get publicity in our supplements, and you'll get it by paying for it,' he told me. 'Why should we give a free ride to anybody? We're a commercial company.' The term 'Kolkata Knight Riders' was in essence a brand, Dhariwal argued, and brands would receive no free publicity in the *Times of India*'s pages.

But wasn't 'Manchester United', I asked Dhariwal, as much of a brand as 'Kolkata Knight Riders'?

'No,' he said. 'Manchester United is the name of a local team. Why isn't the sponsor mentioned there? Why isn't it Barclays Manchester United?'

In similar fashion then, I wondered, shouldn't the *Times of India* have only refrained from calling the team 'Nokia Kolkata Knight Riders'?

'Yes, but in other team names, the sponsor is right there in the name,' Dhariwal said. 'Deccan Chronicle is the sponsor of Deccan Chargers, Vijay Mallya's brand is right there in the Royal Challengers Bangalore. So we had to follow a consistent policy.'

Medianet's immodest beginnings lay in a scheme introduced in 1995, under which companies could buy discounted advertising space to rebut articles that had been unfavourable to them. (One editor labelled it, for his own amusement, the *supari* ad, after Mumbai slang for an underworld hit, 'because effectively the newspaper was taking money to kill its own reports'.) Sucheta Dalal, then the financial editor of the *Times of India*, recalled being aghast at the policy. 'I sent a long note to Pradeep Guha, asking: "Is Response going to go running to people even as I'm doing a story on them?"' she told me. 'Why couldn't companies have just written a letter to the editor or gone to the ombudsman?' The supari ad was discontinued, but its basic premise continued to swirl around the mind of Vineet Jain. In the early 2000s, an editor remembered him saying: 'All these little press releases coming in for *Delhi Times*, for restaurants and so on. Why should we give them space? We can charge them for it.'

In September, I was sent, through a chain of sources, an email from a Bennett, Coleman executive that laid out the rates for Medianet in *Delhi Times*. To feature one of its events over a quarter-page spread, a hotel would need to pay approximately Rs 750,000, or Rs 1,495 per square centimetre. On the front page of *Delhi Times*, a square centimetre of coverage cost Rs 2,530; the lowest rate in the supplement, on the Lifestyle page, was Rs 1,035 per square centimetre.

For a long time after Medianet began operations, its content bore no clear indicators that it had been paid for; even if an article carried a footnote reading 'Medianet', it was not apparent, to the average reader, what that meant. At the beginning of 2011, a strapline below the masthead started to introduce *Bombay Times*, *Delhi Times* and allied Medianet products as an 'Entertainment and Advertising Feature'; the disclaimer was further tweaked a couple of months later to read, as it does now, 'Advertorial, Entertainment Promotional Feature'. There's no doubt that the strapline fulfils *Bombay Times*' obligation to announce that it is stuffed with paid content; equally, there's no doubt that thousands of readers every day must read *Bombay Times* believing it to be the product of genuine, if silly, reporting. I asked Dhariwal if the strapline was a concession to the criticisms that the *Times of India* was misleading its readers. 'I think that would be a defensive way of putting it,' he said drily. 'We wanted it to be clear. We wanted everybody to know that these are advertising supplements, and that they are different from the *Times of India*.'

But talk still circulates, like stale and dangerous air, that advertising and editorial are more tightly linked than they should be. In one example, two former *Economic Times* editors told me that, just before Tata Consultancy Services' public offering in August 2004, instructions filtered down from management to give the event only the most grudging coverage. When I went back into the archives, I found only scanty news briefs, hardly commensurate with the listing of India's biggest IT company. The reason, these editors said, was that the Tatas had blacklisted Bennett, Coleman's publications at the time, buying no advertising in either the *Economic Times* or the *Times of India*. Dhariwal emphatically told me that such withholding of coverage never happened.

In the *Times of India*, two editors told me, in separate conversations, that the journalism under their purview was absolutely blameless, but they were less convinced about the newsroom at large. One of these editors, observing that the newspaper's Response team was carved up into beats just as its pool of reporters was, thought that some journalists might be working a little too closely with their counterparts in Response. The uncertainty that these editors felt seemed to reflect a truth about journalism: that if the line between advertising and editorial is muddied, even if only in a supplement like *Bombay Times*, confidence in the newspaper as a whole can falter. Doubt can worm its way in—even if, as Dhariwal attests, it is entirely misplaced.

Bennett, Coleman's other controversial initiative, Private Treaties, is a more complex animal than Medianet. Starting in 2006, Bennett, Coleman has taken stakes in companies—mostly small and unlisted—in exchange for advertising in its pages. The Bennett, Coleman subsidiary that runs Private Treaties, Brand Capital, has owned equity in nearly 400 companies; among the more well-known ones in its present portfolio are Kingfisher Airlines, Indian Terrain, Emaar MGF Land Limited and Birla Lifesciences. In an interview with the website Medianama in 2008, S. Sivakumar, Brand Capital's CEO, contended that advertising was only being used as a currency, just as cash would be by venture capital firms.

Private Treaties is, according to Bennett, Coleman and other media houses, a win–win situation. Advertising space in newspapers is today an 'unlimited commodity', Dhariwal told me, because 'we can always add more pages'. For a newspaper, the prospect of unsold ad inventory is frightening; in *Paper Tigers*, Jain tells his board: 'An unsold offering is like an unsold airline seat or hotel bed. Neither can be sold the next day. The opportunity is missed forever.' But Private Treaties can also help grow the market, giving small companies with slender budgets a chance to advertise themselves in newspapers. 'So take somebody like Dr Sachdev's Eye Clinic, with no cash flow to advertise,' the head of a rival media house told me. 'They can give us shares, or if it's a real estate firm, they can give us property.' The equity stakes are typically small; Sivakumar, in his Medianama interview, said that each client, on average, swaps equity worth Rs 50–100 million of advertising over three years.

The wonder-drug of Private Treaties has been accompanied, however, by a throbbing migraine of a side effect: the conflict of interest involved when a media house owns stakes in companies it routinely writes about. Suspicions that favourable editorial coverage would be built into the ad-for-equity transaction sharpened when a leaked email dated 29 November 2007, from the *Economic Times* executive editor Rahul Joshi, was published in several places, including the media blog *Sans Serif*:

> At ET, we are carving out a separate team to look into the needs of Private Treaty clients. Every large centre will have a senior editorial person to interface with Treaty clients. In turn, the senior edit person will be responsible, along with the existing team, for edit delivery. This team will have regional champions along with one or two reporters for help—but more importantly, they will liaise with REs (Resident Editors) and help in integrating the content into the different sections of the paper. In this way, we will be able to incorporate PT into the editorial mainstream, rather than it looking like a series of press releases appearing in vanilla form in the paper.

When I asked Dhariwal about this email, he told me, 'I'm sure it was authentic,' but that it dated from the early days of Private Treaties, when the Times Group was feeling its way through the process. 'We didn't know the nature of the beast. It was like trying to build a bloody airplane,' Dhariwal said. The editorial staff described in Joshi's email was tasked with liaising with Private Treaties clients because they would complain, as Dhariwal said, '*Koi hamari baat nahin sunta hai* (Nobody listens to us).'

But rapidly, Dhariwal said, clients started to expect favourable editorial coverage. 'Once we realized this—oh my god, we immediately corrected it. We modified all the contracts, to say: There cannot be any such expectation, and you will not get any priority coverage.' On Brand Capital's website, a Code of Conduct reads: 'Members shall in no manner attempt to influence editorial teams in respect of reporting relating to investee companies of Brand Capital.' Dhariwal claimed, in fact, that the situation had since reversed entirely—that Brand Capital's clients, such as the real estate firm Lavasa, grumble that the newspaper accords them disproportionately negative coverage. In the *Times of India* archives, I found plenty of fluffy writing about the sylvan charms of Lavasa's township in Maharashtra, but I did also find articles about the project's legal and environmental problems.

Neither the *Times of India* nor the *Economic Times* appends a disclosure every time it publishes an article about a company in which Bennett, Coleman holds a stake. Dhariwal told me it was simply impractical to do so. 'Tell me, in the half-hour or one hour that journalists are finishing an article, is it realistic to search to see if Bennett, Coleman owns a part of the company?' he said. The average reader, he argued, doesn't care. 'It's only people in your profession who think it's a big deal.' Sivakumar told Medianama that disclosures are carried only 'when there's an [investment] action possible'—during a public offering, for example. He went on to grouse: 'It has almost become like a crime to carry any news of a Treaties client just because you are invested, which is not fair on our reader.'

It is certainly debatable if newspapers are any more beholden to start-ups in which they hold small stakes than to conglomerates that rain billions of rupees in advertising upon them ever year. But the perception is that the nexus is more worrying in the case of Private Treaties and similar ventures. In mid 2010, the knotted interests trailing ad-for-equity deals in newspapers and news channels drew the gaze of the Securities and Exchange Board of India (SEBI), which prescribed disclosures upon the Press Council of India. These are routinely flouted by Indian media houses. Most newspapers and television channels do not make disclosures in their reports about companies in which they hold stakes, as they're required to do by SEBI. The websites of these media groups—or of the relevant subsidiaries, such as Brand

Capital—also do not disclose the size of the stakes they hold in various companies.

The devastation of the financial markets over the last four years has hurt Brand Capital. Its 2011 annual report reveals a post-tax loss of Rs 266 million and a diminution of the value of its investments of Rs 380 million. Dhariwal admitted that Bennett, Coleman 'has written down a chunk of our Brand Capital investment. But so what? This is money we wouldn't have gotten in the first place. We're very, very happy with Brand Capital. This is the way we will fuel the advertising market in India and protect the print business in India for a long time to come.'

The cocktail of Medianet and Private Treaties has created what Pradyuman Maheshwari, the media analyst, calls 'a crisis of confidence . . . Even if the *Times of India* now does something for legitimate reasons, we as readers will suspect that it's being done for payment.' The stain of 'paid news' has become Bennett, Coleman's damn'd spot; the company and its newspapers bore the brunt of the Press Council of India's criticism in its April 2010 report on media corruption. The journalist P. Sainath, deposing before a Press Council subcommittee, pointed to how three competing Marathi newspapers, including Bennett, Coleman's *Maharashtra Times*, praised the former chief minister Ashok Chavan in 'exactly similar words' and suggested that the articles had been placed verbatim for a fee. Sainath also alleged that another Bennett, Coleman daily, *Vidarbha Plus*, 'carried an advertisement disguised as news' on a Congress candidate in the 2009 Lok Sabha elections.

The Press Council report didn't include a rebuttal from Bennett, Coleman, and Paranjoy Guha Thakurta, a member of the subcommittee, told me that the company sent no response at all. Dhariwal, however, insisted that Bennett, Coleman had sent a rebuttal and that the Press Council 'has chosen not to highlight it'. He pointed out that the report indicted several other publications, and that the Press Council could only find 'in one obscure location, charges against *Maharashtra Times* and *Vidarbha Plus*. Look, it was unfortunate that some of our journalists fell for press release copies. It was press release copy that unfortunately got carried by us, like it was carried by others. But then we were charged with paid news, which is absolute rubbish. We didn't get paid for it.'

The ugly rash of 'paid news' is a symptom that the crisis of confidence diagnosed by Maheshwari infects the Indian media at large. Newspaper and magazine publishers are dependent, to unprecedented levels, upon their advertisers. Most media houses run versions of Private Treaties, and the tangled interests therein are rarely warmed by sunlight. Three of Indian television's four biggest business channels have been colonized by the Ambani brothers: Mukesh Ambani has invested in NDTV and Network18, which air NDTV Profit and CNBC-TV18 respectively, while companies promoted by Anil Ambani own a slice of Bloomberg UTV. (Ironically, for all Bennett, Coleman's detractors, ET Now is the only major business channel that is, on paper, free of the Ambanis' influence.) The Niira Radia tapes, leaked a couple of years ago, showed further evidence of cloyingly close relationships between journalists and corporations.

In such a world, where news can be doctored 'so as to please the piper who is paying', T.N. Ninan wrote in a 2006 essay in *Seminar*, 'bad journalism begins to drive out good'. Editors and managers at the *Times of India* are perfectly justified when they point out that this world—of worrying advertising practices, of commoditized news—is populated by many media houses and not just Bennett, Coleman. But this world is still, very inarguably, the creation of Samir Jain.

VI

In the early 2000s, when an editor left the *Indian Express* to join the *Times of India*, he was asked if he could join Samir Jain in Haridwar for an orientation. He took an early morning train out of Delhi and alighted at Haridwar, where a car ferried him to Jain's home. 'It's like a guest house—really very basic, almost like a hostel, but with marble floors,' the editor told me. 'On the ground floor, it was flush with the river, so you could put your feet into the water. There wasn't a thing on the walls. Samir would personally bring you pomegranate seeds in a *katori*. Lunch would be really basic—boiled food, rotis, maybe a glass of Coke if somebody wanted it.'

Even as Jain has delved ever deeper into Indian journalism to rearrange its innards, Haridwar has become a sanctuary, where he repairs for weeks at a time to read and discuss scripture, to sequester himself from the world, to meditate and think. He telephones his newsrooms only rarely from there, 'and even then it won't be about what to do with the paper, but more to bowl some sort of philosophical journalistic googly', the editor said. 'But then, every time he comes back from one of these spiritual retreats,' another former *Times of India* journalist said, 'he comes back with a new killer scheme for the market, to sell the paper better or to raise circulation by another 100,000.'

The apparent contradiction between Jain's deep spiritualism and his unabashed commercialism, I was assured by many of his colleagues, is really no contradiction at all. Jain simply sees it as his dharma to grow the business he inherited, one former *Times of India* editor told me. 'The money won't affect him in any way, because he is very austere, not at all flashy,' she said. Another editor remembered Jain counselling him: 'Don't confuse being spiritual with being a do-gooder, because the two are fundamentally different things.' It doesn't clash with Jain's view of the world, for instance, 'to sell newspapers with half-naked women on the front page', said the editor who was initiated into the company at Haridwar. 'He may never open *Delhi Times* himself, but he has no problem with its contents. He has partitioned his life quite nicely.'

Jain's turn towards a more sedulous spiritualism may have come at the instance of his mother, Indu, who became, after her husband's death, Bennett, Coleman's chairman, a title she uses in its masculine form. In the late 1980s, she had become a follower of Osho Rajneesh, the Pune-based mystic, and *Times of India* staffers were, along with Samir and his sister Nandita, regular visitors to Rajneesh's ashram. (In one of his books, Rajneesh worked himself up into a fit of pique about these visiting journalists, declaiming that 'to speak to such people is almost worse than speaking to a wall'. He wrote, though: 'But I really agreed for Samir Jain. He is a young man, he has been to the ashram before, he has meditated. He wanted to become a *sannyasin* [ascetic] but his father was absolutely against it, so much against it that if he became a *sannyasin*, his father would disown him . . . He has not the guts to say to the father, "It is perfectly okay, you can disown me," but he has a sympathetic heart.') Indu Jain later moved into the orbit of Sri Sri Ravi Shankar, a path her son too traced; he has also sought the guidance of Jaggi Vasudev, whose Isha Yoga Center sprawls over 150 acres of land just outside Coimbatore.

Towards the end of the 1990s, when he suffered a series of bereavements, Jain's spiritual convictions intensified. In February 1999, Ashok Jain died at the Cleveland Clinic, barely a month after he underwent a heart transplant. Not long after, Samir's son Vardhaman passed away, also in the United States, after choking on a piece of food; he was barely out of his teens. (His daughter, Trishla, who studied English at Stanford, is now a New

Delhi-based artist and a director in charge of business development at Bennett, Coleman; her husband, Satyan Gajwani, was recently named the chief executive of Times Internet Limited.) In May 2001, Jain's sister Nandita, then the group's deputy managing director, died in a helicopter crash over Arunachal Pradesh.

It is perhaps Vardhaman's death that most lends a tragic cast to Samir Jain's life. Very soon after he was born, Vardhaman suffered an illness that left him permanently blind. 'There would be no fluid in his eyes,' M.D. Nalapat, the coordinating editor of the *Times of India* in the mid 1990s, told me. 'It was horribly painful.' Nalapat recalled Vardhaman as a boy with a keen mind and a warm way of dealing with people, although another editor spotted signs of the father's imperiousness in the son. 'I remember one meeting in the boardroom in Bombay when Vardhaman got up and started saying: "We need to turn this newspaper into a lean, mean machine. We need to retrench. There's far too much flab here,"' this editor told me. 'And Samir was trying to hush him up.'

At the time, Vardhaman was, as Nalapat said, 'just a kid', but Jain had already begun to groom him. 'Samir doted on his son. He clearly saw Vardhaman as the future, to help build the *Times of India* into a huge global empire,' Nalapat said. 'So he would ask me to take Vardhaman on my meetings, to expose him to the kinds of people an editor would meet. We went to Nepal once together, and he would come along as a non-combatant observer if I had meetings with ministry officials.' Jain had bought, for his son, the best available computer aids for the sightless, and Nalapat recalled that Vardhaman was fascinated by computers and the Internet. 'As far as I could see, he was looking forward to joining the *Times of India*,' Nalapat said. 'I remember how delighted he was when the *Times* became the number one English newspaper in the world.'

Jain coped with these losses, his colleagues told me, with a frozen calm that was unsettling to witness. On his instructions, the final sentence of his father's obituary in the *Times of India* was: 'He would want us to be *a-shok*—one who is without grief—in the full sense of the Sanskrit word.' When the news of Vardhaman's demise reached the offices in Delhi, a former staffer recalled, Jain 'philosophized the whole thing away. He never showed any emotion. That evening, he even attended a meeting and had a normal discussion. We knew, somehow, that we weren't supposed to go condole with him.' Two people who attended Nandita's memorial service told me that, while Vineet Jain wept for his sister, Samir appeared to be in a trance-like ecstasy. 'In a way, that's what makes him more chilling,' one of these people told me. 'That's why he will never think twice about shutting down a unit, say, or even a newspaper.'

Jain believes strongly, I gathered, in what a spiritual adviser might call the impermanence of the terrestrial realm. 'Life is a game, Samir once said to me, but it is a game you must play in all seriousness, without losing sight of the fact that it is only a game,' recalled a *Times of India* editor who knows Jain well. He directed me to the *Ashtavakra Gita*, a philosophical dialogue that Jain reads avidly, and that posits an unsettling disconnect between a man's thought and his actions. 'Righteousness and unrighteousness, pleasure and pain are purely of the mind and are no concern of yours,' the sage Ashtavakra advises Janaka, king of Mithila. 'You are neither the doer nor the reaper of the consequences, so you are always free.' The body is imagination, only pure consciousness is real, and death, when it arrives, is not to be mourned.

Inevitably, the blaze of Jain's faith has singed Bennett, Coleman's newsrooms. On the third floor of the Times of India building in New Delhi, images of seated Jain *tirthankaras* are emblazoned into the frosted panels on the doors of cabins; in between the thick glass that wraps around other work spaces, mock-ups of pages from old Sanskrit manuscripts are sandwiched into the panes. 'He'd want us to write whole editorials based on the Bhagavad Gita, and if you made one mistake, you had it. On many days, some baba or the other would come to the fourth floor, and we'd all have to go to listen to them,' one former *Times of India* journalist told me. More such lectures were held at Jain's residence, and editors were expected to attend. One editor, during a sermon by Sri Sri Ravi Shankar at Sujagi, found that he had forgotten his spectacles in his car. 'Sri Sri was talking about how a paper shouldn't have bad news, and how it should have only good news or spiritual news, and I got a headache because I didn't have my glasses on. So I was sitting there rubbing my eyes and my head,' the editor told me. 'The next day, I got a call from Dileep Padgaonkar, who was in China at the time, saying: "Boss, what did you do? Sri Sri is really mad at you, that you weren't paying attention to what he was saying."'

The most remarkable twinning of Jain's beliefs and his flair for marketing has been Speaking Tree, a spirituality column so successful that it was spun off, in February 2010, into its own weekly publication. A journalist who worked briefly on the Speaking Tree columns said that Jain had wanted 'a civilized way of discussing religion', and Dhariwal told me that Jain was fed up with the news media's 'obsession with politics, the same old drama that goes on every day, back and forth'. Even Jain's detractors concede, with reluctant admiration, that 'the bloody thing worked'. Vidya Subrahmaniam, who was working on the editorial page when Speaking Tree launched, remembered: 'People would rush up to me and gush about the edit page. But it wasn't about anything I or my colleagues wrote. The praise was for Speaking Tree.' Jain rightly figured, Subrahmaniam said, 'that people who love the *Times of India* are often torn up inside, from just running all the time'. It is the Speaking Tree, and its successful vending of spiritual comfort, that people cite most often as an instance of Jain's marketing artistry, quite forgetting the more obvious example: the newspaper within which it is encased.

Slowly, over the last decade, Samir Jain has become more withdrawn from the newspaper; consensus has it that he has certainly mellowed since the late 1980s, when he was the scourge of the newsroom. 'I do sense that he is letting other people create and innovate, and that he doesn't want to stamp his authority on everything,' Dhariwal said. 'But he's still the best mind in the company. He's still very agile, very active.' Jain has grown less acutely interested in Bennett, Coleman's day-to-day operations and less ravenous in the pursuit of some of his larger goals for his company. He doesn't seem to be still hankering, for instance, to make the *Times of India* into the global media brand he once wished it to be. In the mid 2000s, rumours flitted through India's newsrooms that Bennett, Coleman was considering a bid to buy first the *Wall Street Journal* and then *Newsweek*, but those bids never materialized. Jain had also desired, once, to buy Britain's *Financial Times*, but now that it might be up for sale again, he is said to be showing little interest.

Jain has also been slow to take Bennett, Coleman public, although a listing is now believed to be close at hand. When the financial markets were shimmering hot a few years ago, two former Times Group editors told me, he was seriously deliberating an IPO, his sights set—a little ambitiously—on a valuation of $10 billion. Speaking recently to Ken Auletta of the *New Yorker*, Vineet Jain carefully discussed a public offering 'in the long run', saying: 'We don't need money to grow publishing, but we do to grow television and the Internet.' In December 2010, stock options were handed out to more than 200 senior employees—editors as well as managers—with a promise to compensate these options with cash if the shares are not listed by 31 December 2015.

Although he could not have known it then, Jain entered the Indian newspaper industry just as it was poised on the lip of disruptive change—or, to be reflexive about it, he engineered much of this change himself. Twenty-five years later, the industry finds itself at another crossroads. The business of printing and selling English newspapers in India is at or near its crest; spectacular as the view from the summit remains, growth is slowing, and television and the Internet are leaching away both advertisers and readers. 'Print media is expected to face multiple challenges . . . and some key hurdles,' Bennett, Coleman's 2010–11 Annual Report says, before identifying some of these hurdles: lack of interactivity, abbreviated attention spans, alternative media options. Newspaper readership is 'declining/ stagnant', presenting 'an inability to push our advertising tariffs upwards'. The nimbleness that has been demanded of newspaper companies in the United States is beginning to be demanded of their counterparts here.

In Bennett, Coleman's navigation of these new waters, it may not always be Jain's hand on the tiller or his eye to the sextant, but by filling her holds with cash, he has kitted out his vessel better than any other in the country. Undoubtedly, he has built a rich and mighty corporation; it is not at all as clear, though, that he has improved, or has even wanted to improve, Indian journalism. Instead, he has prized the quantitative over the qualitative, and although by that metric he has thoroughly swamped his opposition, he continues to have an eye or two cocked on the numbers. 'Now, for Samir, it isn't even so much about making money,' one *Times of India* editor said. 'Now it's just about keeping score.'

India's finance minister **ARUN JAITLEY**, with his strong grip over the media, has carefully created for himself the image of a refined, well-spoken, lawyer–politician, unsullied by the reputation of the rabble-rousing Hindu nationalist party to which he belongs. When I started work on this profile in December 2014, my challenge was to go beyond that facade to find the real Jaitley and present him to the reader.

He is a quintessential Delhi insider, and I just the opposite. This meant that I didn't have access to him, but it gave me freedom to be objective. Soon after I started reporting, I was struck by the dual nature of his personality. An off-the-cuff comparison with *Dr Jekyll and Mr Hyde* by a lobbyist gave me a handle over the subject. I found this line in the classic illuminating: 'I saw that, of the two natures that contended in the field of my consciousness, even if could rightly be said to be either, it was only because I was radically both.'

Jaitley is the resident shaman of Delhi's circles of power. I sensed a belief among them that nobody could dare publish anything remotely inconvenient to him. As a result, his friends eagerly met me to contribute to the legend, but his well-known adversaries shied away even from off-the-record conversations. One of the senior politicians from whom I received a rude refusal was seen buying the copies of the issue in question in bulk, I read in the *Economic Times*.

Many of the sixty-plus interviews I conducted were off the record, and I met some interviewees several times: Jaitley is a lawyer with a reputation for vindictiveness, and I went to great lengths to corroborate everything to minimize the risk of legal hassles.

Those who had met me for the story kept calling me to check whether it would be published at all. 'Jaitley will get it killed,' I was told. 'You don't know him.' After the magazine went to press in the last week of April, one person insisted that 'Jaitley will make the copies vanish'. At times it was hard for me not to believe in their confidence in the man.

PRAVEEN DONTHI

Praveen Donthi is a staff writer at the Caravan. *He lives in Delhi.*

Talk of the Town

How Arun Jaitley wins friends and influences people

By PRAVEEN DONTHI | 1 May 2015

I

In 2012, two years before Arun Jaitley became the most important minister in Narendra Modi's cabinet, the news that the ruling United Progressive Alliance's (UPA) allocation of coal blocks may have cost the government thousands of crores and unfairly benefited private interests, incapacitated the Parliament's monsoon session. Bharatiya Janata Party (BJP) parliamentarians threatened to resign en masse, and Jaitley, then the BJP's Opposition leader in the Rajya Sabha, aggressively spoke out against what he called 'the biggest scam in independent India'.

As the stymied Parliament session ground to a halt that August, Jaitley and Sushma Swaraj, his counterpart in the Lok Sabha, released a fierce joint statement. 'We used this session of Parliament to shake the conscience of the people of India,' they wrote. 'This is not merely a political battle. It is a battle for safeguarding the economic resources for a larger public good.' In a press conference, Jaitley called the allocation process 'arbitrary', 'discretionary', and 'corrupt', 'a textbook case of crony capitalism'. In an opinion piece in *The Hindu*, titled 'Defending the Indefensible', he wrote 'the government was so overenthusiastic in continuing the discretionary process in allotment' that it did not institute the 'competitive bidding mechanism' that would have ensured a more just process of allocation.

A few years earlier, Jaitley had offered a different type of opinion to Strategic Energy Technology Systems Private Limited (SETSPL), an ambitious joint venture between Tata Sons and a South African firm, in his capacity as a practising lawyer. When applying for coal blocks in 2008, SETSPL, one of the biggest beneficiaries of the allocation process, sought Jaitley's advice on whether it could avoid sharing a certain part of its profits with the government. Jaitley provided the company with a twenty-one-page legal opinion, via the law offices of his college friend Raian Karanjawala, recognizing that 'the Govt. of India is entitled to adopt a procedure for allocation of coal blocks', and that the company was not legally bound to share the proposed profits with the government. Jaitley's arguments in support of SETSPL indicated that he had been well aware of the prevailing coal block allocation process despite his hue and cry about 'the monumental fraud'.

Shortly after the coal scam broke, the legal opinion was made available to the press by one or more UPA ministers. As the BJP fanned the flames of protest against Prime Minister Manmohan Singh—alleging that he had allowed controversial allocations under his watch as coal minister—the leaked opinion, a potential hot tip, became a hot potato. The document was passed around between journalists, including senior staff at the *Times of India*, the *Economic Times*, Headlines Today, NDTV and CNBC. But in each case, the story of Jaitley's inconsistent outrage was withheld.

A mid-level journalist at Headlines Today said that the office of P. Chidambaram, the Union home minister at the time, gave the channel the story of the leak as 'an exclusive', and that it ran once before being taken off air. The journalist was told by his senior, who said he had spoken to Jaitley, that though he believed in 'the merits of the story', Jaitley had argued the leaked document was 'a private opinion'. 'I have always believed what the editor thinks is right,' the journalist said, smiling, 'so I said okay.'

Another journalist who had the document told me that Jaitley wrote a letter to the vice president, who is chairman of the Rajya Sabha, complaining 'that the intelligence agencies were trying to tarnish his reputation. The vice president's office had confirmed it to me,' the journalist said. 'The bureau chief wanted Jaitley's comment, but he wasn't willing to talk about the issue at all. So the story was not carried.' Only one journalist actually spoke to Jaitley about the opinion, but colleagues who knew about the interview, which never ran, said he was unsatisfied with Jaitley's answers. The journalist didn't want to share details of the meeting to avoid 'creating discomfort' to his colleagues. 'And remember he is the finance minister,' he said. 'I don't want to upset him.'

A year later, the story of the legal opinion finally appeared, but on the non-mainstream news website Altgaze, without the impact it might have had earlier. Several journalists joked with me about Jaitley having rustled up the 'Jaitley Press Corps'—a twist on the Joint Parliamentary Committee—to quell the news.

For leaders with mass support bases, life in the public eye is an exercise in reassuring a particular constituency of one's ability to represent it. A leader like Arun Jaitley, whose support base is his range of contacts in the media, judiciary and corporate world, requires a different public image—in his case the portrayal of the refined, well-spoken Delhi insider who can navigate his less-polished colleagues through the shifting currents of India's national politics as they eddy around the power centre of the capital. For four decades, Jaitley has stayed afloat on these currents, embracing the primary political imperative of change, and impressively adapting to it. Jaitley's steady rise in what one senior journalist with a daily paper called 'the limited talent pool of the BJP', and his importance to his party was affirmed a year ago, when Modi awarded him with the high-profile finance portfolio, as well as the portfolios for corporate affairs and defence. Jaitley had charge of defence until last November, when he took up information and broadcasting.

In a notoriously tight-lipped regime, Jaitley is, to a great extent, entrusted with speaking. He has always loved to hold court, and his door is typically wider ajar than those of his colleagues in the party. The *Telegraph* described a typical encounter in an interview with Jaitley, freshly glowing from his success in managing the 2008 Karnataka assembly elections. Jaitley:

> puts his feet up, settling down for his ritual informal chat with journalists after the daily press briefing. That's when the gregarious college boy in Jaitley comes to the fore. His sharp political insights are then peppered with pithy one-liners, jokes which have him convulsing with laughter more than his assembled audience. He occasionally mimics other politicians.

A news editor called Jaitley 'a raconteur who can regale you with great stories and nuggets of information. It can make you feel part of the club—a heady drug for all journalists and a validation that you are part of something important.' A political editor of a leading newspaper said, 'he wouldn't mind sharing very personal details of his friends for the entertainment of others'.

The political editor told me, 'I am not a BJP-friendly reporter. And I have not been nice to him in print.' But Jaitley 'continues to be friendly to me'. Yet access to Jaitley's durbar comes with its own set of challenges, and some journalists argued that there is a quid pro quo involved. A veteran journalist, who has covered the

BJP for thirty years, told me, 'Either you are with him completely and planted stories on Rajnath and Sushma,'—Rajnath Singh, former BJP president and current minister of home affairs; and Sushma Swaraj, now minister of external affairs—'otherwise his doors will still be open and you can have tea but he will give you no information whatsoever.' Another political editor, who has also covered the BJP since the 1980s, noted that Jaitley's anecdotes 'may not yield a story immediately . . . but if you tuck it away at the back of your mind, you can join the dots and complete the picture some other time'.

The news editor described Jaitley's slightly distracted manner of talking as a 'classic power move' to disorient people and keep them guessing as to whether the information they have is important or not. 'You can't pin him down on any topic,' the senior journalist at the daily paper said. 'He controls the terms and conditions of the discussion.' (Jaitley did not respond to multiple interview requests from the *Caravan*, nor to a list of questions sent to him.)

A journalist repeated a joke he heard from the editor and former BJP member of Parliament (MP) and cabinet minister Arun Shourie that Jaitley is a mass leader—with a mass base of six journalists. Yet his influence belies this as understatement; only a handful of the sixty-eight people I spoke to, most of them journalists or politicians, were willing to talk about Jaitley on the record. 'Half the Delhi claims to know you,' a television journalist told me he once remarked to Jaitley, who reportedly replied, 'Half the Delhi won't be lying.'

I met the self-styled marketing guru Suhel Seth in the executive lounge of Delhi's Taj Palace hotel in early January, about two months before his paean to Jaitley, titled 'My Friend Arun', appeared in *Open* magazine. The two first met during the 1999 general elections, when Seth was hired to design material for Atal Bihari Vajpayee's prime ministerial campaign, and have remained close. Describing Jaitley as 'the life of the party within his circle', Seth told me about a room in his own house called Jaitley's den, 'where he meets the select few' from across professions and party lines. Among the regulars, Seth counted senior advocates Raian Karanjawala and Rajiv Nayar; Shobhana Bhartia, a former Rajya Sabha MP and the editorial director of the Hindustan Times Group; and Congress MP Jyotiraditya Scindia.

'Several times I wanted to shut the bloody den down, but he would open it again,' Seth said. 'Jaitley loves to yak, Raian loves to yak,' and the friends gather to talk about 'the good things in life . . . cashmere, holidays, food'. Jaitley has often stated that being a politician is a financial sacrifice, compared to being a full-time lawyer, but whenever his detractors make fun of his love of expensive shawls, watches and pens, his friends point out that they are all legally bought.

In a 2010 piece for *Outlook*, Jaitley wrote, 'I am a Punjabi by birth and by culture, and as any good Punjabi will tell you—"*Changa khana te changa paana*" (You must eat and dress well).' 'It matters to him how you speak, how you dress, the address where you live, the class to which you belong, the kind of car you drive,' the political editor said. 'He's snobbish in a Delhi way.' Several people, including a former BJP general secretary, told me one reason Jaitley has never been the party's president is the elitism he is identified with.

In the past, Jaitley's projection of himself as modern, moderate and liberal—traits that appeal to a certain segment of Delhi's journalistic, business and intellectual elite—has evoked suspicion among more hard-line members of the BJP, and its ideological affiliate, the Rashtriya Swayamsevak Sangh (RSS). In 2011 *The Hindu* reported a WikiLeaks cable disclosure in which Jaitley was quoted as characterizing the 'talking point' of Hindutva 'as an opportunistic issue' for his party. Jaitley issued a denial, but the idea that his attachment to the BJP is more expedient than ideological pre-dated this controversy, and has persisted beyond it.

Yet his upper-class smoothness has also made him invaluable as the BJP expands. In 1999, the journalist Swapan Dasgupta (who declined to be interviewed, citing his friendship with Jaitley) wrote in *India Today* that, 'In a party plagued by an image problem, he made the BJP respectable among the chattering classes and was rewarded.' He predicted, 'As the BJP moves from the fringes to becoming a liberal, right-wing party, the Sangh Parivar will look to him as a winning face of the next century.' Jaitley's friend Virendra Kapoor, a journalist and an RSS loyalist, told me Jaitley hates the label, often attached to him, of being the 'right man in the wrong party'.

A prominent lobbyist in Delhi, referring to Jaitley's indignation over the coal scam told me one 'part of him is public—that is liberal and modern'. The other 'is the shrewd strategist side that you don't get to see'. Explaining how Jaitley has stayed so close to the centre of power over the last several decades, the lobbyist drew a contrast between him and the prime minister. 'Modi rules by fear,' he said, 'and Jaitley by favour.'

II

Arun Jaitley was born in New Delhi, in December 1952, to a family that had moved there from Lahore via Amritsar during Partition. Jaitley's father, a lawyer, began practising in the capital, where Jaitley attended St Xavier's, a missionary school in Civil Lines. According to a school friend, he was an average student who wanted to be an engineer, but instead joined Delhi University's Shri Ram College of Commerce. Karanjawala told me Jaitley was a B-plus student but an avid debater; he was captain of the debate team and won several gold medals. His image as an erudite public-school boy, refined at university, shaped the course of his political career.

In the early 1970s, India's campuses were political crucibles for Jayaprakash Narayan's growing movement against Prime Minister Indira Gandhi's increasingly iron-fisted policies. Many politicians, including Lalu Prasad Yadav, Sushil Modi, Nitish Kumar, Venkaiah Naidu and Ravi Shankar Prasad, first emerged as student leaders, and Jaitley, too, was introduced into the world of campaigning and elections in this manner.

Jaitley was initially part of what his acquaintances referred to as the 'left club'. In 1971, he met Sri Ram Khanna, a leader of the Akhil Bharatiya Vidyarthi Parishad (ABVP), a right-wing student organization allied with the RSS. 'We were angry young men,' Khanna said when I met him in January. 'Anti-Congress-ism was the mood of the campus politics across the country those days. An entire crop of young people got assimilated in the ABVP.' Several of them, such as Naidu and Nitin Gadkari, later became top BJP leaders. Others, such as Prabhu Chawla and Rajat Sharma, became powerful editors. Khanna, now a professor at Shri Ram College of Commerce, said he 'inducted' Jaitley into politics, nominating him for the post of supreme councillor—one of ten electors in charge of indirectly voting in the president of the Delhi University Students' Union (DUSU). In 1972, Khanna became the DUSU president, and Jaitley replaced him as the president of the Shri Ram College union.

By the next year, Jaitley had embarked upon a law degree at Delhi University—following in the footsteps of his father, uncle and two cousins. He was expected to be the ABVP's presidential candidate for 1973, but instead the ABVP chose Alok Kumar, a member of the RSS. Even Kumar, who went on to become a BJP member of legislative assembly (MLA) from Delhi, told me he thought it was Jaitley's turn, 'because he was more active in politics. I was more into *shakha* work.' However, the defection of the ABVP's first elected DUSU president, Khanna's predecessor, to its Congress-affiliated rival, the National Students' Union of India (NSUI), 'sent panic waves. So the ABVP wanted to pick up a *swayamsevak*,' Kumar said.

It wouldn't be the last time Jaitley, with his friends across party lines and a reputation for fitting in anywhere, was passed over for a candidate seemingly more committed to the ideology of the RSS and its affiliates. But eventually, the very things that made him somewhat of an outsider—'He could speak English fluently, and it wasn't common in the Parishad family,' Kumar said—also made him useful. Khanna told me they had to persuade the RSS to give Jaitley the vice presidential ticket. 'And we literally had to force him to file the nomination because he was so cheesed off,' he said. Denied top billing, Jaitley made the most of an important secondary position.

In 1974, the students' union had its first direct elections. By this time, Jaitley was considered a shoo-in for president, but the banner he would run under was an open question. Pankaj Vohra, a senior editor with the *Sunday Guardian* who was then a member of the NSUI, told me Jaitley 'was considered to be a winner regardless of the party. The Congress also wanted to woo him.' A senior ABVP leader of the time told me it took Prabhu Chawla, the ABVP's Delhi head, and Rajkumar Bhatia, another leader, three days to persuade the RSS to give Jaitley the ticket.

Vohra told me that 'Jaitley was seen being openly approached by Bahadur Singh and Kulbir Singh of the Congress in the Law Faculty', after which the ABVP 'announced his candidature in a hurry'. According to Ravi Gupta, a businessman who was also an ABVP member, the announcement came as a surprise to the NSUI, which was supporting Jaitley. Jaitley 'may dispute it now',

Vohra said, 'but in 1974, he could have as well been a Congress candidate'. For Jaitley, casting his lot with the ABVP paid off, and he won the election by a wide margin.

Jaitley was an effective president, Kumar, Khanna and others told me, due to his managerial skills. 'He had mastered the university calendar, including the statutes and ordinances,' Vohra said. 'The university officers found it difficult to counter him.' He added that Jaitley had the patronage of A.S. Kukla, the dean of student welfare and staff adviser to DUSU: 'As both were Brahmins, Jaitley was able to get things done.'

Jaitley also plunged headlong into Jayaprakash Narayan's movement. He was the convener of Narayan's Committee for Youth and Students Organizations, and travelled to Patna and Ahmedabad to attend conventions. Ram Bahadur Rai, a Padma Shri awardee and a member of the movement's steering committee, recalled that Jaitley organized a public meeting with Narayan at Delhi University, and a two-day student conference in March 1974. According to the friend of a woman Jaitley was romancing at the time, he was so swept up that he missed his own engagement ceremony. 'He came back a couple of days later and told her that his friends took him to Patna for some rally,' the friend said.

After Indira Gandhi declared the Emergency, on 26 June 1975, Jaitley was in the thick of the protests against the suspension of civil liberties. Student activists were among the many dissenters arrested—Jaitley described his own experience in a commemorative Facebook post last June:

> On the evening of 25th June, 1975 a massive rally was organized at Ramlila Maidan which was addressed by JP and several other leaders. After attending the rally I came back home late in the evening . . . At about 2 AM past

> midnight, I received a midnight knock at my residence. The police had come to arrest me. My father, a lawyer by profession got into an argument outside the gate of my house . . . I escaped from the backdoor . . .

The next morning, Jaitley organized what he called 'the only protest against the Emergency which took place that day in the whole country', where about 200 people gathered before the police arrived. Jaitley has also said that he 'courted arrest'; a college friend remembers him running through the university coffee house shouting '*Main bhaag raha hoon*'—I'm running away—before being picked up by the police. 'He knew he was going to be arrested,' Karanjawala told me. 'But nobody really knew how long it would last. Arun may have thought that he would come out in a week.' Jaitley was sent first to Ambala jail, then shifted to Tihar jail in Delhi. He was imprisoned for nineteen months.

Jaitley has often reflected on this time in Tihar with pride. 'I was in charge of the kitchen,' he wrote in the 2010 *Outlook* article. 'I found convicts to make us parathas for breakfast and convinced a kind jail warden to allow us meat, with the result that we got rogan josh for dinner . . . we all left prison looking rather plumper.' In another article, Jaitley wrote, 'For us younger detenus who did not have the burden and worry of supporting families, jail became an elongated spell of a college or school camp.'

In prison, Jaitley's political education continued as he built on the friendships he had forged earlier with RSS workers, ABVP members and socialists from all over the country. He was lodged in a ward with thirteen others, including Virendra Kapoor, who is still one of his closest friends. He also met all the biggest Opposition leaders, including Atal Bihari Vajpayee, L.K. Advani, K.R. Malkani and Nanaji Deshmukh. 'His baptism was in the jail, not on the campus,' Khanna told me. It was 'the biggest test he undertook. He was no more the outsider for the RSS. Probably after coming out of jail, he had the realization that politics is his career.'

Jaitley left Tihar in January 1977 as one of the most prominent student faces in Opposition politics, and became the ABVP's all-India secretary. In March, when the Emergency was lifted and general elections announced, his name even appeared on the national executive list of the newly formed Janata Party. Ram Bahadur Rai told me that the Samajwadi Janata Party's president, Chandra Shekhar, included Jaitley following a nomination by Deshmukh, without consulting either the ABVP or Jaitley himself. 'The ABVP was neither part of the Jan Sangh nor did it want to work under its aegis,' Rai explained, so Jaitley resigned from the position. Jaitley has said in interviews that Vajpayee wanted him to contest the 1977 Lok Sabha elections, but he was a year below the minimum age requirement of 25 years. Instead, completing his law degree that year, he focused on a budding career in the courts. He stayed involved in politics, but peripherally.

'Ours is a centre-stage profession,' Jaitley told *India Today* in 1997, on having a legal career. 'Of course, there is tremendous clout.' He reportedly told the magazine that, 'unlike industrialists seeking favours, lawyers don't need politicians, if anything, politicians need them'. While Jaitley said he 'sort of evolved into law', Karanjawala told me his college friend was practically 'born in Tis Hazari', the north Delhi district court where his father, Maharaj Kishen Jaitley, practised. Jaitley began appearing there himself in the late 1970s, specializing in cases involving the Municipal Corporation of Delhi (MCD) and the Delhi Development Authority (DDA).

In 1979, when he married Sangeeta Dogra, the daughter of veteran Congress leader Girdhari Lal Dogra, Jaitley had a wide network among the political top brass. Both Vajpayee and Advani attended the wedding—as did Indira Gandhi. But over the next few years, Jaitley's experience in the courts brought him closer to the inner circle of the BJP, which he joined in 1980, the same year it was established with Vajpayee as president. Indira Gandhi returned to power that year and, as payback for the *Indian Express*'s critical coverage of her during the Emergency, the DDA tried to revoke a building permit issued to the newspaper by the previous government. When Ramnath Goenka, the paper's proprietor, and Arun Shourie, its executive director, approached Karanjawala for help, he got Jaitley involved, he said, 'since Arun had the speciality that the case required'. The court granted the paper a stay order, and the case strengthened Jaitley's relationship with Goenka, whom he had met as a student.

The *Indian Express* case was just one skirmish in a larger war, brewing through the 1980s, between politicians, industrialists and media owners. Loyalties were divided between the industrialists Nusli Wadia, the owner of Bombay Dyeing, and his rival Dhirubhai Ambani, the head of Reliance Textile Industries Limited; battles played out in courtrooms and across inches of newsprint. Jaitley had many opportunities to engage in legal jousting—especially in a supporting role to senior lawyer and former BJP politician Ram Jethmalani—while also raising his political profile. After the BJP's colossal drubbing in the 1985 general elections, Vajpayee told *India Today*, 'The election result gives us time for rethinking. There is need to project new faces. We have young talent in people like Pramod Mahajan of Bombay and Arun Jaitley of Delhi.'

In 1987, Jaitley was involved in a series of legal matters related to interactions between the Enforcement Directorate, under former finance minister V.P. Singh, and Fairfax, an American detective agency that had allegedly been hired to investigate the illegal stacking of black money overseas. In March 1987, Jaitley and Jethmalani successfully defended S. Gurumurthy, an RSS ideologue and Goenka's financial adviser, from suspicions of passing classified information to Fairfax, soon after Gurumurthy wrote a series of articles in the *Indian Express* against the Congress and Reliance. A commission headed by two Supreme Court judges was appointed to investigate Singh, by then defence minister, who was on the outs with Prime Minister Rajiv Gandhi for his relentless pursuit of tax evaders, including Congress-friendly companies such as Reliance. Singh resigned from his ministerial post, quit the Congress party and hired for his defence Karanjawala, who told me, 'Arun also used to advise him.'

The next month, in April, the tide turned against the Congress when news broke that the Swedish armaments firm Bofors had allegedly paid Gandhi kickbacks to broker a deal worth $1.3 billion with the Indian government. That summer, as the Fairfax probe continued and the Bofors scandal raged, Jethmalani went on the offensive with a series of front-page *Indian Express* articles interrogating Gandhi. According to Nalini Gera's 2009 book *Ram Jethmalani: The Authorized Biography*, he was helped in this endeavour by Gurumurthy, Arun Shourie and several BJP members, 'especially Arun Jaitley'.

Jaitley contributed outside the courtroom too. Riding the wave of the Bofors scandal, in December 1989, V.P. Singh led the Janata Dal to power and became prime minister of the BJP-supported National Front government. *India Today* gave part of the credit for the dramatic improvement in the BJP's election tally—from two seats in 1984, to eighty-six in 1989—to Jaitley. 'The former student leader ensured the flow of funds, and masterminded the BJP's publicity campaign,' *India Today* reported. (Jaitley's college friend Prabhu Chawla was by then a senior editor at the magazine.)

Jaitley, then thirty-seven, was made an additional solicitor general. Karanjawala said Jaitley 'was a great favourite' of Singh's. 'I might have played a small catalyst,' he said. To facilitate this appointment, he was promoted to senior advocate through the Delhi High Court almost overnight, which catapulted his legal career, according to the senior lawyer Dushyant Dave, who shared office space with Jaitley. Karanjawala said that Mukul Rohatgi, the current attorney general, was 'one of our closest friends' and 'had a role in that'.

With lawyers like Jaitley at his service, expectations were high that as prime minister, Singh would determinedly pursue the Bofors allegations. In January 1990, an investigative team consisting of Jaitley, the former enforcement director Bhure Lal, and the CBI deputy inspector general M.K. Madhavan, made high-profile visits to Switzerland and Sweden to investigate the matter. Jaitley had his first prominent national appearance when photographs of the team were splashed across the newspapers.

But eight months later, there were no results. A critical MP, quoted in an *India Today* article, remarked that if the team 'continued their investigations abroad, they would soon be entitled to NRI status'. Still, in the years that followed, Jaitley often brought up his participation in the investigation to burnish his credentials. But in 2012, Sten Lindström, the former head of the Swedish police who had leaked key Bofors documents to the journalist Chitra Subramaniam, spoke out against the team, claiming that it had actually 'muddied the waters' of the investigation.

Lindström explained that while Subramaniam's reports only mentioned five Swiss bank accounts containing Bofors payoff money, the team planted the name of actor Amitabh Bachchan, Rajiv Gandhi's close friend, as the man behind a sixth such account in the newspaper *Dagens Nyheter.* The paper issued a public apology after Bachchan won a libel case in the United Kingdom, claiming it was misled 'in trusting information from persons directly involved in the investigations into the Bofors transaction on behalf of the Indian Government'.

Subramaniam, now the editor-in-chief of the online portal *News Minute*, told me over email, 'It was plantation time galore! Almost everybody and their cousin had a theory, a list, a name.' Over ten years of reporting from Geneva, Bern and Stockholm, 'one saw how governments used and abused the information for their benefit, facts be damned', she said, claiming she had been put under tremendous pressure to implicate Bachchan and aid in the government's investigation.

Her refusal to do so provoked a spate of misogynistic and damning articles. A senior journalist I spoke to recalled that a Bombay tabloid, the *Daily*, insinuated that she and Bachchan were having an extramarital affair. 'The *Indian Express* in turn is questioning her credibility and charging her with suddenly going off on a tangent . . . under the influence of Amitabh Bachchan,' wrote Chawla and Tarun Tejpal in *India Today*, even after Bachchan had won the libel case. Subramaniam, who was 'deeply disturbed' by the articles, told me, 'A few years later I raised these concerns with Mr Jaitley,' and, 'he was open and welcoming of my views'. She did not accuse Jaitley of spreading the rumours, but said, 'He did what was expected of him politically.'

Bachchan was an MP from Allahabad at the time, and the campaign against him had at least one larger political repercussion. V.P. Singh's Rajya Sabha term was coming to an end, and he wanted to contest from Bachchan's seat in Allahabad. After Bachchan resigned in 1987, necessitating a by-election in which he did not compete, Singh alluded to the role the Bofors charges played in his own victory. 'I said I would take on and defeat Bachchan who represents corruption in this government,' he said.

III

In the politically tumultuous years following the 1989 elections, fissures appeared in the uneasy alliance between the Janata Dal and the BJP, which had formally adopted the doctrine of Hindutva at its national executive meeting at Palampur, a few months before it became a part of the ruling National Front. At Palampur, the BJP pledged support to the Vishwa Hindu Parishad's (VHP) Ram Janmabhoomi movement, which sought to build a Ram temple at the site of the Babri Masjid in Ayodhya. As his party's rhetoric became increasingly communal, Jaitley walked a fine line of public neutrality.

In September 1990, when the BJP leader L.K. Advani kicked off his Ram Rath Yatra to Ayodhya, Jaitley 'prepared very effective notes for daily press briefings to be used by Advani', according to an RSS ideologue and former BJP general secretary. When communal riots subsequently broke out across India, Jaitley exerted pressure on V.P. Singh to give in to the VHP's demands. According to Advani's autobiography, *My Country, My Life*, Jaitley and Gurumurthy, the go-between of the government and the VHP, held a 'marathon meeting' with Singh to help the government frame the ordinance that gave part of the disputed territory to the Ram Janmabhoomi movement. During a stalemate, Advani wrote, 'it required Gurumurthy and Jaitley to rescue the kernel from the welter of inessential information'. Though the ordinance was later recalled, Advani called their effort 'so logical and irrefutable that the Prime Minister and his colleagues had no arguments against it'.

That October, when Advani's yatra reached Samastipur in Bihar, he was arrested by the state government, then controlled by Lalu Prasad Yadav, and the BJP withdrew its support for the National Front in protest. On 10 November, Chandra Shekhar—

leading the Samajwadi Janata Party—became prime minister, with the outside support of the Congress. But, despite his party's protest against the government, Jaitley briefly retained his role as additional solicitor general. It was only on 22 November, after economist Subramanian Swamy became law minister, that Jaitley tendered his resignation. A senior leader of the Delhi unit of the BJP told me that as Jaitley claimed he had been nominated to the post by the BJP, 'he should've resigned immediately when the BJP withdrew its support' to the National Front. The senior leader said Jaitley dissociated himself from the BJP after the Babri Masjid was demolished on 6 December, repeatedly referring to it as 'your party', calling its *kar sevak*s 'lumpen elements' and the demolition 'vandalization'.

Whatever his feelings on Hindutva, Jaitley had Advani's approval, even if he still stood a distant second to the party's darling, Pramod Mahajan, who had been promoted to BJP general secretary at the age of thirty-seven. In the 1991 general elections, Jaitley was one of Advani's campaign managers, but managed to secure him only a narrow win in New Delhi over the Bollywood idol Rajesh Khanna. Jaitley had more success defending Advani in court, becoming his primary legal counsel in October 1993, after the CBI filed cases against BJP leaders for the demolition of the Babri Masjid. In the late 1990s, Jaitley also defended Advani against charges in the hawala money-laundering scam, supporting him through what the older politician called 'one of the most challenging periods of my life'. The senior BJP leader from Delhi and a BJP-friendly editor both told me that Advani 'promoted' Jaitley for a Rajya Sabha seat from Delhi in 1994, but was blocked by Vajpayee, who was less enthused about Jaitley than he had been about a decade earlier. According to a BJP MP, Vajpayee said in a party meeting, '*Arun to ho nahin sakta, baaki naam batayiye*'—not Arun, tell me other names.

The BJP-friendly editor, who had lobbied for Jaitley to become Delhi's chief minister when Madan Lal Khurana resigned from the post in 1996, told me Advani felt Jaitley was too young for the job. 'In 1994, we tried to get him the Rajya Sabha seat from Delhi,' he said, but 'Vajpayee didn't like him and Pramod Mahajan opposed his candidature'. Finally, just before the 1999 elections, Advani awarded Jaitley with the post of party spokesperson, which led neatly into his appointment as the minister for information and broadcasting in October 1999, after the BJP-led National Democratic Alliance came to power. Karanjawala told me he thought Nusli Wadia 'played a very positive, very strong, and very supportive role in Arun being made a minister'. By that time, the BJP-friendly editor said, it was clear 'the party needs a minister who is articulate and good with journalists'.

Jaitley was eminently suited to the high-visibility positions of BJP spokesperson and information minister. Sri Ram Khanna, who had drafted Jaitley into the ABVP, told me that Jaitley began making inroads into the press back then. 'We would go to newspaper offices to give out press releases,' he said. 'That's how we learnt our media relations.' By the time he became minister, Jaitley's list of friends in the press was extensive. He had built relationships with media houses, including Ramnath Goenka's Indian Express Group and *Times of India* publisher Bennett, Coleman and Co. Ltd, as their legal counsel, and was also on the board of the *Hindustan Times*.

Television news was changing the way politics was conducted. As Swapan Dasgupta noted in 1999, 'as TV grew in importance, so did Jaitley'. He became such a popular guest that when journalist Vir Sanghvi interviewed him on Star TV soon after his ministerial appointment, he quipped, 'It is unusual for me to have on this programme a guest who has done more television than I have.'

Among the emerging, mass-media-savvy generation of BJP leaders—K.N. Govindacharya, Pramod Mahajan, Narendra Modi—Jaitley had the most comfortable relationship with the press corps. 'Are you a harmless flirt?' Varsha Bhosle asked Jaitley for a September 1999 profile on Rediff.com. 'I presume I am not,' Jaitley replied. 'Which, of course, is high Jaitleyism,' Bhosle wrote, 'the kind that makes us go weak-kneed. It could mean: he's not a flirt; he's a wicked flirt; he only supposes he's no flirt.'

In 2000, *Asiaweek* magazine included Jaitley in a list of India's most promising young political leaders, quoting a diplomat who called him 'the modern face of India, a brilliant man with a clean image'. Even the rare critical article acknowledged his abilities; a November 2003 *India Today* article, headlined 'Under Scrutiny', said, 'Suave, urbane, articulate, Jaitley's public face is mostly visible in television studios, aggressively defending the Government on a wide range of issues, where his sharp legal brain is an obvious asset.'

This public face was ballasted by a fund of private information. 'No two persons can have an affair in Delhi that Jaitley won't know about,' the veteran journalist who has covered the BJP for thirty years said. In his memoir *Editor Unplugged*, the editor Vinod Mehta wrote that 'although hung up on upward political mobility and, possibly, the biggest gossip in Delhi', Jaitley 'likes the company of literate journalists and keeps himself well informed'. When Mehta's *Outlook* magazine did a cover story on 'India's Best Gossips', in 2009, Jaitley took top spot. 'For the lawyerpolitician, gossip is not just social currency or amusement, it is a genuine passion,' the piece said. 'Journalists lucky enough to be invited into his inner circle say . . . he entertains them with his rich fund of stories about the private lives of everyone, including journalists and editors.'

Outlook's list was crowded with Jaitley's friends: former journalist and Congress MP Rajeev Shukla, Samajwadi Party leader Amar Singh, Suhel Seth, and Virendra and Coomi Kapoor. The story characterized the Kapoors as a 'gossip cartel', noting that though 'there's not a thing that goes on in the corridors of power that either one or the other of this power couple is not privy to . . . Arun Jaitley is a no-no area'. Many people I interviewed insisted that journalists sympathetic to Jaitley acted as mouthpieces for the opinions he wouldn't publicly voice.

During Jaitley's initial years as a minister—first of information and broadcasting, and then of law and justice—these opinions contributed to the increasing alienation of Vajpayee, the prime minister, as younger BJP leaders scrabbled for proximity to Advani, who was tipped to take over the top post. In June 2002, in the aftermath of the failed India–Pakistan talks at Agra the previous year, *The Time* magazine ran a cover story on Vajpayee titled 'Asleep at the Wheel?' After a colourful description of the prime minister's dietary habits and ill health, it stated that he 'is given to interminable silences, indecipherable ramblings and, not infrequently, falling asleep in meetings . . . an unusual candidate to control a nuclear arsenal'. The former BJP general secretary called the story as 'a noticeable debriefing' by Jaitley. 'That trait was noticed in him very clearly for the first time' after *The Time* article, he said, 'and Vajpayee was very angry'. Several others also cited Jaitley's 'lack of control' as the reason for Vajpayee's opposition to his advancement.

The BJP MP I spoke to, however, said that Vajpayee was particularly upset by Jaitley's references to his adopted family. A senior journalist told me about a conversation that took place at a BJP national executive meeting in Bhopal, while 'sitting in the Jehan Numa Palace hotel and having coffee after dinner', with two other journalists. 'Jaitley walked up to us . . . and immediately started bad-mouthing Vajpayee and Ranjan Bhattacharya,' the prime minister's son-in-law. 'Jaitley said, "He has a son-in-law who is a failed businessman. A failed businessman is dangerous because they love power."' Vajpayee's family got wind of this conversation: Bhattacharya later ribbed the journalist about the 'long chat session in Jehan Numa'. The senior Delhi BJP leader and the BJP MP said Advani's trust in Jaitley extended beyond professional issues, and that he sought Jaitley's help to resolve a personal matter as well.

Mohan Guruswamy, a special adviser to the finance minister in Vajpayee's government, has known Jaitley since the late 1980s; the two shared a closeness to Advani and met regularly at the India International Centre. He described Jaitley as a 'durbar politician', who, 'after making an argument, looks at everybody for approval with a big smile. That is his characteristic habit.' Even Advani, he said, was not immune from Jaitley's tongue. 'Four, five of us would have lunch at Advani's house,' Guruswamy said. 'We would step out and Jaitley would immediately start abusing him. It was the same with Vajpayee and everybody else. You can't have a conversation with him for more than five minutes before he starts abusing somebody.'

Political journalists thrived on the BJP's internal mud-slinging. Dissecting the 'internecine war', in the BJP in *Outlook* in 2002, the reporter Saba Naqvi wrote that 'the old rivalries and manoeuvrings between second-rung leaders of the BJP like Arun Jaitley, Sushma Swaraj and Pramod Mahajan . . . operates at a very petty level, like the Jaitley camp using friendly publications to plant stories about Swaraj', who took over as information minister in 2000, and Swaraj in turn 'blacking him out of Doordarshan's national network'. (According to the BJP-friendly editor who is critical of Jaitley, when he lost the information ministry, 'Nusli

Wadia helped him get the shipping ministry with a promise of cabinet post soon.')

Virendra Kapoor's gossip column on Rediff.com, Capital Buzz, typically painted Jaitley in a positive light, attacking his rivals and often singling out Swaraj. 'Whenever she comes under media attack, which is quite often,' Kapoor wrote in 1999, 'thanks to her talents in that direction, she starts blaming one or another BJP leader. She would not counter the report with facts, oh no, not she! Instead, she would rush to senior party leaders complaining "look what that man has done to me!".' Kapoor insisted to me that 'Jaitley is not a politician for me, and I am not a journalist for him'. When someone recently insinuated that Jaitley had fed him a story about Modi, he said, 'I felt bad that poor Jaitley is being faulted for no fault of his.'

When *The Time* article appeared, Jaitley had been the minister of law and justice for two years—he took over the position from Ram Jethmalani, who still holds it against him. The same month, June 2002, there was a cabinet reshuffle, and Jaitley was removed from his post. In *Outlook*, Arnab Pratim Dutta, a journalist who knew Vajpayee's adopted family well, wrote that, 'According to sources close to him, Vajpayee, till the end of his tenure, will call the shots. Says a PMO official: "It is another matter that Vajpayee wants Advani to succeed him. But while in office, he'd like to prove that he's not as ineffective as *The Time* magazine has painted him to be."' The political editor who has covered the BJP for three decades remembered Jaitley being 'very, very low—that was the lowest point in his political career'. Despite Vajpayee's ire, however, Jaitley was brought back as law minister after six months, in January 2003; the government needed its best legal brain.

That April, Shamit Mukherjee, a Delhi High Court judge appointed by Jaitley, was arrested for exchanging favourable verdicts for material favours. A few days later, Akshaya Mukul in the *Times of India* noted that the arrest 'has led law minister Arun Jaitley to speed up legislation to ensure transparency in appointments and check cases of improper behaviour by judges'. However, as Mukul reported, the paper had documents suggesting that, in 2001, 'the Union law ministry has itself been willing to overlook questions raised by the Intelligence Bureau about the integrity of candidates'. According to the article, the law ministry had recommended Adarsh K. Goel—a current Supreme Court judge and once the general secretary of the lawyers' wing of the RSS—to the Punjab and Haryana High Court, despite an adverse (IB) finding from the Intelligence Bureau report. According to Mukul, when President K.R. Narayanan did not approve Goel's appointment, Jaitley wrote 'a confidential note', dismissing 'the IB finding on Goel's integrity as a "slur"'. Eventually Narayanan approved the report.

Jaitley sent a rejoinder to the *Times of India* and called a press conference the day after the story appeared. He argued that 'the Government expresses its opinion and is, thereafter, bound by the advice of the collegium of the Supreme Court. The Government in this case acted accordingly.' Mukul replied that Jaitley's confidential note, in which he wrote that 'political leanings per se should not stand in the way of a recommendee for consideration of his case for appointment as a Judge of a High Court' went beyond a government expressing its opinion.

The *India Today* article 'Under Scrutiny' accused Jaitley of various misuses of power both as the law minister and during the six months that he was not a member of the Cabinet. The law ministry wrote a letter in defence of Jaitley; the magazine responded that it had on-the-record statements proving that Jaitley had been indirectly involved in several crucial appointments that he should not have had authority over. A former editor familiar with the story told me the source of these statements was Ashok Saikia, a powerful joint secretary in the prime minister's office. He added that Prabhu Chawla himself had 'got the papers from the PMO'. (Once friends, Chawla and Jaitley had by then fallen out.) Jaitley 'remained quiet' after the magazine's rebuttal to the law ministry, the editor said.

The day after Jaitley's press conference about the *Times of India* article, Satyavrat Chaturvedi, a Congress spokesperson and MP, alleged in a television interview that 'My information is that Intelligence Bureau did not clear' Mukherjee, either—'It was overruled by Arun Jaitley,' he alleged. When I met him recently, Chaturvedi said, 'Arun Jaitley never challenged me on that claim. Neither did he refuse. Silence was his only response.' He added, 'Every issue has its own lifespan in politics.'

In 1999, Jaitley was allotted 9 Ashoka Road, next door to the BJP headquarters, as his official bungalow. Never one to miss an opportunity to play host to the leaders of the day, Jaitley gave up 'his ministerial house to the BJP', wrote Virendra Kapoor, 'so that the party bigwigs who do not own a house in the capital would have a roof over their heads'. Besides the wedding of Virender Sehwag, the house has hosted the nuptials of the children of journalists such as the Kapoors, Shekhar Gupta, and the *Pioneer* editor Chandan Mitra. The senior Delhi BJP leader said that Jaitley courted Murli Manohar Joshi while he was BJP president, in the early 1990s, even offering him 'a flat in trans-Yamuna area to live in'. It was after Joshi's 1991 Rashtriya Ekta Yatra, he told me, that Jaitley also took note of Narendra Modi, who had organized the tour.

The RSS member Alok Kumar said Jaitley had 'the ability to sift people according to their importance and build up on all those who matter'. Of all the relationships Jaitley has nurtured over the years, his careful friendship with Modi—going back to when

Modi was an ambitious *pracharak* from Gujarat—has paid the richest dividends, even if it may be built on a foundation of mutual benefit rather than trust. In many ways, the two complement each other: one a popular leader, the other with an elite following; one an outsider to Delhi, the other the consummate insider. In 1995, when the BJP came to power in Gujarat and Modi was sent to work in Delhi, Jaitley was among the people he cultivated. A senior editor who considers Modi a friend told me that 'Jaitley is the quintessential networker in Delhi, so he would take care of Modi like he would take care of a raft of people. But nobody else did that to Modi and nobody took him seriously at that time.' Many journalists and BJP leaders remember Modi as a regular visitor to Jaitley's house in south Delhi. The lawyer Dushyant Dave, who shared an office with Jaitley between 1992 and 1997, told me Modi visited there as well.

In 1999, Modi and Jaitley expressed their admiration for each other on two episodes of Rajeev Shukla's television show *Rubaru*. Modi dated their relationship to the JP movement, and described Jaitley as 'a rare combination in politics', an 'activist, an intellectual, articulate, very clean, and also a very friendly man'. Though some had doubted Jaitley's abilities at first, Modi said 'the best thing about Arun-ji is his total dedication to whatever work he is given. A person who has such dedication in life rarely fails.' When Shukla subsequently interviewed Jaitley about Modi, Jaitley returned the compliments, calling Modi a 'tough taskmaster', a 'disciplinarian' and a 'creative' politician.

Advani wrote about both Modi and Jaitley as protégés in his autobiography, though he reserved his highest praise for Pramod Mahajan, whose dominance undercut the competition between the others. The former BJP general secretary told me that 'Jaitley, Modi and Venkaiah Naidu emerged as a faction opposed to Mahajan. Later, Ananth Kumar also joined them. They were closer to Nusli Wadia, and Mahajan was close to the Ambanis. First, Venkaiah led the group, with Modi and Jaitley at the flanks. Then, Jaitley led the group, with Modi and Venkaiah at the flanks. Since 2005, Modi is leading from the front.' Mahajan was murdered in 2006.

But Modi's and Jaitley's early political careers ran parallel paths. Modi became the BJP's general secretary in 1998, and Jaitley became a party spokesperson in 1999. Neither had yet won an election, but both were poised for promotions. That year, when Jaitley became the minister of information and broadcasting, he was nominated to the Rajya Sabha from Gujarat. Two years later, Modi became the chief minister of that state. Then, in 2002, when Modi dissolved the Gujarat legislative assembly eight months early—presumably to capitalize on pro-BJP sentiments in the aftermath of the anti-Muslim riots that year—Jaitley was made the party-in-charge for the subsequent elections.

Modi came up against the chief election commissioner, J.M. Lyngdoh, who vetoed polling before the rehabilitation of the riot victims. When the chief minister publicly lashed out at Lyngdoh, attempting to insult him by calling attention to his Christian name, Vajpayee condemned Modi's speech. But Advani and Jaitley supported him, deepening existing rifts in the BJP. Calling Lyngdoh 'a cowboy bureaucrat' who 'thinks the commission becomes God', Jaitley argued that the election commission was constitutionally bound to conduct polling within six months, and convinced his party to challenge Lyngdoh's decision. He argued in favour of the BJP's position in the Supreme Court, in September 2002.

Vajpayee was not pleased. That month, an *Outlook* story headlined 'Unhappy Atal Thinks of Quitting' quoted an anonymous cabinet minister saying, '"The PM has told some of us that Narendra Modi would never have tried to pull off this stunt of resigning in between assembly terms if Jaitley had not advised him to do so." Every time the Gujarat issue is put to rest, the PM feels that it is at Jaitley's insistence that it is again revived.' (Jaitley was 'ballistic' over the story, editor Vinod Mehta wrote later in his memoir, and 'tried to extricate the name of the source'.)

That October, when the Supreme Court upheld Lyngdoh's decision, Jaitley didn't emerge from the scrap looking very good. Rajeev Dhavan, a lawyer who appeared in the case, explained in *The Hindu* how the BJP's 'entire basic legal strategy' was based on a misreading of the constitution, and 'had backfired'. But the whole affair strengthened the relationship between Jaitley and Modi.

So did another incident at the party's national executive meeting in Goa, the April after the riots. Vajpayee planned to sack Modi from the BJP, and Jaitley, following Advani's instructions, played a strategic role on behalf of the party's hardliners. A day before the meeting, he went to Ahmedabad and spoke to Modi, who then offered to quit the next day. The party rejected his offer, saving face while staying intact. By the time the next Gujarat assembly elections were held in December, Jaitley was, as Rediff.com reported, Modi's 'tireless defender'.

IV

On an early morning in July 2005, Jaitley was walking near his home in south Delhi's Kailash Colony with his friend Ranjit Kumar—a senior lawyer who has been amicus curiae in several Supreme Court cases, and who became solicitor general last year—when he started coughing and complained of breathlessness. Within ten minutes, Kumar had rushed him to Escorts Hospital and called noted heart surgeon Naresh Trehan. Trehan lived near enough 'to reach fast, and fortunately everything worked out',

Kumar told me. A few days later, Jaitley, then fifty-two years old, had triple bypass surgery.

Jaitley was at an age when most Indian politicians start reaping the fruits of their careers. But in 2005, as a senior advocate and a BJP general secretary, he still had a long way to go to live up to the title of 'future prime minister' that some of his friends, including Prabhu Chawla, had given him in the 1990s. In December, when Advani stepped down as BJP president, Jaitley may have felt it was his turn: after all, his contemporary Venkaiah Naidu had been elected president a few years earlier.

But the competition within the party was intensifying, as the BJP went through an organizational crisis in the aftermath of its loss in the 2004 general elections. In November 2005, after Shivraj Singh Chouhan became chief minister of Madhya Pradesh, a news report in the Bhopal edition of *Dainik Jagran* claimed that Uma Bharti, who had held the post the previous year, had threatened suicide over the decision. K.N. Govindacharya, a former BJP general secretary close to Bharti, implied that Jaitley had a hand in the article, telling Rediff.com that he had asked Jaitley to speak to Bharti earlier, 'But there are certain things that are kept under wraps . . . I would advice [sic] Arun Jaitley to keep politics away from the personal relationship and desist from off the record briefings. If this is what happens to Umaji then which decent woman would like to join politics.' Govindacharya also told *Tehelka* that, 'Leaders like Arun Jaitley would continue to run slanderous campaigns to tarnish image of leaders with mass following.' He added, 'Internal democracy is being finished in political parties.'

Passing over Jaitley, the RSS supported Rajnath Singh, a Thakur leader from Uttar Pradesh and a compromise candidate, as BJP president. The post was a crown of thorns for Singh, who soon had his hands full with squabbling leaders. He barely had a chance to settle into his position before he too was receiving negative coverage. A series of stories, painting Singh as a country bumpkin who only used Indian-style loos, appeared in the *Economic Times*. A senior editor with the newspaper said that Singh called him in early 2006 to complain about the '*atyachar*'— atrocities—being printed about him in the paper, and pointed the finger at Jaitley. 'I conveyed Rajnath Singh's message to the editor, after which a course correction was done and the frequency of Jaitley pictures and stories came down drastically,' the senior editor said. The 'Jaitley spin', he said, wasn't subtle.

In February 2007, Singh removed Jaitley as the BJP's chief spokesperson after informing Vajpayee and Advani. He also neglected to credit Jaitley, who was managing the Punjab assembly election, for the BJP's impressive results there. 'Jaitley was not part of the bonhomie and camaraderie on display at the party headquarters,' the *Telegraph* reported. 'He did not even shake hands with Rajnath. Since he was removed as BJP spokesperson, Jaitley has not stepped into the party headquarters and the media room except to attend meetings where his presence is necessary.'

But Jaitley's fortunes in the party were on the rise, largely due to the unexpected death of Pramod Mahajan, who had been in charge of the 2004 general elections even though Jaitley had steered the party successfully in a couple of state elections by then. Mahajan died in April 2006, and in 2008, Jaitley's involvement in the BJP's historic win in Karnataka furthered the impression that he had the Midas touch when it came to campaign strategy. That June, his friend Swapan Dasgupta wrote in *Tehelka*, 'With such an enviable track record of election management, it is only natural that many in the BJP would want him to be entrusted with the national campaign for 2009—if only to avoid the disasters of 2004.' Later that year, Jaitley was put in charge of the 2009 Lok Sabha elections by Advani, the prime ministerial candidate.

Sushil Pandit, who has devised the communication strategy for the BJP since 1989, told me that Jaitley 'enjoys a good contest. If he is in the middle of it all, as a captain marshalling his resources, it gives him a high.' G.V.L. Narasimha Rao, a BJP spokesperson and a pollster, who called himself 'an extension of Jaitley's team', told me, 'The politicians always ask, after a survey, "How many seats are we going to win?" But I have not come across any politician who asked me a question like Jaitley asked: "What is our vote share? What is our vote share gap with our political rival?"' According to Rao, Jaitley is a micro-manager. 'In Gujarat, he had managed the media campaign, the advertising campaign and all the legal issues. That's why probably Modi-ji wanted him again and again,' he said.

Jaitley is also seen as a capable ambassador in seat-sharing negotiations. In the run-up to the 2009 elections, Dasgupta wrote on his blog that Jaitley 'is the bridge to NDA partners such as Nitish Kumar in Bihar, the slippery Ajit Singh in Uttar Pradesh and the two Badals in Punjab. He is also the BJP's main fund raiser—a crucial responsibility in these difficult times.' But beyond Dasgupta—'When it comes to the subject of Arun Jaitley, I drop all pretensions of objectivity,' he wrote in 2009—there is little consensus on whether Jaitley is a master campaign strategist, or an opportunist who picks his battles wisely. The BJP-friendly editor, who hasn't always supported Jaitley, said, 'He would always go for the state that is bound to win. For instance, Madhya Pradesh after two terms of Digvijaya Singh was handed out on a platter. How can he take credit for Gujarat? He failed in Uttar Pradesh, West Bengal and Himachal Pradesh. His failure rate is higher.' The political editor who has covered the BJP for three decades wondered 'whether the situation was ripe for BJP to win or was it his clever strategy? In 2009 Lok Sabha elections he failed completely, isn't it?'

A former Congress minister I met described Jaitley's ability to come out on top. 'He first became an additional solicitor general then made senior advocate overnight. He became a minister first, and then was nominated as a Rajya Sabha MP. He lost his election in 2014 from Amritsar, but he became the finance minister,' he said. Many members of the BJP were shocked when, in 2009, even after the party's biggest electoral loss in twenty years, Jaitley was awarded his highest position yet—leader of the Opposition in the Rajya Sabha—rather than becoming a scapegoat as the chief campaign strategist. According to three of the BJP politicians I spoke to, the post was originally meant to go to Venkaiah Naidu, but Advani replaced his name with Jaitley's at the last minute.

In 2009, the BJP won only 116 seats—twenty-two less than its 2004 tally. When the party's national executive met in June to analyse the defeat, Jaitley was holidaying in London, catching up on the India–England cricket series. Nearly everyone who spoke at the meeting attacked Jaitley. Uttar Pradesh MP Maneka Gandhi complained that he seemed to have a lot of time to talk to journalists, but would not pick up candidates' phone calls. The BJP MP Arun Shourie suggested on NDTV that the BJP should 'like once Mao Zedong said, bombard the headquarters. Clean up everybody from the top,' and allow the RSS to take charge of the party. Jaitley started openly criticizing Shourie after this.

Two senior party leaders, Jaswant Singh and Yashwant Sinha, wrote letters demanding that those responsible for the campaign also claim responsibility for its failure, as Mahajan had done in 2004. 'Advani-ji set a fine example of accountability by declining to take up the position of the leader of Opposition in Lok Sabha,' Sinha wrote. 'It appears as if some people in the party are determined to ensure that the principle of accountability does not prevail so that their own little perch is not disturbed.'

Jaitley's critics in the party pointed out that he hadn't shown enough commitment; he had continued to attend court throughout the campaign. A BJP leader close to the RSS told me that Jaitley 'would come after court hours. Because of him the meetings started at 4 p.m. He was the main reason for debacle.' In the run-up to the elections, Jaitley had refused to attend two central election committee meetings, protesting Rajnath Singh's appointment of Sudhanshu Mittal, an acolyte of Mahajan, as the party's man in charge of the North-east. Though Jaitley later patched up with Singh, several senior leaders felt his actions had demoralized the cadre. The political editor who has covered the BJP for three decades told me that Modi's support was a possible reason Jaitley 'escaped disciplinary action'.

Despite rumours that Jaitley would quit the party, he countered by blaming the electoral defeat on the divisive nature of the campaign. 'Sober governance helps, shrillness does not. Moderation and understatement are virtues,' he wrote. This put him in a tricky position. 'It's all very well for Arun Jaitley to call for moderation and an end to shrillness but for many years now he has been Narendra Modi's ambassador in Delhi,' Vir Sanghvi wrote in the *Hindustan Times*. 'He has consistently defended Modi's behaviour during the Gujarat riots, has attacked anyone who dares question Modi and during this campaign, he sang Modi's praises.'

Other journalists close to Jaitley, including Dasgupta, exhorted the party to shun 'the H word'—Hindutva—even as they supported Modi as the party's new hope. Soon after the results, the columnist Ashok Malik called Modi's 'unqualified triumph' in Gujarat 'the saving grace' of the election. 'In 2009,' he wrote, 'Advani led the campaign almost by default, a result of the BJP's TINA (There Is No Alternative) factor. The response to TINA is NITA: Narendra Is the Alternative.'

Prabhu Chawla is fond of saying that 'the only election Arun Jaitley has ever won in his life was on my scooter'—a reference to Jaitley's DUSU days. An anonymous pamphlet distributed in Parliament during the monsoon session of 2012 also pointed to Jaitley's lack of an election record as his Achilles heel. Jaitley, it said mockingly, 'last won a landmark DUSU election from amongst 4000 electorate in 1975'. The former BJP MLA Alok Kumar told me Jaitley once consoled him after he lost an election in 2008 by saying 'we are both not cut out for electoral politics'.

But when Modi made a serious bid for the prime ministerial post in the 2014 general elections, Jaitley faced his demons and contested a Lok Sabha seat from Amritsar. The Delhiwalla awkwardly tried to project himself as somebody with 'a 100 per cent Majhhis ancestry'—that is, from the Majha region of Punjab. Jaitley told *Open* magazine—and every reporter willing to listen—'I belong here from all possible sides.' 'Perhaps,' he said, 'my ability to win polls was earlier less than my utility to organize polls. So my party decided on my political future. But I'm glad that I'm contesting at last.'

But Jaitley's choice of constituency wasn't well calculated. He had allied with the ruling Akali Dal government, despite a great deal of anti-incumbency against them in the state. The Congress then sprung a doughty opponent, former Punjab chief minister Amarinder Singh, upon him. And his campaign manager, Bikram Singh Majithia, had a reputation for being corrupt. A journalist working on the desk at the *Hindustan Times* wrote a snippet noting these difficulties. That journalist was soon fired, according to a former editor at the newspaper, who said the decision 'came right from the top' and that while the journalist was sacked on grounds of 'incompetence', the editor believed this person was 'competent and shouldn't have gone'. Jaitley had his supporters—those who turned out to back him included advocates Mukul Rohatgi, Ranjit Kumar, Maninder Singh and Rajiv Nayar; Shobhana Bhartia; veteran journalist Kuldip Nayar; actors Anupam and Kirron Kher; cricketer Gautam Gambhir; and even former Karnataka chief minister B.S. Yeddyurappa—but ultimately lost the election by over one lakh votes.

Kumar attributed the loss to Jaitley's inability to connect with 'a person on the street'. An editor who described himself as a BJP ideologue and a Jaitley critic told me, 'He has managed to build up every lobby in India except for one, the voters of India.' A popular joke, attributed to the Aam Aadmi Party MP Bhagwant Mann, noted that, 'Jaitley is the only one who could defeat the Modi wave by losing Amritsar.'

Still, Modi had hinted at an important role for Jaitley during his campaign speech in Amritsar. Once he became prime minister, he gave Jaitley the portfolios of finance, defence and corporate affairs, overlooking his electoral defeat. These appointments followed months of speculation on the nature of the relationship between the two politicians.

In the run-up to the 2014 elections, Modi had not quite consolidated his position as prime ministerial candidate and a committed section of his supporters felt that Jaitley was holding him back. M.D. Nalapat, the editorial director of the *Sunday Guardian*, wrote in September 2013 that it was 'disquiet' at Modi's perceived reliance on Arun Jaitley 'that caused Sushma Swaraj and M.M. Joshi to cast their lot initially with L.K. Advani' as the better candidate. He quoted an unnamed BJP leader who argued that Jaitley was only supporting Modi in the secret hope 'that after the elections he will not get the support needed to form the government', after which Jaitley, 'the man closest to Narendra Modi', would 'step forward as the secular choice' for prime minister, as Vajpayee had once done. According to the

BJP MP I spoke to, the article upset both Modi and Jaitley; Modi didn't speak to Nalapat for a few months.

Madhu Kishwar, an academic and the author of the pro-Modi book *Modi, Muslims and Media*, expanded on these theories. In March 2014, she had tweeted: 'BJP insiders: Jaitley belongs to 160 Club—coz he thinks he has bright chance of becoming PM if BJP gets less than 180 seats. Hence sabotage.'

'The BJP insiders those days told me Arun Jaitley was egging Nitish Kumar on,' Kishwar told me, in Kumar's campaign against Modi, 'because he didn't want Modi to be stigma-free.' She broached the issue with Modi during an interview. 'I told him, "One person you have to watch out for is Arun Jaitley." He said, "*Nahin, Madhu-ji, woh mere bade achhe mitra hain.*" I said, "He might be your good friend. But as an impartial observer, I can tell you this friendship will be a millstone around your neck."'

Jethmalani, in an interview to the *Economic Times*, observed that Modi 'keeps his enemies closer', referring to both Jaitley and Sushma Swaraj, who had openly opposed Modi's candidacy but was still given the external affairs portfolio. In *Editor Unplugged*, Vinod Mehta wrote that Jaitley was Modi's 'sole friend . . . if you can call him that'. Jaitley 'has helped him in legal matters', Mehta held, but 'is not close in the conventional sense. Modi finds him convenient at the present time for certain tasks. However, he knows well no one covets his present job more than Jaitley.' However, several senior journalists, including both political editors, told me Jaitley had long ago accepted a secondary role to Modi.

V

Last November, in a cover story on India's 'Axis of Power 2014', *Open* magazine called Modi, the BJP president Amit

Shah and Jaitley 'the three men who rule India'. A week later, *India Today* ran a cover story on 'The Indispensable Mr Jaitley', analysing the same triumvirate. 'Assuming a cross-mythological referencing is allowed in this age of Hindutva,' it said, 'if Modi is Ram, then Shah and Jaitley are his Lakshman and Arjun, two aides who seemingly complete him and he cannot do without.' The article said Jaitley's 'unsurpassable network of contacts across the political, legal and social spectrum makes him uniquely qualified to sit on any side of the Prime Minister', noting that Modi needed to leverage the impressive election results 'across the Capital's several columns of clout, such as the media, the corporate and the diplomatic world'. The truth is, it continued, 'that Ahmedabad is not Delhi—and certainly, Gujarat is not India'.

On the surface, these articles projected a chummy camaraderie between Modi and Jaitley, on the six-month anniversary of the BJP's general election victory. But a month after the *Open* and *India Today* cover stories appeared, the prime minister invited several members of the press to a series of interactions. A senior journalist with a national daily mentioned the *India Today* story as a possible reason for the interaction he attended, which he said appeared to be the prime minister's attempt to create his own direct line to the media. An editor of a south Indian newspaper told me he was informally contacted to attend a similar meeting, which never took place, because, as the man who invited him hinted, Modi felt '*woh log to Jaitley ko pasand karte hain*'—but those people like Jaitley. 'It was an aside,' the editor said, 'but a loaded aside.'

'After becoming PM,' the senior journalist with regular access to the finance minister told me, 'Modi's circle of friendships has multiplied so much that he doesn't need Jaitley beyond a point.' There is still 'a huge gap between number two, Amit Shah, and Jaitley', he said, and to suggest that Modi consults Jaitley as frequently as he consults Shah is 'exaggerated propaganda'.

Jaitley does have a large camp of supporters in the government: Nirmala Sitharaman, Dharmendra Pradhan and Piyush Goyal—respectively, the ministers of commerce, petroleum and power—are among his protégés. And his friends feature prominently on the government's roster of legal officers: the attorney general, Mukul Rohatgi; the solicitor general, Ranjit Kumar; and the additional solicitors general Pinky Anand, Maninder Singh, P.S. Narasimha and Neeraj Kishan Kaul (in whose chamber Jaitley's son Rohan worked as a junior).

In February, soon after he was awarded the Padma Bhushan, Swapan Dasgupta was appointed as an independent director to the board of Larsen & Toubro, a multinational infrastructure company, in which the ministry of finance holds a stake of about 8.18 per cent. Shekhar Iyer, another journalist close to Jaitley, was appointed as a member of the Film Certification Appellate Tribunal, which comes under Jaitley's information and broadcasting ministry, in January.

When it comes to the finance ministry, Modi appears to be keeping Jaitley on a shorter leash, and steadily placing men loyal to himself in its offices. Hasmukh Adhia, who was Modi's principal secretary in Gujarat, was made the secretary of the department of financial services last November. G.C. Murmu, a Gujarat bureaucrat who handled riot-related cases for Modi when he was chief minister, and Raj Kumar, another Gujarat-cadre officer, were appointed joint secretaries in the department of expenditure and the department of economic affairs respectively. A senior journalist based in Gujarat described their absolute loyalty to Modi, and told me that, 'Murmu, in likelihood, will be made the director of enforcement directorate after he is empanelled additional secretary,' pointing out that, 'Modi has kept that post vacant for a while now.'

In a government of relatively closed ranks, Jaitley has still been the target of some criticism. His most vocal detractor is his old nemesis, Ram Jethmalani. When I met the ninety-two-year-old lawyer, he reiterated his statements at the Jaipur Literature Festival this January, when he questioned the choice of Jaitley as finance minister. In a letter to Modi, Jethmalani hinted that Jaitley's appointment would benefit the Congress, and in an open letter to Jaitley he wrote, 'I want to show to the nation that you are determined to see that Prime Minister Modi can never fulfil his pledge to the unfortunate people of India to get back the black money'—a reference to funds illegally funnelled out of the country to avoid taxes. 'You, Mr Finance Minister,' Jethmalani accused, 'are the biggest obstacle.'

'I am living in the departure lounge of god and he's the only one I don't like,' Jethmalani told me. He is one amongst a faction of Modi supporters—some of whom were once close to Jaitley but have now aligned themselves against him—that includes Madhu Kishwar, the RSS ideologue S. Gurumurthy, and, sometimes, Subramanian Swamy. This group alleges that Jaitley has supported P. Chidambaram, the former finance minister, against allegations made by this group, of money laundering and tax evasion, particularly through shell companies belonging to the news channel NDTV.

Karanjawala told me Chidambaram and Jaitley were 'decent friends' who had known each other since the 1990s, when both were lawyers in a succession war at the *Indian Express*. The anti-Jaitley contingent believes the relationship goes deeper, pointing to Jaitley's defence of Chidambaram in a 1997 corruption case filed by Swamy. Last year, after Kishwar made some of the allegations against Chidambaram and NDTV on the website of Manushi, a trust she runs, NDTV filed a defamation case against her. Gurumurthy impleaded himself in the case, and Jethmalani has represented Kishwar in court. K.P.S. Gill, the former director general of police in Punjab and a security adviser to Modi after the 2002 riots, also threw his weight behind the group. In a letter to Jaitley, he argued that the finance minister ought to order a special investigation into the case involving Chidambaram and NDTV and to recuse himself from involvement in it due to his previous legal support for both these parties. In other instances, as Gill pointed out, Jaitley has removed himself from situations in which his work as a lawyer might compromise his judgement as a politician.

In 2006, arguing on behalf of Sushil Modi, then the BJP's leader of the Opposition in Bihar, in a defamation case, Jaitley said that 'in performing his duties and obligations, the leader of the Opposition is supposed to take into account not only what he is today but what he hopes to be tomorrow'. Three years later, as the leader of the Opposition in the Rajya Sabha, he seemed to have few such compunctions. The industry magazine *TelecomLive* raised one example of this in a 2012 cover story that explored Jaitley's position, while leader of the Opposition, on the telecom company Vodafone. While Murli Manohar Joshi, Finance Minister Yashwant Sinha and Sushma Swaraj, the leader of the Opposition in the Lok Sabha, supported an amendment in the income tax law that could force Vodafone to pay as much as Rs 20,000 crore in retroactive taxes, Jaitley and Piyush Goyal vehemently opposed it in the upper house. Citing the fact that Jaitley had appeared five times on behalf of Vodafone in the Delhi High Court in 2008 and 2009, *TelecomLive* alleged that 'Analjit Singh, the present chairman of Vodafone Essar Limited (VEL) has a good relationship with Mr Jaitley. He has been lobbying with Mr Jaitley for his support . . .'

In 2014, when Jaitley became the finance minister, the case was still unresolved, and he did recuse himself, deputing his ministerial authority in the matter. 'I stopped practising as a lawyer with effect from 2nd June, 2009,' he wrote on his Facebook page. 'Prior to that, I had been consulted in the matter by the company on various taxation issues. I therefore considered it appropriate not to deal with the matter as a Minister.'

Like many politicians, Jaitley sees little conflict of interest between his professional actions—in his case as legal counsel to some of the country's most powerful private companies and individuals—and his legislative and executive roles. In 2005, while he was a member of Parliament from Gujarat, Jaitley defended the stockbroker Ketan Parekh against charges of defrauding Madhavpura Mercantile Cooperative Bank in the state of Rs 840 crore. Jaitley got Parekh out of jail on bail (he was later convicted). Angry depositors demanded Jaitley's resignation, and some senior BJP leaders complained to Advani, who was also an MP from the state. Jaitley told the media that legal propriety forbade him from speaking on the matter. In a scathing critique, the business journalist Sucheta Dalal wrote, 'Logically, politically and ethically, it would have been more fitting if Mr. Jaitley's services were available free (pro bono) to the depositors of MMCB.' While Jaitley's position was legally sound, it raised serious questions about his commitment, as a public representative, to the public good.

In January, the former cricketer Bishan Singh Bedi and others wrote a complaint to Narendra Modi about his finance minister. Jaitley had 'misused his position as Leader of Opposition to prevail upon various ministries to spare DDCA of punitive action', they wrote, referring to the Delhi and District Cricket Association. 'Mr Jaitley is now heading two important ministries (finance and corporate affairs) which are supposed to take action against DDCA for infraction of various rules and norms of the companies act, as indeed criminal law.'

As the journalist James Astill wrote in his 2013 book *The Great Tamasha: Cricket, Corruption and the Turbulent Rise of Modern India*, 'No Indian cricket administration is so notorious for nepotism and misrule' as the association that governs Delhi cricket, 'also known as the Delhi Daddies Cricket Association, or the Delhi District Crooks Association'. Jaitley became the DDCA's president in December 1999, less than two years after he became a member of the association and a few months after he became a Union minister. He held the post for thirteen years.

Ashok Malik, the columnist and Jaitley's friend, told me Jaitley was driven by 'his love for cricket', and the 'social cachet'. As Astill observed, 'There is no surer way to be seen by millions of Indians than at a televised cricket match.' To be seen 'ruling over the proceedings', he said, 'is especially useful for politicians, such as Jaitley . . . who are not directly elected to Parliament . . . In such cases, prominence in Indian cricket is almost an alternative to electoral prowess.'

The DDCA is a company that follows an opaque electoral system, which allows proxy voting on behalf of its members, many of whom are small-time businessmen who are never present. In February 2000, *Outlook* reported that this voting could be easily manipulated, and claimed to have 'two proxy forms signed by the same member—one of which is obviously a fake signature but is attested by the court—used during Jaitley's election' as president. However, the association's two rival factions, led by C.K. Khanna (known as 'proxy king') and S.P. Bansal, both supported Jaitley over the years.

The first clear sign of rot in the DDCA appeared in August 2009, when Virender Sehwag, then a star opener on the Indian team, and other cricketers including Gautam Gambhir, Ashish Nehra and Ishant Sharma, threatened to quit the Delhi team over rampant nepotism and corruption. This portended a major embarrassment that December, during the final match of the India–Sri Lanka one-day series at Ferozeshah Kotla stadium. The match was abandoned midway after the visiting team complained of dangerously poor pitch conditions leading to injuries. The DDCA apologized to irate fans and promised to refund their ticket money. The International Cricket Council banned the venue for one year, and the Congress demanded Jaitley's resignation from his post. Jaitley's response to the media was to play for time, saying, 'We have to analyse in a cooler environment.'

Though the Ferozeshah Kotla stadium underwent a massive renovation between 2000 and 2007, the state of the DDCA only deteriorated. The former Delhi captain Surinder Khanna told me about the muck that emerged out of the renovation—a project Malik characterized as Jaitley's greatest legacy. 'He built the stadium which nobody else could,' Khanna said, 'but we had to pay a heavy price as he created a mess.' He alleged that the annual general meetings, in which the association's accounts were put to vote, became a sham due to manipulated proxy voting. The initial budget for the project was Rs 24 crore, but the eventual expenditure came closer to Rs 130 crore.

For a long time, Kirti Azad, a former cricketer and a BJP MP from Bihar, was the sole voice of protest against Jaitley's rule of the DDCA. (For his part, Jaitley tried to deny Azad the party's ticket in his constituency for the 2009 Lok Sabha elections.) But by 2011, many other former players, including Bedi, Maninder Singh, Madan Lal and Surinder Khanna, joined the chorus. Several DDCA members sent letters to Jaitley, but never received responses. 'Ever since you took over . . . I am afraid that the general reputation of DDCA has gone southward,' the association member Dinesh Kumar Sharma wrote in 2011. 'This is mainly due to the fact that . . . the Executive Committee . . . under your patronage have usurped all the financial and administrative powers . . . causing substantial financial losses.'

The cricket journalist Chander Shekhar Luthra told me, 'I once asked Jaitley, "Only Rs 20 crore was spent for the Dharamshala stadium and it is beautiful. How come Delhi's stadium is so bad despite spending so much money?" His answer was a simple one-liner: "People drive Maruti and people drive Mercedes." Till date I have not understood what he meant.' Luthra added, 'But I have seen all these DDCA people from the time when they used to come on scooters to driving Mercedes today.'

In May 2012, Azad wrote a letter of complaint about the 'accounting mess' in the DDCA to R.P.N. Singh, then minister of state for corporate affairs. 'The accounts are blatantly falsified and false bills are shown to account for Rs 30 crore every year,' he wrote. He alleged financial fraud, illegal payments to members without proper clearances and illegal procurement without tenders. He followed this up with a letter to Jaitley that July, in which he wrote, 'I wish to request you not to make snide remarks about me or wife in the manipulated leaks.'

Later, Azad raised the issue in the monsoon session of Parliament, during which Jaitley was loudly accusing the UPA government of corruption in allocating coal blocks. The ministry of corporate affairs constituted a three-member team of the Serious Fraud Investigation Office (SFIO) to investigate Azad's claims. Azad told me he was called 'indirectly through many people', and given 'a lot of offers' to back down.

By the time the SFIO's report was completed, in March 2014, Jaitley was no longer DDCA president; he did not contest the 2013 election, though he was rumoured to be eyeing the top post in the BCCI. The SFIO's report confirmed Azad's allegations, and indicated that the DDCA had not complied with even basic accounting standards, such as using cheques for payments of above Rs 20,000. The SFIO pushed for an internal audit, which exposed even more financial mismanagement. The registrar of companies imposed a compounding fee of over Rs 4 lakh on the DDCA and three of its office bearers—Sunil Dev, S.P. Bansal and Narinder Batra—plus an additional fee on Dev and Bansal. Jaitley, however, escaped any indictment for the corruption under his watch.

'As a president, he can't say "I didn't know,"' Sameer Bahadur, a DDCA member, told me. During the association's 2012 annual general meeting, recorded on video, Azad had challenged Jaitley in a heated moment. 'You have sent in forged proxies here,' he said, 'You file a defamation case against me.' Jaitley responded, 'There are a lot of things I have been choosing to ignore, I will ignore this too.' He also called Azad and others 'a complaint-filing agency', and spoilsports.

Bahadur believes Jaitley stayed out of the 2013 elections because of a change in the Companies Act, which now recommended imprisonment, rather than relatively low fines, for fraud. While the SFIO and Azad were digging for evidence of corruption, Jaitley became its patron-in-chief, an honorary but influential position, instead of president. In August 2014, once Jaitley was finance minister with charge of the corporate affairs ministry, Azad raised the issue of DDCA corruption in Parliament again. This January, the DDCA lodged a police complaint against S.P. Bansal, who had replaced Jaitley as the association's president, and Anil Khanna, its general secretary, for illegally transferring Rs 1.55 crore to some realty companies; both were also sacked by the DDCA's executive committee. Because of the change in the company law, Bahadur told me, 'C.K. Khanna's faction has taken a stand against the president and general secretary.' Earlier, he said, 'they were hand in glove, and would blindly sign all the accounts', while Jaitley looked the other way.

'As they say in Bihar,' Azad told me, '*saiyan bhaye kotwal to dar kaahe ka?*'—when the policeman is your lover, what is there to fear? 'There has been an embezzlement of Rs 30 crore every year. But nobody talks about it. They will talk about the Saradha scam and other scams, but not this.' Jaitley has not been directly accused of corruption in the DDCA. But people like Bahadur hold him responsible for ignoring the warning signs. 'Jaitley couldn't run a company with an annual budget of Rs 30 crore,' Bahadur said. 'What can he do as finance minister of the country?'

Soon after Narendra Modi was sworn in as prime minister last May, reports emerged about his stern attempts to get his ministers in line. Though tensions continued to simmer within the party, details about them rarely leaked out to the press, barring a few glimpses. Yet as the *New Yorker* editor David Remnick observed in his profile of Václav Havel, the former President of Czechoslovakia, 'Political gossip, to say nothing of political journalism, abhors stasis.' Last August, the *Economic Times* reported that Rajnath Singh had complained about 'malicious and false stories', which were 'the handiwork of a party rival, an influential BJP leader', to BJP president Amit Shah and the RSS. In January, Smriti Irani, Modi's minister of human resource development, told the *Economic Times* that the persistent criticism she faced was 'a deliberate narrative, as far as I am concerned, which has been nicely seeded into the media', though she would not specify whether the narrative had been seeded by someone from her own party when asked that question.

Jaitley's image in the media remains relatively untarnished. 'If you do a Google search there is one politician against whom you will not find anything negative,' Kishwar said. 'His own track record is totally sanitized in media despite over four decades in public life.' However, the media did pick up on friction between the finance minister and the Reserve Bank of India (RBI) governor, Raghuram Rajan, over the past year—in a disagreement over interest rates that was unusually public for the two positions. This January, *Open* magazine wrote that both Jaitley and Rajan 'were upset with the concerted efforts by a group of officials to denigrate them', by spreading a 'whisper campaign' that there was a 'wedge' between them. Despite denials, and their united front during the presentation of the annual budget, reports of the rift continued. On 2 April, both Modi and Jaitley praised Rajan at an RBI function. 'There is lot of similarity between the thinking of the RBI and government,' Modi said. 'As a representative of the government, I express my satisfaction. RBI is performing its role and I congratulate Raghuram-ji and his team,' he added. A few weeks later, on 14 April, Jaitley was asked if he was unhappy with Rajan during an interview with NDTV, and he replied, 'There are no personal differences with RBI Governor Raghuram Rajan, just some conflicting viewpoints . . . The Prime Minister has very nice things to say about the Governor also.'

In the same interview, Jaitley also responded to the use of the word 'presstitutes' to refer to journalists by minister of state for external affairs, V.K. Singh, on Twitter. 'I personally don't agree that he should have said that,' he said. 'I am of the opinion that at times even when media commits excesses, it's better to look the other way.' Five days later, Modi came out full of praise for Singh at a meeting of BJP MPs, criticizing the media for ignoring his 'good work' in evacuating Indians from Yemen 'due to other reasons'—a reference to the backlash against the presstitutes remark.

Earlier this year, ahead of his budget speech in February, Jaitley was busy managing the BJP's Delhi assembly election campaign, projecting great confidence for the party. In late January, Jaitley told Headlines Today, 'My analysis is that we are comfortably ahead.' The BJP MP, who called Jaitley Modi's 'consigliere', said that the day before the polling 'Jaitley had predicted a margin of twenty-five seats'. A day after the party lost dramatically, winning an embarrassing three seats in an assembly of seventy, the BJP MP said, 'Modi called Rajnath, Gadkari, Venkaiah and Jaitley for a meeting'. The MP, who heard about the meeting from one of the leaders present, said, 'Modi told Jaitley, "*Kya aap ko koi rajnaitik aakalan hai*?"'—do you have any political sense?

A senior editor, who said he had been friends with Jaitley for twenty-seven years, said after Jaitley became finance minister, he 'has changed his style of functioning as per Modi's advice. He has addressed his limitation.' The editor continued, 'Modi told him "*Aapke pet mein kuch pachta nahin hai, patrakar ko bol dete hain*"'—you can't keep anything down, you talk to journalists. '"Now you have to put a Sellotape and behave like Pranab Mukherjee."' He added, 'Vajpayee's Arun Jaitley is different from Narendra Modi's Arun Jaitley. Now he's become responsible.'

In early December 2012, in a conversation with Vinod Jose, in his small, sequestered cabin, he suggested the idea of a story about the United Progressive Alliance (UPA) government's attorney general, whose involvement in the 2G spectrum allocation scam was the subject of several rumours around Delhi. I had been loosely following the 2G scam, the UPA government's first mega-corruption scandal, but I had never heard of **GOOLAM VAHANVATI**. He was yet to have the ignominy of becoming the first attorney general in the nation's history to depose in a trial court.

Of course, rumours weren't sufficient to substantiate the task at hand. I did some pre-reporting for ten days—a reconnaissance trip to a land that I would have to survey in detail if it turned out to be worth mapping. The survey trip practically became a prospecting one as I discovered rich, unexplored terrain. The story was lying in wait.

Although the attorney general, a constitutional position, is the top law officer of the country, he—every single one so far has been a 'he'—is barely known outside legal circles. This made it easier for me to write about the office, but more difficult to persuade the reader of the importance of Vahanvati. I decided to focus on the responsibility of the attorney general as envisioned in the constitution, and how Vahanvati had diverged from that vision. Instead of being the legal adviser for the rights and interests of every Indian, Vahanvati had become a convenient defender of the government and a personal but powerful adviser to the government's and his own friends.

Near the end of my reporting, the *Caravan*'s senior editor Jonathan Shainin asked me what the most important idea of the story was. Vahanvati, possibly like some other attorneys general before him—if none quite so blatant—was like the government's resourceful chartered accountant; instead of whitewashing black money, he performed that service for their policies. That was the idea, and that was the story.

KRISHN KAUSHIK

Krishn Kaushik is a journalist in Delhi and a former staff writer at the Caravan.

Inside Man

The convenient opinions of Attorney General Goolam Vahanvati

By KRISHN KAUSHIK | 1 May 2013

I

In the cosmos of the Indian establishment, the Supreme Court is a central galaxy. Its brightest stars, the senior advocates, can be seen gliding across the plaza outside the chief justice's courtroom with an imperial hauteur, in their distinctive robes and 'monkey suits' (as lawyers call the waistcoat worn by judges and seniors of the bar). Around each of these seniors orbits a small entourage: not only an assistant (usually carrying phones and bags), but three or four juniors, along with one or more independent advocates—lawyers who have not yet attained seniority, and work with the seniors on a case-by-case basis.

In an era when fortunes can be made and lost on the whims of government policy (or the manipulation thereof), billions of rupees hinge on the decisions of the Supreme Court, which has become the ultimate arbiter in innumerable disputes between corporates and the state. Today, the country's top lawyers, who charge upwards of Rs 10 lakh (Rs 1 million) for a single court appearance, are some of the capital's most powerful figures, Delhi's closest equivalent to the Wall Street investment bankers that Tom Wolfe once dubbed 'masters of the universe'.

It is not uncommon for these stars to quietly fade, due to age or exhaustion. But it is a rare sight when one of the masters gets pulled down to earth, even if briefly, by scandal or misfortune—a spectacle that draws rapt attention from the merchants in Delhi's power *mandi*.

When the spectacle involves not just any top lawyer, but the master of the masters—the attorney general for India, the legal custodian of the public interest of 1.2 billion people, who occupies a constitutional position designed to stand above the petty intrigues of politicians and corporates alike—it is a matter of grave concern that stretches far beyond the capital, for what falls is not just the man but the office.

So on 27 February, all eyes were turned towards an otherwise unremarkable courtroom in Delhi's Patiala House, where Goolamhussein Essaji Vahanvati was appearing before a Central Bureau of Investigation (CBI) special court. Vahanvati, the thirteenth attorney general for India—the Union government's top law officer, with an office on the second floor of the Supreme Court and the right to an audience in any court in the country—was not arguing before the bench. He was standing in the witness box, answering questions about his role in what was, at least for a time, the country's biggest scandal—the fraudulent allocation of 2G cellular spectrum. It was the first time in India's history that the country's attorney general had deposed as a witness in a trial court.

Over the course of two days, Sushil Kumar, the defence lawyer for the prime accused in the 2G scam, former communications minister Andimuthu Raja, peppered Vahanvati with questions. In his cross-examination, Kumar intended to demonstrate that Raja had sought and received the approval of Vahanvati, who was then the solicitor general, while making the decisions that investigators alleged were at the heart of the scam.

The file outlining the revisions to licence allocation procedures had been sent to Vahanvati for his signature three days before the contested licences were issued, and Raja had argued that Vahanvati's opinion gave legal sanction to his policies, though the law ministry had earlier declined to grant that approval. Furthermore, Kumar argued, Raja had consulted with Vahanvati as he formulated a new process for the awarding of licences, suggesting that Vahanvati, who was promoted to attorney general in 2009, had been well aware of the decisions that were now being characterized as a scam.

Claims of this sort—that others in the government knew exactly what he was doing—form the backbone of Raja's defence, which maintains that he has been unfairly prosecuted for decisions that the Cabinet had not seen fit to overrule. But Raja contends that Vahanvati's role was even more significant: Prime Minister Manmohan Singh and other members of the Cabinet had discussed these issues, and even seen files outlining the plans, but it was Vahanvati, Raja says, who gave legal imprimatur to the policy.

While Vahanvati stood uncomfortably in the witness box, parrying Kumar's questions with careful replies, Raja made a display of his disagreement. At one point, near the end of the first day of questioning, Raja interjected in a voice loud enough to be heard by all of the sixty or so people inside the courtroom, exclaiming, 'He is telling all the lies and I am the one going to jail.' Vahanvati, who had thus far avoided looking at Raja, turned towards him with obvious indignation, in disbelief that the tarnished minister would say such a thing in court.

There was more at stake for Vahanvati than mere embarrassment: the judge in the case, O.P. Saini, had the capacity to add Vahanvati to the list of accused if his testimony suggested a deeper involvement or complicity with Raja's actions. But even Kumar, Raja's lawyer, admitted this was not likely, and after two days in the witness box, Vahanvati was excused. He had managed to avoid any obvious missteps, and consistently depicted his role in the scandal as that of a minor bystander, whose legal opinions had been confined to narrowly drawn procedural questions.

Still, his appearance before the CBI special court marked a low point in his tenure as a law officer of the Union government, which has not been without its share of controversy. While much attention has been paid to the 2G scam, and thus to the role Vahanvati played, it is not the only case in which his opinions may have lent legitimacy to questionable decisions. In recent weeks, his name has surfaced in news reports as one of the government officials involved in watering down a CBI status report in the coal allocation scandal; in several other matters, Vahanvati has been accused of tailoring his interpretations of the law for the benefit of influential corporate houses.

Vahanvati is not the first attorney general to find himself mixed up in the messy partisan work of the government he serves; many Supreme Court advocates lamented that the independence of the government's law officers had been corroded by political pressure over the past three decades. But Vahanvati has been more controversial than his predecessors, and not only because this government has been beset by allegations of spectacular corruption.

Over the past four months, while I was conducting interviews with Vahanvati's friends and associates, fellow senior advocates, and Delhi's corps of fixers and lobbyists—who occupy the intersection of government, business, media and law—the attorney general was rarely out of the news, and the news he was in was rarely good. One of his colleagues told me, admiringly, that Vahanvati was a man with 'quick solutions to complex problems of law'; this makes him invaluable for a government whose trysts are mostly with crisis. But even feats of legal agility can't keep an incorrigible client out of trouble forever, and eventually the lawyer is left holding the bill.

Before he was appointed as the Union government's solicitor general in 2004, at the start of the first United Progressive Alliance (UPA) term, Vahanvati had been the advocate general of Maharashtra, a position to which he rose after almost three decades arguing before the Bombay High Court. 'Every lawyer's dream is to practise in the Supreme Court,' Vahanvati told me when I met him in January. 'Earlier I had been coming to Delhi a lot, but I had never had a sustained exposure to Delhi. This was a great change in my life.'

In person, Vahanvati is unfailingly polite and courteous, almost to the point of primness. During our only meeting, at his official residence on Delhi's Motilal Nehru Marg—next to the Taj Mahal Hotel—he spoke so quietly and calmly that I could have heard a caterpillar crawling across his meticulously organized desk.

At one point in our conversation, which lasted about an hour, he produced a small red diary, about six inches by three inches, inside which he had noted, in small and careful handwriting, citations of past decisions, important cases, and legal arguments. It was, he explained, one of the diaries he had carried in his pocket during his early years at the Bombay bar. Back then, he said, junior lawyers spent hours and hours sneezing over dusty volumes of old case law. 'One sentence would come out after three to four hours of research,' he said, adding that today's juniors don't understand how to properly draft their briefs. 'Now,' he sighed, 'everything comes readymade. But I always tell my juniors that unless you research yourself, you will never really improve as a lawyer.'

His friends and critics alike concur that he is a relentless worker, obsessively concerned with details and diligent in his preparation. Janak Dwarkadas, a senior advocate at the Bombay

High Court and a friend of Vahanvati, said he always had 'complete mastery over the facts' of the case at hand. 'He has all three qualities needed to be a competent lawyer,' Dwarkadas said. 'Excellent memory, excellent command over facts and law, and an excellent ability to put his point across to the court.'

After becoming a senior at the bar in 1990, Dwarkadas told me, Vahanvati was involved 'in every single significant case' at the Bombay High Court. 'Don't quote me on this, because it will make me sound foolish,' one of Vahanvati's close friends, a Supreme Court advocate, told me, 'but if there is a genius at the bar today, it is Vahanvati.'

Harish Salve, one of the country's most prominent lawyers, and a former solicitor general, has known Vahanvati for thirty years. The attorney general has 'a very sweet, very understated and gentle style' in the courtroom, Salve said. 'He is definitely a fine lawyer.'

'When you are a law officer,' former solicitor general Gopal Subramaniam told me, 'you have a relationship with the state, as it is your client, but you are also an officer of the law: you have to promote the law, and the rule of law.' The government's law officers—the attorney general, solicitor general and the additional solicitors general—have always been political appointments. But they are expected to give independent legal advice to the government they serve, even while they represent that government before the courts. 'If you have a government that believes in you and has faith in you,' Salve said, 'you can tell them, "Look, if you do this, it won't look nice." And they will say, "Okay, we won't do it."' As the attorney general or the solicitor general, Salve said, 'you're really the conscience-keeper of the government'.

But the government must first decide whether it wants honest advice, or merely legal ingenuity. 'Independent advice from a good law officer can mitigate the number of legal cases against the government,' one senior Supreme Court advocate told me. But too often, he said, 'their opinions are now used to provide a legal sanction to policies that are in a grey area'.

This, in essence, is the case made by Vahanvati's detractors: that as the solicitor general, and then the attorney general, he has more often done what the government asks than what the law requires. One former law officer, who worked under both Vahanvati and the previous attorney general, Milon Banerji, told me that while Vahanvati 'might have a better knowledge of the law' than his predecessor, 'Banerji had greater integrity and dignity'.

Prashant Bhushan, the activist lawyer and Aam Aadmi Party leader, who is involved in several lawsuits related to the 2G scandal, said Vahanvati was 'a competent and intelligent lawyer—smooth in his working style and quite effective in court'. But Bhushan charged that Vahanvati's opinions in several cases showed he was 'willing to give convenient advice, suiting a minister or ministers, who use it as a cover for all their dubious dealings, just as Raja did'.

'A convenient attorney general is very useful to the government,' Bhushan said. 'And therefore they go all out to protect him.' One corporate lobbyist who knows Vahanvati suggested a similar, if more dismissive, summary of his role: 'He's the government's alibi.'

After arriving in Delhi in 2004 as an outsider, Vahanvati rapidly learnt to negotiate the city's networks of power. Few expected that he would succeed Banerji as attorney general in 2009. The consensus was that the job would go to Gopal Subramaniam, then an additional solicitor general, who was a favourite of both Banerji and the then law minister, H.R. Bhardwaj, and also close to the Gandhi family. But after

Bhardwaj was replaced as law minister, Vahanvati was given the post.

'Within a few years he understood the power structure and made key contacts,' the law officer who worked under Banerji and Vahanvati told me. One of these is Ahmed Patel, the political secretary to Congress president Sonia Gandhi. Patel, whose name is whispered with reverence in off-the-record Delhi, was consistently described by people who know Vahanvati as his most powerful ally in the capital. 'Of course he knows how to navigate Delhi now,' Vahanvati's friend, the advocate, responded when I asked him about the attorney general's political savvy. 'I told you: he's a genius.'

But before he came close to Patel, Vahanvati already had a powerful friend in Anil Ambani—whose name came up immediately when I mentioned to any senior lawyer that I was reporting a profile of the attorney general. It's not clear when Vahanvati first met Ambani, but dozens of people testified to their friendship, which dates back to Vahanvati's time in Mumbai. Another law officer who worked with Vahanvati described him as 'very close' to Ambani, while a senior bureaucrat who worked under Finance Minister P. Chidambaram told me that Ambani and Vahanvati had often come together to have lunch with Chidambaram.

For all his proximity to power, the soft-spoken Vahanvati keeps a low profile and attracts very little public attention. 'He's the kind of guy you could pass by without noticing,' another lobbyist said. But Vahanvati occupies a critical junction in the capital's circuits of influence: almost every controversial matter—the policies and decisions that later get challenged in court, disputed by ministries, or probed by the CBI—will likely pass through the attorney general's office before it's resolved.

II

Vahanvati began his legal career at the Bombay High Court in 1972, as a junior to his father, Essabhoy Gulamhusein Vahanvati. 'I was in great awe of my father,' Vahanvati told me. 'Ever since I was a kid, I always wanted to be a lawyer.'

Vahanvati said that his paternal great-grandfather had been a builder of wooden ships—hence the family name: '*vahan*', in Gujarati, is a ship. 'That probably explains why my mind is so wooden,' he quipped. His grandfather had subsequently made a great fortune in the shipping business—in part as an agent for British merchant companies in Mumbai—but 'lost all of his money' during the Great Depression.

The senior Vahanvati joined the bar in 1943, six years before Goolam was born. 'My father was an extremely honest man,' Vahanvati told me. 'No judge ever asked him to justify a statement which he made in court.' Rafique Dada, who served as a junior to Essabhoy in the early 1970s, remembered him as an honest lawyer and a 'great raconteur' who was 'one of the most loved members of the bar'. After the court had adjourned for the day, Dada said, the lawyers would congregate in the library, where Vahanvati 'was so popular that many people gathered only to listen to him'.

In 1975, when Vahanvati was only twenty-six, his father died of an ulcer. 'He died very suddenly,' Vahanvati said. 'He was very young, and my life changed. I just had to put my head down and work. I worked eighteen hours a day.' Dada remembered the young Vahanvati as 'carefree, but very sharp', and 'an outstanding lawyer'. Dinyar Madon, who was among Vahanvati's first juniors in the early 1980s, recalled that he used to get 'sixty to seventy matters each day', and worked longer hours than anyone else in the office.

Vahanvati told me that his father's early death had served as a motivation to succeed. 'Can I be honest with you?' he said. 'Basically, I felt always that my father didn't deserve to die so young. There was always a feeling that I have to bring out his name. It's very difficult for me to describe, but that was my driving force.'

Vahanvati took pains to emphasize that he had little interest in personal enrichment. 'I am not a money-minded person,' he told me. 'What can you do with money? If money is all you want, then don't be a law officer.' He recounted a scene from the Supreme Court, where other senior advocates were showing off their pricey watches. 'I said, "You guys are wearing on your wrists more than what I can earn in a month."' While the desks of senior advocates are typically littered with Montblancs and other luxury pens, Vahanvati called my attention to the compulsively neat row of perfectly aligned pens and pencils on his table. 'Look at my pens,' he said. 'All of them are presents, and they are all cheap highlighters and little things that keep me going.' Later I was told by both Vahanvati's son, Essaji, and one of his good friends, the lawyer Raian Karanjawala, that he had 'an impressive collection' of expensive writing instruments, suggesting that he might have slightly exaggerated his indifference to material possessions.

(At the end of our interview in January, I suggested to Vahanvati that we should meet again, and he agreed. But he declined all subsequent requests for an interview, including more than ten attempts to contact him for comment in the three weeks prior to publication.)

'He doesn't call himself a Delhi person,' Vahanvati's son told me. 'He comes back to Mumbai during every vacation.' In Mumbai, Vahanvati owns one house, which he has given to his son, and rents three apartments in a building called Joyeden, a block from the Taj Hotel in Colaba. (According to the trust that governs the building, the rent for two of these apartments is only Rs 490 per month, while the third rents for Rs 64.) In the 1990s, before he became advocate general, Vahanvati sold an apartment he owned in Pune, and bought a two-acre plot outside the city; in 2003, he purchased two adjacent acres. Janak Dwarkadas, who worked with Vahanvati on many occasions, lives in a farmhouse next door to Vahanvati's property. He described it as 'like a seven-star resort', mentioning a stream that runs across the land, two bungalows, Jersey cows, sheep, and plants and trees from around the world. 'He's a collector by nature,' Dwarkadas said, and recalled walking around the property with Vahanvati, who 'knew the name and details of every tree'.

At the end of 1999, Vahanvati said, he received an unexpected call from Vilasrao Deshmukh, the newly elected Congress chief minister of Maharashtra, offering him the post of advocate general. Vahanvati told me that he didn't know Deshmukh, but 'he had heard about me'. At that point, according to Dwarkadas, Vahanvati was one of Mumbai's top advocates. 'He had a flourishing writ court practice and a good commercial practice, which catapulted him to the advocate general's post,' Dwarkadas said.

One of Vahanvati's good friends in Delhi told me that Vahanvati had called him shortly after the Maharashtra elections in 1999. Vahanvati said he was being considered for the advocate general's post and asked his friend, who was close to senior Congress leader Madhavrao Scindia, then the party's in-charge for Maharashtra, to recommend him. 'I was holidaying in Rajasthan, I remember, and he called me and said can you talk to Madhavrao Scindia. I spoke to Scindia and told him that if you're considering Vahanvati, he will be a good choice.'

Before becoming the state's advocate general, Vahanvati had already become friendly with Sharad Pawar, whose Nationalist Congress Party was Deshmukh's coalition partner. In the mid 1990s, Vahanvati told me, Pawar had been fighting a defamation case against a newspaper that alleged he had ties with the Mumbai underworld. Vahanvati had often worked with J.N. Gagrat, who was Pawar's lawyer, and when he heard about the case from Gagrat, he volunteered to approach the newspaper himself and settle the controversy. 'Without going to the court, I spoke to the newspaper. I said, "This is wrong, what you've done, there is already an injunction." So they apologized. I came to know him briefly then.' As advocate general, Vahanvati represented the Maharashtra State Electricity Board in the state's long-running tussle with the American energy company Enron, whose involvement in the Dabhol power project was the single largest foreign direct investment in India at the time, and the subject of massive controversy, much of it centred around Pawar. Later on, Vahanvati appeared several times for Pawar in a case against the Board of Cricket Control in India, which Pawar headed from 2005 to 2008.

A solicitor from Mumbai who has known Vahanvati for several decades told me that he once confessed that it had been his dream as a child to be driven around in an official car with a red beacon—a status symbol not accorded to state advocates general. His chance arrived when the UPA government came to power in 2004; at that point Vahanvati had been an advocate general for four years, under Deshmukh and his successor, Sushil Kumar Shinde, who now serves as the Union home minister.

Many senior advocates in Mumbai told me that Vahanvati was a top legal mind, whose skills as a lawyer made him an obvious choice as solicitor general. In Delhi, however, opinions were less kind—or more cynical—and many people told me there had been substantial lobbying behind Vahanvati's appointment. A person close to Bhardwaj said he was only concerned that Milon Banerji be made the attorney general, and had no opinion about who should be selected as solicitor general. According to this person, 'a Mumbai corporate lobby' had pushed to have Vahanvati appointed.

Many people told me that Bhardwaj was not fond of Vahanvati, and had argued against his appointment as attorney general in 2009. 'Bhardwaj thought Vahanvati lacked the stature at the bar' that was required of an attorney general, the former law officer who worked under Banerji and Vahanvati told me. A senior Congress member of Parliament, who said 'Bhardwaj couldn't stand Vahanvati', told me that Pawar and Shinde had influenced the decision to promote Vahanvati, which took place only after Bhardwaj was replaced at the law ministry by Veerappa Moily. (Bhardwaj, who is now the Governor of Karnataka, did not respond to multiple requests for comment.)

A few days after Vahanvati's promotion in June 2009, the well-connected journalist Prabhu Chawla, now the editor of the *New Indian Express*, told the lobbyist Niira Radia that Vahanvati was 'an old friend of mine' during a taped phone conversation. 'He is very close to Anil Ambani, everyone knows about it,' Chawla continued. 'Anil Ambani, Nusli Wadia, and our power minister—*kya naam hai* (what's his name)?—Shinde, they all went for him for the appointment. Bhardwaj never liked him. Bhardwaj would not have made him the attorney general *agar Bhardwaj law minister hotaa* (if he was still law minister).' (When contacted for comment, Chawla said Vahanvati was a friend, and declined to be interviewed for this story.)

A close associate of Anil Ambani acknowledged Ambani's friendship with Vahanvati, but insisted that the two men were not unusually close, and that their acquaintance was of relatively recent vintage—after Vahanvati came to Delhi. Ambani, this person argued, naturally had dealings with many powerful people in government, and had only come to know Vahanvati through Ahmed Patel; Vahanvati, he said, was close to other corporate leaders as well—closer, this person said, than he was to Ambani.

III

On the wintry morning of 28 January 1950, the first chief justice of India, along with the chief justices of fourteen high courts, the advocates general of eight states, the prime minister and other cabinet ministers, and a handful of diplomats and foreign envoys, gathered in what was then called the Chamber of Princes in the Parliament building. (The hall is now used as a library.) The proceedings commenced with a speech by Motilal Setalvad, the first attorney general for India, who had assumed his post two days earlier when the Constitution came into force.

'The writ of this court will run over a territory extending to over 2 million square miles, inhabited by a population of about 330 million,' Setalvad said. 'It can truly be said that the jurisdiction and powers of this court, in their nature and extent, are wider than those exercised by the highest court of any county in the Commonwealth or by the Supreme Court of the United States.' His address, which lasted only a few minutes, marked the inauguration of the Supreme Court of India.

Though the attorney general rarely makes headlines, it would be hard to overstate the significance of the position—it is, as Gopal Subramaniam told me, 'one of the most important constitutional posts in India'. The Constitution specifically mentions that the President must select for the post a person 'qualified to be appointed a Judge of the Supreme Court'. Therefore, Subramaniam said, the attorney general 'must be a man of such fearless character, equivalent to that of a judge—with the ability to give fearless advice to government, to the Parliament, to the judiciary'. The same qualities are sought in the solicitor general, he said, 'to be equally independent of the executive'.

Neither the attorney general nor the solicitor general have fixed tenures; they serve as long as they have 'the pleasure of the President', which means they can be replaced whenever the government wishes. Salve said that while the law officers are political appointments, that does not mean that they are not expected to 'rise above their brief'.

'It is a position of great responsibility,' said P.P. Rao, a senior Supreme Court advocate. 'It requires independence, ability, and integrity.' Rao and Subramaniam both praised the first four men to occupy the office, from Setalvad through S.V. Gupte, whose tenure ended in 1979. They were, Rao said, 'men of absolute independence', but 'thereafter, things have been different'. Since then, Rao said, 'political considerations prevailed' within the government, and persons with what Rao called a 'servile mindset' had been appointed. 'You cannot afford to have a pliable person there,' Rao said, 'or the very objective of the office is defeated.'

In late February, a day before Vahanvati's deposition in the 2G special court, I met his son, Essaji Vahanvati, in Mumbai. Essaji, named after his grandfather, is a partner at one of the country's top firms, AZB Partners, and looks about a decade younger than his thirty-three years. It was the first of our two meetings, both at his firm's offices in the Express Towers at Nariman Point. We sat in a conference room named 'Sycamore' and looked out over an impressive view of the sea. Essaji described his father as 'an extremely generous person', very dedicated to his work, compulsive about reading and preparation.

He recalled that his father had been aware, before the 2004 elections, that if the Congress came into office, he might be appointed the solicitor general. When I asked about his sense of Vahanvati's friends in politics, Essaji said, 'In Delhi he did get to know and work with a lot of people over there. He's known PC [Chidambaram] for many years, just to give an example . . . I think he's close to Ahmed bhai [Patel] also.' After his father had become advocate general, a different sort of visitor started appearing at their house. 'There were a lot more government people who had to come,' he said. 'And when they come they don't come in one or twos, they come with their whole band of people.' When Vahanvati was a senior advocate in the Bombay High Court, Essaji said, his friends were more likely drawn from the corporate world, or even Bollywood—'the people he worked for'. I mentioned that a lot of people said Vahanvati had a close relationship with Reliance; did he remember how that came about? 'Reliance, yeah,' he said. 'I am not so sure about what happened exactly.' But as a state's advocate general, he continued, 'a lot of people tend to end up meeting you'.

When Anil Ambani's name came up—as it inevitably did—in my conversation with Prashant Bhushan, he argued that Vahanvati should have recused himself from any matters involving Ambani or his companies. 'Vahanvati told me himself that he is a close friend of Anil Ambani,' Bhushan said. He pointed out that Vahanvati continued to give opinions, or appear on behalf of the government, in cases where Ambani's interests were at stake. 'That, itself, is a conflict of interest.'

Mohan Parasaran, the current solicitor general, argued that talk of this sort, about corporate interests exerting influence on law officers, had been grossly overstated. To be selected as a law officer, Parasaran pointed out, 'you must have had a good private practice as a leading lawyer—these industrialists would have been your clients at some point in time'. Former clients often become friends, he said, and 'it is difficult to cut off these relationships:

I can't say, "Don't come and meet me," no?' But this did not mean the law officers could not issue objective opinions in cases concerning friends or former clients. 'See, these days nobody can avoid controversies,' he said. 'If you're holding a public office, it's easy for anybody to accuse anybody.' Parasaran made it clear that he felt the allegations against Vahanvati were unfair, and said it was too easy for others to assume that identifying the beneficiaries of a given legal opinion provided evidence of favouritism. 'If you go and drink milk under a palm tree,' Parasaran concluded, 'people will think you're drinking arrack.'

Harish Salve, who returned to his lucrative private practice in 2002 after three years as the solicitor general, agreed that it was facile to assume a given opinion had been issued for the benefit of one party. 'Why a law officer holds a particular opinion—does he do it to please the government or does he do it because he believes it—these are matters on which you cannot comment unless you have all the details,' Salve said. But he also suggested that he would find it difficult to be objective about matters that concerned his own friends, and mentioned Mukesh Ambani and Jet Airways chief Naresh Goyal. 'If you ask me about Reliance, I will tell you, "Don't ask me," because my relationship with Mukesh is very deep, so my opinion may not be objective,' he said. 'If I became attorney general, and a file came dealing with aviation, I would decline it, because anything I say is going to either hurt or help Naresh. One of the reasons I would never become a law officer now is that Reliance is in almost every business in the world, so if a file came to me which would either benefit or hurt them, I would have to say no.'

Whatever the nature of Vahanvati's relationship with Anil Ambani, there are at least two cases where Vahanvati authored opinions pertaining directly to Ambani's companies. In these cases, his opinions were both controversial and beneficial to Ambani's interests. The first of these concerned one of the companies implicated in the 2G scandal, Swan Telecom; Vahanvati's opinion forestalled an investigation into the company's ownership patterns, though the CBI later determined it had been set up as a front company for Ambani's Reliance Communications.

By January 2009, one year after the contested 2G licences had been issued by the Department of Telecommunications (DoT), multiple legal challenges had been mounted against the allocation process. Several of these concerned Swan, which had been awarded licences for thirteen service areas.

According to two complaints filed with the Prime Minister's Office (PMO), from the Congress Rajya Sabha member of Parliament (MP) Dharampal Sabharwal, and Janata Party president Subramanian Swamy, as well as a writ petition filed in the Delhi High Court, Swan Telecom had been in violation of the guidelines for issuing mobile licences. These specified that a company already in possession of spectrum in one circle could not own more than 10 per cent of another company applying for additional spectrum in the same circle, as Swan had done. As Swamy wrote in his complaint,

> The documents available disclose that on March 2, 2007, when Swan Telecom applied for Unified Access Services Licences, it was owned 100 per cent by Reliance Communications and its associates.

On 12 January 2009, an internal DoT memo, responding to these complaints, asked whether 'Ministry of Corporate Affairs may be requested to examine the matter', to determine if Swan's ownership pattern had violated the guidelines. In a subsequent memo, dated 5 February 2009, A.K. Srivastava, a deputy director general in the DoT, suggested that the opinion of the solicitor general should be sought, because he was representing the government in the high court. A note on the same page from Siddhartha Behura, the telecommunications secretary, suggested: 'Through the Ministry of Law we may refer this matter to SG [solicitor general].' Three days later, a note by Raja suggested the question could go straight to Vahanvati: 'May be sent to SG directly since the cases are represented by him before the TDSAT [Telecom Disputes Settlement and Appellate Tribunal] and other judicial forums including HC [high court] Delhi.'

The file was not sent to the law ministry. Instead, Vahanvati sent an opinion, issued on his own letterhead, on 25 March 2009. It argued that the ownership of Swan at the time of its application—in March 2007—was irrelevant, because Reliance had voluntarily divested its shares in the company in December 2007, nine months after applying, but one month before the licences were issued. Therefore, Vahanvati concluded, 'the file shows that there has been a full consideration of all relevant material and the conclusion that the applicants fulfilled all the necessary conditions cannot really be faulted'.

In an interview with *Mint* in February 2011, Vahanvati defended his opinion, saying, 'All the facts relating to Swan were known. DoT had gone through the shareholding of Swan and given them an okay.' (A subsequent CBI investigation would show that all the facts were not yet known, revealing an intricate web of cross-holdings designed to disguise the full degree of Reliance's involvement, for which three Reliance executives are now on trial.)

Vahanvati's opinion, according to later notings in the file, was twice cited to block additional requests that the matter be referred to the corporate affairs ministry for further examination. The Comptroller and Auditor General (CAG) report on the 2G scandal admonished the telecommunications department for consulting Vahanvati rather than the finance or corporate affairs ministry, and characterized the department's reply—based on Vahanvati's opinion—as 'evasive'.

In late 2011, the CAG began to circulate a draft report indicating irregularities in the government's allocation of captive coal blocks to private firms, which soon developed into the scandal unfortunately known as 'Coalgate', with a price tag said to be even larger than the 2G scam. One portion of the report focused on Anil Ambani's Reliance Power, which had been given permission to divert surplus coal allocated for an ultra-mega power plant (UMPP) at Sasan in Madhya Pradesh to another power plant nearby. The CAG later estimated that the financial benefit of this concession for Reliance Power would be Rs 29,000 crore (Rs 290 billion) over a period of twenty years.

After the CAG draft report was circulated, an empowered group of ministers headed by Pranab Mukherjee asked Vahanvati for an opinion on whether the Sasan decision had provided an undue concession to Reliance. Officials from the coal and power ministries argued that the decision should be cancelled, but Vahanvati disagreed. In April 2012, the empowered group of ministers cited Vahanvati's opinion—which the *Financial Express* called 'a big relief to the government'—and opted to allow Reliance to go ahead.

The story is a complicated one, and it reflects badly on nearly everyone involved. It began in 2007, when Reliance Power won a bid to operate a UMPP at Sasan; according to the terms of the contract, three captive coal blocks would be allotted, to be used exclusively for power generation at the Sasan plant. Soon after the contract was signed, according to a senior official in one of the concerned ministries, Reliance Power 'started moving in Madhya Pradesh'.

In October 2007, Reliance Power signed a memorandum of understanding with the Madhya Pradesh government to develop another power plant at Chitrangi, which would produce electricity using purchased coal. That same month, Shivraj Singh Chouhan, the chief minister of Madhya Pradesh, wrote to the prime minister requesting that Reliance Power be allowed to divert 'excess' coal from the captive mines designated for Sasan to the plant at Chitrangi. This would increase the profit margins on the electricity sold by the Chitrangi plant, since its tariff had been set based on the assumption of higher costs to acquire coal.

An empowered group of ministers headed by then power minister Sushil Kumar Shinde approved Chouhan's request for Reliance in August 2008. Their decision stipulated that the excess power generated by surplus coal should be sold at rates determined by competitive bidding (which would keep prices low). But as the CAG report notes, the tariff for Chitrangi had already been set, so the savings accrued to Reliance rather than consumers. The group of ministers, the senior bureaucrat told me, had effectively 'tweaked the policy to suit Reliance'.

But Tata Power, which had also bid for the Sasan UMPP, filed a petition challenging the decision before the Delhi High Court in January 2009. Tata argued that the government had retrospectively changed the terms of the contract to benefit Reliance, and that it would not have withdrawn its competing bid if the surplus coal provision had been in place. (Vahanvati defended the government before the high court, which dismissed Tata's petition; the matter is now pending before the Supreme Court.)

In December 2011, an empowered group of ministers once again considered the Sasan decision. According to the senior official, Shinde had started to have second thoughts: 'After the CAG report came out, Shinde got scared,' the official said.

'He thought as the power minister that he would be made the scapegoat, and he wanted to withdraw the allotment to Chitrangi. But Pranab bulldozed him.'

The power and coal ministries had been asked to formulate a blanket policy for surplus coal, which could then be applied to any future UMPP projects. Mukherjee, the senior official said, requested that the ministries 'keep Sasan in mind'. But in response, they proposed that any surplus coal must be sold to Coal India at cost, citing an existing policy that does not allow private companies to earn profits from mining coal. Noting that the original allotment for Sasan had specified similar conditions, the senior official said, the ministries recommended reversing the original decision granting Reliance permission to divert surplus coal to Chitrangi. 'We formulated a policy, but it was withdrawn within three days,' the senior official said. 'There was pressure from Pranab to ratify the policy that was used for Sasan, and we were told to consult the attorney general and come back.'

Over the next several months, the senior official said, the policy was discussed between the power, coal and law ministries. In response to their queries, the law ministry and Vahanvati raised additional questions and responded to them; questions whose answers, according to the official, had direct implications for the Sasan affair. 'We had asked about four questions,' the official told me, 'and he answered about ten.'

The new questions and answers, the official said, were 'totally in line with what Reliance had wanted'. Vahanvati 'interpreted that the clause was open for the government to decide' whether surplus coal could be diverted. 'We said no, the clause did not say that.' Furthermore, the official argued, the documents specified that any excess coal could only be transferred to a subsidiary of Coal India. 'He misinterpreted that the excess coal could be given to a subsidiary of Reliance.'

When the empowered group of ministers convened in April 2012 to consider the excess coal policy, the coal and power ministries presented their position 'in black and white' alongside Vahanvati's opinion. 'We were overruled,' the official said, 'but the CAG report says what we were saying.'

Since then, a senior Supreme Court advocate told me, 'Every time Sasan comes up in court, Vahanvati starts sweating when he has to appear.'

IV

For all the sensational coverage it received, the 2G scandal—arguably the defining scam of our time—essentially consisted of a disarmingly dull sequence of complex policy decisions. Few doubt that A. Raja, in his role as communications minister, was responsible for initiating and executing the contested changes to the spectrum allocation process. The controversial question, which dominated two years' worth of media reports and parliamentary discussions, concerned the involvement of others in the government: if they were aware of Raja's intentions, were they complicit in some or all aspects of the scam, or did they choose to ignore his actions? Or had he misled the prime minister and several others about the true nature of his plans?

The intricate details, involving many subtle alterations to government policies and procedures, recorded in a trail of bureaucratic memos and file notings, are fantastically boring. But the basic outline of the scandal can be summed up by a few key decisions, whose effect was to tilt the playing field in favour of certain companies—including Unitech Wireless, whose proprietors were close to Raja, and Swan Telecom.

After the communications ministry received an unprecedented number of applications for mobile licences and spectrum in late

2007, Raja altered the rules by which those applications were to be processed. First, he changed the cut-off date to an earlier point, eliminating more than 300 of the 575 applications; second, he shifted the criteria for determining the order in which licences would be granted. The now-controversial 'first-come, first-served' policy was already in place, but Raja altered the definition of 'first-come' so that the date applications had originally been filed was no longer relevant. Qualifying companies would be awarded licences in the order in which they fulfilled the conditions in the letters of intent (LOIs) issued by the ministry; in short, whoever deposited their cheques first would get spectrum first.

Many of the individual steps in the evolution of Raja's new policies are laid out in a DoT file, number 20-100/2007-AS-1/ Part C, perhaps the most widely publicized 'secret' document of the past decade. It begins with a memo from a director inside the DoT, dated 24 October 2007, suggesting that the 'Learned Solicitor General' provide his opinion on the proposed methodology to allot licences and spectrum. After a letter to this effect was sent to the law ministry, the law minister, H.R. Bhardwaj, responded that given the importance of the case and its complexity, 'it is necessary that the whole issue is first reviewed by an empowered group of ministers', after which the 'legal opinion of the AG [Milon Banerji] may be obtained'.

Raja found this disagreeable, and sent a letter to the prime minister protesting that there was no need for an empowered group of ministers to decide the issue, since it did not involve 'new major policy decisions' but only procedures for implementing existing policy. Still, in the first week of December 2007, Raja went to meet Pranab Mukherjee, then the foreign minister, who chaired an existing group of ministers on spectrum issues. He was accompanied by Vahanvati, who as solicitor general was defending the DoT in a lawsuit filed by the Cellular Operators

Association of India (COAI), a lobby group that represented Airtel and Vodafone, among others, challenging the criteria for awarding additional spectrum.

The meeting was a brief one, and no minutes appear to have been prepared. But Vahanvati presented Mukherjee with a note, detailing the government's response to the COAI lawsuit, which was later sent by Mukherjee to the prime minister. Under the heading 'The issue of new telecom licenses', Vahanvati described the 'first-come, first-served' policy in a way that left room for Raja's alteration, stating that applicants would be granted their licences and spectrum once they complied with the LOI conditions.

A letter sent by Raja to Manmohan Singh on 26 December and copied to Mukherjee informed the prime minister that Raja had 'several discussions' with Mukherjee regarding spectrum allocation, and that Vahanvati 'was also called for the discussions to explain the legal position'. A memo from Raja, attached to the letter to the prime minister, provides an account of the revised procedures—including, critically, the new criteria for awarding licences according to the order in which applicants meet the required conditions: 'An applicant who fulfils the conditions of LOI first will be granted license first, although several applicants will be issued LOI simultaneously. The same has been concurred by the Solicitor General of India during the discussions.'

Thus far, Raja's revisions to the allocation procedures had not yet been announced. In early January 2008, the DoT prepared a press release that described the new policy for determining the order in which licences would be granted; the same release revealed for the first time that the cut-off date for eligible applications had been retrospectively moved forward, disqualifying all those who applied between 25 September and

1 October 2007. Rather than submitting the release to the law ministry—which had earlier demanded the issue be referred to an empowered group of ministers—Raja made a note on the file, instructing the telecom secretary to 'please obtain Solicitor General's opinion since he is appearing before the TDSAT and High Court Delhi', a reference to the COAI lawsuit.

On 7 January 2008, the telecom secretary, Siddhartha Behura, went to Vahanvati's official residence with the file, including notings and annexures, and a draft of the press release. On the page of the file following Raja's note, under a handwritten 'S.G', Vahanvati wrote: 'I have seen the notes. The issue regarding new LOIs [i.e. the allocation of new licences] are not before any court. What is proposed is fair and reasonable. The press release makes for transparency. This seems to be in order.'

Behura returned with Vahanvati's signature on the file, which Raja interpreted as granting legitimacy to his modifications in the licence allocation procedure, as described in the press release—whose publication, three days later, set the scam in motion.

During Vahanvati's deposition before the CBI court on 27 January of this year, Sushil Kumar pressed the attorney general with a series of questions intended to demonstrate that he could hardly have been unaware of Raja's revisions to the policy, given that he had been consulted at several earlier junctures, and had signed off on the release of the press note whose contents included the two most significant revisions: the new cut-off date for applications and the redefinition of the terms by which 'first-come, first-served' would be implemented.

Kumar's questions about Vahanvati's signature on the file lasted several hours. Vahanvati repeatedly insisted that his note on the file only approved the release, not the policies it described. Behura had called him, Vahanvati said, only to ask whether any developments in the COAI lawsuit might obstruct the release of the press note and the issuing of new licences, after which Behura asked that Vahanvati record his opinion in writing.

Vahanvati said his note and signature did not convey his approval of any policies, which, he said, he was anyway unaware of. His replies to Kumar were a mix of exasperation and lawyerly precision, and featured many variations on a single phrase: 'It is wrong to suggest that the Minister did not ask my opinion on the press release . . . It is wrong to suggest that my opinion was sought through this file on the proposed course of action to be taken by the DoT . . . It is wrong to suggest that I am wrong on this point.'

Though Vahanvati's written reply begins with the phrase 'I have seen the notes', he contended that this statement did not in fact refer to the file in its entirety, but only to the notes on the page preceding his signature, instructing the telecom secretary to obtain his approval on the press release. Two pages earlier, the file contains a memo from Raja to the prime minister, which states in bold text that Vahanvati had concurred with his redefinition of the criteria to determine 'first-come, first-served'. But in response to a question from Kumar, Vahanvati stated that he had not concurred, and that he was not aware Raja had claimed as much, because he did not refer to any earlier pages in the file before giving his approval to the press release.

Neither Kumar nor the lawyers for the other accused asked Vahanvati why he had given his approval to a file that had not been routed through the law ministry, a possible violation of the government's rules of service for law officers. (Raja and Vahanvati both believe, albeit for slightly different reasons, that this was legitimate.)

A few weeks before Vahanvati's testimony, I had asked one of his colleagues whether it was unorthodox for the solicitor general to offer his opinion on a file sent to him directly. The colleague defended Vahanvati, but also said, 'The thing is, it was not as though this was the first time the file had been sent to him. He was being consulted on a regular basis.' This would suggest that Vahanvati had been given many opportunities to acquaint himself with the file. In his testimony before the 2G court, however, Vahanvati stated, 'I had not seen the other pages of the file.'

With regard to the policies described in the press release, Vahanvati argued that he was not aware that the cut-off date had been changed from 1 October 2007 to 25 September 2007, as the release mentioned only the latter date. His statement that 'what is proposed is fair and reasonable' and that 'the press release makes for transparency' was not, he maintained, an acknowledgement of the revised procedure for implementing 'first-come, first-served', even though the release states that 'who so ever complies with the conditions of LOI first' will be granted a licence.

The senior Congress MP told me that within the government, 'it was commonly admitted that Vahanvati vetted the press release'. In its chargesheet, the CBI accused Raja of having 'fraudulently' altered the press release after obtaining Vahanvati's approval, by removing the final paragraph before it was published. The Congress MP, however, pointed out that this was irrelevant. 'Raja has been hit even for the first paragraph.'

The CBI had also accused Raja of fabricating the meeting with Vahanvati and Mukherjee that he described in his letter to Manmohan Singh, stating that 'the investigation has not revealed any discussions with the SG'. In 2011, however, Vahanvati's office revealed in response to a Right to Information query that the meeting had indeed taken place, raising the question of whether Vahanvati failed to mention it when questioned by CBI investigators.

For Raja's defence, the meeting took on particular significance; Kumar proposed to Vahanvati that the meeting proved 'policy and procedures were formulated by the DoT, after discussion with you and the then Minister for External Affairs'. Vahanvati denied this was the case, and insisted there had been no such discussion; he merely presented his note to Mukherjee, who went through it 'very carefully and asked me some questions'. Kumar, in a dramatic flourish, suggested that the details of this meeting would show that Raja had not acted alone, but that the truth would never come out because only three people were privy to the details. 'One is him,' Kumar said, and pointed to Vahanvati. 'One is him,' pointing to Raja. 'And the third is at a position where we cannot reach'—in Rashtrapati Bhavan.

Kumar clearly believes that Vahanvati's role was sufficiently substantial to exonerate Raja of any charge that he deceived the government about his intentions. 'Either Vahanvati is as guilty as the minister,' Kumar told me after the deposition, 'or he is as innocent as the minister—this is my conclusion.' It may not be the case, as Kumar implies, that Vahanvati approved Raja's actions with full awareness of their implications. But the available evidence, combined with Vahanvati's unconvincing account of his own role, suggests either an implausible lack of comprehension or, less charitably, a negligence of his obligation to provide accurate legal advice.

A CBI investigator involved in the case told me that 'based on the facts that emerged from the investigation, there was no criminal evidence against Vahanvati', though many had speculated that he might be named an accused. But, the investigator added, 'It could be speculated that there was passive complicity with Raja.' Vahanvati, the investigator said, was close to Anil Ambani, and 'it seemed this was all done to help Swan'.

According to the investigator, the then CBI director, A.P. Singh, could frequently be heard complaining aloud that the agency had come under intense pressure from the PMO to limit the boundaries of the investigation. Two other people involved in the case—another member of the investigating team and an advocate representing the government—told me separately that the PMO had also worked to ensure Vahanvati would not be among the accused, an allegation repeated by the senior Congress MP. (A.P. Singh refused multiple requests to be interviewed for this story.)

One person who seemed confident Vahanvati had failed to maintain his distance from Raja was the lobbyist Niira Radia, whose taped conversations, leaked to the media in 2010, contain several disparaging references to the attorney general. On 11 June 2009, in a call with her client Ratan Tata about her attempts to secure dual-technology spectrum in Delhi for Tata, she explained that she had met Raja along with Anil Sardana, then the managing director of Tata Teleservices. Raja wanted to grant the available Delhi spectrum to Anil Ambani's Reliance Communications before any other player came into the fray, Radia said, and she told Tata that Raja would obtain legal assistance from Vahanvati, who was then defending the licence allotments before the telecom disputes tribunal. 'I think Raja will be trying to get in the attorney general,' Radia said.

In another conversation, five days later, Radia told K. Venugopal, an editor with *The Hindu Business Line*, that Vahanvati had advised Tata not to fight Raja's decision. 'I know how Vahanvati has called Anil Sardana, and all of us, and said you know, don't oppose minister, don't oppose this, we'll ensure you get your spectrum,' Radia said.

Later in that same conversation, Radia adds, 'I've been party to a meeting, I mean, where Vahanvati has told Anil Sardana, "Do not oppose Mr Raja . . . We will make sure you get your spectrum, I'm giving you my word, isn't my word good enough?" . . . I walked out of that meeting with Anil Sardana, I said Anil do not allow this.'

When I contacted Sardana, he insisted the meeting Radia described had never taken place, and he 'had no familiarity with the person mentioned'. But a person close to Sardana confirmed to me, in two separate conversations, that Sardana said Vahanvati warned him that if Tata tried to block Raja's decision, they would never get spectrum in Delhi. To date, they have not.

V

During my interviews with more than half a dozen current or former law officers, nearly all discussed the difficulty of maintaining one's independence when faced with pressure from the government, at whose pleasure you serve. 'Your government is a client—they want some opinions that promote whatever is their policy,' the current solicitor general, Mohan Parasaran, told me. 'What I feel is, you can bend, but not break. You can bend to a reasonable extent, but you can't compromise on your conscience and integrity.'

The question of how far you can bend before your integrity has been compromised is a subjective one; given the realities of Indian politics, each law officer surely has their own sense of what constitutes an acceptable balance between political expediency and constitutional morality.

Still, it would be hard to deny that in recent years that balance has shifted in the wrong direction: if the government does not respect the independence of the law officers, then the law officers it gets will not be independent. The more that political pressure is successfully brought to bear on important decisions, the more it will be seen as acceptable, and the more it will continue to succeed.

But as Harish Salve told me, it is almost impossible to definitively prove that a specific legal opinion reflects the influence of outside pressure rather than inner conscience; even if there were evidence that pressure had been applied, a lawyer could plausibly argue that he had reached the desired conclusion independently. Nor, for that matter, can an opinion be shown to be 'wrong', except insofar as it misrepresents the facts or the law; the question of which facts and laws are relevant to a given case is invariably open to interpretation.

While it may be improper to draw such conclusions from a single opinion, it can still be the case that examining a body of opinions and their circumstances, over time, can reveal patterns that either confirm a lawyer's integrity or raise doubts about their independence. One opinion that looks convenient may not really be so, but when many look convenient, there may be reason to believe they are.

When a law officer is asked to give an opinion, he or she may have no control over the use to which it is put. But here too, a pattern may emerge: a sample of opinions that appear to serve the immediate political needs of the government may suggest that opinions have been drafted to cater to those needs.

In this regard, there may be no opinion more embarrassing for Vahanvati than the one he produced in November 2008, recommending that a disproportionate assets case not be registered against the Samajwadi Party (SP) president Mulayam Singh Yadav, a little more than three months after Yadav's support saved the UPA in a crucial trust vote in Parliament. The opinion attracted criticism at the time, but it marked the beginning of a legendarily ridiculous chain of reversals and re-reversals in the case, which have, in hindsight, made the opinion look even worse.

The CBI had conducted a preliminary inquiry into the assets owned by Yadav, his two sons, and his daughter-in-law in response to a directive from the Supreme Court in March 2007. Seven months later, after finding prima facie evidence that Yadav and his family had assets disproportionate to their income—even before assessing the full value of the real estate in their names—the CBI concluded that a case should be registered. For an unknown reason, the Court had directed the CBI to submit the results of its preliminary inquiry to the government. Anticipating that it would not act, the CBI filed an application with the Supreme Court in October 2007, requesting the Court to order the case be registered without further reference to the government.

After the Court failed to respond, the CBI filed another application to the same effect in March 2008, to which the Court again did not respond. In the months that followed, the SP stepped in to support the UPA in July 2008, and Yadav's daughter-in-law Dimple sent three letters to the government, accompanied by tax returns, declaring her innocence.

Prompted by Dimple Yadav's complaint, the then law minister, H.R. Bhardwaj, asked Vahanvati for an opinion as to whether the CBI should proceed with the case. Vahanvati's opinion, delivered in November 2008, challenged the premise of the CBI's preliminary inquiry and recommended that the CBI withdraw its application to proceed with an investigation. The central argument of Vahanvati's opinion—which has been called 'absurd' and 'scandalous' by the press—was that it was improper for the CBI to include the assets of Yadav's sons and daughter-in-law in its inquiry unless it could prove that they were being held for him to avoid detection. In other words, the investigation could not proceed unless the investigators could show beyond doubt that the assets were deliberately concealed, a burden of proof that could only be met through further investigation.

But Bhardwaj quickly concurred with Vahanvati's opinion, and recommended the CBI withdraw its application to open a full investigation. The agency complied and requested the application be withdrawn. The Court, however, refused to honour the

CBI's request—which was based on Vahanvati's opinion—and demanded that the agency first explain why it wished to withdraw the case.

At the next hearing, in late January 2009, Vahanvati appeared before the Supreme Court, representing the government, and dismissed his own opinion recommending withdrawal. 'I had given an opinion in this case in November last,' he said, 'and it is no longer relevant.' Now the government argued that it wished for the CBI to consider the merits of the case on its own before coming to a decision on whether to proceed. Two weeks later, Mohan Parasaran, representing the CBI, conceded that the agency had acted on the instruction of the law ministry—again, based on Vahanvati's opinion—in seeking to withdraw its application, an admission that was excoriated by the justices. Vahanvati, again representing the government, now told the Court, 'We don't want to take any decision in this matter. Let the CBI consider the representation and submit report to the court.'

The twists and turns continued: in March 2009, the CBI completed its reversal, asking the court to ignore Vahanvati's opinion and proceed with the case. But in February 2011, Vahanvati was back in court once more, now arguing that the case should again be withdrawn, on the basis that the Court was not allowed to order a CBI probe unless 'fundamental rights' had been violated. A bemused bench told Mulayam's lawyers, 'He is supporting you. In fact, he has argued for you.'

The matter is still not resolved. In November 2012, the petitioner who originally brought the case against Yadav in 2005, Vishwanath Chaturvedi, filed a complaint in a Delhi court charging Vahanvati—along with Bhardwaj and four others—with 'criminal conspiracy' to shield Yadav from prosecution. Meanwhile, the case against Yadav remains in limbo: the Court ordered the CBI on 13 December 2012 to continue its probe, this time without 'obligation to file the status report before the government'.

Last month, Vahanvati found himself entangled in another uncomfortable situation involving a CBI investigation—this time regarding the agency's ongoing probe into the coal allocation scam. A series of news reports revealed that a status report submitted by the CBI to the Supreme Court on 8 March had first been vetted and toned down by officials from the law ministry and the PMO.

Several of these media reports have placed Vahanvati at a meeting, held in the law ministry on 5 March, where the report was amended; others have not mentioned his name.

But four sources, including a lawyer who represents the CBI, confirmed that Vahanvati was present at the meeting called by Law Minister Ashwani Kumar, along with Additional Solicitor General Harin Raval, CBI Director Ranjit Sinha, and O.P. Galhotra, a CBI officer. Raval and Vahanvati, I was told, were already present when Sinha and Galhotra arrived. The men reviewed the report together and changes were suggested; a new report was printed within the law ministry, and submitted to the Supreme Court.

The question of Vahanvati's participation is particularly serious: in the Supreme Court hearing on 12 March, Harin Raval, representing the CBI, was asked if the report had been shared with the executive, which he denied. The bench then asked Vahanvati, representing the government, if he had seen the report. He replied that he had not.

When the first news reports describing the law ministry meeting began to emerge earlier this month, I thought back to something Vahanvati had told me when we met in January, about his admiration for his father. 'My father was a great influence on me,' he said. 'I learned a lot from him. He never misled a judge, and that's why his credibility was so high.'

This profile was published just before a momentous general election in Pakistan, held for the first time after a democratically elected government was due to complete its five-year term. **NAWAZ SHARIF**, in opposition to the Pakistan People's Party government, positioned himself and his own Pakistan Muslim League—Nawaz (PMLN)—as 'anti-establishment'. He did this while nurturing the support of Pakistan's conservative voters, many of whom are fierce supporters of the Pakistani army.

Through the essay, I traced Sharif's once-close relationship with the army, and how, in his ten-year exile at the hands of General Musharraf, he grasped at the notion of taming the military. For the first time in English, the story also explored Sharif's biography in some detail, including the story of his close relationship with his late father, a lasting influence on Sharif.

In the spring of 2013, Pakistan was in the grip of Imran Khan mania, mesmerized by the former cricketer and the rise of his party, the Pakistan Tehreek-e-Insaf. Reporting the story of Sharif and the PMLN, however, made it clear that the election had only one possible winner. It also predicted Pakistan's present, in one bleak sense: it was clear that Prime Minister Sharif, even if he refused to tolerate the growth and influence of the Pakistani Taliban, would accommodate, even support, other elements of undemocratic Islamist power, particularly keen to remake Pakistani society to their liking.

This, too, has come to be. Sharif has cracked down on the Taliban with the help of the Pakistani army, but, just this summer, he also increased the budget of the unelected, orthodox, rather loathsome Council of Islamic ideology, Pakistan's top Islamic advisory body. They recently advised that a Pakistani husband could 'lightly' beat his wife if she defied his commands.

MIRA SETHI

Mira Sethi is an actor and writer living in Lahore. Her debut collection of short fiction is forthcoming from Knopf.

Watch the Throne

Nawaz Sharif on the cusp of power

By MIRA SETHI | 1 April 2013

I

On a Friday afternoon in early March, the two-time former prime minister and current leader of Pakistan's Opposition, Nawaz Sharif, inaugurated the refurbished Pak Tea House in Lahore—the old hangout of progressive Pakistani luminaries such as Faiz Ahmed Faiz, Ahmad Faraz and Saadat Hasan Manto. (It was known as the India Tea House before Partition.) Sharif entered through the front door, surrounded by a contingent of security personnel in plain clothes who pushed through the crowd to sculpt a path for him. As Sharif was making his way up the cramped, winding staircase, a group of young men, presumably uninvited locals from the Mall Road outside, tried to force their way in; Sharif's guards pushed the door on resisting hands and feet and shoulders and elbows until they were finally able to slam it shut.

'Pakistan's writers and intellectuals are its assets,' Sharif said in a calm baritone, upstairs, where tea and fried sweets were neatly arrayed on a thick white tablecloth. 'The reopening of the Pak Tea House is no less important than launching the [Lahore] Metro Bus Service project.' It was a canny little statement—the juxtaposition of two wholly dissimilar initiatives of the Punjab government, which is controlled by Sharif's party, the Pakistan Muslim League—Nawaz (PMLN), and headed by his younger brother, Shahbaz—designed to please the small congregation of left-wing short-story writers and columnists present in the cafe.

Sharif spoke for about five minutes in sophisticated colloquial Urdu, shook hands with everyone present, and quickly exited the cafe to set off for Mardan, 500 kilometres away in Khyber Pakhtunkhwa, formerly known as the North West Frontier Province, where he was due to address a rally later in the afternoon. As soon as Sharif had departed, some prominent columnists flocked around the stooped, bright-eyed, ninety-year-old Intizar Husain, Pakistan's most venerated living fiction writer in Urdu. 'Nice initiative,' the short-story writer Neelam Bashir said. She couldn't help the sarcasm. 'I'm going to vote for Imran Khan. At least he wants change.'

In March, for the first time in Pakistan's history, a National Assembly completed its full five-year term. Campaigning is in full swing for the next elections, while the leading parties are negotiating the composition of a caretaker government that will rule until the polls, which are likely to take place in May. With its traditional rival, the Bhutto family's Pakistan People's Party (PPP), now headed by sitting President Asif Ali Zardari, plummeting in popularity, Sharif's PMLN has emerged over the course of the last year as the front runner in the race to form the next government. Though the former cricketer Imran Khan's Pakistan Tehreek-e-Insaf (PTI) has attracted a passionate following among urban Pakistanis—demonstrated by his massive October 2011 rally in Lahore—and mounted a new challenge to the more established parties, what Khan dubbed the PTI 'tsunami' has not managed to sweep away the traditional bases of support for the country's two large mainstream parties, the PPP and PMLN.

According to several recent public opinion surveys of voting intentions, the PMLN currently appears to be the country's most popular political party. The most thorough poll to date, a survey of nearly 10,000 respondents in 300 villages and 200 urban localities, conducted by the Pakistan Institute of Legislative Development and Transparency (PILDAT) and Gallup Pakistan in February, found 41 per cent support for the PMLN, against 17 per cent for the ruling PPP and 14 per cent for Khan's PTI. In Punjab, Pakistan's largest province and Sharif's stronghold—which represents 148 of the 272 directly elected seats in the National Assembly—the survey found 59 per cent support for the PMLN, with the PTI and PPP trailing at 14 and 10 per cent.

At the rally later that day in Mardan, before a huge crowd from Pakistan's rightist, religious, trading class—Sharif's true constituency—his speech was a more traditional campaign stem-winder, assailing the failures of the PPP government and trumpeting the promises of the PMLN's recently released poll manifesto, with its heavy emphasis on economic growth and development. 'They have given the people nothing but suicide attacks, targeted killings, scandals of massive corruption, high inflation and excessive load-shedding,' Sharif said, adding that Zardari had 'sold the sovereignty of the country to the United States'. The PMLN, Sharif declared, would 'restore law and order to the country', resolve the Kashmir issue, improve ties with Afghanistan, eliminate load-shedding in two years, and bring the development initiatives it had pursued in Punjab to the rest of the country. He focused on projects that are close to his heart: laptop schemes, the creation of industrial zones, loans on easy conditions, the expansion of the motorway system he began in 1998, during his second term as prime minister. Nawaz Sharif is a builder, and holding forth on bullet trains and motorways gets him going. He was so palpably stirred by his own words that at one point, he raised a hand—the fair, unused hand of a wealthy Kashmiri-Punjabi—to stop the chanting crowd from interrupting his speech: 'No slogans right now, no slogans right now, no slogans right now.'

Sharif professes to draw inspiration from Sher Shah Suri, the Mughal-era builder of roads and works who is credited with constructing the Grand Trunk Road that links India, Pakistan and Afghanistan. (On one of the PMLN's official Facebook pages, Sharif's round face has been photoshopped inside Suri's bronze helmet.) In Mardan, Sharif promised the crowd he would build a bullet train from Karachi to Peshawar: the train would leave Karachi after the *fajr* prayer, at dawn, and arrive in Peshawar just in time for the evening *isha* prayer. He pointedly mentioned that passengers would have to perform only the afternoon prayer inside their cabins. It was a classic Sharif image, blending the promise of economic development with the rhetoric of religion. 'The way he frames modern requirements within the framework of religion, or social conservatism, is frankly impressive,' the television anchor and columnist Nasim Zehra told me. 'He's the only one who can do it.'

At the same time, among a certain segment of Pakistani liberals, there has been a wary reconciliation with the idea of Nawaz Sharif. In spite of his flaws—corruption, autocratic tendencies, a limited attention span—Sharif has recast himself as a defender of democracy and a critic of military interference in civilian affairs. In stark contrast to the intrigues of the 1990s, when Sharif and Benazir Bhutto took turns ejecting one another from office in collaboration with the army, Sharif has spent the past five years in the Opposition without attempting to bring down the PPP government, and in fact stood with it against such challenges, to the extent that he has been lampooned as 'the friendly Opposition'. Although Sharif remains a deeply conservative industrialist with ties to Pakistan's religious right, many liberals cautiously admire his stance on three key issues: bringing the army to heel, pursuing peace with India and defending parliamentary democracy—areas in which Sharif's views have clearly evolved in the wake of his own ouster, imprisonment and exile fourteen years ago at the hands of General Pervez Musharraf.

Many in Pakistan believe that Sharif, whose anti-military views have hardened since 1999, has come a long way since he first entered politics in 1981, when General Ghulam Jilani Khan, the Governor of Punjab under the military regime of General Zia-ul-Haq, recruited Sharif into his unelected Cabinet. Sharif, then thirty-one, was a conservative, obedient, pro-military businessman with a grievance against the deposed PPP government headed by Zulfikar Ali Bhutto, which had nationalized the Sharif family's steel mills—all the ingredients the military was seeking in a new leader to offset the populist PPP.

Sharif remains an old master in the realm of Pakistan's politics of patronage, and his strategy for the upcoming elections relies heavily on his traditional vote bank and the formidable PMLN party machine, with everything that entails: welcoming candidates with influence and existing alliances into the party, embracing a non-issue-based politics to attract anyone who can help the party win, and forging ties with powerful local figures rather than national alliances. The PMLN has had a populist tinge to it since Sharif declared autonomy from what Pakistanis call the 'establishment', a euphemism for the military. At the same time, Sharif retains a strong alliance with Pakistan's informal establishment: the country's conservative lobby of businessmen, traders and middle-class professionals. After throwing his weight behind the Lawyers' Movement and its campaign to restore the chief justice, which began in 2007, Sharif has clearly aligned himself with two branches of the state—the judiciary and the bureaucracy—to check the power of a third, the military. In short, he is in understated opposition to the army, while nurturing the support of the country's conservatives, many of whom are conventionally pro-military.

Imran Khan's PTI, by contrast, has staked its campaign on a rupture with traditional politics. According to Khan, feudalism and clan-based alliances, the backbone of traditional politics in Pakistan, are the country's biggest problems. The challenge for Khan, however, is that the tenets of traditional politics still represent the surest path to victory. Where Sharif has been consistent in his electoral tactics—his cold-blooded criterion for recruiting candidates is only that they be likely winners—Khan's position now looks confused. On the one hand, the PTI has just held democratic intra-party elections (a first for Pakistan). But at the same time, Khan has welcomed old stalwarts from the PPP and PMLN, feudal men of wealth and influence like former foreign minister Shah Mehmood Qureshi, and Javed Hashmi, a former PMLN party president. The PTI may be the party of 'change', but this stance has been diluted by the party's piecemeal embrace of traditional politics.

Additionally, Khan is generally regarded as closer to the military than his rivals, a perception that has been bolstered by allegations in the media that the generals encouraged Khan to form a third party and urged PPP and PMLN politicians to defect to the PTI. The military does not trust the PPP, based on the party's anti-army track record (though some would argue this has not been the case under Zardari); the generals distrust Sharif for his open criticism of their interference in civilian affairs. Khan's perceived cosiness with the army may not hurt him with many voters—as in any conservative society, Pakistanis by and large hold the military in high esteem—but it alienates him from liberals who traditionally supported the PPP for its anti-establishment stance and are now seeking an alternative after five years of terrorism, assassinations, economic stagnation and attacks on minorities. To the extent that the PPP is regarded in some circles as pro-establishment without being the establishment party, a kind of role reversal has taken place—Sharif and the PMLN are now positioned as 'anti-establishment', while retaining their traditional conservative vote bank.

After the assassination of Benazir Bhutto, the PPP rode to power on a sympathy vote in the 2008 elections. In 2013, because of the anti-incumbency factor and its astonishingly bad governance, the PPP is expected to get fewer votes. But it is still in contention because of one fact: the PPP's ethnic vote in Sindh—a vote for the martyred Bhuttos tightly wound around feudal fealty—is largely intact.

The PMLN won the majority of seats in Punjab in 2008, and formed a government in the province, but Sharif did not do well elsewhere. Additionally, Sharif's spurning of the Pakistan Muslim League—Quaid (PMLQ)—composed largely of defectors from Sharif's party who supported Musharraf's regime—hurt him numerically in the last election. Now, Sharif has consolidated his vote bank in Punjab and, letting opportunism override personal anger, he has brought back many candidates from the PMLQ, restoring his party's reach. To form a government in Islamabad, a party needs 172 of the 342 seats in the National Assembly. (In addition to the 272 directly elected seats, there are 70 seats reserved for women and minorities, allocated in proportion to each party's share of the total vote.) No party is likely to win a majority outright, but if Sharif sweeps Punjab with, say, ninety seats, and cobbles together thirty from other provinces, he is poised to be the leading contender to form a government.

II

On a cool February morning, I visited Sharif at his 1,000-acre estate in Raiwind, on the outskirts of Lahore. Driving into

Raiwind, Lahore's banks, restaurants, makeshift dental clinics, mosques, marriage halls, and a 'God Bless' beauty parlour gradually gave way to a sunlit semi-rural landscape: the ghostly splendour of eucalyptus, followed by orange trees, mangroves, and finally, blazing rows of mustard. A swirl of corruption allegations surrounded the construction of this estate in the 1990s—in particular, that Punjab government funds were spent to build watercourses and roads leading to the property, along with energy and telecommunication networks. But no investigations were allowed since Sharif, or his brother Shahbaz, have ruled Punjab since the 1980s (apart from the Musharraf years, when the PMLQ controlled the state while the Sharifs were in exile). On the estate, a fenced yard holds peacocks, birds and prancing deer—a small zoo of sorts. As I approached the residence, a gardener was at work, tending patches of cabbage, tomato and coriander.

Inside, the house has the feel of a baroque pavilion, with white pillars, red velvet curtains, calligraphic oil paintings in reds and golds, and sunlight streaming in through tall windows. It was hard to miss the two stuffed lions—the symbol of the PMLN—parked outside the drawing room door. (They had been imported from Zimbabwe, I was told.) Sharif's five-year-old granddaughter stopped in front of the lions as her mother, Maryam, showed me into the room. She swayed on her feet for a moment, contemplating the animals. 'This one,' she said, pointing first to the lion on the right, 'is *nana abbu*.' She pointed to the left. 'That one is Shahbaz uncle.' Though the PMLN is often described as a dynastic party just like the PPP, the reality is more complicated. Sharif's father was not a politician, and his own sons have stayed out of politics. Shahbaz's oldest son, Hamza, does occupy a core position in the PMLN, and appears to be heir apparent, though Nawaz recently took the surprising step—at least for a man of his conservative bearing—of allowing his daughter Maryam to join the party, though her future role is not yet certain. ('She's very intelligent, Mashallah,' he told me.)

In the family's private chambers, Kulsoom, Sharif's wife, sat reading a tattered edition of John Dryden's poetry. On the small table in front of her was an Urdu newspaper and a slim volume of T.S. Eliot's poems; in the margins of its brittle, yellowing pages, she had written 'v.imp', here and there, with a leaky, blue pen. The notes were from her days as a graduate student; she studied, among other things, the influence of English poetry on the Urdu language. It is quite possible that her husband has never heard of John Dryden.

Sharif was wearing a crème-coloured shalwar kameez. The *awami*, or people's, suit—as it has been called since Zulfikar Ali Bhutto popularized it in the 1970s—is meant to conceal divisions of class and power. But Sharif, in his pistachio-green waistcoast and gold-buckled loafers, his face pink and white, freckled along the brow, looked more like a European patriarch than a grassroots Punjabi politician. In the centre of the huge lounge, on a table, was a gold and silver model of Mecca and Medina, a gift from King Abdullah of Saudi Arabia, the monarch who freed Sharif from the coup-making generals in 2000 and hosted him for five years.

As he admitted in the astonishingly frank interviews he gave to the journalist Sohail Warraich between 2001 and 2006, which form the basis of the most comprehensive book on Sharif's life, *The Traitor Within: Nawaz Sharif's Story in His Own Words* (2008), his years in exile provided him time to reflect. The book contains some of Sharif's most uncensored thoughts to date—from the reflective to the absurd to the accidentally honest: 'The Pakistani agencies created the Taliban'; 'Zia was very affectionate'; 'I wanted to see the welcome Benazir received in 1986. I heard the crowds were huge.' He learnt how to use the Internet, a steady flow of party loyalists kept him abreast of Pakistani news, and he began reading newspapers and books.

'I did a lot of soul-searching,' Sharif said of these years, the Western phrase unusually affecting coming from a man most comfortable in Urdu. 'I looked at my mistakes, the blunders I had committed in my life and in the past, as prime minister too.' I waited for a tirade against Pervez Musharraf—how appointing him was a bad idea—but instead Sharif slipped into Urdu, and invoked Allah again and again. 'I thought to myself, Allah, you know better. For what mistake am I getting this punishment? *Tu mujhe itna bata zaroor yey kiss cheez ki saza hai. Takeh mein ainda* repeat *na karoun* (Please tell me exactly for what I am being punished, so I don't repeat my mistake). Whatever has been done, *Allah tou hee behtar jaanta hai* (Allah knows best). As prime minister I did a lot of good things, but I also did bad things, perhaps. *Tou uski shaid mujhe* punishment *mil rahi hai* (Perhaps I am being punished for that).'

His mournful metaphysical tone suddenly shifted to more concrete thoughts: 'Every five or ten years, there have been coups in our country, which have destroyed our country. When I was in exile, I thought to myself: this must not happen again. So I will struggle for that—for the sanctity of the ballot box. This must not happen again.'

It was during his exile that Sharif grasped the notion of taming the military. He realized that conspiring against mainstream political parties played into the hands of the brass. Sharif told me, with the unchecked frankness of a Punjabi politician, that he could have brought down the PPP government had he so desired. 'I could have done a conspiracy,' he said. 'I could have tried to topple the current government, but I didn't.' He added, almost wistfully, 'The time for conspiracies is now gone. That time has totally gone.' When Tahir-ul-Qadri, a dual Pak-Canadian citizen-turned-activist-preacher parachuted into Pakistan with the aim of bringing the PPP government down in January 2013, Sharif brought the Opposition parties together and denounced Qadri, calling his long march a 'circus'. Qadri's thunderous appeals fizzled out soon after.

'But the PPP has failed miserably,' Sharif said, extracting a piece of cardamom from his jacket and putting it in his mouth. 'They could have fixed the problem of power shortage and load-shedding—at least 50 per cent of it they could have fixed, but they didn't make any effort. They were so preoccupied with completing their five years—and I'm very happy that Parliament has completed its full five years, I really am—but what have they delivered in five years? Just making a government isn't enough.'

Since we were sitting in his controversial estate, I brought up the issue of corruption. Allegations abound of the ways Sharif made his money while in power: bending the laws to acquire properties; accepting kickbacks on major projects like a motorway from Lahore to Islamabad; privatization of major banks during his tenure; taking loans from state-owned banks for business purposes, which were then written off on some pretext or the other; illegally converting money into foreign exchange; and unapologetic tax evasion. None of the allegations has ever led to a conviction, and Sharif flatly denies them. '*Dekhein jee*,' he said. 'We started our business in 1937, and even at the time of Partition, Mashallah, we were very prosperous. I've been prime minister twice. We made a motorway and many other big projects. But there is no proof of us having received kickbacks! Not a single piece of evidence.' Khaled Ahmed, an editor at *Newsweek Pakistan* and an expert on the politics of the Punjab, laughed when I mentioned that Sharif paid $10 in income tax in 1999, his last year in office. 'He doesn't like taxation.' Corruption itself is not the problem, Ahmed insisted. 'China and India have more corruption than Pakistan. It is really the shrinking writ of the state and terrorism that is the problem. People are running away, and they are taking their money with them.'

I asked Sharif if he was only criticizing the army now because Musharraf had ejected him from office and sent him into exile. 'I don't criticize the army,' he protested. 'I critique the mindset that creates conspiracies against democracy.' I pushed him further, asking if he would still see it this way if the army had not given him a rough time personally. 'Absolutely,' he said, softly. 'Even if they had not done anything to me, I have come to the conclusion that whatever has happened to us in the last few decades'—the repeated imposition of military rule—'has been terrible.'

Whatever his reasons, Sharif, who had clashed with several army chiefs in the decade prior to his fateful confrontation with Musharraf (and cooperated with a few others to cause Benazir Bhutto trouble during her two terms as prime minister), now finds himself aligned with the intelligentsia's growing resentment of the military's unchecked power. 'It was inconceivable a decade ago that a politician from the Punjab would question the resource allocation and decision-making within the Pakistani army,' said Raza Rumi, a liberal commentator and the director of the Jinnah Institute think tank in Islamabad. 'The world seems to have ignored this major tectonic shift within Pakistan's polity, whereby the largest conservative province has a popular voice, Mian Nawaz Sharif, calling for redressal of the civil–military imbalance.'

'If Sharif comes to power,' a retired military officer recently remarked, referring to the fleet of BMWs and Land Cruisers in which many of the top brass currently travel, 'he will put the generals in Suzukis.' Jehangir Karamat, who was chief of army staff from 1996 until 1998, when he was forced to resign by Sharif, put it to me this way: 'The air force, army and navy chiefs used to get a plot, after retirement, from the government—in addition to other perks. Sharif did away with the plot, and the policy is in place till today. In fact, because he was on an austerity drive, he also told the officers they would not be able to import duty-free cars. A good thing.'

The military in Pakistan runs banks, cement and fertilizer plants, insurance and leasing companies, armaments factories, housing estates. It even makes corn flakes. Retiring senior officers enter the exclusive club of the rich, landed and influential. Serving officers, who don't share Karamat's sober, post-retirement analysis, look far less kindly upon those who would put them in their place.

Sharif may be sincere when he insists that his new-found determination to limit the army's role in civilian affairs is the product of his 'soul-searching' in exile and not merely a desire to settle scores with those who removed him. But when he reflects on his own past errors, his tangle with Musharraf looms large. 'One of the biggest mistakes I made,' Sharif tells me, 'was not appointing the army chief based on seniority and merit'—there were two chiefs ahead of Musharraf. 'But two or three people in my circle supported Musharraf very strongly and I fell in their trap. I should have gone on merit. That was my mistake.' (According to many accounts, Sharif's younger brother Shahbaz was one of two men who pushed for Musharraf.) 'What Musharraf did was not just unconstitutional,' Sharif said with a grimace, referring to the 1999 coup that toppled his government. 'It was revenge. He didn't want to see my face.'

III

On 12 October 1999, Prime Minister Nawaz Sharif finally decided to remove the army chief from office. Sharif had appointed

Pervez Musharraf in October 1998, but had soon come to regret the decision. He had chosen Musharraf because he was an Urdu-speaking *muhajir* soldier whose family had come to Pakistan at the time of Partition. Sharif believed Musharraf would be a pliable and non-conspiratorial chief, with no real sway in Pakistan's Punjabi-dominated army. Musharraf, for his part, was extremely deferential in the early months of his appointment—he knew he had been selected out of turn; he also knew Sharif put a premium on loyalty. Soon, however, like many of his colleagues in the army, Musharraf began to regard Sharif as a paranoid, despotic civilian who didn't fully understand complex matters of national security.

One of Musharraf's early decisions after becoming army chief was to explore the possibility of making headway in the disputed region of Kashmir. In the spring of 1999, soon after Sharif and India's prime minister Atal Behari Vajpayee signed the Lahore Declaration, a bilateral treaty for normalization of relations which included a pledge to find a peaceful solution to conflict in Kashmir, Musharraf gave secret orders to Pakistani troops to cross the Line of Control. In other words, just as Sharif was delicately putting Kashmir on the diplomatic back burner, Musharraf was preparing to internationalize the Kashmir dispute. Pakistani soldiers, posing as Kashmiri mujahideen, scaled the Himalayan peaks until they arrived in the town of Kargil, a base camp for Indian soldiers stationed on top of the Siachen glacier.

Kargil was, in army parlance, an 'unheld area'—an inhospitable region along the Line of Control, abandoned by both sides during the winter. The surreptitiously advancing Pakistani troops escaped the notice of the Indians in the early weeks of 1999, and made initial territorial gains. When the incursion was discovered in the first week of May—Indian army patrols were tipped off by local shepherds—New Delhi did not immediately appreciate the extent of Musharraf's calculations. A carefully crafted narrative, meanwhile, was being rolled out to the Pakistani public by the media managers of the military: Kashmiri mujahideen had 'reclaimed' Indian-held territory.

But cross-border fire increased, as did media-led jingoism in both countries. Given the secretive nature of the operation, Pakistani papers made no mention of the fact that the Pakistani army had been the instigator, and its own soldiers, holed up at treacherous heights with a blocked supply route for food, were reduced to eating snow as the helicopter gunships roared through the Kashmiri skies.

After a decade and a half of silence, the Kargil war has come back into the news in the last few months. Pakistani talk show hosts on private TV channels have openly discussed how the miscalculation of the Pakistani army resulted in confusion at home, defeat in Kargil and humiliation internationally. Most recently, in January, Lieutenant General (retd) Shahid Aziz, a former chief of general staff of the Pakistani army, published a book in Urdu, *For How Long This Silence*, arguing that the Kargil adventure was a 'four-man show', a reference to the gang of four generals—Musharraf and three other top commanders—who conceived and executed it. This is the first time someone so high up in the ranks—Aziz headed the analysis wing of the Inter-Services Intelligence—has spoken with frankness about Kargil. Aziz wrote that Musharraf worked on a policy of 'need to know'. In other words, Musharraf would issue orders to only those who were required to implement them instead of first consulting corps commanders and other military officers.

Sharif's long-standing allegation—that Musharraf kept him in the dark about Kargil—is now generally accepted by Pakistan watchers both at home and abroad, though some argue that Musharraf had briefed Sharif on elements of the operation and the prime minister failed to understand its full scope. When I brought up the subject during our meeting, Sharif replied confidently. 'My position is now being vindicated,' he said. 'I think everyone now knows who the liars are and who the truth-tellers are.' He adjusted himself on the floral-patterned sofa, took out rimless spectacles from his breast-pocket and held them aloft, like a wand. 'This is enough for me.'

Soon after India cried foul, Musharraf pressured Sharif to meet US President Bill Clinton to 'explain' the Kargil 'situation' and bail out Pakistan. 'I did a lot on Musharraf's urging that I regret,' Sharif told me. As he put it to journalist Warraich while in exile, 'Musharraf did the dirty work, but I was made to suffer for it.' Knowing that a political leader who had lost a war would be unlikely to win another election, Sharif clambered on to a plane to Washington, DC, without having secured an appointment with the President of the United States. Worried about the possibility of a wider war between India and Pakistan, Clinton made a special exception on 4 July 1999, to meet the Pakistani prime minister. He made it clear that Pakistan was the aggressor and should withdraw immediately. Sharif had to concede to India's demands; he returned home a defeated man.

For Sharif, things had changed from the heady days of May 1998, when, just over two weeks after India tested its nuclear weapons, Sharif followed suit and triumphantly detonated the world's first 'Islamic bomb'. Two memoirs by Sharif's then cabinet members, Foreign Minister Gohar Ayub (the son of General Ayub Khan), and Finance Minister Sartaj Aziz, have diplomatically suggested that Sharif was hesitant to test. In *Glimpses into the Corridors of Power* (2007), Ayub argues that it was his insistence, in part, that swayed the prime minister to give in to nationalist sentiment at home. During our conversation Sharif said that until India tested its nuclear devices he had 'never even thought about it'. During his rally in Mardan, however, Sharif tweaked his position, telling the crowd of young and old Pashtuns that the US had offered him $5 billion for not testing the bomb, and he rejected the offer in the best national interest.

In Raiwind, he told me, 'We had the bomb, we'd carried out cold tests of the bomb, but nobody had carried out a hot test of the bomb. We never thought, "Let us test our bomb." We knew the implications. If I were mad, I'd have tested much before! The thing is, we have been in a very unfortunate race with India.'

'An arms race?' I asked. 'An arms race,' he conceded grimly. 'We waste all our money on F-16s. They buy tanks, we also buy tanks. We also waste our resources. Both countries have wasted billions of dollars into building up defence.' After a long pause, he said, 'I think we should sit down with India. Both countries—you have to do it together—just as America and the Soviet Union figured it out, India and Pakistan need to figure it out, too.'

Following Kargil, jail and a decade-long exile paved the way for Sharif's avowed distance from the military establishment that had birthed him. When I gently suggested that he, too, was a creation of the 'establishment', he was quick to cite history. 'Zulfikar Ali Bhutto came in Ayub Khan's time, if you remember. General Ayub was a dictator. When I started my career in politics, there was a military dictatorship. Now, one couldn't have fought with them upon entering the political arena for the first time.' It was a dissembling response. 'My real mistake,' he said quickly, 'was to appoint Musharraf.' This fixation on personal enmities represents a narrow view of history, but it suits the political class. Ayub Khan's 'mistake' was to make Zulfikar Ali Bhutto a minister; Bhutto's mistake was to make Zia-ul-Haq the army chief; Zia's mistake was to promote Nawaz Sharif; Benazir Bhutto's mistake was to make Farooq Leghari the President; Leghari's mistake was to side with Sharif over Bhutto; Sharif's mistake was to make Musharraf the army chief; Musharraf's mistake was to cut a deal with Benazir. And so on.

In reality, since Sharif has come of political age, he has had problems with several army chiefs. In 1991, over a disagreement about Pakistan's role in the Gulf War, General Mirza Aslam Beg tried to create space for a coup. Sharif thwarted Beg, narrowly survived, and tried to appoint an army chief of his choice. But under Pakistan's Constitution, the President selects the army chief. President Ghulam Ishaq Khan chose General Asif Nawaz as the chief in 1991. Sharif immediately developed problems with Asif Nawaz over the issue of the writ of the army versus the writ of the government. In 1992, Nawaz wanted to carry out a military operation against the Muttahida Qaumi Movement (MQM), the Karachi-based secular political party known for its routine embrace of violence—with whom Sharif had an alliance. Sharif tried to persuade him against it, but the army went ahead and defanged the MQM. When Asif Nawaz died unexpectedly of a heart attack in 1993, Sharif again sought to select an army chief—this time, he wanted a Punjabi loyalist. But Ishaq Khan, hoping to strengthen his own position, narrowed in on General Waheed Kakar, a Pashto-speaking compatriot who was number five in the military's hierarchy of seniority.

Sharif and Ishaq Khan had developed tense relations by this time: Ishaq Khan accused Sharif of corruption and of hounding his detractors. Within months, Ishaq Khan dismissed Sharif, but the Supreme Court restored him as prime minister. A gridlock ensued, compelling Kakar to show the exit to both and reorder fresh elections. In Sharif's view, the army should have compelled Ishaq Khan rather than himself, a democratically elected prime minister, to resign: he never forgave the army for siding with Ishaq Khan.

After Benazir Bhutto returned to power in 1993, she appointed the mild-mannered General Jehangir Karamat as chief of army staff. When Sharif came back into office in 1997, he first got rid of the President and chief justice, who had opposed Bhutto and were now blocking his autocratic ambitions, and then attempted to control the army chief. Barely three months before Karamat was scheduled to retire in 1998, Sharif sacked him for proposing a national security council to be run jointly by the military and elected civilians, seeing in Karamat's plan a threat to his own power as prime minister. Now, Sharif was rampant: he had a two-thirds majority in Parliament, a loyalist new President in Rafiq Tarrar, and for the first time in his political career, he was poised to handpick an army chief. (He chose Pervez Musharraf.)

When I mentioned that Musharraf routinely told newspaper editors and opinion-makers in the West that Sharif had 'a beard in his belly'—that his true sympathies lay with the fundamentalists—Sharif looked taken aback, and unleashed our meeting's longest monologue. 'He wanted to be the blue-eyed boy of the West so he made statements like that. Musharraf was the one who had an understanding with those elements who have been creating trouble for Pakistan. The establishment needs this type of strength—power, support—from such elements. Because when they want to sideline democratic forces, they need to bolster their support from other angles.

'This problem of Pakistan's, this has been created neither by me, nor by democratic forces. This is the work of the establishment. If democracy had continued its course, if dictators hadn't thrust their way into power, we would not be seeing what we are seeing today. Tell me something: why was there no terrorism in Pakistan on the 12th of October 1999? Musharraf should give an answer to these things.'

Sharif didn't explicitly name the Islamic and jihadi parties who fall into this category of militant zealots. 'Let me tell you: martial law is a breeding ground for extremism and terrorism. Musharraf constantly sidelined the democratic forces of Pakistan: first the people's party, then Benazir Bhutto personally, then our party. To cover up his own doings, he tried to build up that image of me. Otherwise, when I left in 1999, the way that we ran our government was absolutely acceptable to the West. And to the East, to the North, to the South!'

Musharraf's metaphor may rankle Sharif, but the core of his constituency remains Pakistan's conservative, religious class—a fact that gives continued ammunition to Sharif's critics, who are distinctly unimpressed by his more recent criticism of the military. Nighat Said, the director of ASR, a radical NGO that champions women's rights and a secular, demilitarized Pakistan, told me she thinks Sharif has 'not changed in any fundamental way'. Sharif, she believes, has a personal vendetta against the military—'sort of like unrequited love'. His party, she argues, does not share Sharif's anti-military stance. 'Sharif was and remains Zia-ul-Haq's protégé.'

IV

In front of Lahore's Jinnah library, situated in the middle of a public garden of the same name, a fountain shoots long warm beams of water into the air. The building overlooking the fountain was constructed in the mid nineteenth century during British rule; it was a place where the colonial elite congregated for tea, drinks, bridge and dancing. In the 1980s the club was touched by Zia-ul-Haq's civilizing zeal and converted into a library.

Rows of yellow roses and deciduous shrub surround the fountain. It is in this garden, around the fountain, that a young

Nawaz Sharif would pant behind his father in the 1960s. 'I used to follow him,' Sharif remembered. 'Whatever he did, I did that too. If he was running, then I would run too. If he was walking, then I would walk too.'

That he followed his father in 'whatever he did' is a telling admission on a broader level: it was on his father's insistence that a diffident Nawaz got into politics. 'I remember him as the fair, shy son of his father,' said Pervaiz Elahi, a former member of the PMLN and former chief minister of Punjab, who is now an opponent of Sharif. 'When he entered politics and had to make his first short speech in Sargodha, his ears turned scarlet.'

Muhammad Sharif, a Kashmiri whose ancestors migrated to Amritsar, and soon after Partition to Lahore, built a steel business in Pakistan along with his brothers and cousins, which grew into an industrial conglomerate—with interests in steel, sugar and textiles—called the Ittefaq Group. In 1972, Zulfikar Ali Bhutto nationalized Pakistan's major private industries, including the Ittefaq foundries. Reeling from financial pressure, Muhammad Sharif encouraged his eldest son to join politics after Bhutto's fall in 1977 in order to protect the family's business interests.

'I was never interested in politics,' Sharif told me when I asked him how he came to join the Punjab government in the early 1980s. 'I never thought I would enter politics. I used to think, *keh itni* tension *hoti hai, kya karte hain* (there's so much tension involved, what do they do), how do they manage? I had no intention of getting into politics at all.'

'*Buss*,' he continued, looking lost in thought for a moment. 'I don't know how it happened. All of a sudden, I was picked up by General Jilani, and he wanted to induct me into his cabinet. I had graduated only a few years earlier. I was in my own business. But soon after I finished my studies, our factory was nationalized by Mr Bhutto. It fell into the thirty-two factories that were initially nationalized. All of a sudden, we were deprived of everything. *Jo saara* invested *tha woh* lost *ho gya* (All that we invested was lost).'

Back then, it is said, Nawaz Sharif had a friend who was related to Ghulam Jilani Khan, then serving as the appointed Governor of Punjab under Zia. One day, Sharif was taken by his friend to have tea with Jilani, who found the young man good-natured and obedient. The conversation turned to a house Jilani was building, around the periphery of which he wished to erect an iron fence; he asked Sharif if Ittefaq foundries might be interested in building the fence for him. Sharif replied politely that he would ask his father and get back to the Governor with an answer. But when Muhammad Sharif heard what had transpired, he rebuked Nawaz for his naivety. The Sharifs quickly built and delivered the iron fence, and no bill was ever sent.

Generals Zia and Jilani saw the Sharifs as an apolitical business family who hated the Bhuttos, and were ready to express their loyalty to the military. In 1979, the Tehreek-e-Istiqlal, which Sharif had recently joined, was poised to triumph in the polls. But Zia postponed the polls, and Sharif quickly turned his allegiance to the dictator. In 1980 Zia denationalized Sharif's business, and returned it to them with more than their due share of compensation. A year later, Jilani made Nawaz a minister in his cabinet, elevating him later to the choicest slot of finance minister. Sharif duly became the chief minister of Punjab after Zia's non-party polls in 1985 were boycotted by the PPP. The father-and-son business was now ready to profit from a heavy dose of pro-establishment politics.

Zia perished in an air crash in 1988, and the PPP, led by Benazir Bhutto, who had returned from exile two years earlier, came to power in December of the same year amid country-wide celebrations. During the time between Bhutto's return and elevation to prime minister, Sharif's Muslim League had become part of the Islami Jamhoori Ittehad (IJI), an anti-Bhutto political alliance later shown to have been funded by the ISI. The IJI whipped up Punjabi nationalism for the first time under the slogan '*Jaag Punjabi jaag!* (Awake, Punjabi, awake!)' In the 1988 elections, thanks to the assistance of the ISI, the province was captured by Sharif, even as the rest of the country went Benazir Bhutto's way. Having begun his apprenticeship under a military dictator, Sharif had absorbed the conservative, rightist politics of Zia-ul-Haq. It was during Benazir's first tenure as prime minister that Sharif, aided and abetted by the military, emerged as her most determined political foe.

Though an upper-middle-class Punjabi-Kashmiri family, the Sharifs were also Victorian in their way—tightly knit, religious, loyal, conservative. If conflict existed, it was neither described nor defined as an issue of concern. Nawaz was an obedient son: in later years, as prime minister, he repeatedly sought his father's counsel—to the point where it became a national joke. Warraich, the journalist who observed Sharif at close quarters during his time in exile, told me that 'the real love of Nawaz Sharif's life was his father', and recounted a scene from the family's time in Saudi Arabia. 'Nawaz Sharif used to bring his father into the room, on a wheelchair, and put him in front of the family. Even though by then his father could not talk, he used to bring him there, regardless, and talk to him about everything.'

I put the question to Sharif in exactly these terms: was your father the real love of your life? His response was unselfconscious and distinctly Punjabi in its desire to celebrate the obvious: 'Absolutely correct. He was my mentor. I drew a lot of inspiration and guidance from him. When I was prime minister people made a lot of fun of the fact that *aye* Nawaz Sharif prime minister *saara kuj Abba jee kolon jaa ke puchda aye* (This prime minister Nawaz Sharif consults his father on every matter)!' he told me. 'But I felt very proud of it.' He added, in a lower voice, 'Even if people said it tauntingly. *Theek hai jee, agar Abba jee hain tou Abba jee ki* respect *karni chahye* (All right, if Abba jee is there, Abba jee must be respected).'

At the time, however, Sharif was far less sanguine about the jibes. The *Friday Times*, an English-language weekly in Lahore, began to print a satirical column in Sharif's voice—an idiom blending Punjabi syntax with intermediate English—in 1990. Throughout the 1990s, it poked fun at Sharif's relationship with his father: 'Whatever Abba jee is saying,' went a typical line, 'I am doing.' (Full disclosure: the newspaper is published by my parents, Najam Sethi and Jugnu Mohsin.) In 1992, shortly after he became prime minister, Sharif sent his police chief to warn them against publishing any more references to 'Abba Jee'. The threats continued until my mother obtained a meeting with then President Ghulam Ishaq Khan, after which the government backed off. (In 1999, during his second term in office, Sharif had my father jailed for a month on spurious charges of treason, likely in retaliation for an interview he had given to the producers of a BBC documentary focusing on a corruption scandal involving the Sharif family; around the same time, Sharif had arrested two other journalists who had also spoken to the BBC. A month after his arrest, the Supreme Court ordered his unconditional release. Sharif later apologized, and the two men now have cordial relations.)

It was at his father's urging that Sharif, during his first term as prime minister, passed the Shariat Ordinance, making religious observance and practice a constitutional necessity. Then, as now, the PMLN positioned itself as the promoter and architect of Pakistan's Islamic nationalism, and those who remain wary of Sharif invariably point to this track record, and his close relations with the Saudi royal family, to argue his commitment to democracy and civilian rule is merely superficial.

The activist Nighat Said argued that Sharif's stand against the army's involvement in politics was hardly a sufficient reason for liberals to lend him their support. 'I can't look at the civil–military phenomenon in isolation and praise him,' she said. 'What is his record on women's rights? At least with the PPP I have a sense of being able to breathe.'

Nasim Zehra, the TV anchor, thinks Sharif serves a different function in today's Pakistan. She envisions him as a modern man who nonetheless boasts bona fide conservative credentials in an increasingly conservative Pakistan; a man who, via his commitment to free-market economics, porous borders, trade with India and the world, can strengthen Pakistan's democratic moorings. Sharif is the man, she noted, who in his second term shifted Pakistan's weekend from Friday–Saturday to Saturday–Sunday, in line with global custom, by appearing on television one day and quoting a verse from the Quran that decrees Muslims get back to work after the Friday prayer. Pakistan had followed the Western weekend from Independence to 1977, when the privately secular but publicly feeble Zulfikar Ali Bhutto shifted the days to appease religious clerics. Striking down Bhutto's decision was 'something even Benazir, his daughter, failed to do', Zehra added.

For many, Sharif's alliance with the religious right remains a paramount concern, particularly at a moment when the country has been aflame with violent attacks on minority groups, carried out by banned extremist outfits headquartered in Punjab. Numerous media reports have suggested that the Punjab government has resisted calls from the federal government to crack down on terrorist groups like Lashkar-e-Jhangvi (LeJ) and Sipah-e-Sahaba (SSP)—implicated in the killings of hundreds of Shia and other minorities. According to these reports, the PMLN has negotiated seat-adjustment deals with the Ahle Sunnat Wal Jamaat (ASWJ), the 'official' name of the banned SSP, under which the parties agree not to contest against one another in particular seats and to support one another's candidates. The PMLN has denied any formal electoral arrangements with the ASWJ, but ASWJ leaders have confirmed as much to reporters, and evidence suggests the party has lent support to PMLN candidates in the recent past. The Punjab law minister, Rana Sanaullah, a senior leader in the PMLN, is also said to have a cosy relationship with the LeJ: he was seen campaigning alongside an SSP leader during a 2010 by-election, and photographs recently emerged of him addressing an ASWJ rally.

In 1998, during his second term as prime minister, Sharif launched a harsh crackdown against both the LeJ and SSP, in which dozens of militants were killed; the following year, the LeJ attempted to assassinate Sharif by bombing a bridge his motorcade was about to cross. Khaled Ahmed of *Newsweek Pakistan*, a secular expert on Punjab politics, was surprisingly unperturbed when I raised the question of Sharif's cooperative political relationship with the ASWJ, which he depicted as a matter of electoral necessity. 'No party can win in south Punjab until they talk to these elements,' he said. 'Everyone has an alliance of sorts with them.' South Punjab is an impoverished, swelteringly hot part of the country that has long been a recruiting ground for state-sanctioned jihadi groups. The feudal landlords of the region, irrespective of party, pay money to the jihadi groups, partly because they believe in the anti-Shia crusade and partly for protection purposes, Ahmed explained. (Indeed, allegations soon emerged that the PPP had also conducted seat-adjustment negotiations with the ASWJ.)

More than anything, Ahmed said, these electoral alliances tell us something about the weakness of the Pakistani state. 'These non-state actors continue to be used by the army—that's the problem. So Pakistan's politicians have to make adjustments if they want to participate in elections.' I reminded him that Imran Khan has, so far, eschewed such alliances with sectarian hardliners. He laughed, and said, 'Imran can benefit without aligning because of his avowed softness towards the Taliban. Had Nawaz not got in first, Imran might have considered his options with them.'

In their scramble for electoral majorities, Pakistani parties are forced to rely on a variety of gimmicks, shinily packaged welfare programmes (the PMLN's laptop scheme, the PPP's Benazir Income Support Programme), promises of national sovereignty, and deals with extremists. But the fact remains that Imran Khan does not have an open alliance with jihadi groups whereas the PMLN has a record of using political Islam to suit its ends.

The PMLN's critics have been quick to add that the Punjab government's record protecting minorities from sectarian violence leaves much to be desired. Three years after the August 2009 anti-Christian riots in Gojra, Punjab, in which eight members of the Christian community were burnt alive and over 100 houses set on fire by Muslims, the Punjab government is refusing to make public the findings of the Gojra judicial tribunal. Its report was submitted to Shahbaz Sharif in October 2009, seeking an immediate implementation of the recommendations. Though its main conclusions have reached the media, the report has not been made public because of its indictment of the Punjab government in refusing to bring the perpetrators to justice. According to reporter Amir Mir of the *News* newspaper, the 258-page inquiry report held the Punjab police responsible for the events of the massacre, saying the police should have deployed forces in sufficient numbers to stop violence against the Christian community.

Sharif takes succour from the fact that the Islamists' share of the popular vote has declined with every election since the creation of Pakistan—it creates space for his party, after all—but he seems unlikely to confront non-state religious outfits. In early February this year, a video message from a Tehreek-e-Taliban

Pakistan (TTP) spokesperson proposed peace negotiations with Islamabad, but demanded guarantors who would stand assurance against the Pakistani army breaking any agreements. Sharif, named as one of the guarantors, refused to accept this, but publicly asked that the PPP-led government take the initiative. I asked him why the TTP had suggested his name as one of the guarantors.

'I don't know, frankly,' he said. 'Look at the USA! They are talking to the Taliban also! Second, the guy who was killed in the Abbottabad operation—what's his name? Yes, Osama bin Laden. Osama bin Laden was Americans' biggest ally in the 1990s. They were working together to oust the Soviet troops.'

'On certain issues I have very principled stands,' he said to me. 'People don't like that.'

V

If the polls are correct, and Sharif can retain his lead and form a coalition, he will take office as the first person in Pakistan's history to become prime minister three times, and do so as a result of a historic transition from one civilian administration to another. But what does he want to achieve?

Any reasonably intelligent businessman can profit under a 'pro-growth' government simply by knowing a few of the right people, so further money-making seems unlikely to be Sharif's main motivation. Power, on the other hand, comes only from political victory. 'People thought Nawaz Sharif was never going to come back,' Mehmal Sarfraz, a left-leaning journalist, told me. 'More than anything else, in the kind of society Pakistan is, Nawaz Sharif wants to stay politically relevant. He has unfinished business.'

Sharif has not only survived, he has managed, after eight years in exile, to lead his party to the cusp of an election victory—and to do so while being in an understated opposition to the country's most powerful institution, which many of his constituents still trust and respect. When I met Jehangir Karamat, the retired chief of army staff whom Sharif once sacked, he told me he had 'personally never been for the military's overarching influence in politics'. Sharif clearly feels the same way, but he cannot state this too openly, too brazenly, and live to be a practising politician in Pakistan today.

As our conversation was coming to a close, I asked Sharif, out of curiosity, where he had been on the day that Benazir Bhutto was assassinated. He was campaigning in Rawalpindi with a party colleague, he told me. Benazir had called him in the morning, he said, and when he called her back he was told she was in Liaquat Bagh, in the same city, addressing a large crowd and would call him back after the rally.

In 2006, Sharif and Bhutto had signed a Charter of Democracy, establishing an alliance to end Musharraf's military rule and return the country to civilian control. In October 2007, Bhutto took the risk of returning to Pakistan; by that point, Sharif told me, he had developed 'a very good relationship' with his former rival.

'A while after I was told she would return my call after the rally,' he continued, 'somebody called and said, "*Koi haadsa ho gya hai* (Something terrible has happened)."' Then he got another call which confirmed the worst: Bhutto had been assassinated. Sharif dropped his campaigning and rushed to the hospital. 'When I got there, people came to our car saying, "Mian Sahab, what has happened to Bibi? What has happened to our Bibi?" When I saw their tears, I could not contain mine. *Aansou tou balkey kya* (forget the tears), I kept feeling a lot of pain.'

Most reports blamed Bhutto's assassination on the TTP leader Baitullah Mehsud, who was killed in a drone strike in 2009. But subsequent investigations by Scotland Yard and the United Nations also raised questions about the inadequate security Bhutto had been provided, and the hasty move—allegedly on the orders of military intelligence—to wash down the crime scene, eliminating possible evidence. Bhutto had been killed while waving to crowds from the sunroof of a car two weeks before parliamentary elections. Like Sharif, she was a twice-elected prime minister and the leader of a national party, vying for a third term in office. Like Sharif, she had returned, after eight years in exile. Sharif cried out of solidarity, those close to him say, but he was also terrorized and frightened. If they could kill her, they could get him, too.

It is a costly thing, in Pakistan, to disagree on the 'fundamentals' of the exercise of power with certain institutions. Bhutto's death haunts Sharif, and yet, as he sustains his earnest riffs on bullet trains and the ballot box, he continues to defy it. I was reminded of what Khaled Ahmed had said when I challenged his explanation for Sharif's accommodation with extremist religious parties: 'In the run-up to the elections,' Ahmed told me, 'why should he become a martyr? Who does that benefit?'

In an expansive mood while in exile, Sharif told Warraich one evening: 'Once the chief of army staff assumes his title, he begins to think of himself as a king, or super prime minister.' So if Sharif comes back to power, will he really put the generals into Suzukis? He may not go that far, but he will expect the military to heed his legitimacy. He will not rush into embracing India as a long-lost friend, but he will not be drawn into another military adventure. He wants to have a friendly working relationship with the United States and the international community, but he will neither accept them as masters nor spurn them as adversaries. He may once again crack down on the Taliban inside Pakistan—but if he does so, he will still accommodate, as he has always done, the deeply conservative sentiments of religious parties and groups. This, after all, is his history and his patrimony: an old and deep lesson from the real love of his life.

I was surprised when the *Caravan* approached me to do a profile of **VIKRAM**. A good actor, no doubt. A survivor, certainly. But had he really led a life so interesting, and so unique? It's only when I began my reporting that I discovered how remarkable his story was.

The way Vikram turned his life around after his accident is the stuff of bestselling books about can-do-ism. Some crucial dimensions of that story are retold here. Yet in spite of the many fascinating chapters in his life, this story, for me, is what eventually became its last paragraph. I knew the profile wouldn't be complete unless I knew what Vikram really felt—today—about the accident, about the friend who caused it. His exuberance so far seemed to underscore the notion that he had put it behind him. But it's a delicate question to ask. The first few times I brought it up, Vikram said he'd prefer not to talk about it. I asked his wife, so wonderfully cooperative on so many counts during the making of this story. In this matter, she was reluctant to even name the friend.

The last time I met Vikram, I asked him one more time. Somehow, it all came pouring out. We quoted him directly all through to the end: it seemed fitting to play him out in his own words. We haven't met after that day. I wonder, sometimes, what it will be like. Awkwardness, on my part, for dredging up some extremely personal emotions? A sense of betrayal, on his, for taking him into murkier waters than he, or many other Indian actors, have entered in public?

BARADWAJ RANGAN

Baradwaj Rangan is a film critic, writer and deputy editor of The Hindu. *He lives in Chennai.*

Man of Steel

How suffering turned a college lad into a Tamil superstar

By BARADWAJ RANGAN | 1 December 2013

I

It was the best night of Kenny's life. It was the worst night of Kenny's life. And it began on the pitch-black stage of the open-air auditorium at IIT-Madras.

At first the audience at the annual intercollegiate festival thought that there was a technical glitch: they could hear the actors but not see them. They began to fidget. They began to boo. Then, about fifteen minutes in, some of the viewers began to shush the others. They got what was happening: the play—Peter Shaffer's *Black Comedy*, in which Kenny had the lead role—began in darkness but, eventually, the lights would come on. The shushing gradually overwhelmed the booing and the fidgeting. There was silence, then laughs. When the curtains came down, there was a standing ovation. Among the audience that October night in 1986 was Shailaja Balakrishnan, who knew that she would marry Kenny even though he was barely aware of her existence. She watched him get the Best Actor award, beating candidates from all the other colleges. Later she would say *drishtipattuduchu*—someone had cast the evil eye.

Things were going according to plan. Kenny had always wanted to be an actor—at least from 1974, when he was in the third standard at Montfort Anglo Indian Higher Secondary

School in Yercaud. The boys' school was staging a musical named *Steam Boat* and someone was needed to play a cotton-picking slave girl in Alabama. Kenny was chosen. He was dyed black with vegetable powder, squeezed into a white-and-blue dress, and positioned in a corner of the stage. He had no lines; he just had to stand on stage. But that was enough to hook him. He acted through school and at Chennai's Loyola College, where he joined the literature programme in 1983. He acted in small, larkish events. Once, in an interdepartmental cultural festival, he parodied a famous Horlicks ad—in which a little boy says he doesn't need to drink Horlicks, he'd eat it straight out of the bottle—by turning it into an ad for underwear. And he acted in big productions, like the college theatre society's adaptation of Herman Wouk's *The Caine Mutiny Court-Martial*, in which his performance had the city's theatre critics declaring the birth of a star, an endorsement heartily echoed by crush-struck girls from Women's Christian College and Stella Maris.

The Best Actor award at IIT-Madras seemed to be a sign. Kenny was going to finish this last year at college and then he'd become an actor in the movies, in Tamil cinema, like he'd always wanted.

It had been a long day. After the festival, Kenny hopped onto a bike, behind a friend. They zipped out of the IIT campus, took a left and soared off into the night. They had turned right at the corner of the road by the Governor's house when Kenny noticed that his shoelaces had come undone. As he bent to attend to them, he heard a loud sound, and the next thing he knew, he was on the road. His friend had been fooling around as usual, resting his legs on the crash bars, and he couldn't brake in time when he saw the truck speeding towards them near the traffic circle. He accelerated instead and hit the truck. The impact of the collision uprooted the railing around the traffic circle. It was

Kenny's first accident. And he didn't even know how to ride a bike.

Today, he remembers those moments in flashes. He went into shock. There was no pain, only numbness. The pain started when some friends, who were following in a car, reached the spot and lifted him into the back seat. And then there was laughter. Kenny was always high-spirited, and when they reached the government hospital at Royapettah, he found that his sense of humour had returned. He jokingly protested when the medical staff began to snip away his clothes. ('This is imported underwear. Do you know how much it cost?') And as his friends surrounded him, he covered his crotch in mock modesty.

Then things got serious again. A severed artery was emptying blood into his right leg. There was a possibility of gangrene. Strange terms were floating in the air. Haematoma. Thomas splint. Amputation. Consent forms needed to be signed for the amputation, but his mother refused to do so, preferring to take him to the privately run Vijaya Hospital. The ambulance driver took a scenic route to charge more money. And somewhere in the middle of this worst night of his life, there was the ward boy standing beside Kenny when he was hoisted onto a gurney and wheeled into a lift.

He still remembers the dirty khaki uniform on the ward boy. He still remembers asking him if he could hold his hand. But he doesn't remember why. He doesn't remember why he felt so scared in that lift, as the doors closed. He thinks maybe it had to do with lying down and not standing up, as one usually does in lifts. Maybe this change in perspective gave him an inkling that his life was going to change.

The few people who really know the Tamil star Vikram have probably been surprised by this admission of fear. Because even with those close to him, he's always been about the jokes and high spirits and anecdotes that can really punch up a conversation. Like the one about how he ended up with that name. His parents—J. Albert Victor and Rajeswari—named him Kennedy and called him Kenny. He hated the name, even if he had to admit that it was better than the one his ambitious grandfather had in mind: 'Astronaut'. At some point, realizing that if he wanted a name he liked, he'd have to come up with it himself, he took VI from his father's name, K from Kennedy, RA from his mother's, and RAM from his sun sign, Aries. A screen name was born.

That's the kind of story you're likely to hear from Vikram and the people who know him, like Dr P.V.A. Mohandas, a famous surgeon at Vijaya Hospital, who operated on him after his accident. 'He had a huge number of friends,' Mohandas said. 'A big gang used to assemble in the evenings, during visiting hours.' Mohandas told Vikram's mother, 'I have seen so many actors and politicians here, but I've never seen such crowds.'

Shailaja told me another such story, about the day when Vikram had finished his bachelor's degree and enrolled in a post-graduate diploma programme in business administration. He rang her up from a tea stall and said, 'Can I call you every hour?' The second time he called, he said, 'I know I'm basically a Christian, you're a Hindu. Do you believe in the *thaali*?' Shailaja said no, she did not believe in wedding rituals. He said, 'I don't either. So we can get married.' A little later, he called and said, 'I won't be earning anything for a while. But I know that one day I will be able to take you holidaying to the best places in the world.'

None of these stories are about a ward boy in a dirty khaki uniform.

You don't usually hear confessions of weakness from the really big stars—especially the ones in Tamil cinema, whose fans are devoted to their heroes, welcoming each film with firecrackers and giant cut-outs of their idols, which they worship with ablutions of milk. The really big stars like to talk about upcoming films, or about their family, but are careful about saying anything that could disturb the macho facade that their fans buy into. Confessions such as Vikram's sense of fear as he was wheeled into the hospital lift could be considered weakness, and it's not something you expect to hear from him—not because he doesn't have weaknesses, and not because he won't tell us that he has them, but because he won't tell himself that he has them. The relentless positivity and equanimity, the extraordinary manner with which he's conducted himself through the low points in his life, make him seem less a flesh-and-blood person than an amped-up motivational poster.

Everyone I talk to has a story (or three) that intensifies the legend. Sriman, an actor who was struggling to get into films at about the same time as Vikram, told me about trying to convince Vikram to come along with him to perform as a backup dancer at a dance programme organized in Canada in the mid 1990s. It was good money, and he needed it, but Vikram turned it down. He would not be one among many. One day, there would be a dance show called *Vikram Star Nite*, he said, and if Sriman was available, he'd take him along. Ten years later, in Malaysia and Singapore, sell-out crowds watched the top heroines of Tamil and Telugu cinema participate in one such show. Vikram was the sole hero.

The legend-intensifying stories aren't always about his career, or about the movies. Vikram's classmate from Loyola College and good friend, R.M.R. Ramesh, who is managing director of the Tamil daily *Dinakaran*, told me, 'He used to pull me away from the fights I used to get into, around campus elections. The kind of advice we give our kids today, he had that maturity even then.'

Even Shailaja's attempts to humanize her husband end up burnishing his aura. Recalling the days during which Vikram shot for his biggest blockbuster, *Anniyan* (which was released in Hindi as *Aparichit: The Stranger*), she said, 'I felt we should live in two houses. It's not easy to live with a man who can get that eccentric, an actor who wants to be that difficult on himself. I wouldn't say he becomes the character, but there's definitely some kind of internalization.' Being a full-time psychologist, these are not terms she uses lightly.

The only flaw in this man, apparently, is a tendency to spout the occasional cornball cliche. When the Telugu megastar Chiranjeevi asked what kept him going through nearly ten years of struggle, he said, 'Well, I take the cue from my blood group—B positive. I'm an optimist.' The other flaw is, perhaps, his taste in music—though it requires some kind of bravery to declare that one of your favourite songs is '*Can I touch you there*', by Michael Bolton.

II

The first time I met Vikram, at his home near Elliot's Beach in Chennai, on a very hot evening in early May, he was wolfing down dinner—steamed vegetables in a shallow plastic container—using a pair of chopsticks.

He appeared surprisingly small—but then heroes who usually stare out of 70-mm screens can seem so when you see them in person. The shaved head and the alarming weight loss he'd recently undergone added to the impression. This is one of his looks for the hotly anticipated mega-production, *Ai*, from Tamil cinema's biggest blockbuster director, Shankar. Shailaja told me later, 'These past ten months, Vikram has been eating like a hermit.'

This isn't the first time. To appear emaciated in the latter portions of his first hit, *Sethu*, which were set in a mental asylum, Vikram lived only on fruit juice for six months, and once he lost the desired weight (16 kilograms), he maintained the look by subsisting on a scanty diet: an egg white, one glass of beetroot or carrot juice and a single dry chapatti through the day. The film is about a college student who falls for a girl who does not reciprocate his feelings at first—and by the time she does, he's lost his mind. It was shot mostly in sequence—the first scene of the screenplay filmed first, the last scene last—so that a healthy-looking Vikram could be shown slowly deteriorating. Towards the end of the shoot, the first-time director, Bala, had just one instruction for his leading man: 'Have just enough strength to stand up.'

While preparing to play a blind singer in *Kasi*, Vikram practised drawing his eyeballs up into their sockets so that only the whites could be seen. He started with one minute, then two, then five, and then he practised drawing his eyeballs up after dousing his eyes with glycerine, for the scenes where he had to cry. Once shooting started, he would roll his eyeballs up through the whole day on the set. He had to do eye exercises at the end of every day's shoot so that he wouldn't end up with a squint. He said, 'My eyesight changed because of *Kasi*.' He had perfect vision earlier, but now wears glasses to drive, watch movies and work on his laptop.

And now, there's *Ai*. Vikram calls it the toughest film he's ever done.

He showed me a cell phone photograph where his cheeks appeared to be powdered with rouge. But it's actually folliculitis, a rash from his allergy to the prosthetic makeup, which covered his skin for eleven to seventeen hours a day.

He's trying to lose 20 kilograms for the film, eating ten tiny meals a day—half an egg in one, half an apple two hours later, and so on. 'My normal weight,' he said, 'is around 80. Now I'm 63. I want to become 60, but I'm trying to push it to 55. Fifty is insane because I will never be able to get my body mass back. The doctor says okay, but suddenly the BP may drop and you may not be able to get it up.' He smiled the smile of a teenager sneaking out for a cigarette. 'When this movie is released, people will say: how did he do it?'

A more pertinent question might be: why does he do it? Why this need to suffer to the point of self-flagellation? Why this constant desire to be different? After all, the Tamil audience is among the most accepting in the world, with documented indifference to the beauty or the body of heroes. Many of the heroes we see in Tamil cinema today could never be heroes in Hindi cinema, in which the idea of a leading man is more cosmetic. When Salman Khan played the protagonist in *Sethu*'s remake, *Tere Naam*, he appeared in the asylum portions with ripped abs, evidently having improvised an exercise routine using the chains that bound him to the walls. Vikram told me about running into Khan while shooting *Anniyan*. 'He asked me how many films I was doing. I said one. He asked for how long. I said one and a half years. He said, "Are you crazy? You know how many films I am doing? Twenty-three." He asked me why I was doing just this one film. I said because I have to maintain a look. And he said, "Yo, on screen just make sure you look good. That's it."'

The popular belief about this phenomenon is that Tamil audiences—especially those from the lower-income groups who become members of an actor's fan club—like to see heroes who look like them, whom they can identify with, while Hindi audiences like to see heroes who look nothing like them, and whom they can aspire to be. So a Tamil cinema hero who makes movies for the masses can be a number of things the Hindi film hero usually cannot: dark-skinned, unkempt, dressed in the most ordinary clothes, and hanging out with buddies who look like they could be autorickshaw drivers and bus conductors. (One of the latter went on to become south India's most famous star, Rajinikanth.)

However, once you establish a 'look' that fans buy into, you don't deviate too much from it. You just slap on a moustache or change your hairstyle from movie to movie. Vikram, however, puts himself through monastically rigorous transformations even in his purely commercial outings. For all practical purposes, the hero could have looked the same in *Dhil* and *Saamy* and *Dhool* and *Gemini*. 'But in *Dhil*,' he said, 'my character wants to become a cop and those who want to become cops have a small waist. In *Saamy*, where I play a cop, my waist is thicker. Because after you become a cop, that's how you look.'

Bala told me that the reason he chose to make a first film that was so raw was that it would stand out from the mellow, family-friendly entertainers that most first-time film-makers were making in the late 1990s. 'It would make me noticed at once.' Then he said, 'It's also a kind of a mental illness, where someone says, "I will not be like anyone else. I will choose my own path." Only madmen have this disease. If you go to a mental asylum and if you don't talk to an inmate there, he'll throw something at you to catch your attention. I'm like that. I want people to look at me.'

Maybe Vikram, in his own way, wants people to look at him. 'Attention, fame, recognition, money—all that will come automatically,' he told me. 'But I want to do something immortal.' This isn't hubris. He seems to look at acting as some combination of penance and extreme sport. 'I saw this interview with this guy who wanted to jump across a chasm on his bike,' he said. 'Nobody's ever done it. He was about twenty-four, twenty-five. He said he knew he may die, but he's going to die one day anyway, and he wanted to push himself. He wanted that high, that rush. He did die. He hit a rock. But he had that rush. That is what happens to me as an actor. I don't feel complete if I look normal.'

But there must be something about him that's normal. I asked Vikram, only half-jokingly, if he had any skeletons in the closet—perhaps a tendency to strangulate kittens. He said, without missing a beat, 'They're buried in my backyard.'

It's no surprise that he deflects your question with humour and offers his normal self. The Kenny self. The ordinary guy whose favourite food is day-old rice and dry fish, and who likes to hang out in a T-shirt, a faded pair of jeans and rubber flip-flops. We usually met in his immaculate office, which gives no clues about the life that lies beyond—not even a tossed-off, half-read book. A request to observe him on the sets of *Ai* was denied. 'Shankar sir wasn't comfortable,' he said.

What's surprising, though, is that Vikram draws a boundary around him even with his family. 'There's a dichotomy within me,' he said. 'I'm Vikram at work. I'm Kenny at home. When I'm home, I'm a normal father. Nobody outside can reach me. Likewise, at work, my wife cannot reach me. There's no two ways about it. It's very clearly demarcated.'

Shailaja saw this during *Sethu*, during *Raavanan*, and she's seeing this with *Ai*. 'He dialogues with himself,' she said. 'He stands in front of a mirror, observing his moves. And during this process he does withdraw a bit. He likes being alone. He doesn't talk. I have to ask him to tell me what he's doing. I'm not saying it's a schizoid kind of thing, but unless he withdraws, he cannot work this way.'

'Schizoid' would perhaps be the appropriate term to describe Kenny's transformation into Vikram, which happened in the days following the accident.

A week after meeting Vikram at his home, I met Dr Mohandas at the sprawling Ramapuram premises of MIOT International, the multi-speciality hospital complex where he is managing director. 'After the accident, we couldn't operate on Kenny for almost five months because of complications,' he told me. 'He had to be put on traction. We couldn't give him anaesthetics because he'd lost so much blood. If they'd come in three hours later, we'd have had to amputate.' Mohandas told Kenny's parents that there was perhaps a 2 per cent chance of saving the leg, but he would have to stay in the hospital for months and suffer pain throughout. It was expensive, and there was still the probability that a complication could occur and the leg would have to be amputated.

In medical terms, it was a compound comminuted fracture of the leg, with a degloving injury and loss of muscle. In plain English, Kenny's bones were broken to bits, and there was heavy damage to skin and soft tissue from knee to ankle. The fracture needed to be fixed. Flesh and bone needed to be grafted to shape the bottom half of a leg where none existed. Kenny had twenty-three operations over three years, and even after being discharged, he had to return due to infections and complications. And this was a man who was afraid of injections.

But Vikram wasn't. From the accounts of his life that I heard from various people, Kenny appears to be his father's son, Vikram his mother's. Kenny is a dreamer like his father, who, deciding he wanted to be a star, ran away to Chennai from his home in Paramakudi, the town in southern Tamil Nadu most famous today for being Kamal Haasan's birthplace. But he never made it beyond a handful of villain roles, and he now acts in serials. Vikram is a doer like his mother, who was something of a real-life heroine herself. A teacher who joined government service as a revenue inspector, she would eventually retire as deputy commissioner in the revenue department. She'd stop lorries containing stolen sand, despite her son's admonitions that the miners were capable of mowing her down. 'When I began acting in the movies, her name used to appear in the papers more than mine,' Vikram told me. 'I used to say, "Amma, I don't like this." In this aspect, I think I take after her. If she sets her mind on something, she'll do it. If it had been only my father at Royapettah hospital, he would have tearfully signed the consent forms and authorized amputation. My mother refused. The first month and a half I was in the hospital, I never saw her sit. At one point, she was getting ready to trundle out my bed because there was a fire below. I got through that phase only because of her.'

It was a slow, torturous phase. After a few months, Vikram was advised to begin walking with a crutch, so that the leg wouldn't atrophy from lack of exercise. It took him two hours to walk from his bed to the door.

How does someone, however optimistic, come out of something like this with the belief that their dream will still become a reality? The first few times I met Vikram, he just smiled and shrugged, as if it were nothing. 'I just wanted to be an actor,' he said. 'That's what kept me going.' He lapsed into cliches. It's life. You have to go through it. And so forth.

But one day, he told me what really happened. It involves a big name from the film industry, whom Vikram did not want named. He knew the young man wanted to be an actor in the movies, a hero. He could have given Kenny a break, but the only time he called was when he needed junior artists for a movie he was making. Kenny begged off, but he was smarting from the insult, the implication that that was all he was good for. When this man heard about Kenny's accident, he visited the hospital, looked at the college kid who'd been told he'd never walk again and told him, 'Just get well and come out. I'll make you a star.'

Kenny looked at him and thought, 'You know I can act, but you never gave me a chance in any of your films. And now, you're saying you want to make me a hero? Because the doctors said I won't be able to walk again? You know what? I *will* walk. I'm not going to tell anyone that I know you, and I *will* become a hero.'

That was the moment when Kenny really began the transition to Vikram. He began working out: dumb-bells for the arms and shoulders, and for the chest, an improvised bench press—a serving tray loaded with books by favourite writers, like Leon Uris and Wilbur Smith. Doctors began to bring around other patients, who were losing hope, and point at Vikram. 'Look at his attitude,' they'd say.

One day, after watching the movie *Mayuri* on a video player in his room, he had an idea. That film, released in 1984, was based on the real-life story of its heroine Sudha Chandran, a classical dancer who, at sixteen, lost a leg after an accident, got fitted with a 'Jaipur foot', and began dancing again. There were so many parallels to Vikram's story: another youngster with dreams of a performing career; another collision with a truck; another series of bad calls at a government hospital; another transfer to Vijaya Hospital; another frighteningly self-motivated individual. Vikram told his mother, 'I can't work in the movies like this. Let's cut my leg off. Then I can do a film like *Mayuri*. I can be a karate champ who loses his leg and gets a Jaipur foot and returns to doing stunts.' His mother was not amused.

Had that film been made, an emotional scene would have centred on the protagonist saying no to painkillers. Vikram's leg was healing on the outside but not on the inside, so for a while they had to keep the wound open—you could touch the bone. The pain was terrible. They had to reach into his leg and coat the insides with antibiotic powder. 'It was so bad that they gave me morphine. I floated for three days. And afterwards, I began to look out for the sound of the trolley with the painkillers.' Having wanted to be in the movies for as long as he could remember, Vikram was always something of a health freak, who avoided carbonated drinks, chocolates and ice cream. 'I didn't want to get addicted to these things,' he told me. And when he began to realize that he could get addicted to painkillers, he turned them down.

Mani Ratnam, who directed Vikram in *Raavanan*, caught a glimpse of this grit. 'He has a problem with heights,' Ratnam told me. 'We needed a crane shot for a song, and when I asked him to climb on top of a prop, I saw there was some hesitation.' Ratnam asked Vikram if there was a problem, but the actor was not yet ready to confide in his director. He did the song. Later, when the action scenes on the bridge were being filmed over a sheer drop, Ratnam noticed that Vikram would do the shot without looking down. And when the shot was over, he would close his eyes. In the final shot, the character had to be shown falling into a ravine. Vikram had become comfortable with Ratnam by then and admitted to the director that he had a problem with heights. He, added, however, that it wasn't going to be a problem this time. He would be looking at the sky.

III

Shailaja had always known that Vikram was her soulmate. She told me that she was a 'devotee' of Brian Weiss, the American psychiatrist and past-life regression therapist. 'I'm keyed to these things. And it was predicted that my soulmate would be someone drastically different from me. That's how it's turned out. I'm a pessimist. He's an optimist. He can laugh at anything. I can't. I'm very judgemental. He's not. I can do sympathy but not empathy. But he's very good at empathizing with people.'

She had gone to the hospital with a group of friends to express her sympathy. She was shocked to see him lying in bed and cracking jokes. Ever the entertainer, he would play the guitar, sing songs, paint and flirt with girls who came to see him even though he was now restricted to bed. It was after he came out of the hospital, on crutches, that Shailaja finally got to talk to him, at a get-together organized by a common friend. She knew that it would be a very important day in her life. She walked up to him and asked him what he planned to do. He told her, 'I am going to be a star.' She thought he was delusional.

Vikram realized that this was the girl for him, and he began to woo her like he'd woo women in the movies one day. He bought her a sari from the ration shop. He took her to the beach and sang for her—'*Nilavevaa*' from Mani Ratnam's *Mouna Raagam*, the big hit of 1986. And he charmed her parents. Her father asked him what he was going to do. He said he had applied for a job in Lintas—the advertising agency that's now Lowe Lintas & Partners—but eventually he wanted to act. 'My dad didn't know what to say,' Shailaja said. 'Then he told me that if this man has this dream even after such an accident, then he couldn't say anything.'

Years later, when in Berlin for a workshop, Shailaja showed the nuclear scan of Vikram's leg to a German orthopaedic surgeon. He asked her what Vikram did. She said he was an actor who often worked in action films. The doctor told her it couldn't be the doing of medical science. 'It's all His doing,' he said.

I asked Vikram if he was a believer, as tragedies have a way of turning people spiritual. 'I know there's a universal something,' he said, 'and my perception of it changes over the years. In school, I was punished if I didn't go to church, and that can really drive you away from Christianity and God.' His early influences were far less clerical—the book that he says changed him was *The Fountainhead*. 'Like a lot of people, I saw myself as Howard Roark. For me, it's never been about being No. 1, but about doing something you believe in. But later in life, you want to believe in something. Today, I say the rosary. "Our Father, who art in Heaven." But it's more about the universe. Live well, let live.'

After leaving the hospital, Vikram still had a year of college to complete. His English lecturer, Professor G.M. James, obtained the necessary permissions so he could do his dissertation from home. It was titled 'Strong-willed Women in Shaw's Plays'. For his exams, though, he had to go to the college. His father would bring him in a Maruti Omni, where he could stretch his leg in the back. His friend R.M.R. Ramesh said, 'He walked with a crutch. He had a slight limp. Otherwise you couldn't make out anything was wrong.'

Vikram isn't the first man who worked hard at overcoming a setback, but what makes his story slightly different is the magnitude of his dream. He wanted to become a hero; it was that or nothing. He said no to Mani Ratnam when offered the role of the heroine's sister's fiance in *Alaipaayuthey*. He said no to Mani Ratnam again when offered the role of Nandita Das's husband in *Kannathil Muthamittal*. He told himself, instead, 'I want people in Kerala to recognize me. I want my films to do well in Andhra Pradesh. I want to be known in the north.' This was either the world's most foolish man, or the bravest.

Vikram's dream was incubated in boarding school, to which he was packed off when he was nine. He learnt to play basketball. He was the swimming champion—breaststroke and butterfly. He learnt horseback riding. He was the boxing champion. He took up the guitar and saxophone. He was a part of several teams—

dramatics, music, art—and played a number of games (even if he was just a substitute). 'If I am an actor today,' Vikram told me, 'it is because of the facilities there. Actors who haven't done these things end up looking fake when playing a guitar or throwing a basketball. But I can do all these things to an extent, so I can fake it convincingly.'

The students used to do small plays in class, for an audience of twenty kids. Then they did plays in front of the school, watched by 500 kids. And then in the girls' school across the hill, before 1,000 kids. Vikram, who was then in the eighth standard, loved it. He also realized that cinema would give him the biggest audience. By this time, his mother's brother, Thyagarajan, had become a popular actor in Tamil cinema. Vikram used to buy film magazines, and if there was something about his uncle, even if it was just one line, he'd read it over and over.

As he did in the film world many years later, Vikram lurked in the fringes of the school's theatre for a long time. He played a guard, or did backstage work—anything to ultimately be in front of the audience. When he was in the ninth standard, the lead actor in the Molière comedy *The Doctor in Spite of Himself* contracted chickenpox. The director looked around and realized that there was only one possible replacement, the junior artist who always knew everyone's lines. The play was a hit, and his performance was praised. This was his *Sethu* moment long before *Sethu*. 'After that,' he said, 'I got bigger roles, and I'd always get the Best Actor award.'

One day, in a pile of books on a pavement outside the school, Vikram spotted a volume of photographs. 'It was by some lecturer. 150 pages, 150 pictures. He'd photographed himself as a postman in one picture, then a fisherman, then he was a sweeper. He looked different on every page. I was shocked.' Vikram said 'shocked' as if replaying the emotion to me, voice rising, eyes widening like a silent-film actor. 'You can see Sivaji Ganesan do something like this. But this was some ordinary guy. And at that age, I said, when I do films, this is what I'll do. I should not just look different, I should *be* different.' And he began looking out for 'weird' roles. In one play, he was a guy talking to his dead father, who's in a chair. In another, he was a hypochondriac who never left his bed, until, finally, he's told the house is on fire. 'When we did *Julius Caesar*, I was offered Caesar. I said no, I'll do Brutus or I'll do Cassius.'

Molière and Shakespeare can hardly be thought of as steps to a flourishing career in Tamil cinema, but there was more. 'My sister and I used to speak only in English,' said Vikram, relishing the irony of a 'Peter'—south Indian slang for an English-speaker—making it big in one of the most rooted regional film industries. In school, they used to think he was Anglo-Indian because he didn't speak much Tamil and what little he spoke was with an Anglicized accent. 'My grandfather was a headmaster in Paramakudi. My father used to tell this story about how amazed the other kids would be when he recited "Twinkle twinkle little star", that the headmaster's son spoke such good English. So that fascination for English was always there in the family.'

James, the English teacher, told me that the last thing he thought Vikram would become was an actor in Tamil cinema. 'I have seen him talk only in high-flown English. One of my courses was copywriting, and I always felt he would go and set up an excellent ad agency and do very well. I don't know how and where he picked up such good Tamil.'

Vikram knew that he couldn't be in Tamil cinema without speaking Tamil, so he began to read Tamil newspapers out loud. Later, when he started making movies, he chose to follow up *Sethu* with films where he played villagers—films like *Kaasi*, *Vinnukkum Mannukkum* and *Dhool*. 'It was my insecurity,' he told me. 'I didn't want people to think I was this English-speaking guy.' When people saw him as Remo—the smart and stylish 'dude' character he played in *Anniyan*, one of the protagonist's multiple personalities—they thought he was playing out of his comfort zone. 'Actually, a Remo is what I am.'

IV

When Vikram could finally walk again, he did everything he could to keep himself busy. He did a copywriting stint with the advertising agency Lintas. He did a course in computers, learning BASIC and COBOL. And to keep his acting dream alive, he packed in a few ad films and an anti-drugs short film and a six-episode television serial called *Galatta Kudumbam*, which aired on Doordarshan between November and December 1988.

I asked him why he did ad films and a television serial when he wanted to become a movie star. 'I needed a start somewhere,' he said. 'I knew people would notice and someone would call me for another film and then another film till the big break happened.'

One of those who noticed was an employee of Indian Bank, who, with several of his colleagues, was turning producer for a small-budget experimental film named *En Kadhal Kanmani*. It was about a smoker who has to kick the habit if he wants to marry his girlfriend. Midway through the shooting, Vikram learnt from his father that the well-known director C.V. Sridhar was looking for a new hero. Sridhar asked Vikram if he'd done any films. Vikram said no. It wasn't a lie, exactly—*En Kadhal Kanmani* hadn't yet been released. Sridhar was a legend. One of his most popular and fondly remembered films is the 1960s' romantic comedy *Kadhalikka Neramillai*, which was remade in Hindi as *Pyar Kiye Jaa*, but by the 1990s, he was seen as something of a spent force.

Thanthu Vitten Ennai, which was released in 1991, with Vikram as hero, would be the director's final film. Still, as shot-in-the-dark strategies go, the decision to work with Sridhar wasn't completely misconceived. 'In my mind,' Vikram said, 'he was a big director at one point. He *could* make a comeback.'

Vikram's next film was *Kaaval Geetham*, with another big director at one point who could make a comeback—S.P. Muthuraman, the director who gave Kamal Haasan and Rajinikanth some of their biggest hits. Then Vikram was signed on for *Meera*, whose director P.C. Sreeram was Mani Ratnam's usual cinematographer. 'That was my first glimpse of stardom,' Vikram said. 'I'd go to the set and look at the way he'd lit it up and go, "Whoa, am I a part of this?"'

R.M.R. Ramesh wasn't as impressed. He felt that these roles were trivial when compared to the parts Vikram played on stage. Shailaja told me something similar. 'I began to wonder if this was the field for him because these roles were nothing compared to what he did on stage. But he never brought the flops home and felt bad—except when Mani sir's film didn't happen. I remember him getting very emotional.'

The call from Mani Ratnam's office came when Vikram was shooting for *Pudhiya Mannargal*. It was another film with a big-name director, Vikraman, who had burst onto the scene a few years ago with a smash-hit first film called *Pudhu Vasantham*. It would turn out to be another flop.

The Mani Ratnam film was *Bombay*, and Vikram was called for a screen test with Manisha Koirala. He thought it would be a video shoot, which is the usual practice, but it turned out to be a photo shoot. 'Now I can do photo shoots blindly,' he told me, 'but then, I was terrified of the still camera. Mani sir was giving me a non-stop stream of instructions. She's coming. You're looking there. You're turning. She's turning. I froze. I was trying to hold one expression for the camera, and he said, "No, no, no, just be free, be natural."' Vikram had grown his hair long and had a beard for the *Pudhiya Mannargal* part, but Ratnam wanted someone with close-cut hair and just a moustache. 'I was on a break between schedules,' Vikram said. 'I could have even shaved my head. But I was an *actor*, you see. It was all about continuity.'

He was dejected for a few hours. Then he resumed his routine: the dance classes, the exercises—loading his right leg with iron rings and raising and lowering them. He resumed his fight training, learning how to twirl a stick in the martial art known as *silambam*, which is popular in the action sequences in Tamil films. But, of course, he had to be different—while others trained with sticks, Vikram opted for an iron rod used to dig up roads. And he resumed his acting classes. Sriman and some other strugglers would troop to Vikram's house after their dance class, and as Vikram was the only one with acting experience, he'd create situations for the others to perform, requiring them to effect variations in the delivery of a word or a line—like '*enna*?' (what?).

'*That* kept me going. If I hadn't done that . . .' he trailed off, recalling the decade between his first film and his first hit. 'Those ten years, I cannot dismiss them as just ten years. At that age, in your twenties, it's a *lot* of time to stay focused on a goal, especially when a friend comes by and talks about a job opening. There are so many people who wanted to be in the movies and now they're working in some cubicle somewhere. Once you get that money, once you move into your home, you can't stop and say you're going to follow your dream.'

In 1994, eight years after the accident, four years after *En Kadhal Kanmani* sank without a trace, two years after *Meera* failed to make him a star, Vikram and Shailaja got married, twice—first in the church at Loyola College, and then, because Shailaja is a Malayali, in a Guruvayoor temple. James told me, 'The church ceremony was over quickly. We didn't even have dinner afterwards. They got into a car and drove off. And then we left.'

The career front was equally low-key. Stardom seemed so near, yet so far. The big banners, big directors kept calling. Vikram was cast as one of the heroes in *Ullasam*, the first Tamil venture of Amitabh Bachchan Corporation Ltd. The film flopped. An opportunity to feature as one of the two leads in *Raman Abdullah*, a film by the well-regarded director Balu Mahendra, slipped away because of date clashes with the *Ullasam* schedule.

But his financial situation wasn't dire. Somewhere in the haze of his impossible dreams, there had been a reality check. He needed a livelihood. After *Meera*, Vikram was chosen to play the lead in the Telugu film *Chirunavvula Varamistava*, and a supporting role in the Malayalam film *Dhruvam*, which had Mammooty in the lead. If any of these films clicked, Vikram was ready to move to that industry and make his career there. But he hoped the big break would come from a Tamil film. 'Because that's your mother tongue, you want to do the right stuff,' he said. 'That's why I never did anything but hero roles in Tamil.' But he admitted that doing commercial cinema in Telugu, where he wore 'glittery outfits' and 'belted out lines loudly and melodramatically', and in Malayalam, where 'the actors are so good, you always pick up a trick or two', gave him a sense of balance. 'Today, I can do a very de-glam role. I can also do something outrageous. It all helps you.'

Vikram also began to dub for other actors. Here, too, he had standards. He wouldn't dub for religious films that involved, say, wish-fulfilling snakes—but he became the voice of Abbas and Prabhu Deva, and he lent his voice to the protagonist of *Satya* and for a portion of *Gandhi* when these films were dubbed in Tamil. 'For me, dubbing is where actors excel,' said Vikram, who doesn't like live sound. 'I like to change my voice while dubbing, and I put in a lot of effort in the modulation.' He was, in his own way, having fun.

And then Bala put the brakes on it.

V

'Everyone is some kind of actor, no?' Bala asked me in his office, where the air-conditioned air was infused with freshly exhaled cigarette smoke. 'I'm talking to you now. Maybe 90 per cent is the truth, but the rest is acting.'

After working under Balu Mahendra for seven years—until *Marupadiyum*, the Tamil remake of *Arth*—Bala decided it was time for his first film, and he based it on the trials of a friend who fell in love and lost his mind and ended up in chains at a mental asylum. While looking for his protagonist, 'an actor who could sacrifice everything', his eyes fell on Vikram. He hadn't been impressed by any of Vikram's films, but there were some expressions—'just two or three shots'—that had grabbed his attention in the 'O butterfly' song sequence in *Meera*, where Vikram studies the colourfully garbed heroine with the rapt awe of a lepidopterist gazing at a Painted Lady.

Bala and Vikram had been friends, hanging out with the same group of strugglers. So Bala approached him and said he had a script ready, and instead of telling the actor what the story was, and what his character was like, he rattled off a list of conditions. Vikram would have to reduce his body weight by 20 kilograms, shave his head, stop doing small roles in other films and give up dubbing work. 'There could be no distractions,' Bala said.

Vikram finally found himself in the hands of a film-maker whose intensity matched his own. He threw himself into the project with such dedication, transforming his appearance so drastically that when the first scene at the asylum was shot, with some 300 extras—all with shaven heads, all in uniform, a dirt-coloured vest and shorts—Bala couldn't tell where his leading man was. During these stages of the shoot, the actor was so weak from starvation that Bala had to keep tapping him and asking if he'd heard and understood what he was supposed to do. 'If I called out, he couldn't hear me,' Bala said. 'His ears were blocked, and his eyes were often out of focus.'

Bala began to wonder if it was right to 'torture' a man like this. 'Had it been another actor, I wouldn't have bothered, but he was someone who'd had a major accident—and I've seen the condition his leg was in. What I was doing was worse than the accident. An accident is an accident. But this was deliberate. I was using him for *my* self-interest, for *my* film to become a hit.'

The film, whose shooting was inaugurated with a puja in April 1997, took two years to make and it was plagued with problems, beginning with a Film Employees' Federation of South India strike that stopped shooting for six months, from June to December that year. 'I still don't want to recall that period,' Shailaja told me. 'He was on a diet that went on and on. To have this person who's at home all the time and not eating normally, just saying the strike will get over, shooting will happen, the strike will get over, shooting will happen . . . It's not easy. He used to have that look, that *Sethu* look. I used to tell him, "Don't look at me like that." I knew that there was so much hard work on his side, but I didn't verbalize it and give him the warm-fuzzies. I was not an encouraging wife, honestly. He encouraged himself. It was his sole journey.'

Sriman, who played the role of the protagonist's friend in *Sethu*, had left the unit after finishing one schedule with the normal-looking Vikram. When he returned, he found an emaciated wreck who was surviving on four scoops of papaya every two hours. 'I asked him if this was necessary. But Kenny said this is it. This is life or death.'

Shailaja gave him an ultimatum. If *Sethu* didn't work, then he'd live his dream through television or theatre. He was not the kind of person who went to producers and handed out photos or introduced himself. He was just someone who had talent. And in television and theatre, you could get by if you just had talent. To convince him, she sought the help of James, whom Vikram regarded highly. But Vikram begged them to back off. 'He was in so much pain,' James said. 'But when I saw the look in his eyes, I told Shaila not to talk to him about this any more.'

When the strike was called off, the producer ran out of funds and decided to abandon the project. Vikram and Ameer, an assistant director on *Sethu* who would go on to make *Paruthiveeran*, met the producer and begged him to return. Shooting resumed in January 1998, in fits and starts, whenever the producer could scrounge up some money, and the film was finally ready in June 1999.

But there were no buyers. Bala and Vikram kept organizing preview shows with Shailaja's money to impress distributors. 'For months and months I kept doling out money,' Shailaja said, and laughed. There was such a demand for preview shows that, at some point, it appeared to Vikram that all of Chennai had seen *Sethu*—and while everyone doled out generous words of praise, no one actually bought the film. Vikram remembers thinking, 'Even if this gets into theatres, who's left to buy tickets now?' He hadn't been on another set in two years. He hadn't done any dubbing. He was out of circulation. There was Rs 25,000 in the bank. He went into a shell.

A friend who was working at the National Institute of Information Technology offered him a job, but Vikram chose to occupy himself in ways connected to cinema. He directed a serial, with Ameer as his assistant—its title, *Mounam Pesiyathey*, became the title of Ameer's first film. He did a telefilm called *Siragugal*, which was about a Tamil family settled in London. It was well received and he got offers to do more telefilms. 'But,' he said, 'I realized that if I took up these offers, I'd be called a "TV actor". They're not going to touch me in the movies.'

On 10 December 1999, nine years after the release of *En Kadhal Kanmani*, *Sethu* was released, with no publicity, in a musty theatre called Krishnaveni in Chennai where the ushers couldn't be bothered to close the doors after the screening began. Sriman went along with Vikram and Bala on the opening day, but they didn't watch the film. They watched the audience. The response was so ecstatic that Sriman feels it to this day. He pulled back his shirt sleeve and extended his arm to me. There was gooseflesh. Vikram told me that they heard someone swear as they walked out of the theatre. It was a viewer wiping his eyes, remarking, 'Those motherfuckers. They made me cry.' Bala was ecstatic. There could be no bigger compliment.

Sun TV came out with a rave review, as did the Tamil press. The reviews brought more people in. These people told other people, and so on. The film became a word-of-mouth sensation. Vikram finally had his first hit. He was thirty-three years old.

'My life is always before and after *Sethu*,' Vikram says today. He had to learn the rules of stardom. His mother wanted to see *Sethu*, so he asked her to come to Abirami theatre, where he'd wait in the foyer with the tickets. Suddenly, there was a shout. The crowd that was coming out of the earlier show had recognized Vikram, and began to mob him. The security personnel had to come and rescue him. '*Saar*,' they said, 'when you have a hit film, you shouldn't come to the theatre.'

When the next screening began, his mother wasn't watching the film. She was watching the crowd's reactions and giving her son a running commentary: they're laughing, *da*, they're clapping, *da*, they're whistling when you make an entry, *da*.

His father was silent. Every time Vikram asked him what he wanted for his birthday, he'd say 'give me a good film, a hit film, and become a big hero'. He'd finally gotten his gift. He'd never made it to the big league, and there was probably no one who understood better what his son had achieved. Vikram spoke about the time his father, who is a heart patient, took a small role in Vasanthabalan's 2012 period epic *Aravaan*, which was being shot on a hill near Madurai. At some point during the shooting, he collapsed and had to be flown back to Chennai for treatment. At the hospital, he told Vikram, 'Imagine, how wonderful it would have been if I'd died on the set.' Vikram told me that he scoffed at the sentiment then ('dying on the battlefield' his father called it). After which Vikram said, 'I may think that too at some point.'

The success of *Sethu* left Vikram with two acquisitions—a black Lancer with the licence-plate number 2000 ('because that was the year I made it. I was the millennium kid.'), and the prefix of 'Chiyaan', which is how the character, a good-hearted but rowdy youth, was affectionately addressed in the film. But it also left him wondering what to do next.

Vikram did not take on another film for two months. No script was worthy enough, he felt. He had made it. Now he had to maintain it. He chose films carefully, some because they appealed to the actor in him, and some because he knew that no leading man ever became a star by only doing films that appealed to the actor in him. The hits began to happen. *Kasi. Dhil. Dhool. Saamy*. And then came the two high points of his career.

He reunited with Bala in *Pithamagan*, playing an animalistic graveyard attendant, a character the director wrote for him. A few months after the film's release, Vikram was in the gym, lifting weights, when his assistant called and told him that he had won the National Award for Best Actor.

Following *Pithamagan,* Vikram scored the biggest hit of his career—Shankar's *Anniyan*, in which he played a meek lawyer who transforms into the titular vigilante after stumbling upon writings in an ancient text that prescribe horrific punishments to evil-doers. It was released in the summer of 2005. The film's success changed his life. Vikram said, 'I've got used to people recognizing me. But when someone in Mumbai comes to you and says they've seen your film, you feel good, because that's not your usual audience.'

Vikram has not been able to recapture this high. The films that followed were either flops or modest successes, but there's been nothing definitive, as James put it. '*Sethu* became the proverbial portrait of the doomed lover, just like the character in *Saamy* was the proverbial police officer,' he told me. 'With *Sethu*, *Saamy* or *Anniyan*, people could parody the performance, emulate it, incorporate it into jokes and in casual conversation. "Don't be a Sethu, *da.*" It was so distinctive that it became the last word. The films that weren't proverbial didn't click.' After *Anniyan*, Vikram has played everything from a costumed superhero (*Kandasamy*) to an emotional gangster (*Bheema*) to a visually impaired avenger who's skilled in echolocation (*Thaandavam*). What he hasn't played is something 'proverbial'.

After *Anniyan*, Vikram was on par with Vijay, the biggest name in the generation of stars after Rajinikanth and Kamal Haasan. Unlike Vikram, Vijay has been happy to play to the gallery, making the same film over and over. This acceptance of formula is something that could have helped Vikram, feels Sreedhar Pillai, a writer, trade analyst and long-time industry watcher. 'Vikram had established himself as an action hero, and in order to become a mass star, he should have continued playing action heroes. Because that's where the money is, and that's what a majority of the fans like to see. They want an actor to do the things they like him to do. They don't like him to experiment too much.'

Pillai told me that becoming—and remaining—a star in Tamil cinema isn't just about acting prowess or delivering hits. 'You have to move along with the political current. Many top stars have had political ambitions. They choose their roles with an eye on that position. They cultivate a fan base with that in mind. These fan bases are important because the more fans you have, *loyal* fans, the more tickets you sell during the all-important opening weekend. But Vikram has never been the political sort. He has refrained from cultivating a huge fan base.'

Vikram has to, therefore, ensure hits in other ways, and one of these ways is to pick what he called 'commercially viable projects'. (It's a different matter that many of these projects sank at the box office.) In the recent—and much-reviled—*Rajapattai*, he played a gym instructor who dreams of becoming a villain in the movies. He explained that he wanted to do something commercial after a 'soft drama' like *Deiva Thirumagal*, and he thought that if a 'realistic' director like Suseenthiran, the maker of critically acclaimed dramas like *Vennila Kabadi Kuzhu*, made a hard-core masala movie, the film would benefit from a mix of both sensibilities. About *David*, Bejoy Nambiar's portmanteau drama about three eponymously named men across decades, he said it was supposed to be only in Hindi, a chance for him to cut loose in front of an audience that did not have any expectations of him. 'David is a drunkard. He's irreverent. He's *nothing*. And the only way the performance would succeed is if I just let go. I loved that. But I knew it wouldn't work in Tamil. They cheated me and did it in Tamil. I didn't even know it was happening.'

But the market doesn't care about explanations. 'The market only looks at the current scenario, not what his last hit earned if it was many years ago,' Pillai told me. Still, he placed Vikram among the top ten Tamil stars today. 'Because only a star gets an opening. He will be able to fill theatres up for three days, even if his opening power has eroded over the years. Also, he is not from a film family. He has come up the ranks. He is a self-made star. The Tamil audiences respect that. *Ai* is a solo-hero film, a Shankar film. If it works, then Vikram will be back in his old position.'

In a sense, then, it's the *Sethu* days all over again. Vikram needs a hit, a big hit, the kind that can make him shoot past the competition, and he is banking on *Ai*, which shares many similarities with *Sethu*. This is another film with a long gestation period. This, too, has occasioned starvation and extreme weight loss and obsessive focus. Vikram doesn't even take his mobile phone to the sets, as he wants no distractions. He doesn't want to talk to *anyone*.

Shailaja has learnt to accept it. She said, 'I just want him to do good roles. That's what makes him happy. And as long as he's happy, I'm fine. I've become less nagging and more understanding over the years because his passion has rubbed off on me.'

But that's just Vikram. Kenny is still the father he's always been, the friend he's always been. Mala Burman, who worked as a secretary and public relations officer at Vijaya during Vikram's stay in the hospital, still sees him as the same Kenny. She told me about the time he was upset because she designated him chief guest for her daughter's *arangetram* in 2003 when instead he wanted to be like family, helping with the girl's make-up and hair. She also told me about the time, just recently, when he decided to drop in quickly and surprise her at the supermarket where she was shopping. Her husband had to tell him he couldn't do that any more—he would be mobbed.

I asked Shailaja if Vikram was in touch with the friend who drove his bike into the truck on the best and worst night of his life. She hesitated, and then said no. I asked her what his name was. She didn't want to answer.

I asked Vikram the same question when I met him for the last time, but he said he didn't want to talk about him, or even mention his name. He was willing to talk about the accident, though, and about what he could do with his right leg today. He said he could do 10 kilometres per hour on a treadmill, and then he stood up to demonstrate how flexible (or inflexible) the leg was. As he bent to roll up his trackpants, I noticed streaks of silver beginning to grow in his hair. He can bend his leg up to a right angle, but he cannot squat, and he cannot sit cross-legged. 'This always creates a problem in my wedding scenes,' he joked. 'The director has to do some cheating, with me sitting on a small stool or something.'

When he said this, it sounded to me like a minor inconvenience, a small price to pay when all your dreams have been fulfilled. Vikram seemed to sense I was thinking this. He lowered his leg and focused his gaze squarely on me, and began to speak with uncommon seriousness for the man I'd come to know off the screen. 'That's why I don't want to talk about him,' he said. 'Because every day of my life, *every day of my life*, there is a problem. I'll fall on a step. Or when I run, one leg will do what my mind wants it to do and the other won't. Or I'll be sitting somewhere and it'll start hurting. Which means I think of him almost every day. I was very upset at first. It's not because he escaped unhurt. But he never came to see me. He lived just one street away from where I lived. I could see him go past on his bike, and he would look the other way. Recently, I met him at an Old Boy's meet. He acted as if nothing had happened. He came up and said, "Hey big shot. Have you forgotten me?" I took him aside and said, "I can't forget you, you bastard. Every day, I think of you. Every hour I think of you. You fucked my life. You may think I've become a hotshot hero and all that, but nobody knows what I'm going through. I'm fucked. My life is not the same. So don't come up and ask me if I have forgotten you." His wife said he was feeling guilty, and wants to be friends again. But I can't. I don't want to fight, but I don't want him coming to me and saying, "Remember me?" He caused the accident. He put his legs on top. I always told him not to ride like that. And he never came to the hospital. He could have come once. And now, he's approaching me as if it's something on his bucket list. I don't want to be on his bucket list.'

After this outburst, which unfolded with increasing intensity, Vikram went silent for a minute.

Then he said, 'You see, I'm very normal after all.'

In early 2011, when I began working on a profile of then Prime Minister **MANMOHAN SINGH**, the shitstorm hadn't hit his government in its full fury. Manmohan Singh still enjoyed a lot of goodwill for the nuclear deal he had orchestrated with the United States in his first term, which was supposed to make India energy-sufficient, and only two years ago, in 2009, he had led the Congress party back to power for a second term, making him the first prime minister since Jawaharlal Nehru to be re-elected after a full five-year term. Plus, there was the recurring long-term dividend that he had gained in public opinion for opening India's market in 1991.

The no-nonsense, hard-working, non-politician prime minister that modern India needed was more or less the public image that Manmohan Singh enjoyed for a long time. But by early 2011, it was clear that something was just not adding up. Singh's government was, by then, credited with what was being termed as the biggest scam in Indian history, the 2G spectrum allocation, and his reaction to it, as the captain of the ship—first, indifference, then defending the indefensible, then action, when push came to shove—began giving the impression that it was time to know Manmohan Singh, the man, a little better.

'Coalgate' was still a few more years away from gaining public attention. And the anti-corruption movement, which humiliated his government, was still being scripted from a little-known activist's apartment in Indirapuram. But as I was reporting I found that the current against the Manmohan Singh government was so strong that I could barely keep pace with the news events. So an effort was made to understand the man, his make and mettle through the distant as well as most recent past.

Why did Singh behave the way he did? What were the transitions he made to transform from a bright star in academia to a bureaucrat to, finally, a politician? Can they shed any light on his personality? Was Singh an underestimated politician and an overestimated economist? With regard to the 2G matter, when the files made the rounds of his table, could he have stopped the scam then? What legacy, reading the events from 2011, was he going to leave as the thirteenth prime minister of the Republic?

VINOD JOSE

Vinod K. Jose is the executive editor of the Caravan.

Falling Man

Manmohan Singh at the centre of the storm

By VINOD K. JOSE | 1 October 2011

I

On the morning of 15 August, India's Independence Day, it was raining cats and dogs in Delhi. By 7 a.m., Prime Minister Manmohan Singh was atop the ramparts of the seventeenth-century Red Fort, hoisting the flag and saluting the assembled soldiers and citizens from behind a glass enclosure. Amid a sea of umbrellas, children who had gathered to watch the parade ran about, as if at a disorderly festival ground; the soldiers and paramilitary troops paraded on the wet asphalt, completely drenched.

It was an unusually gloomy Independence Day, and not merely because of the inclement weather. After a cursory presentation of his government's achievements over the past seven years, Singh devoted almost the entirety of his eighth Independence Day speech to a series of crises: the recent terrorist attacks in Mumbai; the ongoing 'challenge of Naxalism'; inflation and rising food prices; the 'tensions caused' by land acquisition; and, most of all, 'the problem of corruption'—'a difficulty for which no government has a magic wand'.

After his speech, Singh was driven to the Congress headquarters at 24 Akbar Road for the party's own flag-hoisting ceremony. Traditionally, the Congress party president presides over the flag raising, but with Sonia Gandhi hospitalized in the US, many predicted Rahul Gandhi would seize the moment and hoist the flag himself. Instead, he passed on the duty to the senior Congress leader Motilal Vora, and Singh stood nearby with the party's senior leaders as they saluted the flag and sang: *'Jhanda ooncha rahe hamara, vijayi vishwa tiranga pyara . . .'* ('Let our flag always be lofty, this world-conquering, beloved tricolour'). Manmohan Singh, in his iconic powder-blue turban, and the home minister, P. Chidambaram, were the only ones not wearing the Gandhi cap—a one-time symbol of the party of Independence, that had more recently become the emblem of its newest and most popular nemesis, Anna Hazare.

The Maharashtrian activist had announced his plan to begin an indefinite hunger strike in Delhi the following day, and Congress leaders were buckling under the pressure: one-quarter of Singh's speech at the Red Fort had been devoted to corruption and the Lokpal Bill, whose passage Hazare was demanding. After the flag hoisting, Rahul Gandhi called Singh, Chidambaram and Defence Minister A.K. Antony, into a meeting in the party office to discuss Hazare. Finance Minister Pranab Mukherjee, the party's most reliable problem-solver, had already left the premises, so Rahul sent someone to retrieve him.

According to accounts provided by three party insiders—two members of the Congress Working Committee (CWC) and a top Congress functionary—Rahul expressed his displeasure with the personal attacks on Hazare that had been launched in his absence, and suggested that greater tact should be employed to deal with Hazare's impending fast.

Unlike his mother, who is said to be firm and precise in her orders to senior party leaders, Rahul's directions proved insufficiently forceful to avert the looming disaster. After the meeting, according to the three party sources, Chidambaram took charge of the situation in concert with Human Resource Development Minister Kapil Sibal, and the two lawyers-turned-politicians devised a plan to prevent Hazare from staging his fast. Citing the best legal justifications—Section 144 of the Criminal Procedure Code, and Section 188 of the Indian Penal Code—Chidambaram sanctioned Hazare's arrest the following morning, and then all hell broke loose. Agitated crowds massed outside Tihar jail, while Hazare took maximum advantage of Chidambaram's error, refusing to accept release until his conditions for the fast were granted. Hazare and his allies had humiliated the government, and the ensuing spectacle at Delhi's Ramlila Maidan soon became Indian television's most successful reality show, with record-setting ratings for the non-stop coverage on every single news channel.

Singh's prime ministership, already battered by twelve months of scandals and setbacks, seemed to have hit a new low; his impeccable reputation as an incorruptible man of integrity—which served for so long as a firewall against criticism—no longer shielded him from the consequences of his government's failings. If the prime minister privately expressed any opposition to the decision to arrest Hazare, he seems to have done nothing to prevent it.

'It was Manmohan Singh who lost face, since it was his decision to leave everything in the hands of Chidambaram and company,' one of the CWC members said. 'The people who make mistakes keep making them, and the ministers—especially those who are professionals—are so arrogant.' While the nation's attention was fixed on Ramlila Maidan, the upper echelons of the Congress drew their knives in private—and they did not spare the PM: 'Everyone called up everyone else, and they were all so furious at Chidambaram, Sibal and Manmohan Singh,' said the party functionary.

The 'professionals' were soon pushed aside in favour of Pranab Mukherjee, who managed to negotiate a resolution with

Team Anna to bring an end to the fast after a special session of Parliament voiced its near-unanimous assent to a Lokpal Bill that met Hazare's conditions. 'When it was finally decided to let Pranab deal with the Hazare thing, it meant snubbing Chidambaram and Sibal', and sidelining Singh, according to the CWC member. 'What was it, if it wasn't a public snub, that Manmohan Singh had to hand over the political leadership to Pranab because he wasn't capable of defending his own colleague's blunders?' the party functionary added.

During the marathon Parliament session on 27 August, which began with Mukherjee's solemn warning that 'the largest functional democracy of the world is at a very crucial stage', more than two dozen parliamentarians stood up in the Lok Sabha to speak on corruption and the Lokpal Bill; another 102 presented written statements. Manmohan Singh did not utter a word, and sat like a mute witness, his face fixed with an impassive grimace against the barrage of criticism from the Opposition benches.

The harshest blow may have come from Sushma Swaraj, the leader of the Opposition in the Lok Sabha. In a fiery speech delivered in Hindi, the Bharatiya Janata Party (BJP) MP did more than criticize the prime minister: she mocked his reputation as an ineffectual figure even among his own colleagues. *'Waise toh hamare pradhan mantri bolte nahi hain, aur bolte hain to koi unki sunta nahin hain,'* (Normally, our prime minister doesn't talk, and when he does, no one [in his Cabinet] even listens to him.) she said.

II

That Manmohan Singh's star has fallen—and far—may be the closest thing to a consensus in Indian politics today. The cautious smiles that briefly graced Singh's face two years ago, in the wake of the Congress general election victory and his Indo-US nuclear deal, now seem a distant memory. The Anna Hazare fiasco was merely the latest in an apparently unending string of debacles for Singh and his government, which have steadily ground his formerly impeccable reputation into dust—at first slowly and then all at once.

While the newspapers and television channels continue to lay siege to the government—feasting on a rich diet of unfolding scams, ongoing investigations and the arrests of former ministers and MPs—the *aam aadmi* has been hit hard by skyrocketing food prices and runaway inflation, denting, both, the loyalty of Congress voters and the reputation for economic wizardry Singh earned by presiding over the liberalization of the Indian economy as finance minister in 1991.

It was Manmohan Singh, himself, who said, in a 1996 interview, that 'it is only a crisis that concentrates the mind'. But faced with too many crises to count, his government looks to be indisarray, and the man who helped steer India through its most perilous financial crisis and into an age of explosive growth—whose image has always been that of a swift, purposeful manager, too busy solving problems to play political games and preen for the cameras—now appears as a technocrat in way over his head, overwhelmed and out of steam, pale-faced and emotionally spent.

'The fall has been so dramatic,' said a former Union cabinet minister who has known Singh since the 1960s. 'There is a visible drift, without any direction, and he appears to be helpless. People will say that of course he is an honest man, and nobody doubts his personal integrity, but when you are presiding over an outfit that is dealing in corruption, you have to answer for that. How do you defend it? You can't defend it.'

'Just look at the cartoons,' the former minister continued. 'He is shrinking in size every day. He must be feeling awful.'

'He is facing the worst situation in his life,' said Sanjaya Baru, a business journalist who served as Singh's media adviser from 2004 to 2008. 'In politics, it's all right to be loved or hated, but you should never be ridiculed. And his problem today is that he has become an object of ridicule.'

With senior members of his own party openly speculating that he will be replaced before the next general election—the prospect may be unlikely, but the volume of such talk is significant nonetheless—it seems clear that Singh, now seventy-nine, is nearing the end of a long and extraordinary innings in public life. Before becoming finance minister in 1991 at the age of fifty-eight, he had held every top economic policy position: chief economic adviser, finance secretary, deputy chairman of the Planning Commission and Reserve Bank of India (RBI) governor. As the finance minister and then as prime minister, Singh quietly but decisively presided over the dismantling of the two foundational principles that had, for decades, defined both the Congress party and the nation: a socialist planned economy and a non-aligned foreign policy. In that sense, Manmohan Singh—who once answered a question about his legacy by saying, 'I hope I've earned a footnote in India's long history'—may one day be credited with having transformed India more dramatically than Indira and Rajiv Gandhi combined.

At the moment, however, the prospective judgements of future historians can hardly comfort the beleaguered prime minister: escaping the harsh verdict of the present already looks like an impossible task. The prominent historian Ramachandra Guha, who has described the current administration as 'inept and incompetent beyond words', told me that he now regards Singh 'increasingly as a tragic figure'.

'He's intelligent, upright, and possesses all these vast experiences of working in the government for over four decades,' Guha said.

'But the timidity, complacency and intellectual dishonesty will make him a tragic figure in our history.'

Contemplating the case of Manmohan Singh throws up more questions than answers. An intensely private man, whom friends and associates invariably describe with adjectives like 'shy', 'reticent', 'modest' and 'decent', Singh prefers to shut himself away from the media and the public. His personal feelings and emotions are more closely guarded than state secrets—a trait he shares with the woman who appointed him, and one that lends the country's most significant relationship an impregnable opacity. 'He is basically a loner,' the former Union cabinet minister said. 'I don't think he has many friends. He is a very shy person, and he must be hating the adverse publicity he is getting—he must be thinking, 'What the hell did I get myself into?''

But somewhere between the mythic hero of 1991, the accidental PM of 2004 and the diminished leader of 2011 lies the real Manmohan Singh, though the man himself offers little assistance to anyone seeking to better understand his life and work. Through his office, the prime minister declined numerous requests to be interviewed, as he has done, with very few exceptions, for almost all media inquiries in the past seven years.

This story is, therefore, based on the accounts of others, gathered over the course of four months of research that included lengthy interviews with over forty people who have known and worked closely with Manmohan Singh in his private and public life during the last half-century.

Singh's legendary reticence is no myth, but from the collected accounts of his associates, friends and relatives, a complex and sometimes contradictory picture can be assembled: self-effacing but confident; modest but ambitious; diffident yet determined; stubborn in his convictions but often selective in their application.

His weakness and meekness as a politician have been greatly exaggerated, along with his subservience to Sonia Gandhi.

To the larger question of what led him to this unpleasant juncture in an otherwise exemplary career, only Manmohan Singh can provide a definitive answer, and his overwhelming reluctance to narrate his own story thus far suggests that readers are unlikely to find his memoirs in stores any time soon.

In a 2006 interview with the American talk-show host Charlie Rose, Manmohan Singh described himself, with ostentatious modesty, as 'a small person put in this big chair'. Singh's detractors would say that he has too often lived down to this self-portrait, while his defenders would take it as a sign of his admirable humility; all that can be added, in the present context, is that the former have begun to outnumber the latter.

III

For a man of such modesty and reserve, Manmohan Singh entered the national—and international—spotlight at a moment of great drama and upheaval, emerging from the relative anonymity of the higher bureaucracy as a slayer of socialist shibboleths who issued oracular pronouncements like 'India needs to wake up' to admiring foreign journalists.

When P.V. Narasimha Rao took office as the newly elected prime minister in June 1991, the world was in the throes of a rapid and abrupt reordering: communism had collapsed in Eastern Europe, the two Germanys had been reunited, the Soviet Union was within months of dissolution and the United States had gone to war to roll back Iraq's invasion of Kuwait. The situation in India was even more volatile: two governments had fallen in the brief interval between November 1990 and March 1991, and the Congress party's candidate for prime minister, Rajiv Gandhi, was assassinated while campaigning in May 1991, leaving the party without a Gandhi as its leader for the first time in twenty-five years.

Rao, a shrewd Andhra politician who spoke more than a dozen languages and had earlier served as Rajiv Gandhi's foreign minister, inherited an economy on the cusp of disaster. India's debt to foreign lenders had nearly doubled between 1985 and 1991, and a series of external shocks—including the sudden spike in oil prices that accompanied the Gulf War—had reduced India's foreign currency reserves to less than the amount required to finance two weeks of imports. The government was so desperate to raise funds that it had pawned 20 tonnes of gold confiscated from smugglers, which were secretly shipped to the Union Bank of Switzerland in exchange for $200 million. When that proved insufficient, another 47 tonnes from the RBI were sent to England and Japan to secure loans worth an additional $405 million. In a country where pawning the family jewellery would be an act of final desperation, the sense of alarm was palpable.

On the day Rao was elected to head the Congress Parliamentary Party (CPP), a few days before he was sworn in as prime minister, he received an urgent visit from the Cabinet secretary, Naresh Chandra. 'I rang him up and said there was something very important he had to see,' Chandra told me. 'I had prepared a seven- or eight-page memo on the crisis. When I gave it to him, he asked me, "Do you want me to read this right now? I'm very busy building the Cabinet." I told him that could wait a few minutes, he should read this now. When he finished, he asked, "Is it as bad as this?" I said, "In fact it is even worse."' Chandra—accompanied by Finance Secretary S.P. Shukla and Chief Economic Adviser Deepak Nayyar—told Rao he could either continue the unsustainable status quo of emergency borrowing or announce that the government planned to liberalize the economy. 'If it is our new policy,' Chandra told Rao, 'there will be less criticism than if it seems we were asked to do it by the IMF [International Monetary Fund] and World Bank.'

Facing an economic catastrophe, Rao knew he needed to reach beyond the ranks of the khadi-clad senior Congress leaders to select a finance minister, for three separate reasons: first, he would need a skilled economist to conduct negotiations with the international financial institutions; second, in the event of a backlash against the radical policy changes, an 'outsider' would be easier to dismiss from the Cabinet; and third, if the new finance minister was successful, he still wouldn't pose any threat to Rao's own position in the party. To some extent, the blueprint for liberalization had already taken shape, given India's desperate need for huge loans; what remained to be determined were the details of its execution.

P.C. Alexander, a close friend of Rao's, who had been an influential principal secretary to Indira Gandhi, helped with the search. 'Alexander would sit with PV, make calls, write names, try combinations, strike them out and then write again,' recalled the former Union cabinet minister. After Alexander's first choice, the former RBI governor, I.G. Patel, declined the offer, he called Manmohan Singh, Patel's successor at the RBI. Singh was delighted and said he would eagerly accept the job, the former Cabinet minister told me, but two days passed without any follow-up from Alexander.

On the morning of 22 June, a Saturday, Singh got a call in his office at the University Grants Commission, where he had been appointed chairman three months earlier. It was Rao, who was scheduled to take his oath as prime minister that afternoon. 'PV asked Manmohan, "What are you doing there? Go home and change, and come straight to Rashtrapati Bhavan,"' the former Cabinet minister said.

Singh was among a handful of Cabinet ministers who took their oaths with Rao that Saturday afternoon, and he started the job immediately. 'Manmohan started working from home on Saturday and Sunday,' said Mani Shankar Aiyar, who later served as a minister in Singh's first Cabinet. 'He was already consulting with other economists and making plans to borrow funds.'

On Monday, his first day in office, Singh held a press conference to announce the scope of the impending reforms; he promised to clear the 'cobwebs of unnecessary control' that had impeded economic development and decreed that 'the world has changed, and the country must also change'.

The next day, Singh had his first official meeting with Rao, whose commitment to serious reform was still unknown. According to a senior secretary then in the finance ministry, 'Manmohan was at sea, and still very nervous.' Singh told the prime minister that the country immediately needed a huge standby loan of at least $5 billion. To manage the current financial year would only require $2 billion, he suggested, but it would be prudent to take a larger loan from the IMF in anticipation of ongoing problems in the following year. 'There was no ambiguity in Rao's mind,' the senior secretary recalled. 'He was more convinced than Manmohan Singh.' Rao approved Singh's proposal on the spot, and the new finance minister returned to his office and immediately drafted a letter to the managing director of the IMF, Michel Camdessus, specifying India's requirements and promising to undertake the necessary structural reforms in a manner consistent with 'India's social objectives'.

The following month would prove crucial: Singh had to prepare a Budget that would pass muster with the IMF and any other international lenders looking for evidence that the commitment to liberalization was sincere. 'During that month of Budget preparation, the Cabinet Committee for Political Affairs met almost every day,' the senior secretary told me. 'Manmohan was so indecisive and nervous that Rao ended up doing most of the talking and convincing the others himself.'

Singh's starring role in the 1991 crisis was already enshrined in history by the time the term 'Manmohanomics' was coined, within a year or two of his first Budget. The prime minister has modestly insisted that 'no single person could claim credit' for the reforms, but time has steadily effaced the critical part played by Rao, who is today rarely credited with anything more than having selected Singh as his finance minister. 'Manmohan was actually a convert, from the old system to the new,' the senior secretary said. 'So like every convert, he was unsure, even if he gave the impression that things would all be fine. PV, who was known to be very indecisive—at cabinet committee meetings he couldn't even decide between tea and coffee—was surprisingly sure that India had to deregulate and open its markets, and he gave Manmohan the crucial confidence to make those moves.'

'He feared he would be attacked by the party,' another top bureaucrat who worked with Singh at the finance ministry told me, 'because he had authored the current Five-Year Plan when he was the deputy chairman of the Planning Commission, and he was now implementing policies which were totally contradictory. The PM and all of the secretaries told him it was okay, but it took time for this to sink in.'

On 24 July, a few weeks after presiding over a two-stage devaluation of the rupee, Singh stood up in the Lok Sabha to present his first Budget, which laid out a series of structural reforms and fiscal adjustments: relaxation of industrial licensing, abolition of export subsidies, reduction in fund transfers to public enterprises and massive cuts in fertilizer subsidies and welfare programmes. At the close of his two-hour speech, the novice politician demonstrated a flair for rhetorical drama, uttering the lines that would be repeated in the thousands of subsequent articles about Singh and the breakthrough of 1991:

> I do not minimize the difficulties that lie ahead on the long and arduous journey on which we have embarked. But as Victor Hugo once said, 'No power on earth can stop an idea whose time has come.' I suggest to this august House that the emergence of India as a major economic power in the world happens to be one such idea. Let the whole world hear it loud and clear. India is now wide awake. We shall prevail. We shall overcome.

Singh's Budget, which would come to symbolize the unleashing of the Indian economy, met with a cold reception within the Congress party. At a meeting after the Budget speech to discuss the new economic policies, a sizeable crowd of MPs vented their outrage: they may have had little sense of how the macroeconomic changes would impact their political careers, but they were certain that slashing fertilizer subsidies, among other measures, would spell doom at the polls. 'There was considerable unrest in the Congress ranks,' a CWC member and former Cabinet minister told me. 'There were as many as sixty-three backbenchers who spoke against Manmohan. PV really had to save him in that meeting.'

IV

On 22 July 2008, almost seventeen years to the day he delivered the Budget speech that launched his political career, Manmohan Singh stood once again in the Lok Sabha to stave off its demise.

The fateful trust vote that threatened to bring down his government over the Indo-US nuclear deal was minutes away, and Singh rose to defend both himself and the nuclear pact.

The speech that Singh prepared but did not deliver—after an uproar from the Opposition benches cut him off—closed with a rare allusion to the story of his own life:

> Every day that I have been prime minister of India I have tried to remember that the first ten years of my life were spent in a village with no drinking water supply, no electricity, no hospital, no roads and nothing that we today associate with modern living. I had to walk miles to school, I had to study in the dim light of a kerosene oil lamp . . . On every day that I have occupied this high office, I have tried to fulfil the dream of that young boy from that distant village.

The basics of Singh's journey from a tiny village, in what is now Pakistan, to 7 Race Course Road are well known, but the prime minister has typically refused to make political use of his rise from humble beginnings. When I mentioned Barack Obama's skilful employment of his own biography to Sanjaya Baru, the PM's former media adviser, the frustrations of his earlier job came boiling to the surface. 'He always shied away,' Baru said. 'He prevented me from telling his story; he said to me, "No, no, I don't want to build my image. I'm just here to do work." He is afraid of being a political personality.'

'In fact, his life story is far more inspiring than Obama's—with the background he came from, the struggle he went through and the heights he has reached,' Baru continued. 'The tragedy is that he hasn't allowed anyone to tell it. But I think now it is too late.'

Singh was born in 1932 in a village called Gah, about 60 kilometres south of what is now Islamabad; his family were Punjabi traders of the Khatri caste. His father, Gurmukh Singh Kohli, was a small-time dry-fruit trader who bought wholesale stock from Afghanistan and resold it in smaller towns in the Punjab. Singh's mother, Amrit Kaur, died when he was only five months old, and so he was raised largely by his paternal grandmother, Jamna Devi, whom he called Dadi. Singh's father was often away from home, but his principled business conduct still exerted an influence on the young boy, who everyone then simply called Mohana. In Amritsar earlier this year, I met Prem Kumar, a trader of tea leaves who had lived next to the future prime minister and his family after Partition. 'Gurmukh had a reputation of staying away from foul tricks,' Kumar told me. 'He was a silent worker, and he chose to speak very little.' His maxim, Kumar said, was *'Imandari se kamai huyo ik roti bemani ki do rotiyon se acchi hai'* (One roti earned through honest means is better than two earned dishonestly).

Singh attended an Urdu-medium village primary school until he was ten, at which point he shifted to an upper primary school in Peshawar, obtaining top marks all along. Early in the summer of 1947, the year that Singh sat for his matriculation examination, the family fled Peshawar for Amritsar: Singh's father had anticipated the violence that would follow Partition and, shortly before the bloodshed began, he moved his family into an upper-floor apartment along the narrow lanes behind the Golden Temple.

The alleys of Amritsar's old city haven't changed too much in the intervening decades, but the building where the future prime minister once lived is now a dilapidated wreck. Known in the neighbourhood as Sant Ram da Tabela, it's been sealed for several years as a result of litigation between the owner and a bank, and has become a sanctuary for rats and crows. Sunlight barely falls on the narrow alley, and I smelled the pungent odour of rotten groceries mingling with baking sweets. 'The air wasn't any different sixty years ago,' said Prem Kumar, who was a neighbour to the Singhs beginning in 1947. Nor, it seems, was the prime minister: 'Manmohan would sit on the staircase and read the whole day,' Kumar recalled. 'He barely got out on the lanes, nor played with anyone. He studied like there was an examination every tomorrow.'

After arriving in Amritsar at a moment of great political and economic instability, Singh firmly resisted his father's demands that he join the dry-fruit trade. He wanted to go to college and earn his degree, and pleaded that he would earn a scholarship and still lend a hand with the business—as his father's accountant. He eventually prevailed, thanks to the intercession of his grandmother, and began his degree in economics at Hindu College in Amritsar.

Singh had a meteoric rise through academia, funded by a succession of merit scholarships, from Amritsar to Chandigarh to Cambridge to Oxford. Between his Cambridge degree and the completion of his PhD at Oxford, he became the youngest professor at his own alma mater, Panjab University in Chandigarh. 'He was a very serious teacher,' said H.S. Shergill, one of Singh's students who later became a professor of economics at the university. 'He always started the classes on time, and marked the papers very stringently.'

It was in Chandigarh that Manmohan Singh first met Gursharan Kaur, a BA student. Gursharan has said they became engaged without ever having seen each other, but Manmohan's younger brother, Surjeet Singh Kohli, told me with a smile that theirs was a love marriage. 'They were an affable, romantic couple, totally happy with each other,' said R.P. Bambah, one of Singh's colleagues at Panjab University. 'Manmohan had a bicycle, and on Friday they would go together to Kiran Cinema,' then the only movie hall in the city that played English films. Kiran is still standing, but it's been outclassed by fancy new multiplexes. 'We can't offer the facilities that the theatres in the malls offer,' the manager told me. 'So we're B-class now—meant for the autorickshaw drivers.' Little did he know that the man who opened India to malls and multiplexes used to bicycle to his theatre.

The austere habits of Singh's university days have stayed with him through the decades. 'Manmohan and Gursharan haven't changed at all,' Bambah said. 'Gursharan remembered that I liked rajma, so she had it for me on the table when I visited them recently. Even after sixty years, it looked as if we were sharing the same meal we once shared in the university staff quarters.'

The second of his three daughters, Daman Singh, told me that her earliest memory of her father was of a 'workaholic'. 'As children,' she said, 'we just assumed that's the way all fathers are. He hasn't changed at all.'

'All of our birthday presents were books,' Daman recalled. 'For any of our birthdays he used to take us to bookshops like the New Book Depot and Galgotia at Connaught Place. We can pick any books, and he will pay—that was the gift. He never asked us to buy what he thought was important for us.'

In the past forty years, Daman said she could only remember her father taking one vacation—a three-day family trip to Nainital, a hill station five hours from Delhi. Seven years into his tenure as prime minister, he still hasn't taken one. Sanjaya Baru recalled that it was difficult to convince Singh to take even a single day to relax. 'We were going to Goa one day, to inaugurate the Birla Institute of Technology in Panaji,' Baru said. 'We were to fly there in the morning, inaugurate the Birla Institute and fly out in the evening back to Delhi. I said to him, "Sir, it's a weekend. Why don't we stay Saturday night, spend Sunday morning on the beach and come back Sunday evening? You won't miss a working day." You know what he asked? "But what do I do there?" Only Manmohan Singh could ask what he could do in Goa.'

V

With each major chapter in his life, Manmohan Singh has moved gradually and deliberately from the abstractions of academia to the calculations and compromises of politics. The first of these shifts brought him into the bureaucracy, where he served for nearly twenty years under six separate governments—rising rapidly through the ranks with a combination of talent, determination and political instinct. Singh's reputation as an economist had brought him to the attention of the finance ministry as early as the late 1950s, when one of his Cambridge professors recommended Singh to then finance minister T.T. Krishnamachari. But at the time, his obligations to Panjab University prevented him from taking up a government post.

Singh left the university in 1965 for a stint in New York at the United Nations trade body, the United Nations Conference on Trade and Development (UNCTAD), and then one at the Delhi School of Economics, which brought him into contact with powerful bureaucrats like P.N. Haksar and P.N. Dhar, two top secretaries to Indira Gandhi. In 1971, he took a lateral entry into the civil service and became an economic adviser to the ministry of foreign trade; within a year, he had been promoted to chief economic adviser in the finance ministry, where he earned his first small measure of public acclaim by taming runaway inflation. His ascent continued with positions as finance secretary, member secretary of the Planning Commission, RBI governor and deputy chairman of the Planning Commission.

The prime minister's detractors have mounted various attacks on his tenure in the bureaucracy, ranging from the simple accusation that he helped implement counterproductive economic policies to the more damning and less substantiated insinuation that he was (and therefore still is) an ardent socialist whose rise reflected favouritism rather than merit. But in an era when doctorates in economics from Oxford weren't exactly queuing up to serve the Government of India, Singh was unquestionably among the best-qualified technocrats on hand, and he quickly earned a reputation for delivering results—without stepping over the line to challenge his superiors. His capacity to adapt to shifting political winds was nicely captured by the *Times of India* in a 1991 editorial: 'Manmohan Singh was perfectly happy with the *garibi hatao* phase of Mrs Gandhi, then with the Emergency, then with the Janata Party, then with the return of Mrs Gandhi. He was accessible to Chandrasekhar as an adviser with Cabinet rank. He's accessible to everyone. That's a miracle.'

Singh navigated these turbulent years under the tutelage of a series of mentors, beginning with P.N. Haksar, then the influential private secretary to Indira Gandhi, who is said to have helped Singh shift from the trade to the finance ministry. After Haksar turned against Gandhi's increasingly authoritarian tendencies in the run-up to the Emergency, Singh became close with P.N. Dhar, who had succeeded Haksar as Gandhi's principal secretary, and R.K. Dhawan, an intimate of Sanjay Gandhi. When Indira was ejected and the Janata Party came to power, Singh worked closely with H.M. Patel, whose position was almost diametrically opposed to that of Dhawan, his previous mentor.

It would be too simple to conclude, on the basis of Singh's capacity to survive such turnabouts, that his ambition had already shifted from economics to politics; that turn was still more than a decade away. At the time, there were merely intimations of his future identity—as an economist among the politicians and a politician among the economists.

It is similarly difficult to draw firm conclusions about Singh's vaunted conversion to the free market after two decades spent helping to administer controls over the Indian economy. When the question of this apparent contradiction was first raised in June 1991, at Singh's first press conference as finance minister, his response was unguarded: 'I agree that I had played a role in getting the economy into a mess, and now I want to play a role in getting the economy out of the mess.' A few weeks later, shortly before presenting his first Budget, he presented a more assertive answer to the very same question: 'What I am saying now is what I have been saying since I came into the government. It is true that I have lived within the system and that I have not been able to change the system's thinking earlier.'

The record is complicated further by an episode from Singh's tenure as the deputy chairman of the Planning Commission: Rajiv Gandhi had come into office backed by an enormous parliamentary majority after his mother's assassination, full of energy and eager to transform India overnight. At a meeting in early 1985, Singh presented the new prime minister with a draft of the Seventh Five-Year Plan, and Rajiv made no effort to hide his disapproval. 'Rajiv lost his cool,' said Natwar Singh, who was then a minister of state. 'He said it was rubbish.' C.G. Somiah, who served with Singh as secretary in the Planning Commission, recalled in his autobiography that Gandhi 'wanted us to plan for the construction of autobahns, airfields, speedy trains, shopping malls and entertainment centres of excellence, big housing complexes, modern hospitals and healthcare centres. We were shocked into silence.'

According to Somiah, Singh called an internal meeting of the Planning Commission, whose members agreed that Rajiv had an 'urban-centric' orientation without proper regard for the vast population of poor villagers. After Singh 'deliberated at length on the negative economic indicators prevalent in the country' at the next meeting with Rajiv, Somiah writes that the prime minister 'made some hurtful and derogatory remarks'; a few days later, he called Singh and his planners 'a bunch of jokers' in a meeting with journalists.

Six years later, Singh would be the one implementing a radical break with the planned economy, but back in the mid 1980s, he was still 'living within the system', as he later put it, and he unhappily decided to offer up his resignation in the face of Rajiv's public mockery. He was persuaded by Somiah to stay on, but left Delhi with pleasure two years later for a job in Geneva as the secretary of the South Commission, an outgrowth of the non-aligned movement, whose mission was 'to plan an alternative development strategy for the countries of the South, drawing from their unique conditions of poverty, poor resources and unfair trade relations with the countries in the North'. The commission's final report, published in 1990, had positive words for trade liberalization and economic cooperation among developing countries, but its dominant tone was one of harsh criticism for the inequalities of the global economic system and the international lending agencies with which Singh would soon be negotiating.

Within the Congress party, which presided over liberalization and has since sought to corner the credit, there is still lingering unease over India's tryst with capitalism—regarded by some as a deviation from Nehruvian socialism, not to mention a losing card with rural voters. Singh's struggles over economic policy since 1991, therefore, have often pitted him against his own party.

In 1998, after the BJP had come to power and Sonia Gandhi had assumed the Congress presidency, the party's heavyweights gathered at the Madhya Pradesh hill station of Pachmarhi for a 'brainstorming session' intended to put the stumbling party back on the road to victory. Singh, who was the leader of the Opposition in the Rajya Sabha, chaired the subcommittee on economic affairs. Mani Shankar Aiyar, who would later serve in Singh's Cabinet, was then the party's chief draughtsman, typing up pages of the policy resolutions. 'One page on economic vision came to me with the word "planned" cut out and the word "balanced" written in the margins,' Aiyar told me. 'I thought the phrase "planned development" had been with the Congress party from the Karachi Conference of 1931, so in all innocence, I put "planned and balanced economy".'

When Aiyar returned the draft, he said, 'Manmohan Singh was very, very angry. He said, "I cut out the word 'planned'. Why did you put it back in?" I protested that the word had been used since the Karachi Conference.' But Singh would not relent. Natwar Singh, another working committee member, came over to intervene, tugging at Aiyar's kurta and telling him, *'Chhod do'* (Leave it). Aiyar yielded to the seniors. 'If you say *chhodo, chhodo,*' he recalled. 'I went back and cut out the word.'

VI

After Singh entered the upper echelons of the Congress in the late 1990s, the party gave him a ticket to contest a Lok Sabha election in 1999 from south Delhi—a posh constituency of middle-class voters who had reaped great benefits from the liberalized economy. His challenger was an unseemly state-level BJP leader, V.K. Malhotra. 'It was meant to be a cakewalk for Doctor Sahib, a very sure seat for the Congress,' said Harcharan Singh Josh, a local party leader who served as Singh's campaign manager. 'In the previous year's state election, ten out of the fourteen assembly seats were won by the Congress MLAs. The Muslim and Sikh populations came to more than 50 per cent of the constituency. And everyone was buying the foreign brands in the South-Ex market, brought to India by Doctor Sahib. Malhotra had *jhero* chance.'

But there were problems from the start. Singh was still an outsider in the party, a talented bureaucrat who had been swept into politics after his successes in the finance ministry, with neither the aptitude nor the appetite for the dark arts of campaigning. Sonia Gandhi had personally given Singh the ticket, but that hardly guaranteed him the support of the party's cadres.

'The AICC [All India Congress Committee] gave us Rs 2 million, more than they paid for other constituencies,' Josh said. 'But that wasn't sufficient to keep the MLAs, municipal councillors and the party workers active. He did not know anything about these intrigues—he was having the impression that since the Congress party has given him the ticket, the MLAs and municipal councillors will all work together.'

'For the first ten days,' Josh said, 'we had no funds, and industrialists came from as far as Calcutta, calling to ask for appointments to hand over election contributions. But he refused to meet them.'

'One day I told him, "Doctor Sahib, we're losing the election. We have no money,"' Josh said. 'Everyone [in the party] said they'll give money,' Singh replied, but Josh regretfully informed him that further inquiries had demonstrated the emptiness of these promises. Josh told Singh the campaign needed at least Rs 10 million. *'Councillor kahta hai mujhe paisa do* [Councillors are asking for money]. *Kya karein? Minimum do lakh toh mangte hain na?* [What can we do? They ask for Rs 200,000 minimum, right?] Office *kholna hai, jo log aayenge, unko chai pilana hai, car chahiye* to go this way, to go that way, flags also, banners. So all these things require money,' Josh said.

'But he was a different man. He had never dealt with money. So ultimately, one day, I sat with Doctor Sahib, his wife and his daughter Daman. He said, "I will not meet anyone." I said, "Doctor Sahib, we'll lose the election—money *bina, paise ke bina*—we'll lose without money."'

According to his campaign in-charge, Manmohan Singh, who had at first 'stood like a rock', finally yielded to the ethically dubious practices of Indian electioneering. 'It was decided that people would come to Doctor Sahib—*sir, kuch seva bataiiye mujhe* (Is there any way for me to be of service?). So Doctor Sahib used to say, "I want only your good wishes. Nothing else." Then the money will be delivered to Madame [Gursharan] in the next room.' (After the election, Josh said, Singh passed the unused funds—about Rs 700,000—to the AICC.)

'The entire corporate sector was with him,' Singh's rival V.K. Malhotra told me. 'They got appeals issued by Khushwant Singh, Javed Akhtar; the entire media supported him—the *Times of India, Hindustan Times*, Star TV.' But elections are not won on the strength of elite opinion, and Singh lacked the ability to reach out to voters or mobilize the Congress ranks. 'Several senior party men worked against Doctor Sahib, and the councillors who had affiliations with those senior leaders did not work for Doctor Sahib either,' Josh said.

Singh lost by almost 30,000 votes, shocking his supporters and admirers and cementing his image as a man ill-suited to politics, a 'weak politician' who would rather sit comfortably in the unelected upper house than face the judgement of the voters. When various party figures came back to Singh in 2004, promising to put him in a safe seat and ensure his election, the humiliation of 1999 still loomed large, and he refused all offers.

The defeat, recalled his daughter Daman Singh, was 'very hard' on her father. 'He felt very alone after that,' she said. 'It was a huge blow, sort of like a *dhakka* for the whole family.'

'He was very subdued and depressed' after the election, the former Union cabinet minister told me. 'It took him almost a year to really come to terms with it. His graph had always been upward, and suddenly it went down—he couldn't take it. The tragedy was that the Congress men made sure that he lost it. They said, "Who is this chap who has come from outside?"'

After his loss in 1999, Singh retained his seat in the Rajya Sabha, and continued to draw closer to Sonia Gandhi, joining her inner circle of trusted advisers—a position for which his apparent lack of political ambition was likely a considerable asset. When the members of the CPP gathered to select their leader on Saturday, 15 May 2004—two days after the surprise Congress general election victory—it was Manmohan Singh who presided over the election and announced the unanimous result in favour of Sonia Gandhi. Singh was also present the following day when Gandhi called a small informal meeting of party leaders—including Pranab Mukherjee, Natwar Singh and Ahmed Patel—to reveal that she would decline the opportunity to be PM. When Gandhi went to see President Abdul Kalam on Monday to explain that she would not head the government, she took Manmohan Singh along. At a CPP meeting later that afternoon, Gandhi formally announced her decision, tears welling up in her eyes, to a chorus of shouts and wails from the assembled parliamentarians. The session adjourned without mention of a replacement. But while top party leaders were speculating about the identity of their next prime minister—and a handful of ambitious Congressmen were eyeing the job—Gandhi was at home writing a resolution to elect

Manmohan Singh, which was circulated to every Congress MP that night. By the time the parliamentary party met for a third time the next day, Singh's election was a mere formality.

It's not hard to see what led Sonia to select Manmohan from half a dozen more seasoned and more powerful Congressmen: his loyalty, integrity and his international reputation as the architect of 1991.

'He didn't put money into his account. He followed very simple personal habits. And his children didn't run amok. All this helped him slowly create an image of respectability in politics,' a senior secretary, who worked closely with Singh in the finance ministry, said.

Singh's house was soon overrun with well-wishers. 'I remember they put a tent at the back, an area for refreshments and cold drinks in the garden, under a big sort of shamiana,' Daman Singh said. 'It took some time to get organized, because obviously nobody was expecting something like this.'

The accidental finance minister had become the accidental PM, thrust into the prime ministership by Gandhi's surprise gift—circumstances that only seemed to confirm Singh's reputation as the quiet man of Indian politics, too decent and modest to grasp for the throne himself. But Singh's ambition and determination have always been underestimated, a misperception he has rarely tried to correct.

'He was principally an outsider—he didn't expect to become the prime minister,' said the former Union cabinet minister. 'I am not saying that he is totally lacking in ambition—in this game, nobody is not ambitious. But he was very subtle about it.'

In a 1996 interview, Singh had been asked point-blank about his aspirations for the top job and his response was uncharacteristically blunt: 'Who doesn't want to be prime minister?'

In fact, Singh was secretly approached two years later, in 1998, with a proposition to put him forward as a prime ministerial candidate. The Congress was fractured at that point in time, and the era of unstable coalitions had begun. A senior Congress leader who had joined Mamata Banerjee's breakaway Trinamool Congress told me that he and Banerjee had hatched a plan early in 1998 to approach Singh—who was then unhappy in the Congress—and offer him a safe seat in North West Calcutta. They were confident that the upcoming snap elections would deliver a repeat of 1996, with no party as a decisive winner, and believed they could cobble together a coalition with Manmohan Singh as the prime minister.

'I went to his Safdarjung Road residence and put this proposition to him, to join the Trinamool Congress,' the senior leader told me. 'I said, "I'm authorized by Mamata Banerjee to offer you a ticket from North West Calcutta, the constituency of the aristocratic Bengalis—the *bhadralok*. There is no way anyone could beat you there, and after the elections the prime ministership will be offered to you on a platter."'

'Do you know what Manmohan Singh said?' the leader continued. 'He said, "This country will not accept a Sikh as the prime minister."'

VII

That Manmohan Singh became India's first Sikh prime minister as the head of the party that led the 1984 anti-Sikh riots was only the first of several ironies in his appointment. After vanquishing the BJP in a campaign that revolved around the saffron party's 'India Shining' slogan by appealing to the hundreds of millions left behind by liberalization, the Congress selected the man most associated with that liberalization as its standard-bearer. Five years later, when Singh became the first prime minister since Nehru to win the re-election after completing a full term, the scales were tipped by two pro-poor policies associated with Sonia Gandhi rather than Singh—the National Rural Employment Guarantee Act (NREGA), which provided low-wage labour to 20 million households, and the farm-loan waiver, which forgave Rs 60 billion in debt.

The shadow of Sonia Gandhi has led some to caricature Singh as a puppet prime minister, which plays well in cartoons, but has little resemblance to reality. Indeed, in what may be remembered as the two most significant events of his tenure—the apex of the nuclear deal and the nadir of the 2G scam—it was Singh's own instincts that were decisive. At no other moments has the inscrutable PM revealed so much of himself: in the first case, the stubbornness and strength of his convictions; in the second, the selective nature of those convictions.

The nuclear saga began in 2005, when Singh and George W. Bush announced their intention to sign a civilian nuclear agreement. At the time, the Left parties offering outside support to Singh's coalition government voiced their objection, but they were preoccupied with economic matters, like blocking further public sector disinvestment. By 2007, Bush had delivered on his half of the deal, pushing two bills through the US Congress, and a formal agreement negotiated by Pranab Mukherjee and the US Secretary of State, Condoleezza Rice, was released to the public in early August.

The Left turned up the heat in response, but Singh fired a warning shot. When he saw the *Telegraph*'s Delhi editor, Manini Chatterjee, at a public meeting, he dangled the prospect of an exceedingly rare exclusive interview. 'He said, "Manini, it's been a while since I've talked to you. Why don't you come over to the office?"' Chatterjee recalled. Singh kept the conversation focused entirely on the nuclear deal, and issued a challenge to the communists in their hometown paper: 'It is an honourable deal, the Cabinet has approved it, we cannot go back on it . . . If they want to withdraw support, so be it.'

But the Left parties soon demonstrated their willingness to take Singh up on his offer: Prakash Karat, the general secretary of the Communist Party of India (Marxist), declared the Left would 'not support a government which surrenders India's national interest to the Americans. The ruling party will have to choose between the deal and its government's stability.' The Congress party's survival instinct kicked in: nobody was in the mood for an early election, including the leaders of the coalition's three largest partners—Sharad Pawar, Karunanidhi and Lalu Prasad Yadav—who contacted Sonia Gandhi and urged her to halt Singh's nuclear ambitions. By October, Singh was on the back foot, announcing at the Hindustan Times Leadership Summit that failure to carry the deal through 'is not the end of life'. Later that day, at the same event, Gandhi said, 'The Left's opposition to the nuclear deal was not unreasonable . . . the party is not in favour of early elections.'

The nuclear pact seemed to be dead, but the government needed to engineer an elegant way out. The US Congress had already amended two laws to permit nuclear cooperation with India, and Washington had sent word to the forty-five countries in the Nuclear Suppliers Group that the deal would soon be under way. Singh felt that backing out now would be a personal humiliation and a national embarrassment—so the Congress and the Left devised a secret strategy for Singh to save face internationally.

On 22 October, at an informal meeting of the United Progressive Alliance (UPA)–Left Committee, which had been established in an attempt to broker a compromise on the nuclear agreement, the government's chief negotiator, Pranab Mukherjee, offered terms of surrender. 'Give us an honourable exit, and we'll not go ahead with the deal,' he said, according to a member of the committee.

Mukherjee and Defence Minister A.K. Antony proposed a covert deal to the Communist Party leaders Prakash Karat and A.B. Bardhan: the Congress promised to abandon the nuclear pact, but the Left would allow the government to take it forward to the International Atomic Energy Agency (IAEA) and conduct a few rounds of negotiations, at which point India would cite one clause or another proposed by the IAEA as a pretence to withdraw from the deal without offending the US. The Left leaders agreed, on the condition that the nuclear deal come before Parliament before approaching the IAEA.

A few weeks later, on 10 November, a working lunch meeting was held at the prime minister's residence to formalize the secret arrangement. The only participants were Manmohan Singh, Sonia Gandhi, Mukherjee, Karat and Bardhan, and the five agreed on a clear roadmap to give the nuclear deal a dignified burial.

'Manmohan Singh just sat there, sulking,' the committee member said. 'He didn't say a word.' Singh's nuclear deal had been sabotaged by the Left's anti-American dogma and his own party's lack of resolve. But he was already hatching a few plans of his own.

Two days later, he paid a private visit to his predecessor, A.B. Vajpayee, for an hour-long discussion on the nuclear deal. It was Vajpayee, after all, who had initiated India's close relationship with George W. Bush, and Singh hoped he might help rescue the deal. But the very next day, L.K. Advani, the leader of the Opposition in the Lok Sabha, spilled the beans in an effort to embarrass Singh: Advani ridiculed the government's 'opportunism'. 'Now, they have reached out to talk when they are at the verge of falling,' he told reporters. 'It is too late now.'

In the meantime, Parliament discussed the nuclear pact, the government approached the IAEA and the Left did not threaten the government, just as they had promised. For the next several months, while negotiations with the IAEA were under way, the Left remained quiet, and Singh knew he had to act quickly to retain any hope of saving the deal.

According to accounts provided by multiple sources—top leaders in two allied parties and one CWC member—after the BJP refused to lend support, it was Manmohan Singh, and not the Congress party, who made the first approach to Samajwadi Party (SP) leaders Mulayam Singh Yadav and Amar Singh. After losing power in Uttar Pradesh, the SP bosses were fighting for survival against a spate of cases filed by their victorious opponent, Mayawati, and a disproportionate assets probe from the Central Bureau of Investigation (CBI); Sonia Gandhi had frozen out the SP leaders ever since Yadav had ridiculed her during the 2004 campaign. 'Everyone on the inside knew it was Manmohan Singh who opened the first channel of conversation with the Samajwadi Party,' one of the allied party leaders said. 'The Congress leaders didn't even know this at that point. They only intervened later.'

Once the talks with the SP were under way, Singh pressed his advantage with Sonia Gandhi. She knew she had to keep her word to the Left or watch her government fall, but Singh stood his ground. 'Privately, he threatened to resign,' a former official in the Prime Minister's Office (PMO) told me. The allied party leader put it less kindly: 'He blackmailed her—he said he didn't want to continue unless she allowed the deal to go through.' Singh convinced Gandhi that the government could obtain the required support, 'so Sonia backed out and decided to go with the Samajwadi Party', the former official said.

'Don't forget, he learned realpolitik from Narasimha Rao, who was a clever old goat and a master craftsman,' said Sanjaya Baru. 'I keep telling people, never underestimate Manmohan Singh.'

As documented in the US diplomatic cables released by WikiLeaks, a round of intense bargaining between Congress and Samajwadi leaders soon ensued. The Left parties were outraged and held a press conference on 8 July to withdraw support for the government. But it was too late. Singh initiated a vote of confidence in Parliament before anyone in the Opposition could move a no-confidence motion. Two weeks later, the government prevailed by three votes in the Lok Sabha, amid widespread allegations that votes had been bought to ensure the razor-thin victory—charges that recently landed Amar Singh in jail.

Addressing the media that night, Singh beamed with confidence and declared that the vote 'gives a clear message to the world that India's head and heart are sound, and India is prepared to take its rightful place in the comity of nations'. For the moment, the tarnish of the cash-for-votes allegations was easily forgotten, and the media sang hymns of praise to the 'warrior king' who had shed his timidity at long last.

But the former senior secretary who worked with Singh at the finance ministry told me the PM's unexpected guile came as no surprise. 'Some of us—economists who've known him for a very long time—like to say that Manmohan Singh is an overestimated economist and an underestimated politician,' he said.

'The nuclear deal proved that where Manmohan Singh had a political conviction—when he wanted something done in a particular manner—he would go all the way,' the leader of a Congress ally said. The nuclear showdown demonstrated that Singh could defy Sonia Gandhi; the details revealed above indicate his ability to play first-class power politics. But this additional evidence of Singh's steely determination in 2008 raises another troubling question: How did he allow the 2G scam to proceed under his watch?

VIII

The fraudulent allocation of cellular spectrum licences in 2008—which sold off scarce public resources at prices well below market value in an irregular and corrupt process that favoured specific telecom companies—appears to be the largest scandal in the history of India. According to the government's own accounting firm, the Comptroller and Auditor General (CAG), the decision to allocate spectrum at 2001 rather than 2008 prices—in spite of the exponential growth in cell phone users over the same interval, from 40 million to 350 million—caused a loss to the exchequer estimated at Rs 1.76 trillion.

According to the CBI, which is prosecuting the case, the figure is about Rs 300 billion. But if you inquire with the current minister of communications and information technology—whose predecessor is in jail for his role in the scam—the total losses were 'zero'.

Even if you tried to design a scandal intended to tear a government's credibility to shreds, you would have a hard time improving on the 2G scam. The sums were mind-bogglingly astronomical; the guilty parties were unabashedly venal and unquestionably corrupt; and the government's ineffectual reaction to the defrauding of the exchequer—which had been carried out almost in plain sight—seemed to confirm the worst allegations of its critics.

In the two years since the initial reports of the 2G scam emerged, Manmohan Singh's government has floundered in its public response at almost every juncture and in almost every possible way. In the press, spokesmen dished out a haphazard mix of unconvincing and contradictory defences; in the Cabinet, months passed before the corrupt ministers were forced to resign; and in the Parliament, the government stonewalled, for three months, against the Opposition's demand for a Joint Parliamentary Committee (JPC) inquiry—wasting an entire session—only to concede to the very same demand after two more months.

But the government's inept management of the aftermath has only obscured a more fundamental failure—to stop the scam before it started. On the basis of the available evidence, it is clear that Manmohan Singh was aware of the prospective revenue loss. He knew that something fishy was under way, and studying his interventions during the crucial period between 2006 and 2008 reveals at least three instances when he could have decisively changed the course of the spectrum allocation process and yet chose not to do so. In all three cases, Singh's intuitions were correct, but on each occasion his reservations were dismissed by one or more of his ministers, and rather than enforce his authority, he backed down.

The first of these episodes took place in 2006, when Singh constituted a six-member group of ministers to supervise the allocation of spectrum held by the government, in part to avoid leaving the decision of fixing the prices in the hands of a single minister. But when Dayanidhi Maran, who was then telecommunications minister, protested that the pricing of spectrum should be left solely to his ministry—citing a policy decision taken under the previous BJP government—Singh conceded without a fight.

By the time of Singh's second intervention, A. Raja had taken over from Maran at the telecom ministry and continued to exploit the policy set by his predecessor. The PMO had received several complaints from telecom companies alleging favouritism and kickbacks in the sale of spectrum, and on 2 November 2007, Singh wrote a letter to Raja raising five concerns about the ongoing allocation of 2G licences. The most significant of these was the prime minister's suggestion that prices should be increased or determined by auction. Raja replied on the same day with a wordy letter intended to deflect each of the PM's concerns, cleverly arguing that it would be 'unfair, discriminatory, arbitrary and capricious to auction the spectrum to new applicants' since that would deny them a 'level playing field' with existing licence-holders.

Singh declined to press the matter, but in a speech at an international telecom trade conference the following month, he publicly voiced his preference for the auction of spectrum, noting that 'governments across the globe have harnessed substantial revenue while allocating the spectrum'. Raja was unpersuaded and sent another letter to the prime minister on 26 December defending his policies with a skilful appeal to Singh's free-market inclinations. 'My efforts in this sector,' Raja wrote, 'are intended to give lower tariff to the consumer and bring higher teledensity in the country.' Singh did not pursue the correspondence any further.

The third of Singh's missed opportunities involved his senior Congress colleague P. Chidambaram, who, as finance minister, had to approve the prices set by the telecommunications ministry. On 15 January 2008, Chidambaram indicated he shared Singh's position in a letter which argued that 'the price for spectrum should be based on its scarcity value and efficiency of usage. The most transparent method of allocating spectrum would be through auction.' But by 4 July 2008, Chidambaram had evidently changed his mind: in a meeting with the prime minister, Raja and Chidambaram informed Singh they had reached an agreement on spectrum charges that included neither an auction nor an increase in fees from the 2001 rates still in use. Once again, Singh deferred to the decisions of others in spite of his own stated preferences, a choice he later defended by suggesting he felt that he did not have the authority to 'insist' on an auction.

These three episodes present the prime minister as a man who has the decency and intelligence to recognize that something is amiss, but who lacks the conviction to fix it—someone who doesn't exactly look the other way in the face of wrongdoing, and yet gives up all too easily when his initial efforts to confront it fall flat. 'He is not a stern person,' the former Union cabinet minister told me. 'Temperamentally, he's such a nice person. I think it hurts him to take drastic action and see people suffer.'

A fourth incident completes the picture in a most unflattering way: after Singh had abandoned his perfunctory efforts to intervene with Raja, another file from the telecom department on spectrum allocation came to his office on 23 January 2008. On the document, which was uncovered by the Parliamentary Accounts Committee earlier this year, a note written by Singh's private secretary suggested his desire to wash his hands of the matter; it said the PM 'Does not want a formal communication and wants PMO to be at arm's length'. (In July, the PMO took the unusual step of issuing a press release to challenge what it called 'unwarranted inferences' about the note.)

'Manmohan Singh is an honest man in a pecuniary sense, but not in the high political–moral sense, as someone who wants to correct wrongs in governance by taking on dishonest people or practices. That's not him,' said the former senior secretary, who worked with Singh in the finance ministry and has known him for more than four decades. 'Look at his responses on 2G—he says, "I never knew" or "No one told me." That fits a pattern, having seen him closely in the government.'

In the assortment of excuses and rationalizations deployed by the prime minister and other senior Cabinet members since the revelation of the scam, one finds little to refute the former secretary's judgement. After Raja was finally compelled to resign in the wake of the CAG report estimating the cost of the scam at Rs 1.76 trillion, his replacement at the telecom ministry, Kapil Sibal, called a press conference where he attacked the auditor and asserted that Raja's actions had incurred 'zero loss' in revenue. It was a widely mocked statement, but it also ironically and unintentionally lent weight to Raja's own defence—that he had merely followed policy set by the previous government and that his superiors, including the prime minister and the finance minister, knew exactly what he was doing.

The debating points and legalistic justifications that issued forth from the Cabinet failed to resonate with an increasingly angry public, but they accurately reflected the sensibility of the prime minister and his core team of advisers on the matter, which included Sibal, Chidambaram and Singh's close family friend, Montek Singh Ahluwalia, an Oxford-trained economist who worked at the World Bank and IMF, and now serves as the deputy chairman of the Planning Commission.

It's easy to forget today—after the investigations and arrests, the Opposition protests and the hunger strikes against corruption—that, for months, top figures in Singh's Cabinet essentially argued that the scam was not a scam at all. Ahluwalia went so far as to defend Raja after the scandal broke, and reportedly argued that the dramatically underpriced 2G licences were 'a spectrum subsidy', akin to food subsidies. Even after the release of the CAG report, with its massive loss estimate, Ahluwalia defended Raja's policies in a television interview and attacked the auditor: 'We were not trying for revenue maximization . . . It has been the consistent policy of the government not to treat revenue maximization as its objective,' he argued—suggesting, in other words, that distributing spectrum at discount prices to private firms (several of whom are among the largest corporates in India) was not an accident: it was the policy. Raja abused the policy on behalf of his benefactors, to be sure. But the prime minister and his most senior Cabinet colleagues held the door open for him to do so, leaving the distinct impression that they were not merely helpless in cracking down on corruption but were also indifferent to its causes and origins.

IX

In mid September, I met with two very senior former officials who had served in the current government and are intimately familiar with the 2G case. Although neither man accused the prime minister of wrongdoing, both suggested that he may still come under legal pressure, and could be summoned to court as a witness or even to face prosecution. 'I hope it doesn't happen,' the first official told me. 'But the court can actually even prosecute the PM for the violation of transaction of business rules.'

'The PM is in a bad shape, and unless there's a very credible lawyer who can take care of the 2G case, the government will be in trouble,' the second official said when I met him on 17 September. 'The PM is very concerned about himself and Chidambaram—only today morning both of them had a meeting to discuss 2G.' The home minister is facing petitions against him in both the Supreme Court and a CBI court, arguing that he should be prosecuted over his agreement with Raja on spectrum prices, and has already indicated, in private, his willingness to step down if either court acts against him. 'Chidambaram will go,' the second official said. 'He has said to me, "If anything happens, I'm going."'

It seems certain that the 2G scam will continue to haunt the government until the end of its term. A more significant question for Manmohan Singh is whether it will come to colour future considerations of his prime ministership and even his legacy. His reputation for honesty may remain intact, but the course of this particular scandal—and a host of others that have transpired under his watch—suggests that honesty alone is an insufficient defence in crises that demand more from leaders than personal decency. It has been Manmohan Singh's misfortune to run the country at a moment of proliferating corruption, which has had the unfortunate effect of highlighting his own inability or disinclination to confront it.

It may be instructive to return briefly to the first scandal of Manmohan Singh's political life: one considerably less significant than the 2G scam, but perhaps indicative of a troubling tendency that now threatens to overshadow the rest of his impressive career.

In April 1992, barely ten months into his tenure as finance minister, the booming Bombay Stock Exchange had what was then its biggest-ever crash, falling 13 per cent in a single day. The collapse had been caused by a stockbroker named Harshad Mehta, who had colluded with senior officials in public sector banks—which come under the control of the finance ministry—to siphon funds from the banks into the stock market, which crashed when the fraud was revealed. According to an official in P.V. Narasimha Rao's PMO, when internal intelligence reports about the fraud first reached the finance ministry in March 1992, Singh anxiously called an emergency meeting with Cabinet Secretary Naresh Chandra; Finance Secretary Montek Singh Ahluwalia; and Economic Adviser Ashok Desai, to discuss the situation.

The former PMO official recalled that Singh's initial response had been a decidedly defensive one. 'It was a systemic failure,'

Singh proposed. 'One thing led to another.' When one of them suggested to Singh that nobody would buy this argument and that Mehta should be investigated and forced to offload his shares, Singh demurred. 'Then there will be a lot of noise,' he said. 'People will write about it, everyone will know.' A few weeks later, news of the scam leaked anyway. An investigation began and a JPC was formed in August 1992 to probe the scandal.

Then, as now, not even Singh's opponents alleged any impropriety on his part, but the finance ministry faced severe criticism for its failure to detect the scam and its sluggish pursuit of the perpetrators. In another echo of his present troubles, Singh's first reactions left the impression he was untroubled by the scandal; under attack from the Opposition in Parliament, he famously quipped that he did not 'lose sleep simply because the stock market goes up one day and falls the next day'.

Singh would be cleared of responsibility in the JPC's final report, but the committee took note of his remarks and criticized his apparent indifference: 'It is good to have a finance minister who does not lose his sleep, but one would wish that when such cataclysmic changes take place all around, some alarm would ring to disturb his slumber.'

Those cataclysmic changes, which Manmohan Singh helped to unleash, are now two decades old. At some point this year, the size of the Indian economy is expected to surpass $2 trillion, growing at the second-fastest rate in the world; in the past decade, per capita income has tripled, and India now boasts the world's fourth-largest group of billionaires. But with this explosive growth have come dramatic increases in income inequality and an age of endemic corruption—much of which emanates from the shadowy crossroads where the state and capital meet.

A 2009 study sponsored by the Asian Development Bank warned of the 'risk that India will evolve towards a condition of oligarchic capitalism' unless steps are taken to challenge the 'links of power between politicians, the state and the private sector'. In a similar vein, the influential political analyst Pratap Bhanu Mehta, hardly a radical leftist, suggested in a column earlier this year that 'the recent scandals have put private capital beyond the pale of acceptability':

> From being generators of wealth, they are now being branded as appropriators of public wealth. This is true not just of upstart miners like the Bellary brothers. The uncomfortable fact is that this perception is now shadowing even the exceptional Tatas and the global powerhouse Reliance. The perception is widespread and real, and will need to be addressed directly.

Manmohan Singh cannot bear sole responsibility for all that came in the wake of liberalization, but as the prime minister he has too often appeared unprepared to reckon with the conflict that remains unresolved two decades later, over how to negotiate the proper balance between the state and the market.

The leader of a party allied with the Congress described to me a meeting with Manmohan Singh in December 2005, two months after the release of the UN report investigating abuses in the Iraq Oil-for-Food programme. The report had implicated Natwar Singh, then the minister of external affairs, and he had been forced to resign as a result, but it had also named Reliance Petroleum Limited as a beneficiary in the oil-for-food scam. The party leader said he had raised the issue with the prime minister, saying, 'Sir, the report mentions not just Natwar, it also prominently mentions Reliance. Why are you not taking any action against Reliance?'

'With a sigh,' the party leader recounted, 'Manmohan Singh said to us, "After all, what can I do? It is India's largest corporate."'

In the course of the last twenty years, Manmohan Singh has been at the centre of two major public debates, both of considerable historical significance: first, over the shift from a socialist planned economy to a liberalized free market, and, second, over the turn away from a non-aligned foreign policy and towards stronger ties with the United States. In the waning years of his political career, he now seems likely to occupy a central role—if perhaps a symbolic one—in a third era-defining debate, over corruption and its causes and cures.

Manmohan Singh himself does not symbolize corruption in the way that he has become an emblem of liberalization and Americanization, and even if many call his government the 'most corrupt' India has ever seen, that record may yet be broken. But the debate over corruption is not really about scandals and bribes, or about the devious schemes of amoral persons inside and outside of government: it is about the increasingly common fear that the system itself is broken, and about the inaction and apathy of those who should be positioned to lead in its repair.

In the end, the fate of Manmohan Singh's legacy is out of his hands. If the intractable structural crises troubling India somehow get resolved, then his place in history will be far larger than a footnote. But if the centre cannot hold, then Manmohan Singh will be seen as the man who let loose a storm, but failed to bring it under control—who sowed the wind and reaped the whirlwind.

'Most good writing,' says the pitiless V.S. Naipaul, 'undermines its subject.'

But what if you feel like writing a sympathetic appreciation? A wistful, exultant, half-mad love letter to an artist you have intimately known but never quite understood?

My profile of the Pakistani ghazal singer **FARIDA KHANUM** flouts all the writerly rules that I had until then amassed and vigorously practised. For once I didn't set out to 'deconstruct' or 'unpack', to launch an argument or drive home a point. I simply allowed my impressions of the singer—with whom I had engaged in an informal apprenticeship over ten years—to flow out in the most expressive way possible.

I now see I was writing a ghazal-like piece: wayward and fanciful but grounded in a mitigating metre. It could even be said I was paying tribute to Khanum in her idiosyncratic *ang*. In any case, I was writing a non-linear and un-secular piece, and I am grateful to the *Caravan* for allowing me to proceed in that 'hazardous, semi-free vein'.

One reader, expanding on the title of the piece, left this comment on the web: '*Aap nay toh Writing ka Djinn khada kar diya.*' (You have summoned the djinn of writing.)

Thank you, Amit. I really hope I can do it again.

ALI SETHI

Ali Sethi is a writer and musician. He lives in Lahore.

The Djinn of Aiman

Farida Khanum returns to sing in Calcutta

By ALI SETHI | 1 April 2014

January: It was afternoon in Lahore, there was a power outage on Zahoor Elahi Road, and Farida Khanum had finally woken up.

We were sitting among shadows in her living room: I on the carpet and she on a cushion that was both a mark of prestige (she is 'The Queen of Ghazal', the last of her generation's iconic classically trained singers) and a sign of advanced old age (she can no longer sit like a mermaid, with her legs folded beguilingly beneath her). I had come to prepare Khanum for a concert she was to give in a week's time in Calcutta, and was trying to engage her, in this fragile early phase of her day, with innocuous-sounding questions: which ghazals was she planning on singing there, and in what order?

'*Do-tin cheezaan Agha Sahabdiyan,*' (Two–three items of Agha Sahib's.) she said in Punjabi, her voice cracking. She was referring to the pre-Independence poet and playwright Agha Hashar Kashmiri.

'*Daagh vi gaana jay,*' (You must sing Daagh too.) I said. '*Othay sab Daagh de deewane ne,*' (Everyone there is crazy about Daagh.)—Daagh Dehlvi, the nineteenth-century poet.

'*Aa!*' she said, and stared at me in appalled agreement, as though I had identified an old vice of Calcutta's citizens.

'*Te do-tin cheezaan Faiz Sahabdiyan vi gaa dena.*' (And you can also sing two–three pieces from Faiz Ahmad Faiz.)

'*Buss*,' she said, meaning it not as a termination (in the sense of 'That's enough') but as a melancholy deferral, something between 'Alas!' and 'We'll have to wait and see.'

I knew she was nervous about the trip—the distance, the many flights, the high standards of Bengalis—and to distract her I removed the lid of my harmonium and held down the Sa, Ga and Pa of Bhairavi. I was *chhero*-ing the thumri '*Baju band khul khul jaye*'.

'*Farida ji, ai kis taran ai?*' (How does it go, Farida ji?) I asked, all goading and familiar.

'*Gaao na*,' she said.

I screwed up my face and began the *aalaap*.

'*Aaaaaa . . .*' Her mouth became a cave, her palm came out like a mendicant's.

'*Subhanallah*,' I said, and pumped the bellows.

Her singing filled up the room: she climbed atop the chords, spread out on them, did somersaults.

'*Wah wah, Farida ji! Mein kehnavaan kamal ho jayega! Calcutta valey deewane ho jaangey*,' (Bravo, Farida ji! It will be extraordinary! The people of Calcutta will go crazy.) I said.

'*Haan*,' she said, looking away and making a sideways moue that managed to convey deliberation, disinterest and derision all at once.

The concert was the brainchild of Malavika Banerjee, who organizes the annual Kolkata Literary Meet. I met Banerjee—'Mala'—at last year's KaLaM, and told her I was making a documentary film about Farida Khanum. Our conversation took place one night in a car; we were weaving past rotten old buildings near the Victoria Memorial and I was telling Mala about Khanum's Calcutta connection. Her older sister, Mukhtar Begum, was a Punjabi *gaanewali* who came to the city in the 1920s to work for a Parsi-owned theatrical company. Within a few years she was a star of the Calcutta stage—she was advertised on flyers as the '*Bulbul-e-Punjab*' (the Punjabi bulbul)—and had moved into a house on Rippon Street. Khanum herself was born, sometime in the 1930s, in these now-decrepit parts.

Mala was held: she asked if I could bring Khanum to next year's festival. She also asked, in a sort of polite murmur, 'She's still singing and all?'

'Of course!' I said, mainly to serve my own interests: I was looking for a reason—a ruse, really—to bring Khanum to Calcutta and film her in the locations where she had passed her childhood.

'*Theek hai*,' Mala said. 'Let me work on this.'

One year later, I was headed to Calcutta with Khanum and her two daughters, her fifteen-year-old granddaughter, and the film's archivist. There had been crises. Some weeks before we left I was told that Khanum's passport had expired; strings had to be pulled, and a new passport procured within a week. This was compounded by a panic about visas—I had to meet the Indian High Commissioner in Lahore and urge him to release ours on time. And we did, despite Khanum's protests, have to take a wheelchair with us from Pakistan: she would not be able to cross the Wagah border and navigate India's airports entirely on foot.

'*Kar laangi*,' (I'll do it.) she announced on the day her new passport arrived.

To which her daughter Fehmeda, an endocrinologist, responded in a tone of practised refusal: '*Ami aap hargiz nahin kar saktin*.' (Ami, there's no way you can do it.)

As Fehmeda had explained to me, a trauma to the sciatic nerve had led to a loss of sensation in Khanum's left foot. She could travel only if it didn't involve the use of her feet.

'But she will go,' Fehmeda had said. 'She must. The doctor has said she should stay active. We shouldn't let her sit at home all the time.'

Fehmeda was referring to Khanum's debility of the last three years, which has been accompanied by hospital visits, physiotherapy and rounds of medication. (Khanum herself described the ordeal to me in terms of demonic sensations: her foot going numb, a tube entering her throat, being forced to swallow strange pills and feeling a subsequent whirling in her head.) But worse, I had sensed, was the gloom accompanying this illness—an awareness of the body's vulnerability that led constantly to thoughts of mortality, wistful ones not unlike these lines from Khanum's most famous song, '*Aaj jaane ki zid na karo*':

Waqt ki qaid mein zindagi hai magar
Chand ghariyan yehi hein jo azaad hain
(Time cages life but / Just now we're free)

A few days before we left for Amritsar she asked me, in the middle of a frivolous conversation, in a detached and mildly quizzing tone, '*Main kar laangi?*' (Will I be able to do it?)

And I was sly and cavalier with my response: '*Araam naal, Farida ji. Tuaanu pataa vi nahin chalna.*' (With ease, Farida ji. You won't feel a thing.)

I came to Farida Khanum, like most people, after encountering her rendition of Fayyaz Hashmi's '*Aaj jaane ki zid na karo*'. But I feel lame putting it like that—saying 'rendition' and ceremoniously attaching the song's title to the writer's name, as though he were a major poet and this some lofty *kalaam*. The truth is that '*Aaj jaane ki zid na karo*' started out as an ordinary film song, a *geet*—so many people in their enchanted ignorance have called it a ghazal—that was commissioned for the 1974 Pakistani film *Badal aur Bijli*. A Memon from Karachi by the name of Habib Wali Mohammed sang the original, which was sullen, randy and liltingly hummable—a young man's plea for gratification.

What it became in Khanum's rendition—a widely circulated recording from a *mehfil* in the 1980s—is a bewitchingly layered lullaby, a song with a cajoling, comforting, almost foetal ebb and flow to it, but also with the plunges, scrapes and gasps of a ravenous consummation. It has bliss, strife, love, sex.

Of course, Khanum will never say any of this. She only ever speaks about her music in sweet nullities: the song was 'fast' and she made it 'slow'; the song was 'light' and she gave it '*soz*' (pain); the original was sung in the 'filmi style', and to make it her own she decided to sing it in a 'somewhat altered style'.

A formal analysis of the rendition yields something of a trail or path. The song is set in Aiman Kalyan, also called Yaman Kalyan, the evening raag associated with young love. Khanum leans on the raag repeatedly for results: her '*yunhi pehlu mein baithay raho*' (just stay beside me) is so persuasive because she is literally holding the note, in this case the *Gandhar* or Ga of the raag, which happens to be its *vaadi,* or dominant, *sur.* Then there is the song's beat-cycle—here the Deepchandi *taal* of fourteen *matras*. Khanum is notorious for singing in a hazardous *aarha* style—she remains slightly off the beat, creating an additional tension between her voice and the tabla that is resolved occasionally when the two converge at the *samm,* or first *bol*, of the cycle. Her '*Aaj jaane ki zid na karo*' is delivered in this semi-free vein: her wilful, uneven pacing of the lyrics creates the illusion of a chase, a constant fleeing of the words from the entrapments of beat. (This technique, which has the mark of her teacher—the erratic and perennially intoxicated Ustad Ashiq Ali Khan—bears its sweetest fruit in Khanum's ghazals, where strategic lags and compressions in the singing can enhance the pleasures of a deferred rhyme.)

But what after these outlines have been described? How to account for the slightly torn texture, the husky tone, the maddening *rass* of the voice? And what to do about Khanum's devastating deployment of the word '*haye*' in the phrase '*haye marr jayein gey*'? I once heard the Bollywood playback singer Rekha Bhardwaj exclaim, '*Yeh gaana hai hee "haye" pey.*' (This song is all about the '*haye*'.) I think she is right, in that Khanum's transformation of that word—from a jerky exclamation in the original to a dizzying upward glide, a veritable swoon, in her own version—has made of it a mini-*mauzu*, or thematic locus, of the lyric.

Can such phenomena be broken down? Not on the keys of a harmonium. I once placed my *baja* before Khanum and asked her to show me the note-by-note progression of her '*haye*'. But she could only produce it with her voice, and then too with a mysterious effort that seemed to marshal her whole being: she would close her eyes, put on a smile, tilt her head, throw a hand in the air and let the '*haye*' out.

Not everyone has been wowed by Khanum's musical abilities.

Mehdi Hassan, the Pakistani ghazal singer who was her great peer and rival, and who passed away in 2012, used to complain that she was given to 'mixing'—taking a passage from one raag and joining it arbitrarily with another for an easy resolution of melody. This is essentially an accusation of cheating—contrast it with Hassan's showy detailing of raags, which is often interspersed with tiresome commentaries about the rules of classical music and delivered in the middle of his performances. But the same observation—that Khanum is given to mixing—can also be taken as a compliment, an appreciation of her knack for improvisation.

There are those who think Khanum is an over-complicating singer, one who can't sing a 'straight' tune. This view, contained in the mocking-pitying remark, '*Seedha nahin ga saktin,*' was common among Pakistani music directors in the 1960s and 70s, and cost Khanum a lucrative career in playback singing. She was incensed by the critique—'It reached my ears,' she told me cryptically—and got a chance to disprove it in 1976, when she was asked to sing Athar Nafees's ghazal '*Woh ishq jo humse rootthh gaya*' for the Pakistan Television (PTV) programme *Sukhanwar*. Though Khanum sang the ghazal with uncharacteristic simplicity, she used all her reserves of sinuousness to secure the assignment: she had heard the song, composed in Bhairavi by Master Manzoor, and gauged its potential for popularity. But she wanted to ensure the PTV officials in charge of the programme didn't give it to another singer. So she undertook an elaborate *nakhra* to confound them: she pretended not to want to sing the song, insisting that it was 'not her style'. This spurred the officials into assigning her the song as a punishment.

Finally, there are those who consider Khanum an undereducated singer, one who can't abide by the rules because she doesn't know them. Such people—I know a few 'experts' in Pakistan's radio and TV bureaucracy who hold this view—see in Khanum's tussles with beat and melody the proof of an unfinished *taaleem*. (Comparisons are drawn, inevitably, with Mehdi Hassan, the 'natural' Noor Jehan, and the studious but unadventurous Iqbal Bano.)

There is, to be sure, an element of truncation in Khanum's musical trajectory: she has said many times that Partition, which resulted in the loss of her Amritsar home, signalled the end of her training and forced her to make compromises—personal as well as musical. For a few years, while living in the alien hill-bound city of Rawalpindi, Khanum shuttled regularly to Lahore to sing for radio and act in films. But she failed to make an impact. Soon she surrendered to marriage, and gave up singing at the insistence of the industrialist who offered her the securities of a 'settled life'.

Later, when she returned to music, she took up not khayal or thumri but the accessible and mercifully 'semi-classical' Urdu ghazal.

But here too we have an artful complication, contained in a remark she once made before me—when asked to explain her peculiar style, or *ang*—about the way she was trained as a child. '*Saanu sikhhaya hee aistarhansi,*' (This is how I was taught [to sing].) she said. Her ustad, it is true, was a musical maverick, a man who emphasized ingenuity and dynamism over fidelity to rules. (His own voice was coarse and reedy, and his reputation—like that of Nusrat Fateh Ali Khan in our time—rested on sensational gimmicks and gambles with the beat rather than mellifluousness or emotional *taseer.*) There was, at the same time, Khanum's childhood exposure to the liberal attitudes of north India's courtesans, the *bibi-jis* and *bai-jis* who looked upon music as a device—one of many workable wiles—and were not bound by obligations of form and lineage. (Khanum was particularly influenced by the anarchic charms of the ghazal singer Begum Akhtar, who was a friend of her sister's and a regular visitor to their house in Calcutta.) The courtesans valued *adaayigi*, or presentation, more than *qanundari*, or lawfulness, and placed a premium on heart-stopping quirks. Their music was distinct in crucial ways from that of the *khansahibs* or *gavaiyyas*, whose prowess was measured to a much larger extent by their ability to showcase the laws and structures of raags and taals. This difference can be discerned even in the 'light' art of ghazal-singing: the cultural commentator Ally Adnan is beautifully precise when he says that Mehdi Hassan and Ghulam Ali, eager to show their grasp of taal, are bound to race towards the samm and explode it like a 'climax', whereas Farida Khanum will render it a surprising and more interesting 'anticlimax'.

Finally there is the tricky business of pleasure, which dislikes explanations and resists the isolation of technicalities.

Farida Khanum is the purveyor of a holistic agreeableness, an overall sensory delight that doesn't require division into cynical categories. What a pleasure she is—to hear, watch, *experience*. (In the realm of Hindustani music, at least, the last is a vital mode of analysis—and a real alternative to the ravages of 'pure' theory.)

The best description of Khanum's gifts is perhaps this remark from a PTV producer: '*Mehfil lootna koi unn se seekhhay!*' (She sure knows how to bring the house down!) That ability—to revel in solutions, to *make do* or *make work*, even if it requires bending the rules—is the hallmark of a born performer. It is also interpersonal—it requires an intuitive appraisal of the whole of a situation—and can really only be experienced during a live performance.

In October, three months before the concert in Calcutta, Farida Khanum moved an audience in Lahore to tears.

This happened at the Khayal Literature Festival. I was interviewing Khanum, in a session pleasantly titled 'The Love Song of Pakistan', about her life in music. Adding star power to our panel was the ghazal singer Ghulam Ali. I had spotted Ali—urbane in black kurta and rimless glasses—in the audience at the start of the show and asked him to join us with a spontaneous announcement. The people in the hall were mostly bourgeois Lahoris, though a relatively diverse set from within that limited lot. (There were students and teachers, parents and grandparents, women and children.) The atmosphere, even before Khanum appeared on the stage, was one of uncritical veneration, and it was suffused with a weighty melancholy when she emerged from behind a curtain, held by her daughter and stumbling and tarrying on her way to a chair.

'Farida-ji,' I said, switching on the shruti box I had placed before her. 'Could you please, for just a little bit, sing for us the *bandish* in Aiman that you learned as a child? Just a small sample, please.'

This part was rehearsed. I had suggested to Khanum earlier in the week that she present on stage a 'thread' of Aiman: she could start with a classical piece, then proceed to ghazals and geets—including the crowd-pleasing '*Aaj jaane ki zid na karo*'—all in her favourite raag. This would give our session a musical coherence, I had said, and make it easy to follow.

'*Achcha*?' she had replied. '*Sirf Aiman karna ai?*'(Really? You want to dwell only on Aiman?) She pinched her lips, in her inscrutable way. Then, with a steady and mildly warning look, she said, '*Theek ai. Ay achcha sochya ai.*' (Fine. This sounds like a good plan.)

Now, on stage, she ceded to my request for the bandish with a wide, indulging smile. What happened next surpassed everyone's expectations. Khanum's voice, in contrast to her ailing frame, was robust, full-throated, steady, flexible. Everything she sang glowed with energy: she unfolded an aalaap, a bandish in teentaal, Faiz's ghazal '*Shaam-e-firaaq ab na poochch*', Sufi Tabassum's ghazal '*Woh mujhse huway humkalam*' and her signature '*Aaj jaane ki zid na karo*'. She was bringing out the raag in different forms, showing its familiar movements, making it reveal its secrets. But she was also compressing a century of cultural evolution: interspersing the singing with anecdotes about her childhood in Calcutta, the *riaz* with her ustad in Amritsar, her post-Partition collaborations with poets and music directors at Lahore's radio station, and the fortuitous way in which she had come to sing '*Aaj jaane ki zid na karo*' (someone had asked her to sing it in a mehfil). For the lay Lahore audience, the overall experience—one of observing a constant or eternal thing (the raag) endure in ephemeral or perishable contexts—was eye-opening, cathartic and extra-musical.

The young writer Bilal Tanweer, who was in the weeping, clapping audience that day, later described what he had witnessed as a kind of shamanism. '*Unhon ne Aiman ka djinn kharaa karr diya,*' (She brought out the djinn of Aiman.) he said to me. I thought that was profound. A djinn—a spirit or presence—has to be channelled or conjured up. Summoning these djinns is the function of all great musicians. (Their existence is confirmed, in Hindustani music, by the special terms *upaj* and *aamad*—spontaneity and inspiration.) Within music, it is singing, more than any other art, that draws attention to the artiste as a medium for conjuring such spirits. Why do so many singers look frazzled or bewildered after an especially good concert or recording? The better the performance, the greater the musician's feeling of emptiness, of having been possessed and vacated.

In the case of a singer like Farida Khanum, her role as a transmitter of djinns is magnified by social and historical contexts. When she sings '*Aaj jaane ki zid na karo*', she is passing on the cumulus of centuries—the laws of Aiman, according to one legend, were laid down by Amir Khusro in the thirteenth century—in an accessible, contemporary, but fundamentally uncompromised form. And the process is made poignant and ironic by our ignorance: how many of the amateurs who upload videos of themselves singing '*Aaj jaane ki zid na karo*' on YouTube and Facebook know what they are really channelling? The enduring appeal of a singer like Khanum is nostalgic, yes. But it is also heightened by our condition, which is one of rootlessness and over-mediation, and by our corresponding thirst for what is true, rare, original and sublime.

As for Khanum herself, I don't think she knew how popular she was with young people until I sat her down one day and placed a computer on her lap.

'YouTube,' I said.

'Oho,' she said, affecting curiosity.

'*Ai kee ay?*' (What is this?) I asked, pointing to the video links on the screen.

Khanum peered at the screen. Then she gave a start. '*Ai te mein aan,*' (That's me.), she said.

I played for her several covers of '*Aaj jaane ki zid na karo*', and read out some of the comments under her (now erroneously-deemed-original) version: 'Soulful!'; 'What a beautiful voice!'; '133 dislikes—for what??'; and 'My all-time favourite ghazal.'

'*Ae hunay hee aya ai?*' (Did this one come just now?) Khanum asked, tentatively pressing a finger to the screen.

No, I told her, the comments had been accumulating for years, and would continue to gather for as long as people listened to her song.

'*Mein hairat mein hun,*' (I am amazed.) Khanum said. '*Ai* magic *horyaai*, magic.' (This is magic, this is magic.)

We went to India, then, for old times' sake.

It required the artful breaking up of our itinerary: we crossed Wagah, spent a night in Amritsar, flew to Delhi in the morning and took a connecting flight in the afternoon to Calcutta—or Kolkata, as it is now known. (We adjusted our tongues on the plane, softening the K and elongating the O.) A wheelchair was involved at several stages, but Khanum's aversion to it was diminished by our calling it the 'chair'—glossing over the existence of the wheels somehow transformed the dreaded device into a luxury, a privilege, something befitting a legendary person.

It also required shielding Khanum from unwanted attention. When the media called for interviews—'We would *re-ally* like to talk to her for *just* five minutes'—we said in the most conciliatory tones, 'She is resting, she is resting, please.' Whereas really she was preparing: taking mysterious medicines and guzzling a ginger-and-honey drink and being told constantly to talk less and preserve her voice.

'*Haye*,' she said on occasions when her foot hurt, feeling real pain. Whereupon I improvised, telling her how good she looked, how much people loved her, how wonderful the concert would be. '*Saara Calcutta afra-tafri vich ay*,' (All of Calcutta is in a tizzy.) I kept saying, although I had no proof of it. And: '*Saaray ticket vik gaye nay*.' (All the tickets have been sold.)

On the night of the concert, a final hurdle appeared. I had gone to the GD Birla Mandir, the venue of the show, for a sound check. There I was told, an hour before the concert, that Khanum would have to go down several flights of stairs in order to reach the auditorium.

'What are we going to do?' I asked one of the organizers, a woman in a sari who stared back at me uncomprehendingly.

Then she said, 'Wait.'

Approximately twenty minutes later, a little before 7 p.m., a white car carrying Khanum pulled up at the GD Birla Mandir. The legendary singer emerged in a pink-and-gold sari, and was led by helpers and admirers into the foyer. Then the Mandir's doors closed, and the foyer was emptied of people. Khanum, who had only just sat down in a chair, spent the next few minutes in a state of miraculous airborne transport, gripping the chair's arms and muttering the lord's name under her breath, until she found herself seated in her usual, regal way on a stage decorated with flowers. '*Ya Ali Madad*,' (Help me, Ali.) she said, invoking the Prophet's heir and fourth caliph of Islam, before the curtain went up.

'*Ek muddat ho gayi hai*' (It has been an age), Khanum said, shivering a little but looking serene before her Calcutta audience, which was comprised of young and old alike. '*Innhon ne kaha aap chalein, buss thhora sa safar hai*.' (They said I should go, the journey is not long.)

She stuck to the rules: she sang two ghazals from Daagh, two from Faiz, the thumri in Bhairavi and '*Aaj jaane ki zid na karo'*. I had the privilege of sitting next to her on the stage and holding open the book that contained the words to her songs. I marvelled at her composure—and, yes, at the soundness of her training—when I saw how she conducted the audience, the accompanying musicians and the sound technicians behind the curtain with her hand movements and facial expressions. And I saw—a novice observing a master, a mortal observing a living legend—how she managed her voice: the expansions in the middle octave, the careful narrowing at the higher notes, the strategic truncation of words and notes when she was running out of breath. Occasionally, when I feared she was going to skip a beat, I found myself clenching the book in my hands and glancing at the audience for signs of a crisis.

But there were none, because even the odd anticlimax, when it did occur, was a pleasure.

I began working on a story about Pushpa Kamal Dahal, Nepal's Maoist-guerrilla-turned-prime minister, better known as **PRACHANDA**, in the summer of 2012. Most of my waking hours in the autumn of that year were devoted to Prachanda: I cultivated sources, met his close associates and read everything about him I could get my hands on. I turned the draft in at the end of the year, and the story appeared in early 2013.

I sent two copies of the magazine to Prachanda, but it was not until months later that I learned what senior Maoists, part of his cohort, thought of it. Agni Sapkota, a Maoist leader who had helped me gain access to Prachanda, met me following a press conference in Kathmandu, clearly upset over the portrayal of his leader. I don't recall his exact words, but he referred to hagiographies on China's Chairman Mao (including the American author Edgar Snow's *Red Star over China*), books about Karl Marx and Vladimir Lenin. In contrast, Sapkota said, my article deliberately showed Prachanda in poor light. I defended my work, but the exchange became so heated that fellow reporters stopped to ask me what was wrong.

Over the years, particularly since their defeat in the last general election in 2013, the Maoists have faced a series of setbacks that underscore how untenable this bent of ideological criticism is. Long-overdue commissions on truth and reconciliation, and enforced disappearances have begun their work; the Maoist leadership (and the top brass of the Nepal Army) awaits the possibility that they will be charged with war crimes. This was part of the peace agreement, but it has, nevertheless, deeply worried Prachanda himself. War in Nepal has ended, as I write this. For its architect and former revolutionaries, however, its legacies will haunt them throughout their lives. And since Prachanda's story is inseparable from Nepal's own, it remains to be seen what his future means for that of this country.

DEEPAK ADHIKARI

Deepak Adhikari is a freelance journalist based in Kathmandu. His work has appeared in Nepal and abroad, including in the New York Times, *the* Guardian *and Al Jazeera, English.*

The Fierce One

Prachanda's long tussle for power in Nepal

By DEEPAK ADHIKARI | 1 February 2013

I

On the afternoon of 16 November 2012, Padam Kunwar stood in line at Kathmandu's Bhrikutimandap exhibition complex, waiting to shake hands with Nepal's former prime minister, the Maoist revolutionary Prachanda. Several marquees had been erected in the gated entertainment park, which thronged with thousands of people, including journalists, politicians, former government officials, foreign diplomats and supporters of Prachanda's ruling Maoist party. The function, organized by the Maoists to mark the ethnic Newari New Year 1133, had a festive air. Inside a huge tent open to the streets, Prachanda, the Maoist party chairman, sat on a stage, draped with his party's hammer-and-sickle banner, flanked by Nepal's current prime minister, Baburam Bhattarai, a long-time party rival, and by opposition leaders from the country's centrist Nepali Congress and Unified Marxist–Leninist parties. Around 3 p.m., Prachanda, a former guerrilla commander who led Maoist forces in a decade-long revolt against the state, gave a short speech stressing the need for political consensus. Afterwards, he began to shake hands with people in the eager crowd.

Kunwar had not intended to visit the event. He had only learned about it earlier that afternoon, during an idle shopping trip to the city centre, he later told me. As he haggled with a roadside clothes vendor, the twenty-seven-year-old overheard people talking about the reception and decided to attend. Approaching the venue, amplified sounds of Maoist leaders making speeches had reached him in the street. He looked forward to meeting some of these former guerrillas, who just six and a half years before had come overground to participate in electoral politics. Perhaps, he thought, he could complain to them about woes his family was facing. When he learned that Prachanda was shaking hands with supporters, he queued up. It would be his first chance to meet the former revolutionary—a memorable day.

While Kunwar waited in line, the country's one-time leader greeted dignitaries and chiefs from Opposition parties, and Kunwar found himself growing irritated. He had seen senior Maoists arriving at the venue in fancy cars, and they were now jumping the queue of commoners, in which he stood, to hobnob with Prachanda and other worthies. The proletariat party leader himself, it had been widely reported, was living in splendour in a Kathmandu mansion, right next door to one of his former military foes, a senior Nepal Army general and former adviser to a king from Nepal's now-dissolved hereditary monarchy. On stage, men who were once sworn enemies embraced. For Kunwar, the hypocrisy, and the prolonged wait, rankled. He tried to subdue his rising anger, but could not. Soon, he was seething.

As the commoners' line crept along and his ire mounted, Kunwar was flooded with memories and stories from the violent uprising and civil war initiated by Prachanda and the Maoists in 1996. Kunwar's elder brother, who had fought for the party and in 2003 helped capture a local administrative headquarters in the upland district of Myagdi in west-central Nepal, still had shrapnel throughout his body. Kunwar's elder sister, with whom he now lived on the outskirts of Kathmandu, had been one of the most popular Maoist leaders in their home district of Baglung, several hundred kilometres north-west of Kathmandu. While organizing a party meeting, she and her fellow cadres had come under attack from government security forces; two of her colleagues were killed and she was left for dead. She dragged herself, bleeding, into a small bush, where she lay wounded for three days, until another Maoist fighter, who is now her husband, found her on the verge of death. Although she served the party, and almost died for it, the party later sidelined her. The rest of their family, poor farmers who lived in a remote village in Baglung, had been brutally terrorized by the Nepal Army during the war; soldiers would forcibly enter their home, break furniture and aggressively question Kunwar's parents about his siblings' whereabouts. Kunwar's mother, unable to cope with the family's tragedies, was now suffering from deep depression.

Kunwar himself had also become a party member. During the war, Prachanda had promised an equal society and an end to poverty. This call attracted Kunwar; like many Nepali youths, he had failed to graduate high school and had few skills or job prospects. In an attempt to support himself, he had travelled across the border to Punjab to work as a tea boy at a tractor supply company. He then moved to Kathmandu, where he applied through a local labour agency for construction jobs in the Gulf. Later, he discovered that the agency was cheating unemployed workers by charging them placement fees for positions that never materialized. Despite this setback, in 2005, he managed to join the ranks of tens of thousands of Nepalese migrants working in the Arabian peninsula in oppressive conditions; the construction company for which he worked in Doha, for example, didn't provide its labourers with water during lunch. In 2007, he and his 3,500 co-workers staged a strike to protest the privation, and, although an agreement was reached, Kunwar was later dismissed. On his return to Nepal in 2008, he worked odd jobs to supplement a meagre savings and joined the Maoist Young Communist League. The party welcomed him with open arms and made him a district committee member in Baglung. But life didn't improve: employment remained unsteady and, eventually, his savings ran out. In 2012, following a split in the party, Kunwar quit, disillusioned, he told me, by the 'difference' between the Maoists' 'words and deeds'. He moved to Kathmandu to live with his married sister and train as a chef, preparing himself for yet another gruelling stint abroad, but his frustrations and disappointments trailed him like shadows. Even though every member of his family had contributed in some way to the Maoist struggle, the party had provided them with next to nothing.

As Kunwar inched closer to Prachanda, he recalled, these frustrations returned in agonizing flashes. Finally approaching the front of the line, his anger continuing to intensify, Kunwar decided to act. Soon he was face-to-face with Prachanda. He pressed his hands together to say namaste, and, when Prachanda offered him a hand to shake, Kunwar slapped the former prime minister, hard, across the face. Prachanda screamed and his glasses fell, broken, to the floor. A shock went out through the crowd. Kunwar was hauled from the stage to the ground and attacked; members of the Maoist Young Communist League kicked him in the groin and rained blows down on his head. 'We should kill him! We should not spare him!' he remembered people shouting. Finally, the police were able to break up the melee and drag Kunwar, his face smeared with blood, from the scene. The event dominated Nepalese television news channels for days.

'I was not afraid,' Kunwar assured me a month after the event. 'I knew that I would not be able to slink away.' We met at the ramshackle offices of a new, anti-Prachanda Maoist splinter group, to which hundreds of alienated cadres were being welcomed. Kunwar had come, with his brother-in-law, to hear a speech condemning Prachanda's policies, but said he had not known he would be attending an initiation. When I pressed him again about the November attack, he admitted: 'At the time, I was worried that I might be beaten to death.'

II

Six summers ago, Pushpa Kamal Dahal, better known by his nom de guerre Prachanda, arrived in Kathmandu to a hero's welcome. Although he had been living in relative secrecy for a quarter-century, the Maoist party chairman had, in many ways, become the country's dominant political figure during the preceding decade of internecine violence. The relatively small guerrilla force he controlled had fought the country's professional army to a ceasefire, and allowed the Maoists to gain de facto control over 80 per cent of the country. On the morning of 16 June 2006, Prachanda, his wife, Sita Poudel (whom he married when he was only fifteen), and his then deputy, Bhattarai, had been helicoptered to the Nepali capital from Sikles, a village in the Annapurna foothills, where the three had lived under the protection of a Maoist militia for the past several months. Krishna Prasad Sitaula, the home minister in a recently reconstituted parliamentary government led by the Nepali Congress president and then prime minister, Girija Prasad Koirala, had been dispatched to Sikles to pick them up. On the ground in Kathmandu, Sitaula shepherded the guerrilla leaders, under the escort of a Maoist security unit, to Koirala's spacious, heavily fortified official residence.

There, Prachanda and Bhattarai held a marathon meeting with Prime Minister Koirala, Sitaula and the leaders of six other parliamentary parties, including the Unified Marxist–Leninists. Earlier that year, the Maoists and the seven parliamentary parties had warily joined together to lead a successful popular movement that displaced the country's centuries-old monarchy, ruled by a dynastic Hindu family called the Shahs; now, the uneasy coalition was trying to lay the groundwork for a new constitution and to find a peaceful resolution to the preceding ten years of Maoist rebellion and civil war, twenty-five years of failed attempts at democracy and over 200 years of almost unbroken autocratic rule.

The uprising that Prachanda had launched in 1996 later escalated into a civil war that killed more than 15,000 people, including nearly 5,000 in its bloodiest year. In the largely remote mountain districts that his Maoists controlled, they had set up parallel, if makeshift and capricious, public administrations, including a terrorizing network of tribunals dubbed the People's Courts. He had battled Nepal's Shah monarchy and former democratic governments. He had called for a secular country, decrying Nepal's enshrined Hinduism, and for the redistribution of land to the landless. He had even called for a war against India and its purported expansionism, which—he sometimes claimed—was the principal enemy in the fight for people's rule in Nepal. Without his assent, there could be no hope of a credible peace or a lasting democratic union.

Outside the prime minister's residence, approximately 300 local and international journalists had converged. The Maoist security contingent that had escorted Prachanda and Bhattarai to the meeting now cordoned off the building. Displaying improvised placards scrawled with messages reminding the guerrillas about the importance of press freedoms, some journalists staged an impromptu protest. By late afternoon, many were exhausted from hunger and the endless wait, but all were eager to hear from Prachanda, who they hoped would appear in front of the professional media for the first time since he had gone underground, two and a half decades before.

Although rumours of previous, clandestine discussions between the Maoist leader and the prime minister were circulating, this was the first confirmed meeting between Prachanda and Koirala, the leaders of Nepal's two parallel governments. The octogenarian prime minister was suffering from respiratory disease, and due to fly the next day to Bangkok for treatment; he was desperate to get Prachanda on board then and there. As the afternoon wore into evening, things outside the residence grew tense. Finally, around 7.30 p.m., Prachanda, Bhattarai and a bevy of leaders from the other parties emerged from their day-long conclave. (The ill Koirala was conspicuously absent.) A press conference was hastily convened under a swiftly pitched canopy on the prime minister's front lawn. Reading through a statement, Sitaula explained the summit's outcome: a series of crucial steps had been outlined to bring the country out of civil war and create a democratic polity. The tentative ceasefire between the Maoists and the Nepal Army would be converted into a formal peace. The so-called People's Government, which had been formed by the Maoists in their strongholds across the country, would be dissolved. Dates for elections to a new Constituent Assembly—a decades-old mainstream demand, left unfulfilled by previous regimes—would be announced. This assembly would form a fresh government, with Maoist participation, charged with drafting the constitution for a 'new Nepal'.

Then it was Prachanda's turn. Speaking without an amplifier, his face glowing from both the light of a naked bulb and camera flashes, he did not disappoint the crowd. He mocked the '*purano satta*' (old regime) for failing to provide electricity and derided its dysfunctional state. The marathon talk and the resulting agreement were, he claimed, an 'ice break' in Nepal's history. 'We are trying to develop the multiparty parliament system in a new way,' he told the crowd that had waited with bated breath all day for him to speak. 'In that sense, the experiment we are spearheading is not a simple political game. This is a new experiment in history. In our view, this is a great experiment.'

In the difficult years since that experiment began—years between the 'ice break' and Kunwar's angry slap—the fortunes of Prachanda and Nepal have been intricately intertwined, and, throughout the tribulations of this period, Prachanda has remained arguably the most powerful, and certainly the most polarizing, man in the country. 'He continues to be the key leader and a person who carries not only people's hope, but also their frustrations,' the political commentator Bishnu Sapkota told me. Sudheer Sharma, the editor-in-chief of the nation's influential *Kantipur* daily newspaper, agreed: 'Other leaders are weak. Their politics revolve around reacting to what Prachanda says or does. The Maoists are the ones who set the agenda. The opposition is not in a position to offer anything new to the people.' According to Kanak Mani Dixit, the editor of *Himal Southasian* magazine, no one in the country can match—let alone contest—the Maoist commandant's stature: 'There's no giant individual to take him on.'

Prachanda, however, is a giant indeed. After ten years commanding a brutal revolutionary war, he managed to bring the Opposition, and his own party, to the negotiating table—not only achieving a peace that has largely held since 2006, but also forging Nepal into a democratic republic of which he was the first prime minister. At the same time, he has transformed his guerrillas, who once ruled the Nepali countryside by force, into the most popular political party in the nation: he now leads an organization with over 300,000 members and dozens of affiliate groups. And, although he has long since lost his premiership, Prachanda continues to dominate Nepal's as yet untempered democratic politics.

For a man at the centre of his nation's politics, little is known about Prachanda and his journey from radicalism to power. Even his face was a mystery to the media and the general public until 1999, when the Maoist guerrilla, who is now fifty-eight, leaked a staged black-and-white photograph of himself to the press. Many of the stories that do circulate about his youth and the quarter-century he spent underground come from Prachanda himself. Even today, Prachanda remains largely opaque. 'Their lives aren't transparent,' Sapkota said of Prachanda and other Maoist leaders. 'They are shrouded in mystery.' What can be gleaned about the man from former associates suggests that he is both canny and cunning. Indeed, despite the assurances that Prachanda made to the crowd of reporters on the evening of 16 June 2006, many observers believe that a political game is precisely what he has been undertaking—albeit not a simple one.

'His weakness is the vaulting ambition,' Mani Thapa, a former Maoist leader who is now general secretary of a small radical group, told me. 'He is weak in terms of principle and belief. His politics is devoid of values. His ultimate goal is to achieve power.' Sharma took a similar line: 'Prachanda's is a utilitarian approach. He thinks that he can use all the political forces in Nepal. He thinks he is the smartest politician.' At the same time, Sharma believes that Prachanda is committed—at least instrumentally—to Nepal's still tenuous democracy. 'Instead of becoming an autocratic strongman, he wants to gain power through democratic means,' Sharma told me. 'But he wants to be an absolute leader in Nepal for at least a decade. He hasn't changed his goal, he has just tweaked the means to achieve it.'

This vaulting ambition may explain some of the transformations that Prachanda has undergone since his birth in 1954—how a rural schoolteacher, the son of a Brahmin smallholder, became the leader of a Maoist revolutionary party that held out to poor, marginalized Nepalis the promise of economic prosperity and political empowerment, while at the same time being accused of human rights abuses, including extrajudicial killings and the forced conscription of minors, and how this revolutionary then became prime minister. It may also be the key to understanding how Prachanda lost that very premiership in a mere nine months—and why even that hasn't stopped him from remaining the country's most important political figure. Now, he faces the challenge of fulfilling the promises that were made in 2006. The charter for a 'new Nepal' has yet to be written, and, in November last year, in the wake of a final missed deadline to draft one, the Constituent Assembly that Prachanda helped to create was dissolved. As was the case in 2006, without Prachanda, the republic's other leaders may stand little chance of resolving this ongoing political gridlock, which has kept Nepal, the oldest nation state in South Asia, without a stable constitution.

In the meantime, Prachanda has shifted his platform from one of communist revolution to a regional federalism based on ethnic identities. He has effectively ceded his army, which the United Nations once reckoned at over 19,000-strong; but he has now formed tentative alliances with parties representing far larger constituencies in Nepal's rural southern plains, where over half the country's 27 million people live, many of them from marginalized ethnic groups who have been fighting for social equality and regional autonomy for many years.

Some critics, including Dixit, have slammed Prachanda for such shifts, seeing them as evidence of his expedient breed of politics. According to Dixit, one of the Maoist leader's most vocal detractors, Prachanda is an 'opportunist' who has 'used his cadre, his opponents, the international community, the South Asian neighbourhood—all with the sole goal of getting ahead personally'. Prachanda's politics, he added, are 'demagoguery'; he has only 'remained top dog within Nepal by triple-speak'. 'Some people call it dynamism,' Gunaraj Lohani, a former confidant of Prachanda, told me. 'But it is not.' Thapa, it seems, would concur. Prachanda, he said, 'has risen through conspiracy, lies and deception'. 'He is a good salesman,' Thapa said. 'He knows what can be packaged and sold in the marketplace of politics.'

Whether through demagoguery and personal ambition, or through a genuine desire to uplift his country, in the past few years the Maoist chairman has begun to talk more and more about Nepal's economic potential, especially in hydropower and tourism. Nepal, which has the lowest gross domestic product per capita in all of South Asia, and is in the lowest decile globally, also has some of the highest levels of unemployment and income inequality in the world. Its development over the years has been extraordinarily poorly distributed between groups and regions, with urban centres, such as Kathmandu, seeing the vast majority of economic progress. Prachanda has broadly outlined his vision as the economic growth and rapid industrialization of the impoverished country, and has argued that the nation can benefit from the increasing international heft of its two gargantuan neighbours, India and China. For this to happen, one of his close aides told me, he wants to create, and then secure, a new position atop Nepal's government; he aspires to become an executive president of the country for at least ten years.

Some observers believe that such an eventuality is unlikely. Jhalak Subedi, a Marxist political commentator who heads a think tank called the Nepal South Asia Centre, said that although Prachanda 'displays a capacity to manoeuvre among the political forces of Nepal', the ex-guerrilla 'lacks a vision to guide the country'. The former Maoist leader Mumaram Khanal went further; Prachanda, he told me, is now at the beginning of a final descent. 'We are witnessing his fall,' Khanal assured me. 'His fall has begun and it will plunge deeper. I don't think he will rise again from the ashes.' Although Thapa thinks that Prachanda has yet to reach a dead end in what he called the 'labyrinth of Nepali politics', he told me that the former guerrilla leader may already have squandered the historical opportunity that began to open up to him in the summer of 2006.

One of the challenges Prachanda faces in raising Nepal, and himself, to new heights is that he needs the support of Prime Minister Bhattarai, with whom he has had a rocky and at times openly antagonistic relationship. Bhattarai, who has a doctorate in development from New Delhi's Jawaharlal Nehru University, is widely recognized as the intellectual powerhouse in the Maoist party, and, unlike Prachanda, he has maintained relatively close ties with India, culturally and historically Nepal's closest neighbour. Bhattarai, too, is not lacking in ambition; he has already shown success in using his own political instincts and leverage to elevate himself in the face of Prachanda's objections. At the same time, however, Bhattarai does not seem to have sufficient political and popular support to remain in power without Prachanda's backing. If the two men cannot maintain a delicate balance, Nepal's immediate chances for stability, progress and democracy may be doomed.

Although Prachanda's perch on the summit of Nepali politics is less than secure, there are no doubts about his lofty political aspirations or the single-mindedness with which he will pursue them. Sharma, for one, believes that Prachanda still has an opportunity to transform Nepal; but the Maoist leader and former prime minister will have to go beyond mere rhetoric. 'People are desperate for delivery,' Sharma told me. 'His final test will depend on whether he can deliver on the promises he made during the war.'

Following his dramatic return to Kathmandu and the June 2006 press conference on the prime minister's lawn, Prachanda travelled across the country, speaking to local cadres about their imminent conversion from a guerrilla force to a party thrusting itself into electoral politics. He then returned to the capital, where he continued to hold talks with Opposition party leaders. In order to move towards a long-lasting peace, it was agreed that a United Nations mission would be invited to monitor both the national and Maoist armies.

Though the ceasefire agreement had held since earlier that spring, the relationship between the battle-hardened Maoist forces, which Prachanda and his colleagues had styled the People's Liberation Army, and the Nepal Army remained fraught. The Maoists had deeply wounded the army's pride by fighting its superior force of 90,000 well-armed soldiers to a stalemate. The Nepal Army, which identified itself with the country, had also long supported the monarchy; as far as it was concerned, its interests and those of the king and nation were one.

To the Maoists, the Nepal Army was among the country's greatest forces of oppression. Like the rebel forces, the Nepal Army had been accused of significant human rights abuses, including extrajudicial killings, forced disappearances and torture. Prachanda did not baulk from pointing this oppression out; at the 16 June press conference, he had provoked his military adversaries by asking: 'Where did the Nepal Army show its bravery except killing Nepali people and raping our women?'

Prachanda also stated that he wanted to downsize the army to a militia of 20,000, which was to include former Maoist guerrillas. Attempting to integrate the two militaries would prove a politically treacherous task, especially given Prachanda's outbursts, which army pressure soon forced him to retract. This should have been a lesson to Prachanda, giving him a sense of what lay ahead in Nepal's fractious political landscape, especially where the Nepal Army was concerned.

For the time being, however, he was able to bring his party closer to the mainstream and to national power. After a further series of meetings with the seven parliamentary parties, Prachanda and Koirala finally emerged, on 21 November 2006, with an accord, the Comprehensive Peace Agreement, that formalized the terms outlined at the June summit and brought an official end to Nepal's brutal civil war.

Elections were announced for 10 April 2008. With popular slogans promising peace and a liberal constitution, and with a nationwide network they had built throughout the war while other parties had been forced to retreat from rural constituencies, the Maoists jumped into the electoral fray. Prachanda, in his underground years, had acquired a popular mystique. In Kathmandu, where he contested the election from a Newar-dominated and largely anti-monarchy hilltop constituency called Kritipur, overlooking the city, the streets were festooned with posters of his face and banners proclaiming his name. He also contested the elections from the Maoist heartland of Rolpa, a remote district in the western hills. At rallies, Prachanda spoke of old and new Nepal: his party was for the transformation of the country, which would only be possible after dismantling the remnants of the old feudal order that had been represented by the king.

Pundits in Kathmandu had predicted that the former insurgents would come a distant third; but, in an election then certified as fair by the international community, Prachanda's party swept constituencies across the country, defeating Nepali Congress and Unified Marxist–Leninist stalwarts, and winning nearly 40 per cent of the seats in the 601-member Constituent Assembly. (The legitimacy of the election has since been called into question after reports surfaced that the Maoists used intimidation tactics, and created a climate of fear, to garner a significant number of their votes.) At victory rallies in the streets of the capital, a leonine Prachanda, his brow smeared with vermilion and his neck maned with garlands of marigold, delivered fiery speeches declaring that the people, by voting in the Maoists, had given their mandate to peace and a democratic constitution.

'It was a miracle,' Prachanda told me, when I visited his spacious red-and-white-brick Kathmandu mansion in November 2012, ten days before Kunwar's slap. 'You won't find this sort of transformation anywhere in the world. Remember, we had an army, the People's Courts, our base areas and we joined the peace process. And then, we participated in elections and became the largest party. We had raised people's agendas. They were fed up with the old parties and they also wanted peace.'

In the months that followed, the Constituent Assembly voted to make the country a republic, officially ending 240 years of royal rule in Nepal. A fight for control of the new government, centring on the respective powers that would be granted to the positions of president and prime minister, and on the parties that would be allowed to control those positions, promptly ensued. By August, after a series of tortuous negotiations, accompanied by threats to withdraw from the political process and hold violent street protests, Prachanda and the Maoists successfully convened a coalition government. On 16 August 2008, the Constituent Assembly elected Prachanda as the first prime minister of republican Nepal. It was a remarkable accomplishment: the former revolutionary was now at the apogee of power. Could the guerrilla commander, who had so successfully fought against the centre from the margins of civil life, now hold that centre? Or would the forces arrayed against him—including the Opposition parties and the barracked but by no means tractable

Nepal Army—and his own vaporous ambition haul him back down to earth?

III

Prachanda's road to power began with a belief about himself. The rural schoolteacher, who had grown up dancing to Bollywood songs and reading Dale Carnegie's *How to Win Friends and Influence People* in a farming village in Chitwan district, which borders Bihar in Nepal's southern plains, judged himself to be destined for more. 'I felt I shouldn't spend my life as a teacher in a government school,' Prachanda told me in November. 'I felt I should seek a greater role.'

Prachanda had had a high-caste but relatively modest upbringing and an unpromising youth. He graduated both his local high school and a middle-tier college with second division marks, and was then packed off by the government to teach at a remote, upland school in eastern Nepal. At the end of a five-day trek into the hills, at times in drenching rain, Prachanda, who in earlier days aspired to become an airline pilot, was told that his humble job had already gone to another teacher. In 1978, after suffering this and a number of other personal humiliations, the twenty-three-year-old Prachanda decided to join the Communist Party of Nepal. 'I think that I was sent to a remote district because there was no one at the education ministry who would lobby on my behalf,' he told me, with lingering bitterness. The communists offered something more. He was made a Chitwan district committee member, and, against the objections of his father, he plunged into underground life.

Prachanda soon ascended the communist ranks, continually choosing the most radical in a set of perpetually splintering factions. Intentionally or otherwise, his ideological commitment to revolutionary violence appears to have coincided with a savvy opportunism: whenever Prachanda switched groups, he inevitably rose. Prachanda's climb was 'unnatural', the former Maoist leader Thapa told me. 'He seems to have harboured a wish to join the ranks of top leadership as soon as he joined the party.'

'In the early 1980s, Prachanda started to assert himself as a leader,' his former fellow radical Khanal recalled. It may also have been during this period that Prachanda, who then used the alias 'Bishwas' (Trust), started popularizing a story about his childhood that he has often told, in various forms, to reporters and fellow cadres. The story seems to have served for the Maoist chief as a sort of personal foundation myth, explaining why he became a communist and eventually took up arms. In the version Prachanda told me, when he was ten or twelve he used to accompany his father, Muktiram Dahal, a farmer, to a local bazaar to sell rice. On one of these trips, Muktiram pleaded with a businessman to give him a better price for his grains, but the man humiliated him. In another version, recounted to me by Khanal, who said Prachanda had told it at a 2001 party meeting, Prachanda was in his early teens, and the businessman would humiliate his father on a regular basis. In a third version, which Prachanda related to the *Times of India* in 2001, and which was quoted in an admiring 2008 biography of the Maoist chairman, Prachanda said that one day he saw a moneylender insulting his father. 'My father fell at the moneylender's feet,' Prachanda told the *Times*. 'But the moneylender kicked him. It lit a fire inside me. It was a political lesson I never forgot. It changed the course of my life.' Without casting doubt on the veracity of this particular story, Sapkota, the political commentator, attacked the myth of Prachanda, insisting there was 'nothing revolutionary' about the man. 'Look at his life,' he told me. 'It's full of contradictions. He comes from a typical hill, middle-class Brahmin family and has carried all their conventional, traditional, unsophisticated legacy.'

By 1985, Prachanda was a confirmed proletarian radical. He had switched parties at least three times, finally joining Mohan Baidya, a soft-spoken ideologue with a deep knowledge of communist classics, in a faction advocating immediate preparations for a protracted uprising they called a People's War. The two men were brought together in part by the realization that their other radical colleagues 'would just talk about revolution, but would never actually initiate it', Baidya, who goes by the alias Kiran, told me in an interview this past November.

Their first attempt at armed insurgency was a risible failure, but the political consequences catapulted Prachanda to the party's top position. In 1987, as part of a boycott on elections for members of a party-less, palace-controlled regime called the Panchayat, faction leaders in Kathmandu planned to attack police posts across the city. In the event, all the attacking cadres managed to do was pelt the police with stones and smear soot on the face of a statue of a former king. Following the pathetic sortie, several local leaders were arrested. This sparked a row in the party over who should be held responsible for the debacle. To avert a schism, Baidya proposed that he and a few senior leaders be demoted, effectively leaving Prachanda at the top. There were other capable leaders in the faction, Thapa told me, but Baidya 'sidelined them all'.

'I wanted to encourage him,' Baidya said to me of his decision to elevate Prachanda. 'We had decided to launch a communist revolution in Nepal.' Following his ascension, Prachanda relocated to Kathmandu, and, jettisoning his benign alias, Bishwas, adopted the sobriquet 'Prachanda'—the Fierce One. It was a name befitting his new stature: at age thirty-five, he had gained control of a radical fringe party of sixty hard-core, full-time members, with strongholds in the remote Nepali districts of Rolpa, Rukum, Sindhupalchok and Sindhuli—all of which would serve as launch pads for the People's War.

Over the next few years, Prachanda held a number of military camps for his faction's senior commanders, and travelled to a guerrilla stronghold in Bihar where he studied warfare with combatants of the Maoist Communist Centre (MCC), at that time one of the largest Maoist groups in India. He also began to reach out to former comrades within Nepal; according to Thapa, the botched 1987 attack had taught the faction leaders that they could not instigate armed insurrection on their own.

In the spring of 1990, the Nepali Congress, together with another moderate party, led nationwide pro-democracy protests that forced Birendra Shah, the king, to resurrect a multiparty parliamentary system that his father had abolished in 1961. After establishing a coalition with two of his former factions, Prachanda and his party had participated in the protests, though independently of the moderates. Following the democratic victory, the old communist colleagues became deeply engaged in a debate over how to proceed under the new dispensation, which would make it possible for them to take part in elections and the formation of a government. At the time, Prachanda maintained that the change was cosmetic and that conditions for a People's War were ripening. When I spoke to him in late 2012, however, he claimed that he was pressured to start the war by an international revolutionary group that was supporting his coalition. 'I was very clear about the need to participate in parliamentary politics,' Prachanda told me. 'But our party was under pressure from the Revolutionary Internationalist Movement not to do so. They told us that if we fought elections, we will deviate from the revolutionary ideals,' he said. In truth, the *Kantipur* editor, Sharma, argued Prachanda and his partisans 'realized that armed struggle was the surest way to reach the pinnacle of power'.

In the short term, the coalition prepared to contest elections through an overground political wing headed by Bhattarai, then thirty-seven, who had returned from completing his PhD in New Delhi five years before. At the May 1991 polls, the communists won nine seats, making them the third-largest party in Parliament. Despite their modest electoral success, the rift over instigating a People's War grew wider as the months wore on. In May 1994, the less radical members broke away from the coalition, leaving the hardliners, including Baidya and Bhattarai, to unite with Prachanda under the banner of a new party, the Communist Party of Nepal (Maoist), which agreed to move forward with Prachanda's vision for a People's War.

Prachanda was coming closer to achieving the conflagration, and the power, that he sought. In March 1995, he and a dozen of his lieutenants travelled to a cave outside the village of Sirubari in central Nepal's Gorkha district, where they had secretly deposited a cache of rudimentary arms, including home-made pistols, kukris and two .303-calibre rifles—only one of which, according to Prachanda's biographer, could fire. They then received military training from a former Nepal Army captain—'The first challenge was to unite the party for the war,' Prachanda told me—and went back to their command posts to propagate the conflict ideology.

In early February 1996, Bhattarai, accompanied by another senior cadre and scores of supporters, handed over to the government a list of forty demands, which included abrogation of 'all discriminatory treaties between India and Nepal', regulation of the Indo-Nepal open border, and bans on Indian number-plate vehicles and 'vulgar Hindi films, videos and magazines'. They also stipulated that the country should be declared secular and that 'land under the feudal system should be distributed to the landless'. If these conditions were not fulfilled in two weeks, the document declared, the Maoists 'would be forced to adopt the path of armed struggle against the existing state power'.

On 13 February 1996, before the deadline on their demands had even expired, Prachanda and his comrades launched the People's War in the mountain districts of Rolpa, Rukum, Gorkha and Sindhuli by attacking banks, police posts and even a local landholder whom they branded a 'feudal lord'. When I asked Prachanda if he feared for his life, he said the preparations for the war—collecting ammunition, training, indoctrinating the cadre—had readied him for the day. 'We were sure that we will either be arrested or killed,' he told me. In leaflets they distributed throughout the country, the militants declared that they were fighting to 'establish the dictatorship of the proletariat, marching to communism, the golden future of humanity'. Their avowed goal was to bring about a permanent democratic revolution by abolishing the monarchy through armed struggle. 'I could not sleep the night before that,' Prachanda recalled. 'I was thrilled with the anticipation of the dawn of a new era.'

The war's first casualty was an eleven-year-old boy from Gorkha district who was shot dead by the police. Then, on 17 February, the police killed six young men from a single family in Rukum. These seven deaths in less than a week scared the Maoist leaders into fleeing Kathmandu. They first sought shelter in the countryside, and then abandoned Nepal all together. One by one, Prachanda, Bhattarai and other Maoist commissars snuck across the border to the town of Siliguri in West Bengal, where Prachanda would live for the next three years, posing, according to his biographer, as a 'research scholar attempting to complete his thesis' or a local schoolteacher.

This left day-to-day military operations to Prachanda's conscripts. Of four regional commands the Maoists soon established, only one, the Kathmandu propaganda bureau, was in Nepal; the others were in Siliguri, Lucknow and New Delhi. From time to time, the Maoist leaders would smuggle themselves back into Nepal for secret meetings in remote villages, where they met with the men conducting the revolution on the ground. By way of explaining his exodus, Prachanda said that communists all over the world had used foreign soil to wage war inside their nations. 'It was only Mao who didn't have to go abroad because of China's enormous size,' he told me. Prachanda's former confidant Lohani, however, saw this as a turning point in the war. 'The problems began after he left Nepal within months of launching the war and took shelter in India,' Lohani said. 'He didn't have first-hand experience of war until late 2004.'

In the first few years of the conflict, the insurgents focused on sabotage: they bombed factories and continued to attack police posts. Initially, the government in Kathmandu did not take the insurgents seriously, but, in May 1998, heavily armed police task forces were sent to sweep up suspected rebels in the countryside. Rural citizens were brutalized during the crackdown and indignant locals were driven into the Maoists' arms. In addition to these immediate grievances, and chronic unemployment, Sharma told me recruits were also attracted to the Maoists by 'Prachanda's mysterious aura' and 'the power of the gun'.

As a result of this injection of fresh blood, the Maoists were able to step up their efforts. In one of their major offensives, in September 2000, they slaughtered at least twelve policemen and injured a further three dozen in an attack on a rural police command. The Nepal Army, following a policy of non-engagement set by the palace, had refused to aid the police. It was an aloofness the army would soon be unable to maintain.

During the same period, Prachanda was consolidating his power within the party. In collaboration with Baidya, he moved to contain the growing influence of the party's intellectual force, Bhattarai, by promoting himself from general secretary to chairman of the party, a shift that gave him unquestioned authority. It soon became mandatory for other leaders to quote him in their formal communications. Then, a more profound change occurred, one which likely alienated Prachanda from his former mentor Baidya, a relentless supporter of armed conflict: in early 2001, a five-year review of the war led Prachanda to reconsider an engagement with democratic politics and to espouse a commitment to the idea of a Constituent Assembly, a body which he hoped he could leverage into Maoist control of the government. It seemed to be dawning on Prachanda that the war could never elevate the party fast enough, and that, without an initial political compromise of some sort, he could never hope to accomplish a takeover of the state.

Although Bhattarai had much to do with the ideological formulation of this new approach, the Maoist chairman made sure it would be known as the 'Prachanda Path'. Inside the core cadre, however, Bhattarai received credit. 'This was Bhattarai's line and he was very happy with the decision,' Thapa, the former cadre, told me. Prachanda and Bhattarai then began to reach out furtively to the palace, seeking a peace that would clear the way for Constituent Assembly elections. If they hadn't made this decision, the Maoists 'wouldn't have arrived this far', Thapa said. 'We would have been crushed.'

In summer 2001, a cataclysmic event radically changed Nepal's political dynamics. On 1 June, King Birendra's son, Crown Prince Dipendra, allegedly drunk, high on drugs and upset by his mother's refusal to let him marry his girlfriend, killed his mother and father, his brother, a sister, an aunt, two uncles and two cousins. Then he shot himself. The crown prince was anointed king as he lay unconscious in a military hospital.

He died two days later, and the throne passed to his bellicose uncle Gyanendra.

With the monarchy in chaos, Prachanda asked the parliamentary government to engage in talks. The administration reciprocated and a ceasefire was called. At the same time, however, Maoist forces, now dubbed the People's Liberation Army, were preparing for more aggressive attacks. On 21 November 2001, Prachanda, through a statement, withdrew from the negotiations, citing an unwillingness on the part of the government to engage in Constituent Assembly elections. The 'imperialist and reactionary forces have contributed to the failure of the talks', he declared. More likely, the Maoists' bargaining hand was not yet strong enough to secure the political outcome they desired.

Two days later, they ended the four-month-old ceasefire by carrying out their most audacious operation yet: in a pair of synchronized assaults, they opened a front against the Nepal Army. Scores of soldiers and a number of policemen were killed in the strikes, and seventy Maoist comrades were freed from jail. King Gyanendra promptly declared a state of emergency, thereby mobilizing the Nepal Army for the first time since the Maoists launched hostilities five years earlier. The war rapidly escalated and over 100 people were killed in the next three days.

Within a year, an increasingly aggressive King Gyanendra suspended the government and initiated a crackdown on civil liberties across the country; the retrenchment effectively foreclosed the possibility of a peaceful rapprochement between the combatants. This was compounded by the fallout from the 9/11 attacks in the USA: Gyanendra was trying to take advantage of the growing antagonism towards extremism to garner US support for his war on 'Maoist terror'. Year-on-year casualties soared more than sevenfold to over 4,600.

Over the next two years, a number of Maoist leaders were arrested in India, where they lived and maintained links with Indian revolutionary groups. This finally forced Prachanda, who had been residing in New Delhi following his time in West Bengal, to move back to Nepal. 'When we gathered that the Indian ruling class was against us, we decided to transform our war into a movement for national independence,' Prachanda told me. 'We prepared ourselves for the eventual war with India.' Thapa, who left the party a few months after the decision, elaborated: 'The idea was to dig tunnels to wage war against India, but in reality it was the old Maoist rhetoric of raising the fears of Indian invasion and cashing in on the anti-Indian sentiment in Nepal.' It was a desperate move; Prachanda must have realized that the war at home would drag on indefinitely, preventing him from fulfilling his ambition of taking over the government—but he had no one left with whom he could negotiate a way into power.

In late 2004, the chill between Prachanda and Bhattarai grew colder. Although Bhattarai was dissatisfied with the distribution of power within the party—Prachanda controlled both its military and its political activities—the dispute ostensibly centred on the identity of the insurgency's main antagonist. Prachanda continued to fulminate against India and its alleged expansionism, and, in his hopelessness, proposed to reach out again to the palace. Bhattarai argued that domestic feudalism, represented by the monarchy, was still the biggest enemy. After Bhattarai openly criticized Prachanda, the angered chairman expelled him and his wife, Hisila Yami, from the party and sent them to a labour camp. 'We took action because he violated our party's norms,' Prachanda told me. 'He should have voiced his dissent in the central committee. He shared it with the cadre.' Khanal, Prachanda's former fellow radical, had another reading of the situation: 'He cannot hear a single word of criticism'—a trait exacerbated by the fact that

Prachanda 'doesn't have a consistent position'. Prachanda was now left both without potential allies at the centre, and without the strategic support of Bhattarai, on which he had relied. 'It is said that he has many antennas by means of which he keeps abreast of the activities inside the party,' Prachanda's former confidant Lohani put it. 'He may have information but doesn't have acumen to interpret it in the right way.'

Circumstance would soon bring the rivals together again. On 1 February 2005, King Gyanendra launched a full-on coup, dismissing the entire government and instituting autocratic military rule. This disconcerted the international community and initiated yet another shift in Prachanda's strategy, this time away from the palace. His change of tact was reinforced that April when a Maoist battalion, now under the direct operational control of their supreme commander, was brutally put down; in a humiliating defeat, Prachanda lost more than 200 fighters while trying to gain control of a hilltop army base. 'We were taught to hold our head high even in the face of defeat,' Prachanda's former confidant Lohani told me. 'I was surprised to see our commander lamenting the loss.'

Having lost any political and military leverage over the palace, Prachanda was now forced to turn towards his avowed enemy, India. The country was willing to aid the Maoists in order to neutralize the unpredictable Gyanendra, who was attempting to court its major regional competitor, China. New Delhi also hoped that if the Nepali Maoists entered into a peace process, it would prompt home-grown guerrillas to follow suit. Prachanda rehabilitated Bhattarai and sent him to New Delhi, where the Indian government helped mediate talks between the Maoists and seven parliamentary parties, including the Nepali Congress and the Unified Marxist–Leninists, that had been ejected during the king's putsch. Indian Foreign Secretary Shyam Saran,

Research and Analysis Wing chief Hormis Tharakan and senior government adviser S.D. Muni all had direct contact with the Maoists during this process. On 22 November 2005, the Maoists and the parliamentary parties struck a twelve-point deal to end the armed conflict and resume peaceful protests against the king.

At the time, Prachanda couched this reversal in typically ideological terms, promising to his party members that they would now launch an urban insurrection. But the future he foresaw without a ceasefire was bleak. 'Most of our leaders would be arrested and killed,' he admitted to me when we spoke at his mansion in November. 'People would suffer more. They would be terrified and the beneficiary of such a situation would be the foreigners. So, we decided to forge an alliance with the parliamentary parties and fight against the king's autocracy.'

Clandestine negotiations continued throughout the next six months, while the Maoists and the parliamentary parties geared up for nationwide anti-monarchy protests. In the spring of 2006, thousands demonstrated across the country, and, in April, nearly a million marched through the streets of Kathmandu, forcing the king to step down and reinstate the Parliament that was dissolved in 2002. That June, following the success of the protests, the Nepali Congress leader, Koirala, dispatched his deputy Sitaula to retrieve Prachanda and Bhattarai from Sikles, where they were holed up under the protection of Maoist guards. In November, when the Comprehensive Peace Agreement was signed to wild applause in front of crowds at Kathmandu's Chinese-built International Convention Centre, Prachanda invoked Gautama Buddha to explain his turn towards peace. Hard-line party members, including Baidya, felt that Prachanda had sold out; Prachanda told me that they were 'too dogmatic' to accept his 'ground-breaking move'.

IV

The euphoria following Prachanda's prime ministerial victory in August 2008 was short-lived. Complex allegiances within his coalition government and a constant threat that it, or the entire Parliament, would be dissolved created a treacherous administrative landscape, one that Prachanda was not accustomed to navigating. 'It was the first time I was heading a government,' an apologetic-sounding Prachanda told me. 'It was a new experience for me. Therefore, I made some mistakes which were inevitable.'

Part of the problem was that Prachanda did not know how to operate in consensus-driven political conditions that were not amenable to his authoritarian style. 'After becoming prime minister, I realized how weak our state was,' Prachanda explained. 'We couldn't do anything on our own.' But this didn't stop him from trying to push through his policies. 'I tried to change everything at once,' he admitted. 'It has now dawned on me that I should have effected change gradually. We tried to do everything and ended up doing nothing particularly well.'

At the top of his agenda was to integrate People's Liberation Army soldiers into the Nepal Army, a process that was necessary to prevent further outbreaks of military violence, but was also likely to extend Prachanda's influence among former adversaries. Barely nine months into his term, Prachanda entered a bitter row over the issue with then army chief Rookmangud Katawal, a staunch royalist on the verge of retirement who had resisted democratic control of the military. Katawal actively opposed Prachanda's policy of integrating Maoist combatants, who had been sequestered in twenty-eight United Nations-monitored cantonments. At the same time, Katawal defied government orders by extending the tenure of eight brigadiers (thereby ensuring a concentration of monarchist sympathizers at the top of the military hierarchy) and withdrawing army soldiers from Nepal's annual national games. Angered by Katawal's non-compliance, Prachanda peremptorily dismissed him.

It was an irrevocable mistake. 'Katawal would have retired after three months,' Prachanda reflected when we spoke. 'But we acted in haste.' The *Himal Southasian* editor, Dixit, had a more critical reading of Prachanda's actions at the time. 'The party leadership, especially Pushpa Kamal Dahal, took us through a road of devastation which continues to this day because they cheated on the peace process,' Dixit told me. 'When they came above ground, it was clear that these guys were for a one-party state. The idea was that their party would take over the country and the international community will be presented with a fait accompli.'

But, in some senses, it was Prachanda who had been brought under the control of the state and not vice versa: forming and attempting to run a coalition government had increased the Maoists' influence at the centre, but defused their ability to get anything done. The country's first president, Nepali Congressman Ram Baran Yadav, who was expected to play a largely ceremonial role, stepped in to reverse Prachanda's decision. In an about-face from its recent pro-Maoist policy, the Indian establishment backed Yadav and Katawal. Prachanda claimed that Yadav's overrule created two power centres; as a result, in May 2009, he angrily stepped down 'to save the country from a bloodbath'. 'If he hadn't resigned, there could have been bloodshed and a big crisis,' Sharma, the editor of *Kantipur*, agreed. 'He saved the country from that.'

Many of Prachanda's supporters, however, did not see him has a saviour; they argued that Prachanda, by embracing democracy in the first place, had mortgaged the revolution. 'That was when the inner struggle resurfaced in the party,' Prachanda admitted to me. 'Some of our friends started to voice their position against the party's policy of peace and constitution.' Prachanda's former confidant Lohani put it differently. 'Before launching the war, the leaders had pledged that they would not lay down arms unless the revolution was achieved,' Lohani told me. 'Prachanda not only betrayed us, but also squandered the achievement gained through the People's War.'

Whether to maintain control within the party or in a genuine attempt to regain power—or both—Prachanda came back around to the radical view, and once again encouraged his cadres to revolt. That summer, the party invited members from across the country to gather in Kathmandu in 'a show of force' to demand 'civilian supremacy'. In the capital, angry Maoist protesters waved black flags at government ministers and blocked their convoys in the streets. In a second wave of demonstrations, the Maoists shut down transport, industries, schools and colleges across Nepal. Next, they mounted a six-day nationwide strike, which reportedly cost the country's fragile economy an estimated $300 million. The bandh was called off after widespread anger led to counter-protests. At the end of the six days, thousands of Maoist supporters gathered in an open theatre at the Kathmandu city centre, where Prachanda promised to fight on. 'This is only a dress rehearsal,' Prachanda warned. 'We will put on a real show in the days to come.'

Despite his rhetoric, Prachanda seemed to realize the political inexpediency of the bandhs, and nothing came of his threats. 'Our goal was to transform the framework of the state through the protests, but our calculations were proved wrong,' Prachanda told me. 'We weren't in a position to use violent means to transform the state.' This left Prachanda in another political limbo; once again he tried in vain to pursue a democratic path to power. In seven different rounds of prime ministerial elections, Prachanda failed to reclaim the premiership. 'The forces inside our country and outside didn't want me to win,' Prachanda told me, in what I took to be an oblique reference to India. To the political commentator Sapkota, the existence of such forces is dubious. 'It might have been necessary to identify an enemy and motivate others to take up guns during the war, but even after it ended, he has been creating imaginary enemies,' Sapkota said. Sharma, the *Kantipur* editor, had another explanation: 'He continued to put his feet in two boats: peace and constitution, and state capture. This fluctuation severely damaged his credibility in national politics.'

Taking advantage of this damage, Bhattarai and Baidya formed an unlikely alliance to shift their party's balance of power away from Prachanda. Prachanda would remain party chairman, but Bhattarai would be put forward as its candidate for prime minister. Bhattarai was able to garner support from the hardliners, and, through a coalition government with ethnic-Madhesi–dominated parties of the southern plains, was elected the prime minister in August 2011, a position he has held ever since. 'Bhattarai was keen on becoming a prime minister and had India's backing,' Sharma told me. 'Prachanda did his best to stop Bhattarai, but the alliance between Bhattarai and Baidya proved insurmountable.' For his part, Prachanda acknowledged that Bhattarai's growing stature was a challenge to him, but said that they complemented each other. 'I asked Baburam-ji to get ready to head the next government,' Prachanda told me. 'I needed to concentrate on resolving the divisions within the party, and vying for the same position would not look good.'

Prachanda may also have remembered the crippling experience of his time in office—an experience that Bhattarai has not been spared. Ever since the general election in 2008, Nepal's political parties have been struggling to draft a lasting constitution; in May 2012, under Bhattarai's watch, the Constituent Assembly was dissolved after missing its final deadline. The parties could not agree on the contentious issue of dividing Nepal into federal states based on ethnicity. The centrist parties refused this arrangement, but the Maoists and Madhesis would not compromise. It was a serious blow to the Maoists—the Constituent Assembly was one of the main reasons they had been willing to give up arms—but the Madhesis are an essential ally in their bid to maintain power over the centre. 'We made many compromises, but we didn't want to go to the extent where we would lose the people's support,' Prachanda told me. 'We would have lost not only our supporters but also the grounds on which we stood.' While the Opposition calls for fresh elections, Prachanda is lobbying to reinstate the assembly under the current Maoist administration. A sense of urgency regarding the fashioning of the constitution, and the fact that successive coalition governments have failed to bring about the desired result, may serve to promote Prachanda's ends, allowing him to push through provisions for the strong executive position he seeks.

But another one of Prachanda's post-war plans has come up short. In April, clashes erupted in the Maoist cantonments after combatants accused their commanders and the party of siphoning off their allowances. Nepal Army soldiers were deployed to defuse the situation and finally take charge of the Maoist forces. Nearly 7,000 guerrillas were offered integration into the army, but only 1,500 chose to join their former enemy. The result was a massive embarrassment for the party, which has allowed the clout its militia once possessed to ebb away. 'He has lost everything including the military wing of the party,' Khanal told me. 'He compromised so much that he forced the fighters to accept a humiliating deal.' Prachanda agreed that the integration had not worked as he had hoped, but claimed it wasn't a failure. He accused a recently formed breakaway faction of Maoists, led by Baidya, of inciting the violence that led to the army's intervention. 'They wanted to dismantle everything,' Prachanda said of his former colleagues. 'But we knew that at some point, we would have to join the Nepal Army. We should trust the Nepal Army. We should not see it as our enemy.'

Although Prachanda's optimism regarding the army may partly serve a rhetorical purpose, it may also mark a larger shift in his approach. In the years since his embarrassing prime ministerial showing and its aftermath, Prachanda seems to have decided that engagement with democratic politics and promoting a slowly rising economic tide in Nepal is the best way forward. 'Let me tell you one thing,' he said to me. 'After my resignation, I realized that our party should not remain in Opposition. We would be strong only if we are in government.' In April, six years after his landmark press conference on the lawns of the prime minister's house, Prachanda made 'peace and constitution' his party's official platform, finally abandoning any allegiance to revolutionary means.

Prachanda now presents himself as a former insurgent gingerly treading Kathmandu's messy political terrain. 'This is quite complicated,' the potbellied politician said of his time since the peace accord in 2006. 'During the war, things were clear, there was an enemy and we were fighting against him. Now I have to deal with many constituencies. Instead of common people, I have to meet big businessmen, capitalists and even agency people.' (I took him to mean intelligence agencies, but he refused to elaborate.)

With these changes in Prachanda's approach has come a change in the way he is perceived by the nation. The revolutionary mystique that once surrounded him has now faded like Kathmandu's morning mists. The day I interviewed him, *Kantipur* published a dispatch from the village of Thabang, in the former Maoist heartland of Rolpa. At the height of the war, Prachanda's face was painted, alongside portraits of the communist pantheon—Marx, Engels, Lenin and Stalin—on the walls of Rolpa's two-storey, tin-roofed houses. But people in Thabang, *Kantipur* reported, had now disowned Prachanda, accusing him of selling out the revolution. Their former messiah was no longer welcome. The *Himal Southasian* editor, Dixit, for one, expressed a sentiment with which Thabang locals might agree. 'I don't accept that it was a people's war,' Dixit argued. 'It was a Maoist insurgency. You cannot hold a knife behind your back and use others just by repeating the words that I'm for the marginalized and deprived.'

Other betrayals have occurred closer to home. In October 2011, when Prachanda's father, Muktiram, died at age eighty-five at his home in Chitwan, Prachanda took advantage of the occasion. Instead of shaving his head and performing Hindu funeral rites as Muktiram might have wished, Prachanda wrapped his father's body in a hammer-and-sickle banderole and brought several Maoist leaders to the ceremony. 'That was a political act,' Prachanda's younger brother, Gangaram Dahal, fifty, told me from his home in the United Kingdom. 'Where were they when he was bedridden? Neither my brother nor the party extended any help in his hour of need. What's the use of covering his body with a communist flag after his death?' Gangaram described Muktiram as an independent and religious person. 'He was a peace-loving person,' Prachanda's brother said. 'He never endorsed violence. He consistently held views against the war.'

Prachanda may have used his father's death to propagandize for his party, but he may also be selling out the party's revolution (as the Rolpa villagers claim): one of the initiatives he now sponsors is the Maoist Guerrilla Trek, which runs guided expeditions in regions where the former rebels fought their decade-long war. 'Many countries that have emerged from war have tried to capitalize on the memory of war,' Prachanda told a crowd of 500 attendees at the company's launch this past October. 'A huge political change occurred in Nepal, but we cannot sustain it unless there is an economic transformation. I hope the Guerrilla Trek will play an important role in that.'

Prachanda also appears to be attempting to capitalize on peace. In a lavish ceremony at a five-star hotel in Kathmandu this past November, Prachanda, in his capacity as the chairman of a high-level government committee, signed a memorandum of understanding with Linus Xiao Wunan, executive vice chairman of the Hong Kong–based NGO Asia Pacific Exchange and Cooperation Foundation. Prachanda, who has no known bank account or sources of income—apart from a modest allowance from the state for fuel, security and housing—is also a vice chairman of the foundation. Their aim is to develop Lumbini, the birthplace of Buddha, into a commercial Buddhist mecca in a project rumoured to cost $3 billion. Unlike Bhattarai, who has remained close to India, Prachanda has advocated cultivating links with China as well; what he stands to gain beyond prestige in this particular project, however, isn't quite clear.

A week after Kunwar slapped him, Prachanda appeared in public again for the first time since the incident. In an interview on Kantipur Television, Nepal's most influential news channel, he tried to connect Kunwar's act to the larger political process. 'Personally, I haven't taken the incident seriously,' he said, sporting new spectacles and appearing exuberant. 'Soon after, I told my party colleagues that we should not take it as anything huge. It appeared that in the past, he and his family were involved in our party. He might have grievances. Therefore, I have my sympathy for him.' On 11 December, Prachanda's fifty-eighth birthday, Kunwar was released on bail. The funds were deposited by an aide of the Maoist leader.

When I met Prachanda in early November at his home, I asked him what legacy he wanted to leave. We were sitting in a spacious office, adorned with images of the Buddha and Mount Everest, and with two flags—Nepal's national double pennant and the Maoists' crimson banner. He told me he wants people to remember him 'as a person who played a role in ushering in an epochal change in Nepal.'

'Do you think that they will remember you in that way?' I asked him. 'They will have to,' he said.

In my early years in Carnatic music, when, to me, its nuts and bolts seemed to be supreme, I belittled **M.S. SUBBULAKSHMI**'s musicianship. But as I immersed myself in music, searching for the intangible, fathomless moments of art, I discovered MS and, in the process, music itself. I learned that to live in art, you must be vulnerable and surrender yourself to it.

The complexities of her life came through in every raga that she unfolded. Her life and music were in harmony, revealing the struggles of a lone woman in an upper-caste, upper-class man's world. She sang to her heart's content, conveying so many inner stories that were beyond the literal. Perhaps she hoped that we were listening.

While writing this essay, MS also became my reflection, revealing to me my own prejudices in which built-in notions of musical purity were just violent discriminators. Some have seen this piece as an insult to her memory. But I have celebrated her in what seems to me the best way possible—telling the story of a woman who was a brave devadasi, a Brahmin housewife, an exquisite, renowned musician and a quiet seeker, all in a lifetime.

MS is also extremely important to the times we live in, when the cultural majority in this country is justifying misogyny, casteism and religious discrimination in order to consolidate political power. She may not be a typical feminist, but she fought and fought hard for her space, and found it between the *swaras* she adorned.

Her music moves us; may her life transform us.

T.M. KRISHNA

T.M. Krishna is a Carnatic music vocalist living in Chennai. He is the author of A Southern Music: The Karnatik Story.

MS Understood

The myths and misconceptions around India's most acclaimed musician

By T.M. KRISHNA | 1 October 2015

In a private conversation sometime in the late 1980s, a sharp-tongued young, aspiring musician made an extraordinary statement about Carnatic music's most iconic figure. 'M.S. Subbulakshmi,' he said with disdain, 'is the greatest hoax of the twentieth century.' Many readers will leap to accuse me of blasphemy for even citing this rather obnoxious remark. But it has stayed with me ever since, and I have a somewhat severe explanation for why.

This musician's assertion was based on the argument that it was packaging and marketing that made Madurai Shanmukhavadivu Subbulakshmi the global face and voice of Carnatic music; her music was otherwise intrinsically hollow and lacked 'stuff'. The Carnatic hinterland would not employ the word 'hoax' to describe her, but would consider, with varying levels of empathy, the hypothesis that she was stage-managed. The marketing of MS—orchestrated, as is well known—by her mentor, husband and business strategist, T. Sadasivam, was undoubtedly astounding and far ahead of its time. But to claim that what he sold to the world was intrinsically empty is unacceptable.

The world of Carnatic music, and its nerve centre, Chennai, is an intense, and intensely insular, world. Its norms of adherence, practise and evaluation are unforgiving. Through conversations, informal criticism, even hints, learned musicians and seniors, working in tandem with informed listeners, bestow various degrees of so-called classical value upon musicians. These value judgements become harsher as the popularity of a musician rises. Some of these musicians have publicly offered MS gestures of admiration, even adulation. Many use her performance techniques to enhance their own. But serious critical and technical appreciation has been rare. MS's contemporaries, and even her juniors, have received weightier musical approval.

This was as true at the crest of her fame as it is now, over a decade after her death—and in this, her centenary year. Quintessential Carnatic connoisseurs and musicians differentiate between the real *rasika*, or aesthete, and the *janata*, who attend concerts to hear merely melodious music. The only praise that the hard-core section of this small universe bestows upon MS with honesty is that she had the most beautiful and pitch-perfect voice, and immaculate presentation skills. But let me make this clear: musicians don't consider that combination a compliment. It usually means that there is nothing in the music to really write home about. I gather, from those close to her, that MS herself used to get quite upset when people only admired her voice—or worse, went on and on about the exquisite sari she was wearing.

There are also those who may want me to stop right here, because this is not the MS they venerate—a figure through whom every god spoke and continues to speak. That MS is the voice through which Shakuntala and Meera sang. Through her renderings, the works of the poet saints Tyagaraja, Kabir and Surdas came alive. Every *swara*, or note, she sang is a precious gem; every musical rendition a jewel of grace and dignity. This MS is a divine vehicle to the deities—so divine that she has become a deity herself. This is MS as seen by people whom the aesthetes are likely to call ignoramuses and outsiders.

The narratives around MS have usually followed one of two paths. The most popular and sociologically captivating one is that of the personal history. The dramatic emergence of a Brahmin musical superstar with a devadasi background is a storyteller's dream. Comparisons with Bharatanatyam's great diva, T. Balasaraswati, are inevitable: Balasaraswati, born in Chennai in 1918, stuck to her devadasi roots and, in fact, flaunted her antecedents.

The second strain of writing about MS has focused on her music. This has been mostly hagiographical. Words have failed almost everyone who has tried to describe its effect—considered transporting and transcendental by many. But can we look at her life and her musical movements as a single thread, trying to understand one by the other?

Both the life and the work of M.S. Subbulakshmi bear investigation, to see whether it was her choices or compulsions—I use these words, which mean the opposite of each other, deliberately—that are responsible for the two differing views of her. There was a constant friction between MS's choices as an artist of great resources and her compulsions as a woman of equal vulnerability. The early MS sang in the idiom of her inheritance, to popular acclaim. The later MS sang in the syntax of a spiritual revisionism, to popular worship. It was an extraordinary transition from what was great to what became grand.

The basic facts that can be retrieved from the mythology surrounding MS's early life run thus: Subbulakshmi was born in Madurai in 1916 to a senior devadasi, known and respected in the town as a veena player. In keeping with devadasi practice, Subbulakshmi retained her mother's name, Madurai Shanmukhavadivu, which formed her famous initials. Shanmukhavadivu was an unwed single mother, the father of her daughter having retreated into the mists of anonymity. According to MS, he was Subramania Iyer, a Madurai-based Brahmin lawyer.

MS was introduced to the world at the age of ten, on an HMV *thattu* (in Tamil, records used to be called thattu, meaning plate) rendering the Tamil song '*Maragathavadivu*' in raga Jenjooti. It would be unfair to judge her music at that stage, but there are some remarkable aesthetic indicators. In that recording, made in 1926, she comes across as a young girl with a sharp, brave musical expression. Her voice is already fast-moving, with the ability to render speedy phrases with aplomb. Her musical accent is natural and free; there is nothing contrived in the way her voice negotiates the twists and turns of the composition. Today, when I replay that recording, I imagine in my mind's eye a girl with oiled, plaited hair, dressed in a *pavadai–sokka*, singing with the calm nonchalance of a maestro in the making.

Her strength of character is evident in her delivery. It is the work of a tough, almost audacious, aspirant, singing with abandon, knowing full well that she is exceptional. There is also the innocence of a child who probably knew of nothing but music. She sings without an iota of self-doubt.

These very qualities gave her the courage to exit her mother's vulnerable home, on Madurai's Hanumantharayar Koil Street, when she was just twenty, in 1936. She left for Madras and chose the settled rhythms of the household of T. Sadasivam, a middle-class Tamil Brahmin. Sadasivam was an enterprising advertising manager for the celebrated Tamil magazine *Ananda Vikatan*, and a close friend of its famous editor, Krishnamurthy. Sadasivam was deeply involved in the Indian independence movement, and both he and Krishnamurthy were devoted adherents of C. Rajagopalachari, the Tamil statesman whom Mohandas Gandhi referred to as his conscience-keeper.

MS had briefly met Sadasivam on an earlier visit to Madras, when she had performed at the city's renowned Music Academy. Now, upon her return, she was undoubtedly seeking Sadasivam's protection, taking a huge risk by placing herself in the hands of a man she hardly knew. That she did so with conviction is quite astonishing. Theirs became a partnership of two very independent and strong individuals. Each knew what he or she wanted, and knew, too, the potential of the other.

Shanmukhavadivu had done all that she could to advance her daughter's career opportunities, but MS had outgrown her environment in Madurai. Madras was becoming the hub for all things Carnatic, and MS's thirst for music was certainly as compelling a reason for her move as the obvious fantasy of making it big.

Sadasivam, for his part, was a married man when he started to provide shelter to the young devadasi from Madurai. I am certain the conservative expression *ellarum yenna sholluva?*—'what will people say?'—flashed across his mind. Apart from his love and affection for her, and beyond his progressive zeal, Sadasivam probably saw musical greatness in MS and knew he had to be by her side.

The musical voice is a complex phenomenon. Just as every person speaks at her own pace, every musician has a range of speed at which her voice is most comfortable. A vocalist's musicality emerges from physiological as well as psychological traits; each voice is unique in its malleability. This does not remain constant even within an individual musician's practice, however. Musical maturity, and the wear and tear on the vocal muscles, leads to unconscious adjustments to her thoughts and actions. Nevertheless, unless some serious damage occurs to her voice, any change in a singer's musical direction is likely to be in the form of a progression.

MS's music in the early years of her stardom is a continuance of what we hear in the voice of the ten-year-old. She had, what we would call, a *briga* voice, a voice that could render a musical phrase fast, irrespective of its complexity, with precision, elan and finesse. Her renditions moved with great accuracy, without ever compromising on musical definition. There was no apparent conscious effort, no contrived intellectualization—this aesthetic seemed second nature to her.

There was something in her singing then that was very avant-garde, stylish, modern and carefree. This should not be taken to mean it was free of care, but free of fear—that is, the fear of going wrong or falling short. Her style had a quality that was fleet but not hasty, quick of movement but not jerky. The modern and the avant-garde are, after all, born from unbound flight: musicians achieve the most elusive artistry when they reach out for the high skies without a second thought.

Her early recordings create the impression of a very contemporary young musician, liberal and feminist, who didn't care a damn for what people thought. This attitude, as others have observed, is well in keeping with the devadasi tradition of music. Artists of devadasi origin had to be, if anything, supremely assertive and artistically self-confident, in a bid to protect their lives from exploitation as far as possible. They were not to be fooled around with or taken for casual performers. In aesthetic terms, this meant their work was to be respected; they were to be given time and space to perform, to create that unmarked zone in which they were sovereign. There is a clear streak of a non-patriarchal, non-conservative musical democracy born out of the organic nature of devadasi learning.

But MS's music was strikingly different even from that of the dominant devadasi musical tradition in Madras, from the school of the legendary Vina Dhanammal, who rose to prominence at the turn of the twentieth century. This music was slower, with a focus on softer curves and gentler phraseology, with intricate aural filigree. For the Carnatic community, the Dhanammal variety of music, later propagated by her grandchildren—T. Brinda, T. Mukta and T. Vishwanathan—has come to be accepted as the universal representation of the devadasi tradition. We seem to have forgotten that devadasi homes nurtured diverse ideas of musical aesthetics, but the early MS reminds us of this reality.

There are also musical reasons for the difference of texture. Some of MS's biographers, including the journalist T.J.S. George, have speculated that her father may have been the star musician Madurai Pushpavanam, a contemporary of Shanmukhavadivu's, said to have had a very racy and dynamic interpretation of Carnatic music. It is at least possible that MS heard about his approach from her mother. Shanmukhavadivu herself seems to have taught MS music that packed a punch. And then there was G.N. Balasubramaniam, or GNB, as he came to be called—a dashing musician six years older than MS, whom we now know she not only admired but was also infatuated with. The feeling was mutual, as evident from the fact that he kept all her love letters safe until the end of his life.

GNB's love for MS has been underplayed, thanks to the latent patriarchy of Mylapore, the Brahmin neighbourhood at the heart of Chennai where music and temple rituals merge like the warp and weft of Kanjeevaram silk. By the late 1930s, GNB had revolutionized the tone, thought and method of rendering Carnatic music. He brought into its practice a kind of Western analytics, which is often attributed to the fact that he was the first Carnatic musician of note who was also a college graduate—he took an honours degree in English literature.

GNB had a magical voice. Unprecedentedly, he sounded most Carnatic when he sang at stunning speeds. All of a sudden, this genius had given the music an exciting, youthful expression, and he became all the rage among Madras's young upper classes. MS's music from this period through to the 1950s sounds akin to GNB's sound. This was probably the result of her conscious internalization of his music, as well as his subconscious impact.

MS and GNB can be said to have collaborated, although not in the sense that they sang together regularly. In 1940, both starred in the film *Sakuntalai*, in which GNB played the king Dushyanta, and MS his love, Shakuntala. Their duets in this film bear testimony to my observations. If anyone could match him, phrase for phrase, it was MS. I am certain that anything he might have thrown at her, she would have given back with interest. In colloquial Carnatic parlance, we would use the Tamil phrase *sangati ellaam palapalapalannu vizhum*, meaning that her sangatis, or musical phrases, unfurl with clarity and lustre. There are no approximations or sly escapisms in MS's execution. Her voice and her music are perfectly paired—and propelled by her tenacity.

There is a 78-rpm recording, released around this period, in which MS sings a brief *alapana*—a kind of improvisational form—of raga Harikamboji. Just before concluding it, she sings a sparkling, ascending musical phrase that is utterly GNB-esque. I bring it up to highlight just how razor-sharp and adventurous her music was, and not superficial by any standard. This is exactly what we would say about GNB too.

By mid 1940, MS had become a name to reckon with, both as a singer on the rigorous stage and as an actor on the fluid screen. Both roles were complementary; on both, she became, quite simply, a star. In July that year, she and Sadasivam were married, after the passing away of Sadasivam's wife. It marked the officialization of their relationship and the point after which everything began to change.

What happened next can be called the transformation, or the psychological realignment, even the taming, of Subbulakshmi. The free-spirited young woman was to become the embodiment of the ideal Brahmin housewife, seen among the elite as the epitome of purity and devotion.

The patriarchy that surrounded the Carnatic world governed every aspect of MS and Sadasivam's social and cultural life. Sadasivam's politics were emancipatory, but he was personally a conservative patriarch. He was instrumental in choreographing MS's transformation. She may have wanted the legitimacy that came with it herself, of course. The security of social respect and acceptance among the cultural elite was probably important to her.

MS's own baggage was her life and past in Madurai, and the contrast between it and being with Sadasivam. On the practical side of things, she was aware that Sadasivam knew exactly what to do professionally. She was on the verge of something really big and he was, after all, a master of marketing. *Ananda Vikatan* had reaped the benefits of his savvy; so would *Kalki*, a popular Tamil magazine he had promoted with his friend 'Kalki' Krishnamurthy.

For MS's transformation to occur, the social memory of her had to be redrafted and then filled in with new details, which meant MS had to be redesigned, both in image and in music. We can see clearly how MS's style changed just from her attire. Gone were the puffed sleeves and casual saris. Even more dramatically, gone was the MS of that early, fun photograph in which she is pictured with a young Balasaraswati, in a Western-style sleeping suit, sporting an unlit cigarette in her mouth. We can now only visualize her in conservative *smarta-brahminkattu*, the style in which she draped her sari.

Between 1938 and 1947, MS acted in five movies: *Sevasadanam, Sakuntalai, Savitri, Meera* in Tamil, and *Meera* in Hindi. In those early years, it was the norm for south Indian films to star Carnatic musicians, as they depended heavily on their music for success. Her movie career was also a business endeavour for MS. She played Narada in *Savitri* to raise money for the launch of *Kalki*. Then came *Meera*, a point of inflection in the lives of Sadasivam and MS.

There are two sides to the *Meera* story, one personal and the other professional. Close associates of MS have said that her experience of playing the title role was deeply emotional, even spiritual. In her mind, she had become the '*dasi* Meera', the poet–saint known and revered across India, and that connection would never leave her. Professionally, of course, *Meera* was a national success, launching a small-town south Indian singer into the headlines. For the first time, a Carnatic musician was recognized in the corridors of power up north. Political and corporate leaders bowed before MS now, and she became known by the titles conferred on her by Jawaharlal Nehru—'the Queen of Song'—and by the nationalist and poet Sarojini Naidu, who, it is claimed, said she surrendered her own title to MS—'the Nightingale of India'. They and the general public must have seen echoes of MS's experience of transcendence in the role—the feeling of actualizing Meera in herself.

But this was only the beginning. In what turned out to be a brilliant marketing move, Sadasivam ensured that MS never acted again; thus etching the image of Meera forever on the frame of MS. After 1947, I don't believe MS ever presented a concert that did not feature Meera's bhajans. The decision to drop out of cinema also erased a potential conflict: a woman becoming the perfect Brahmin housewife could not, after all, also remain in the film industry without creating contradictory images. Ending that chapter of her life only further established MS's Mylaporean conformism.

There was, however, more to this transformation. Just a decade after *Meera*, MS's aesthetic transition was clearly visible. By the late 1950s and early 1960s, her concert tours across India had become processional, like Dasara in Mysore. They were great events, replete with social celebration and musical rejoicing. Here, the striking changes in her music are first discerned in the texture of her voice. It starts sounding heavier, even a little suppressed, as though forced into containment. Musically, the carefree abandon disappears. She still does sing those beautiful 'runs', but they sound more structured. All of a sudden, the kite is tied down by a heavy boulder.

Some may argue that this was the result of Subbulakshmi's maturing, but I beg to differ. In the maturing of a musician, the spirit behind her music is not manipulated. With MS, there seems to have been a kind of reverse engineering: the core was dislocated in order to accommodate the realignment of mind and voice. After *Meera*, and her becoming a quasi-saint across India, her music had to reflect her new status.

We cannot pass judgement on matters of personal faith. But the change unquestionably affected MS's music. She did not stop at Meera bhajans; encouraged by her husband, she acquired and recorded a wider repertoire of religious music, including the work of Tulsidas, Kabir, Nanak, Surdas and Tukaram. She also learned Rabindrasangeet. She acquired many identities in her music. When in Kolkata, she was Tagore. In Pune, she brought Tukaram to life. In Delhi, Tulsidas was reincarnated. On her home turf, in Madras, Tyagaraja sang through her.

Being all these characters was not just about surrendering personally to a godhead or philosophy. It also meant that she was reorienting the aesthetics of her art. It is one thing to learn an assortment of compositions, completely another to have to perpetually juggle musical approaches. MS was intensely involved in every work she rendered, which meant giving up something of herself to its composer, form and intent.

She was also simultaneously updating her Carnatic repertoire and expression. She learned from many greats, including K.S. Narayanaswamy, and, before him, Musiri and Semmangudi. It is said that a leading musician from Madurai, a member of the Isai Vellalar community, once remarked that MS used to sing beautifully until she came under the tutelage of two Iyers. The story is unsubstantiated, but even concocted tales can reveal something of the inner workings of the environment that produced them. It points to the underlying friction between communities in the Carnatic world. As a musician, I can only interpret it to mean that the musician felt sparkle and spirit had given way to predictability.

MS loved to sing, and to learn more and more music, whether it was Carnatic, Hindustani or even—unfortunately—English. In 1966, she was given 'Here under This Uniting Roof' to sing at the United Nations on the occasion of UN Day. The song was written by C. Rajagopalachari and tuned by the respected Chennai-based Western classical musician Handel Manuel. But whatever the value in their contributions, the song was musically hollow and aesthetically limp. Did these frequent shifts cause any internal conflict? Did MS view all these roles as one and the same, or was she painting and peeling identities constantly? We cannot know how she reconciled the contradictions within herself.

Still, her expanded repertoire demands recognition for one astounding quality. Even as MS was singing songs of great diversity, she had the capacity to prevent each from being marred by the aesthetic dimensions of the other. Never was her rendition of a Muthuswami Dikshitar composition muddled by the musicality of Rabindrasangeet; nor her offering of a Meera bhajan by lapses into the heaviness of the Carnatic accent.

This was a tremendous achievement, but one that has gone entirely unnoticed. Her hopscotch between genres gave her music a stronger emotive layering. People may have complained about MS's accented Hindi, but they adored her music, its mellifluousness and its sanctity. In the eyes of the public, she became the spiritual heir to the rishis of this land or even something more, perhaps: the goddess Saraswati incarnate.

Fame had its repurcussions in the inner world of Carnatic music, where MS's national positioning began to skew people's perceptions. She was soon thought of as a bhajan singer, which led to a certain amount of trivialization. For a serious musician of any form, respect from her own contemporaries, seniors and connoisseurs is essential. By the time MS received the coveted title of Sangita Kalanidhi from the Madras Music Academy in 1968, that respect, paradoxically, had begun to dwindle.

Even after *Meera*, MS's concerts contained all the elements that would pass muster with the Carnatic world. She presented many rare compositions, such as Maha Vaidyanatha Iyer's magnum opus, the *Melaragamalika*. She rendered numerous *ragam–tanam–pallavis*—three-part improvisational presentations, considered the greatest test of a Carnatic musician's abilities—set to challenging tala structures, in chaste Carnatic ragas such as Begada, Todi and Bhairavi. Very rarely was she applauded for them. It was most unjust, but the ragam–tanam–pallavis were simply drowned out by bhajans such as '*Morey to Giridhara Gopala*'.

I will say that it was MS who increased the importance of what we call the *tukkada*, or ostensibly lighter section of a Carnatic recital, which follows the virtuoso performance. In the minds of rasikas, the focus of MS's concerts moved away from the first two hours of art music to the last half hour of tukkadas, during which she sang devotional music. She rendered every piece with great beauty, but listeners became obsessed with the religiosity of the shorter pieces and forgot her musical acumen. Even her rendering of serious Carnatic compositions began to be received by many listeners as some form of divine deliverance.

MS's contemporary D.K. Pattammal was the first Brahmin woman to become a celebrated concert performer. In particular, Pattammal was considered a master of the ragam–tanam–pallavi. This conferred on her the status of being, somehow, equal to men in the eyes of Carnatic musicians and connoisseurs. She also uncovered many unknown compositions by Muthuswami Dikshitar, but, unlike MS, she was constantly lauded for these and other efforts by the critical core of the musical world. This must have really hurt MS.

The release in 1963 of MS's recording of the *Venkateshwara Suprabhatham* was a popular coup. But it was musical free fall as far as the serious listener was concerned. This, however, did not prevent MS from continuing to release many recordings in the religious and devotional genres. I am certain Sadasivam knew of the rasikas' perceptions of these. He may not have cared, since by now MS had escaped the clutches of Mylapore. But we may not be able to say the same of MS's feelings.

Sadasivam's control over MS and her music was not only that of a producer; he was also her director and screenplay writer. It was he who decided which ragas and compositions to present at any concert, and even stipulated the duration of each rendition. She also received instructions from him during concerts. The worst of these interruptions would occur when someone of importance was part of the audience. MS would be deep in the Carnatic idiom, preparing to elaborate a raga, when Sadasivam would suddenly ask her to render, say, a Surdas bhajan. The reason: some Hindi-speaking dignitary was leaving early and would not be present to hear her sing the bhajan towards the end of the concert. Those who knew the workings of MS's mind during her concerts have told me that this irked her no end.

These manipulations affected both her own flow and the image of Carnatic music itself, since she was its best-known symbol. Stipulating the duration of an interpretation is not prudent planning. In fact, it dismantles the essence of what drives not just music but every creative art. A concert's balance is calibrated by an invisible inner gauge that an artist develops over time. Each concert is an experience in itself; every composition or improvisation is born from the creative impulse of the day. To destroy this was simply another way of belittling MS's musicianship. It is quite unfathomable that an artist of MS's calibre was tied down by rules set by a non-musician, even if it was her own husband.

To top it all, there was the Shankarabharanam quagmire. If ever a person can be said to have epitomized a raga, MS epitomized raga Shankarabharanam. It is said that Sadasivam invariably wanted her to present it as the main feature of her concerts, believing that this would lead to the success of the performance. MS would gently protest now and again, expressing a desire to sing, perhaps, the Bhairavi or Saveri ragas instead, only to be vetoed.

Ragas such as Shankarabharanam and Kamboji possess the swara known as *anthara gandhara*, a sharper variety of the swara we sing as 'ga'. Anthara gandhara can be used as an anchor in the higher octave, especially while rendering the alapana. Using it as a sustained note, an artist can weave multiple phrases, particularly in faster speeds, leading to a theatrical climax. In MS's music, almost every time, as she ended her dramatic explorations at the anthara gandhara, she sang a final flourish that took her to the *panchama* (the swara 'pa') in the higher octave. This always won applause.

Perhaps Sadasivam's fascination with Shakarabharanam came from its capacity to generate applause, rather than any real musical feeling for it. It led to the perception that MS was incapable of rendering other ragas with the same ease as she did Shankarabharanam. She changed the *kirtana* that she presented in the raga every time, but some listeners began to grow bored. Everyone forgot that her interpretations of Anandabhairavi or Kharaharapriya were just as gorgeous.

A fundamentally more serious charge was levelled against her creativity. Many Carnatic musicians and rasikas will say that MS's improvisations were rehearsed and pre-planned; that she was a mere reciter. At face value, this rings true. There is no doubt that her alapanas, *neraval* and *kalpanaswaras*—all types of improvisational techniques—operated within a frame and with a kind of route map already drawn within the outlines. She was certainly not a creative genius of the order of, say, the nagaswaram maestro T.N. Rajaratnam Pillai.

But the truth is more nuanced. This did not mean that every alapana MS sang was a photocopy of a previous rendition. It is worth noting, too, that others of great repute have followed the same custom no less assiduously. The improvisations of Ariyakudi Ramanuja Iyengar, the godfather of twentieth-century Carnatic music, also adhered to a plan and structure. There was most certainly ideational repetitiveness in his performances. But I have rarely heard anyone bravely proclaim that he lacked the creative spirit. Instead, Ariyakudi is revered as the 'Margadarshi', or path-finder. No musician would dare question his abilities. Musicians such as D.K. Jayaraman and K.V. Narayanaswamy also followed templates, but their music is seen as spontaneous, in-depth and thoughtful.

MS was, and is, an easy target. She was often considered more of a parakeet than a nightingale, though her alapanas, neraval and tanam renditions were free-flowing and intuitive. There was never any indication of artificiality in her vocalization or in its creative development. I would argue that the same cannot be said of D.K. Pattammal, the critics' favourite, whose alapanas were creatively limited and whose articulation was laboured. Rasikas do not complain about this.

A third front of criticism had to do with the fact that MS practised regularly with her accompanists. Customarily, Carnatic musicians do not sit together and practise; they meet on stage. In fact, such rehearsals are scorned: the assumption is that musicians who require them are incapable of creativity on the fly. But MS and her team practised extensively, and the overall effect in performance was impeccable.

This was especially evident in the 1960s, when her accompanying musicians were V.V. Subramaniam on the violin, T.K. Murthy on the mridangam, V. Nagarajan on the *kanjira* and Vikku Vinayakaram on the ghatam. Listening to this team can sometimes give the impression that there are three human voices: that of MS, of her stepdaughter Radha, who provided vocal support, and of V.V. Subramaniam's violin. The percussionists always seem to know exactly how to respond to every movement in the melody.

While devotees of MS will argue that the rehearsals only enhanced the listening experience, I must accept that there is some weight to this criticism, since, to my mind, there is a flaw in this conception of what is perfect. MS sought a unified, error-free concert presentation, and accomplished that. Whether that made her concerts great art is another question. The experience of life, after all, is not one of correctness. Perfection is the search for the pure, experiential quality born from surrendering oneself to art. The artist gives her all and stumbles upon perfection by accident. It is quite possible that there will be moments of technical imperfection in that process. Yet, when such perfection is attained, it takes us beyond the personal to the abstract.

But what was behind this obsession with practice? Over time, MS had come to represent a flawless human being and become, in the public eye, a haloed personality, complete in every sense. Her graceful saris, her measured words, her hairdo, even the way flowers adorned it—everything was perfect. South Indian Brahmin women began to emulate the MS demeanour. The music of such a blemish-less person had, of course, to be mistake-free. A false note from MS was unimaginable. There could not be a stumble, let alone a fall. Her concerts had to be as impeccable as her personality. Repeated practice was the best way to achieve this.

MS never tired of it: she was willing to sing a song a hundred times if needed, and she did. Her moments of ethereality came in spite of this, not because of it. Throughout her musical life, there were unmonitored moments in which the MS of Madurai made a guest appearance, stunning us with a phrase that illuminated the horizon, like a flash of lightning over the open seas. If the initial freedom heard in her music is anything to go by, we may well have witnessed spectacular creativity from her if she had been allowed to just be.

By 1970, MS had been singing for nearly four decades. She was also constantly doing what someone or the other expected of her, rather than what her genius expected of her. The songs she sang on stage were always meant to please some constituency. Her singing itself was about satisfying what her husband saw as music. She had become mother, woman-saint, deliverer and model, as well as singer.

Sadasivam was a man of great integrity and self-respect, but he submitted himself to the political and corporate hierarchies of the time. His long and close association with Rajagopalachari, and his involvement in the latter's Swatantra Party, drew him into many circles of power. MS was constantly singing, both informally and formally, at gatherings organized by her husband, either in their own large residence, Kalki Gardens, or at those of others in their circle. Ever so often, it was to please or felicitate visiting bigwigs from elsewhere in India or abroad.

No count exists of the number of such performances; they must run to several hundred. I wonder what the musician in her felt about these indulgences. I don't have an answer, but I can speak as a musician myself: such concerts most certainly belittle the seriousness of music. I am referring not to spontaneous renditions of a song but to situations in which MS's art was taken for granted.

By the 1980s, she had toured and been honoured across the globe. She had sung at the United Nations. She received the Ramon Magsaysay Award in 1974. In 1998, she was awarded India's highest civilian decoration, the Bharat Ratna, becoming the first musician to receive that recognition. It would have pleased Sadasivam immensely, but he was no more by the time she received it. The Carnatic community may have criticized her art, but it had to accept her stardom and offer her recognition, even if murmurs about her musical ability continued. Since unabashed adulation had come from the outside, she received grudging acceptance from within.

But in all this, where was MS? Did she even know where to find herself? These are difficult questions and I do not raise them as an insider who was privy to her personal life. A musician's personality is revealed from the music she offers us. In MS's case, the signals were all too confusing. Her sincerity was unquestionable, yet there seemed to be so many acts and facades. These were not put on to cheat her listeners; she internalized her roles to such an extent that she was subsumed within them.

It is unanimously agreed that MS was a kind, humble human being, who bore no one any malice. She was soft-spoken and never rude. Her laughter occasionally lit up a room. But she was also a mystery. Access to her was restricted. The outside world knew nothing of her musical process. We may never know how deeply she thought about her music.

MS was certainly not a tortured soul, but there was a sadness in her, and I think it may have emanated mainly from the restrictions on her musical life. I am not saying that she did not love all that she sang, but she knew that it was not on her terms. She knew, moreover, that she would die without getting her real due from the Carnatic world. It was in singing bhajans and thumris that she received approbation, but it was in the kirtanas, *padams*, *thillanas*, *varnams*, *viruthams* and *javalis*—all types of Carnatic composition—that she sought validation.

Set everything else aside for a moment, and try and inhabit the 'MS space'—where an intangible, intense, deeply moving moment arises and takes your breath away. There is something there that comes from the depth of a partnership between the singer and the sung, the two in a union that is both private and open for all to hear and witness. When MS sang with all her being, which was invariably the case, she sang with her eyes closed, lost to us.

What was she? What did she find? I have dissected her music, even said that she performed to please others and gave herself up to do what her husband said. I am now saying something that contradicts all that—or am I? Once engulfed by the music, an artist finds a freedom and openness within, even if everything constructed on the exterior is limiting. So is there more to the 'divine MS' experience?

I have struggled with this question for a very long time, because the power of MS's music is irreplaceable and incomparable.

I have one probable answer. I do believe she was unable to be fully herself. The scaffolding around her was Sadasivam's construction and she had to remain within it, grateful for the security that it provided. Musically, too, she was locked in a vault. But when she sang, forgetting everything around her, all her suppressed sadness, regrets and experience burst into music.

It is this honest and pure outpouring that still shakes us. Her art was MS's only outlet. Every time she sang, she allowed every moment of her life experience to imbue the melody, letting go of all her inhibitions, abstracting herself into the raga. Once in a great while, we experience an unadulterated sense of what is real, so tender and vulnerable that our fences break down when it touches us, and we see ourselves like never before. MS, more than any other musician, can gift us these moments of self-realization.

She is an unsolved mystery to me. Every time I engage with the idea of her, a new strand appears. Her life and history is open to many interpretations. Since she herself said so little about it, we can only grapple with third-person narratives and use her music as a window into who she was. Her emotions were bundled up so tightly that even her closest friends and family saw only glimpses of her inner struggles, each one taking away his or her own personal impression like a private trophy.

She was determined, strong, focused, committed and brave. She was also introspective, innocent and fragile. The Carnatic world, for its part, has simplified her music and boxed it into either of two categories: the celestial or the ordinary. But her music was both, and everything that lies in between. She, and her music, will never cease to bewitch us. They will only ever continue to raise the unanswered question about where the real MS resides.